Funerary Spectacle

Applied Digital Humanities in the Roman Forum

CALIFORNIA CLASSICAL STUDIES

NUMBER 11

California Classical Studies publishes peer-reviewed long-form scholarship with online open access and print-on-demand availability. The primary aim of the series is to disseminate basic research (editing and analysis of primary materials both textual and physical), data-heavy research, and highly specialized research of the kind that is either hard to place with the leading publishers in Classics or extremely expensive for libraries and individuals when produced by a leading academic publisher. In addition to promoting archaeological publications, papyrological and epigraphic studies, technical textual studies, and the like, the series will also produce selected titles of a more general profile.

Also in the series:

Number 1: Leslie Kurke, *The Traffic in Praise: Pindar and the Poetics of Social Economy*, 2013

Number 2: Edward Courtney, *A Commentary on the Satires of Juvenal*, 2013

Number 3: Mark Griffith, *Greek Satyr Play: Five Studies*, 2015

Number 4: Mirjam Kotwick, *Alexander of Aphrodisias and the Text of Aristotle's* Metaphysics, 2016

Number 5: Joey Williams, *The Archaeology of Roman Surveillance in the Central Alentejo, Portugal*, 2017

Number 6: Donald J. Mastronarde, *Preliminary Studies on the Scholia to Euripides*, 2017

Number 7: Olivier Dufault, *Early Greek Alchemy, Patronage and Innovation in Late Antiquity*, 2019

Number 8: Todd M. Hickey, James G. Keenan, *Edgar J. Goodspeed, America's First Papyrologist*, 2021

Number 9: Christopher A. Faraone and Sofía Torallas Tovar, *Greek and Egyptian Magical Formularies: Text and Translation*, Volume 1, 2022

Number 10: Nicola Reggiani (ed.), *Papiri da Tebtynis pubblicati dal Seminario di Papirologia dell'Università di Parma (P.Tebt. VI)*, 2025

FUNERARY SPECTACLE

APPLIED DIGITAL HUMANITIES IN THE ROMAN FORUM

Christopher John Johanson

Berkeley, California

California Classical Studies
c/o Department of Ancient Greek and Roman Studies
University of California
Berkeley, California 94720–2520
USA
https://calclassicalstudies.org
email: ccseditorial@berkeley.edu

ISBN 9781939926203 (paperback), 9781939926210 (eBook: Adobe PDF)

Library of Congress Control Number: 2026934584

To Camila, Nicolás, and Zannie

CONTENTS

PREFACE

Many of the formative ideas for this book were generated during my initial years in Los Angeles, where I pursued a Ph.D. in Classics and worked in the UCLA Cultural Virtual Reality Lab and later the Experiential Technologies Center. Multi-year projects devoted to scientifically rigorous reconstructions of archaeological sites guided my thinking: while it is impossible to reconstruct the past, it is entirely possible to model and represent evidence and its various interpretations.

Stuart Dunn once asked me whether I chose first the subject or the method for this study. This question seems wiser by the day. I was drawn to the funeral because I wished to study spectacular phenomena set in the Republican Forum. Why the Forum of the Republic? Because most of the material remains have been lost, so it naturally seemed to be a project rooted in ideas, texts, and documents, rather than material. Reconstructing the Imperial Forum requires knowledge of structures and a visual fidelity that is simply not possible for the Forum of the Republic. Put simply, when substantial remains of a building exist, one is tempted to trace its outline with exactitude. My own thinking on this point has changed, however, and future studies will work with abstract models of even the more well-preserved buildings. Nonetheless, the funeral in the Forum became my focus because it conveniently brought together major elements of spectacle in a symbolically charged environment. Initial drafts of this project focused on each spectacular element without concern for their relation to each other. Years of reflection have changed my view on this point and have led to the overarching argument of this book. I have also reconsidered how to interpret Polybius and his assessment of aristocratic funerals in general. To understand Rome during this time period requires consideration of the way a funeral with *imagines*, like that of Lucius Aemilius Paullus, activated historical and cultural forces by interacting with the built environment and by harnessing the full spectacular apparatus available at Rome.

It is also difficult to overemphasize the importance of virtual experimentation in the development of this manuscript. The book represents decades of work in a virtual laboratory. The genesis of this book led to the creation of tools that expanded its range and depth. My RomeLab team, consisting of students, faculty, and staff at UCLA, along with collaborators during the funded period for the Humanities Virtual World Consortium, helped launch a generic virtual world platform that became the basis for virtual world experiments.

All routes and sightlines were explored at length in multi-player virtual worlds; images resulting from those experiences appear in this volume. Students using modern avatars have stood on top of the Capitoline Hill and waved to a group of us below. We have dropped experimental theaters and amphitheaters throughout the Forum. Avatars walked, ran, and, as often happened at the beginning of each class using this material, flew and landed atop buildings accompanied by real-world laughter. This project is serious, but the material generated for these 3D investigations is rooted in a sense of playful and creative experiment. The images generated are all relatively conservative in appearance, precisely because they were purposefully built with extreme constraints discovered through radically creative experiments in RomeLab. The work was almost always accompanied by students and colleagues. How did sound attenuate? What might be heard or seen? What did the Forum look like during a rainstorm? What if we visualized all *imagines* of all known Roman aristocrats in one place within the Roman Forum? What if we could fly around them? What does an original musical score add to the experience? What if we were to create 3D versions of physical books that would open up to reveal a 3D version of the Forum? Exploring these and many other questions led to the imagery and words you will read. This book would not exist without this coupling of creativity and experiment combined with careful and relatively restrained execution.

ACKNOWLEDGEMENTS

Various funding agencies generously provided me the opportunity to collaborate with others, develop my thinking, and create the digital tools to aid discovery. The support of the Mellon Foundation for the coalition of the Humanities Virtual World Consortium was critical. This book would look very different were it not for support from the National Endowment for the Humanities, its Summer Institute program, and the Office of Digital Humanities, as well as broader support from the MacArthur Foundation, the Keck Foundation, the National Science Foundation, and the Ahmanson Foundation.

There are many who helped me directly or indirectly as I devised, wrote, rewrote, and regenerated the material in this book. I first wish to thank Donald Mastronarde, Editorial Board Chair of California Classical Studies, for creating such an important contribution to the field and to scholarly communication. I am also deeply grateful to Robert Morstein-Marx, whose never-waning support and substantial feedback on many drafts have made the book better in every way. Leanne Bablitz, whose invitation to speak at a graduate seminar based on her spontaneous reading of my dissertation over a decade ago, made me think that the project should be completed. I owe much to John Bodel, whose direct and indirect support over many years has been critical, and to David Fredrick, whose work and critique have been transformative.

I am grateful to have worked with Sander Goldberg, whose instantaneous feedback during the early stages of this project was invaluable, and with Robert Gurval, who read initial drafts; later reflection on our early conversations helped sharpen my overall argument. A mentor and close collaborator, Diane Favro, read early drafts and has been supportive in countless ways; her experimental and courageous investigation of the ancient world suffuses and motivates my own work.

It is also the case that the images of this book would look very different were it not for collaboration with Marie Saldaña, whose sense of design and interest in procedural modeling fundamentally transformed my own processes for computationally representing the past.

All Ph.D. programs are different, of course, but few achieve the kind of broad training for its students compared to that of UCLA during the early 2000s. Much of what I write responds to Steven Lattimore, who taught me that one can and should spend a lifetime with one text. Ann Bergren's insistence on a quote for all questions applies to this work as well: *O passi graviora, dabit deus his quoquo finem*. Each seminar experience and professional interaction contributed to my interdisciplinary view and appreciation of the ancient world, and I am in general deeply indebted to the faculty of the UCLA Department of Classics. In particular, Amy Richlin's interest in and support of my work has always carried me forward. Alex Purves' collegiality and appreciation for creative scholarship has meant a great deal to me. Brent Vine ensured early on that I would never overlook epigraphic material.

My use of computational technology and three dimensional computer graphics to explore historical phenomena would not have been possible without Iowa State University's Honors Program and its mentoring system. Early guidance from Judy Vance, Carolina Cruz-Neira, Margaret Mook, and James Ruebel led me to create a virtual reality reconstruction of the Roman Forum—my first steps in front of the Temple of Saturn were taken in Ames, Iowa, in the first CAVE installed in the Black Engineering Building. We all write for someone aside from ourselves; every sentence of scholarship I create, I write with Jim in mind.

Views regarding reconstruction, representation, and reality were interrogated at the Cultural Virtual Reality Lab and its UCLA-based successor, the UCLA Experiential Technologies Center, and I am grateful to Bernard Frischer for inviting me to join his team so many years ago. In those labs, conversations with Dean Abernathy made me a passable architectural critic and have influenced every aspect of my approach to thinking about the built environment and my keen desire to make things to help us learn. I was fortunate to work on project teams, at one point all housed within UCLA Academic Technology Services, that spanned the globe and helped advance my thinking. In this capacity I learned a great deal working alongside Phil Stinson, Ewan Branda, Mantha Zarmakoupi, Rebeka Vital, Renee Calkins, Gregor Kalas, John Dagenais, Margo Reveil, Paul Hoffman, Marsha Smith, Joan Slottow, Pieter Lechner, Lisa Snyder, Michael Benjamin, David Beaudry, and Jeff Burke.

I owe much to Todd Presner, whose generosity and calm demeanor are a model of collegiality. Our many collaborations, first on the HyperCities project, and later on the development of the UCLA Program in Digital Humanities, focused my critical thinking regarding DH: if humanists do not make tools for our disciplines, who will?

The Humanities Virtual World Consortium led directly to the development of RomeLab, and helped me explore what was and was not possible in virtual worlds and on the printed page. I am eternally grateful to my collaborators who I met for the first time on that project: Hugh Denard, Richard Beacham, Susan Schreibman, David Germano, John Fillwalk, and Chris Collins.

My thinking about the built environment and the monumentality of Roman architecture was expanded through collaborations with Vedat Idil and Musa Kadıoğlu at Nysa on the Maeander and with Orhan Bingöl and Görkem Kökdemir at Magnesia on the Maeander. Chance walks and conversations with Fikret Yegül were highlights. Within the context of my work in Turkey, I had the pleasure to supervise small teams of UCLA graduate students on site, and I benefitted greatly from my time spent with Pelin Yoncacı Arslan, Ece Okay, Michael Rocchio, and Brian Sahotsky.

Though the intellectual work of this project takes place in an abstract space of ideas, time spent in actual Rome and in the Forum was invaluable. I am deeply indebted to Monica De Simone for conversation while on site and on a Vespa. I also learned much working closely with nascent architects, Itay Zaharovits and Steven Guban. Time in consultation with Carla Amici and Cairoli Giuliani helped me think more carefully about the use and misuse of material evidence.

As the blues musician Chris Smither is wont to say in concert, it's funny how small acts of kindness and a few positive words make all the difference. To this end, I thank Penelope Davies, Matthew Roller, Peter Heslin, Alyson Gill, Johanna Drucker, Patrik Svensson, and John Clarke, all of whom have helped me move forward. I owe a special debt of gratitude to Stefania Tutino and our DH^2 and InkCode collaborators, Giovanna Ceserani and Stefania Pastore. It is impossible to overestimate how meaningful their collaboration has been. I would not have completed this book without them. Lastly, though I am certain they won't remember their contributions, observations from Helen Morales and Isabel Köster respectively made me refine my claim that a funeral occurred in three acts, and made me reflect on the chronological relationship between gladiators and *imagines*.

My interdisciplinarity was cultivated in Forest City, Iowa, and I would not have written this book in this way were it not for the freedom, play, and intellectual curiosity fostered by Linda Mekelberg, JoAnn Sundermann, and Lyle Wignes.

Family carried me to the finish line. Special thanks are due to my suegros, Oswaldo and Zannie Sandoval, who have been stalwart fans from the beginning. I am deeply indebted to my parents, Linda Kasperbauer Johanson and Steven Johanson, especially for trusting that I would mostly make good decisions. Lastly, I am grateful to my children for their inspiration and joy, and to my wife, for her love, patience, and support.

The book took shape near Wilshire and Westwood and in an apartment just south of Pico and Sepulveda. Its chapter on processions was outlined in Testaccio, adjacent to the parade of Santa Maria Liberatrice. Final revisions were completed in the pervasive humidity of the Pacific Ocean near Marina del Rey and on the outskirts of Lima.

ABBREVIATIONS

Most items are referred to by author's name and date as they appear in the Bibliography at the end of the book. But a few key works and online resources are referred to by name only, as indicated here together with other standard abbreviations.

BMCRR	*Coins of the Roman Republic in the British Museum.*
CIL	*Corpus Inscriptionum Latinarum* (1863–).
DPRR	*Digital Prosopography of the Roman Republic.* https://romanrepublic.ac.uk/.
LTUR	M. Steinby (ed.), *Lexicon Topographicum Urbis Romae*, 6 vols. (1993–2000).
MRR	T. R. S. Broughton, *The Magistrates of the Roman Republic* (1951–2); Suppl. (1986: supersedes Suppl. 1960).
RE	Pauly, A., and Wissowa, G., eds. 1884–1978. *Realenzyklopädie der classischen Altertumswissenschaft*. Leipzig.
TLL	*Thesaurus Linguae Latinae* (1900–).

LIST OF FIGURES

Some images in the text use color to pick out key elements; those using a print copy are advised to consult the online PDF at escholarship.org for best understanding of the images.

Funerary Spectacle

Applied Digital Humanities in the Roman Forum

CHAPTER 1

Visual Argumentation: Analysis of Funerary Spectacle

This project investigates the funeral of Lucius Aemilius Paullus Macedonicus, who died in 160 BCE. This study is deliberately grounded in a tightly circumscribed set of evidence relating to a specific time, person, and place. As I will discuss below, no complete description of Paullus' funeral exists. Yet it has the most robust body of extant evidence for any mid-Republican funerary event, and for this reason, I focus on Paullus' funeral over all others. Paradoxically, this focused approach also can allow for broader, more ambitious interpretations. The degree to which Paullus' funeral was exceptional or instead reflective of more general funerary practice is a tension that runs throughout this book, however. Ultimately, the conclusions reached here apply specifically to this one funeral and to its unique time frame, yet they also provide a framework that may be applied, with caution, to other Roman funerary events in other chronological contexts.

My investigation takes three innovative turns.

- I consider the entirety of Paullus' funeral to be a complex, highly integrated multi-act spectacular performance—consisting of the procession, the funeral eulogy, and the funeral games—in which viewing and performative priorities of one act influence those of the other two.
- I integrate the surrounding space and place of the Roman Forum itself into all aspects of my investigation through the use of three-dimensional computer graphics and a geographic information system (GIS) in order to document, interrogate, and disseminate space-based arguments.
- I contend that the Roman aristocratic funeral of the second century BCE is inextricably connected to the built environment of the Roman Forum.

I harness the affordances of a three-dimensional, visual argumentation system to reinvigorate study and interpretation of a historically well-studied topic. By working behind the scenes within a fully interactive, 3D model of the Roman Forum, I am not only able to see evidence for the first time within its surrounding three-dimensional context, but I can also address spatial and performative research questions in ways hitherto impossible. What were once theoretical discussions become transformed into practical and experimental investigations.

THE FUNERAL PROBLEM

A Roman aristocratic funeral was spectacular. Polybius asks, "What spectacle could be finer than this?" (τί δ' ἂν κάλλιον θέαμα τούτου φανείη; 6.53.10–6.54.1). Modern scholars echo this sentiment.[1] At its most extravagant, the funeral could comprise a spectacular triad: a procession (*pompa*), a speech—the eulogy for the deceased (*laudatio funebris*), and subsequent public games (*ludi funebres* which might include "gifts," *munera*, of gladiators). While each of these components of the funeral has received individual treatment—in the case of the gladiatorial *munera*, extensive—no detailed, comprehensive discussion of aristocratic funerary practice of the mid-Republic exists. The fault lies in the evidence and in the available epistemological toolsets. The spectacle of the Roman funeral presents a particularly difficult scholarly problem. It was a relatively common and well-known event in antiquity; it was fundamental to the continuity of Roman political and social life; and it largely took place in the most important civic and cultural area of the ancient city, the Forum. Yet it rarely received a detailed description.[2] Our sources reveal only glimpses of the practicalities of the display. It is deeply concerning that, in some cases, a lone source provides the scholarly justification for the existence of a significant aspect of the ritual. References are made to funerals notable for their luxury, size, or other unusual quality, but they lack the sort of comprehensive detail

[1] For specific treatments on the "spectacle" of the Roman funeral, see Bodel 1999; Beacham 1999: 17–19, 37–39, 151–153; Flower 2004: 331–337. For more general studies that focus on visual elements of the funeral, see Flower 1996, who addresses the visual effect of *imagines*: 91–157; Purcell 1999, who considers the effigy for the deceased and its effect on the audience; Holliday 2002: 122–154, who examines the visual elements of the funeral through the lens of Roman reliefs and Etruscan wall-painting; and Morstein-Marx and Byrne 2025, who pinpoint when waxen masks were no longer employed. For treatments on the use of funerary spectacle for political ends, see Hölkeskamp 2023: 272–340 and Flaig 1995; Flaig 2003: 49–68, on the *pompa*, and 232–260, on the *ludi*; and Sumi 2005: 16–46, esp. 25–29 and 46; see as well Campbell 2021 for an analysis of the funeral procession at Pompeii.

[2] It was an event that had no blueprint or specific script to follow. Like similar activities of Roman daily life, it also may have required no description; Flower 1996: 97 concludes: "We have no detailed description by any Roman author, let alone one entitled to such a funeral, of a practice which was central to aristocratic life during the Republic. Numerous passing references to be found in the extant sources show how natural it was for Roman writers to assume a knowledge of these customs in their audience." Or as Hope 2018 notes, in a section that articulates the problematic nature of the study of ancient ritual, "[To access Roman funerary practice] is an assembly job that lacks any real sense of chronological and geographic specificity."

that might help the modern scholar understand the totality of the event. The fundamental source is a Greek immigrant to the Roman world. The *locus classicus* for the funeral, Polybius' description of, primarily, the parade of famous ancestors on display in the Forum (Polyb. 6.53–54), though incomplete, forms the backbone of all scholarly discussions pertaining to aristocratic funeral practice in Rome. The chronological dispersion of the already sparse textual and artistic evidence distorts the rest of the scholarly debate. Hence, the unavoidable tendency has been to conflate, project, and retroject the evidence.[3]

An overreliance on Polybius can obscure two crucial details.

1. Polybius' description is incomplete and is at odds with other fragments and testimony. It glosses over the kinetic and spectacular details of the procession to focus solely on the presentation of the waxen masks (*imagines*) and the praise of the ancestors for reasons that should not be ignored.

2. The Roman aristocratic funeral is a site-based ritual performance, and the particular site, the Roman Forum, is a complex, material palimpsest—all the more difficult to understand because the bulk of the spatial evidence comes not from the archaeological record but from ancient testimony.

Regarding the latter point, imagining what the Imperial Roman Forum might have looked like is difficult enough. There are fragments and foundations of Imperial buildings extant at the modern site. For the Republican phase, the small amounts of material remains are buried beneath later pavers, monuments, and the overpowering influence of Imperial representations.

Views of these reconstructed monuments dominate modern visual depictions of the space.[4] The versions of the Forum we find in the *Plastico di Roma*, in the images from the Beaux-Arts tradition of architectural drawing, in Piranesi, and in modern cinema and television have given us a highly ordered image of *Imperial* Rome.[5] While HBO's television series, *Rome*, for example, depicts the confusion, architectural disorder, grime and filth of a living city—perhaps itself exaggerated—its Forum, which in no substantive way aligns with the actual evidence *in situ*, is an amalgamation of influences from the late Republic, Augustan Rome, and Pompeii. Even when these representations are sensitive to the extant archaeological remains found in the Forum today, the images bear little resemblance to the mid-Republican Forum, filled with Tuscan-style buildings and open competition

[3] Hope 2007: 86: "The danger remains that we will merge together primary sources and secondary interpretations to create a composite picture of a Roman funeral that may never have been a reality."

[4] In fact, there are relatively few who have tried to represent the Republican Forum beyond schematic plans. For the primary examples from the last thirty years, see Welch 1994, Stambaugh 1988, Carandini and Carafa 2012, Gorski and Packer 2015, Hanses 2020, and Muth, n.d.

[5] For a survey of various scale models, see Haselberger 1997. The winners of the *Prix de Rome* extrapolated only from the remains they could see; for a collection of images, see Cassanelli and Massimiliano 2002.

among private citizens to gain a monumental presence in the public space. It is tempting, though risky, to view the Republican Forum through a later lens.

Contexts of two kinds lie at the heart of this study: the textual and the geographic. Since most of the textual evidence about the early aristocratic funeral is testimony extracted from sources whose primary intent was not to document the event, the various literary contexts cannot be ignored. The time and the source of the textual evidence matter and are too often overlooked. By studying these contexts and re-evaluating their meaning within the larger purpose of the respective work, new avenues of scholarly inquiry can open. In the case of an event understood solely through fragmentary evidence, perceived truisms coupled with preconceived notions of the spatial context assemble an impossibly clean historical narrative. It is only through a close reading of the textual evidence that we can tease out the gaps in our knowledge and discover areas that demand investigation. What the sources omit is often the focus of this investigation. The second form of context is rooted in the topographical, the spatial, the visual, and the experiential. The Roman funeral, like many historical phenomena that are event-triggered and site-specific, was influenced by its staging space. In practice, only certain staging choices were possible, only certain paths for a procession were probable, and only a limited number of audience/performer configurations were allowed by the space. In theory, the overt power of place in the Roman world and the ever-prominent visual battles of symbolic capital formed the visual backdrop for the funeral.[6] The funeral itself was filled with these same elements. Such a visually charged event held in a symbol-laden location requires more than textual analysis can offer. Indeed, the digitally reconstructed Forum itself can serve as a source text.[7]

In my study I perform a first-person experiential interrogation of the evidence by modeling a multiplicity of spatial configurations and visual mappings of ideas and historical phenomena suggested by the textual and material evidence.[8] This study focuses primarily on an analysis of the funeral of L. Aemilius Paullus held in 160 BCE. This specific geo-temporal moment serves as an organizing principle for the marshaling of evidence. By focusing on the event of 160 BCE, I assemble the evidence to understand how the Forum might have looked at that one time, and how the event might have unfolded therein. In general, throughout this study, the textual and relevant material sources are adduced to serve an argument about this specific funeral in 160 BCE; the further removed from this time period, the less relevant they become. There are few historical funerary events that suit such an approach. The fortuitous convergence of sources that either treat the funeral of

[6] For the power of place in Rome, see Vasaly 1993, esp. 40–87. For the power of place as envisioned by geographers and cultural historians, see Gallagher 1993 and Hayden 1997. On symbolic capital, see Hölkeskamp 2004, 93–105, and Hölkeskamp 2010, esp. 107–124. On architectural manipulation in the political sphere see Steinby 2012 and Davies 2017, and on the specific political manipulation of the Forum space, see Russell 2016: 77–98.

[7] See Schreibman and Papadopoulos 2019 on 3D reconstructions as critical editions.

[8] The sections in this chapter that pertain to modeling have been derived from Johanson 2009.

Paullus specifically or are contemporaneous and pertinent does not offer a comprehensive description, but it does provide stronger textual foundation for study than any other aristocratic funeral prior to that of Julius Caesar at the end of the Republic.[9]

The fundamental source for the Roman funeral is Polybius 6.53–54. He provides the most detailed description of the constituent parts of the Roman funeral procession and eulogy, but he has an agenda to pursue. Although his description of the funeral occurs in the midst of a short political and social ethnography of the Roman people, he introduces the funerary event as evidence for a larger argument. He explains the ways Roman institutions give the Roman people a distinct advantage over the Carthaginians, their nearest rival, by encouraging a pursuit of bravery at all costs.

> διαφέρουσι μὲν οὖν καὶ φύσει πάντες Ἰταλιῶται Φοινίκων καὶ Λιβύων τῇ τε σωματικῇ ῥώμῃ καὶ ταῖς ψυχικαῖς τόλμαις· μεγάλην δὲ καὶ διὰ τῶν ἐθισμῶν πρὸς τοῦτο τὸ μέρος ποιοῦνται τῶν νέων παρόρμησιν. ἓν δὲ ῥηθὲν ἱκανὸν ἔσται σημεῖον τῆς τοῦ πολιτεύματος σπουδῆς, ἣν ποιεῖται περὶ τὸ τοιούτους ἀποτελεῖν ἄνδρας ὥστε πᾶν ὑπομένειν χάριν τοῦ τυχεῖν ἐν τῇ πατρίδι τῆς ἐπ᾽ ἀρετῇ φήμης.
>
> By nature, all the Italians are superior to the Phoenicians and Libyans both through their bodily strength and the courage of their souls; but also in part through their institutions they create a great desire for this in the youth. One example will be sufficient proof of the zeal of the governmental institution to make men ready to endure everything for the sake of obtaining fame in the homeland for their courage.[10]

This "institution," as described by Polybius, is a specific combination of activities that occur upon the death of a prominent Roman citizen:

- the parade of the body in a conspicuous position into the Forum to the Rostra;
- the eulogy, given by his son or another relative on the Rostra in which the virtues and achievements of the deceased can be heard by all;
- men wearing the masks of prominent ancestors in character, riding chariots, display the rank of the deceased, and seat themselves in a row on ivory chairs at the Rostra;

---

[9] References are made to many other funerals, but they all lack the chance combination of surviving sources: Val. Max. 2.4.7 (D. Junius Brutus Pera, 264 BCE); Livy 23.30.15 (M. Aemilius Lepidus, 216 BCE); Livy 31.50.4 (M. Valerius Laevinus 200, BCE); Livy 39.46 (P. Licinius, 183 BCE); Livy 41.28.11 (Flamininus, 174 BCE); Livy *Per.* 48 (the funeral games of M. Porcius Cato's son, 154 BCE); Cic. *Leg.* 2.57, Livy *Per.* 90, Plin. *HN* 7.187, Plut. *Luc.* 43.3, Plut. *Sull.* 38.1–6, Plut. *Pomp.* 15.4, 81.3, App. *BC* 4.1.105–107 (the funeral of Sulla, 78 BCE); Suet. *Iul.* 6.1 (funeral for Caesar's aunt Julia 69 BCE); by the time of the funeral of Julius Caesar we are far removed from the texts critical to this study, and the topography has changed drastically.

[10] Polyb. 6.52.10–11. All translations are my own unless otherwise noted.

- at the conclusion of the funeral the *imago* of the deceased is placed in a shrine within the house.

Polybius is making a tightly constrained argument that these particular elements elevated the Romans above all others. He does not profess to give a detailed account of the spectacle of the Roman funeral during the mid-Republic. Instead, he wishes to adduce examples of the institutionalized instillation of virtue in Roman culture.[11] He highlights the *imagines* and the veneration of the ancestors, but ignores other aspects of the funeral, many of which would have been detrimental to his argument. The entire passage must be viewed with this context in mind. Polybius' description can be used to investigate the Roman funeral, but it cannot be used to limit the investigation. What is included, omitted, and possibly exaggerated by Polybius in his description is governed by his argument and not by the event.

In addition, Polybius is a frustrating source for Roman topography. He was one of a few eyewitnesses from second-century Rome who might have been able to write at length concerning the surrounding built environment. Instead, he rarely offers detailed descriptions of spatial relationships within the city, and he avoids referring to buildings with any specificity.

Polybius purports to describe a somewhat generic Roman aristocratic funeral, but traces of a specific event may appear in his account. He was most likely an audience member during the funeral of L. Aemilius Paullus.[12] Upon the defeat of Perseus of Macedonia at Pydna in 168 BCE, Polybius was one of a thousand Achaeans who were deported to Italy and detained there without trial. Polybius was sent to Rome. By chance, Polybius befriended the young Scipio Aemilianus, who was the adoptive son of P. Cornelius Scipio (son of the more famous Scipio Africanus), and who also was the natural-born son of L. Aemilius Paullus. Polybius, by request, remained in Rome when the rest of the group was distributed to the provinces, and his friendship with Scipio Aemilianus continued apace. The first evidence for Polybius' travel outside of Italy seems to have been a journey in 151, when he traveled to Spain with Scipio. Therefore, he was in Rome at the right time and was connected directly to the family of L. Aemilius Paullus. It is likely that he attended Paullus' funeral, and that his personal observations of this specific funeral informed his report.

---

[11] Connolly 2007: 211 notes how the description of the funeral connects to the end of book 6, where Polybius represents Roman moral superiority by describing Rome's refusal to ransom 8000 men captured by Carthage. See also Sommer 2013, whose main conclusion applies, *mutatis mutandis*: "He may have written his history for a Greek and Roman audience, but his perspective was entirely Greek. His questions were Greek, and so was the specific angle from which he approached his subject: Polybius' purpose was not to deliver an accurate description of the political functioning of the Roman republic, the procedures and processes that kept the Roman state running, but a theoretical—ideal-typical in the Weberian sense—explanation for its superiority over the other Mediterranean polities."

[12] What follows is a brief summary of the relevant details in Walbank 1970: 3–6, which recounts the reconstructed life of Polybius and provides source citations.

While Polybius' discussion of the archetypal funeral omits the rest of the funerary activities, the funeral of Paullus is known to us not for the *laudatio*, but for its famed procession, the number of attendees, the associated games, and their costs. Much later in his work, Polybius recalls the funeral of Paullus to illustrate his surviving sons' familial devotion (31.28.5–7): they spent 30 talents on gladiatorial games, a considerable sum.[13] Diodorus Siculus (who was writing a century after the event) included a section on the funeral of L. Aemilius Paullus. Only fragments of his treatment survive. In his description of the opulence of L. Aemilius Paullus' funeral, Diodorus adds that actors who had been employed to observe the deceased during his whole life portrayed him at the funeral. The rest of the ancestors on display, whose rank would be clearly marked out for spectators by their costumes, were represented as well, but we cannot say by whom.[14] This funeral was noted for the number of spectators it attracted. According to Diodorus, people came from surrounding cities to attend.[15] Plutarch reports that the character of L. Aemilius Paullus was such that not only his friends, but also his conquered enemies (who chanced to be present), joined the procession and helped carry the bier.[16] It was at the funeral games of L. Aemilius Paullus where the *Adelphoe* of Terence was staged for the first time, and the staging of the *Hecyra* was apparently interrupted for a second time.[17] Livy also must have remarked on the death of L. Aemilius Paullus in 160, but that book is lost and what remains is a perfunctory note in the *Periochae*, with no mention of the funeral or games.[18]

ROMAN SPECTACLE

Roman spectacle has received considerable attention in recent years, but its study has been limited by spatial and kinetic demands required to examine an ephemeral

[13] Diod. Sic. 31.27.6 also reports on the gladiatorial games.

[14] An innovation of the Paulli? The use of men "similar in form" is associated only with this funeral, but is presented as custom; Diod. Sic. 31.25.2 (Photius Bibl. p. 383 B): τῶν γὰρ Ῥωμαίων οἱ ταῖς εὐγενείαις καὶ προγόνων δόξῃ διαφέροντες μετὰ τὴν τελευτὴν εἰδωλοποιοῦνται κατά τε τὴν τοῦ χαρακτῆρος ὁμοιότητα καὶ κατὰ τὴν ὅλην τοῦ σώματος περιγραφήν, μιμητὰς ἔχοντες ἐκ παντὸς τοῦ βίου παρατετηρηκότας τήν τε πορείαν καὶ τὰς κατὰ μέρος ἰδιότητας τῆς ἐμφάσεως. For the most part Diodorus echoes Polybius, but notes the mime of the deceased, perhaps retrojecting from Imperial times (cf. Suet. *Vesp.* 19.2). Whether actors, family members, or simply hired members of the funerary trade played the roles of the ancestors, we can never know. For a different reading of μιμητὰς, see Blasi 2010, who argues that they were "craftsmen" not actors. Morstein-Marx and Byrne 2025: 334n23 are skeptical of the applicability of this passage to Republican practice and argue convincingly that the translation should be 'imitator' and not 'actor.' I will continue to use the term 'actor' in the sense, not of a professional actor, but of someone who puts on a mask to play a part for a specific occasion.

[15] Diod. Sic. 31.25.1 in *Const. Exc.* 2(1) p. 285.

[16] Plut. *Aem.* 39.6–8.

[17] See below, p. 156 and p. 147n46. Ter. *Ad.* 15 gives a potential reference to Paullus himself, and Ter. *Hec.* 39–42 describes the moment when the play was interrupted due to rumor of a gladiatorial performance. See Goldberg 2018 for a detailed analysis.

[18] Livy *Per.* 46.13–14.

event from antiquity.[19] Bergmann notes the difficulties in using text-centered readings:

> No thorough study of public displays in Greece and Rome exists. In recent years, however, historians and philologists have begun to reveal the primary role of performance in the transmission of Greek and Latin texts, to understand the logistics of producing plays, and to underscore the prevalence of role playing among all members of society from king or emperor to slave. These often text-centered readings tend to neglect the essential role of physical sites, special effects, choreography, props, and visual representations.[20]

Studies specifically aimed at investigating spectacle tend to paint a picture that is temporally conflated. They gather together a number of illustrative images taken from ancient painting and sculptural relief, and amass textual passages that emphasize visual elements (e.g., the color of the togas worn in a procession, a parade of wild beasts, wax *imagines* worn by actors) in order to underscore the importance of spectacle for the selected theme. They often attempt to capture the overwhelmingly sensorial nature of the event, as, for example, Beard 2003 and Brilliant 1999, on the triumph in which the masses of people, their shouting, the treasure, the imagery, the trumpets, and the chariots are assembled and presented in detail with extended text and lengthy footnotes.[21] Another approach has been to focus on specific historical and literary problems to reveal new insights from an investigation into the logistics of spectacle. I will combine these two approaches, but supplement them with a visual analysis of its spatial and temporal dimensions.

Triumph, oratory, and drama have each benefited from focused studies that consider the topographical context and visual experience. Scholars have elevated the importance of topographical context in historical investigations and literary analyses, particularly as it relates to performative spaces in the Roman Republic.[22] The impact of monumental structures on Roman performers—members of a procession, orators, actors and gladiators—and their audiences, what could and could not be seen during their performance, as well as the significance of *monumenta memoriae*, directly affected the shows then and the reading and interpretation of

---

[19] See Beacham 1999, Bergmann and Kondoleon 1999, Köhne 2000a, Kyle 2001, Beard 2003, Flower 2004.

[20] Bergmann 1999: 9 with extensive bibliography on prior text-centered studies of spectacle.

[21] This method is a kind of "thick description" (see Geertz 1973); for a powerful and comprehensive example of this method applied to performance, politics, and visual symbols in the Roman Republic, see Hölkeskamp 2023.

[22] Coarelli 1983, Coarelli 1985, Vasaly 1993, Millar 1998, Mouritsen 2001, and Morstein-Marx 2004 all represent book-length treatments in which the argument revolves, in part, around the reconstruction of or interaction with political performance space; see as well Davies 2017 for a broader discussion of political activity and the built environment in the Roman Republic. Hanson 1959, Goldberg 1998, Marshall 2006, Goldberg 2018 represent the major works concerning spatial characteristics of Republican theater. For general acknowledgment of the importance of spectacle and context, see Bergmann and Kondoleon 1999 and Flower 2004.

the records they have left us now. Surprisingly, the Roman funeral has not received this treatment, though it includes similar events.

Despite recognizing the relevance of the natural and built environment, the aforementioned spatial analyses share a problem inherent in their representational methodology. They attempt to reconstruct the monuments and surrounding context, which are inherently multi-dimensional, by means of textual description and two-dimensional plan.[23] Beacham pinpoints the problem:

> Spectacle is three-dimensional and sequential, realized by taking place over a period of time, and its place, circumstance, and unfolding fundamentally shape what an audience both expects and experiences.[24]

Three-dimensional, sequential analyses require new tools. The impressive and stimulating studies to date have pushed the boundaries of text-based investigation. A new methodology that injects interpretations of textual and material data into a geo-temporal, digital space offers a possible way forward. More importantly, it lets us transform the physical fabric of the Forum itself into an additional and legible "text" to be part of the evidentiary toolkit.

MODELING THE FUNERAL OF LUCIUS AEMILIUS PAULLUS

This project uses the spatial tools and methods of Digital Humanities to explore, contextualize, and model a specific historical event, the funeral of Lucius Aemilius Paullus, held in 160 BCE in the Roman Forum.[25]

In this book, images generated from a reconstructed 3D Roman Forum serve as backdrop and as evidence to help us understand how the funeral of Paullus might have been staged. In general, such models are built as follows. Before extruding the three-dimensional built environment from 2D plans, the two-dimensional plan must first be made geographically aware. The plan is georeferenced into the GIS through a simple translation and rotation defined by three control points. In a two-part process, the topographical lay of the land is then approximated from hypothetical contour lines and the extruded three-dimensional buildings are dropped onto the elevated skin of the land. The extruded buildings must accomplish the following:

1. Connect the hypothetical plan of the monuments to the geographic coordinate system. (See fig. 1.1.)

---

[23] For example, Morstein-Marx 2004: 104–106, whose magisterial work describes the topographical picture of commemorative monuments by listing the related textual sources in nearly page-length footnotes. The footnotes are necessary, but could be augmented by three-dimensional images.

[24] Beacham 1999: 24.

[25] I have previously developed the methodologies and tools employed in this study in Johanson 2009, and Johanson 2015. The 3D models were constructed procedurally using the Roman City Ruleset, which was developed at UCLA RomeLab; see Saldaña and Johanson 2013 and Saldaña 2015.

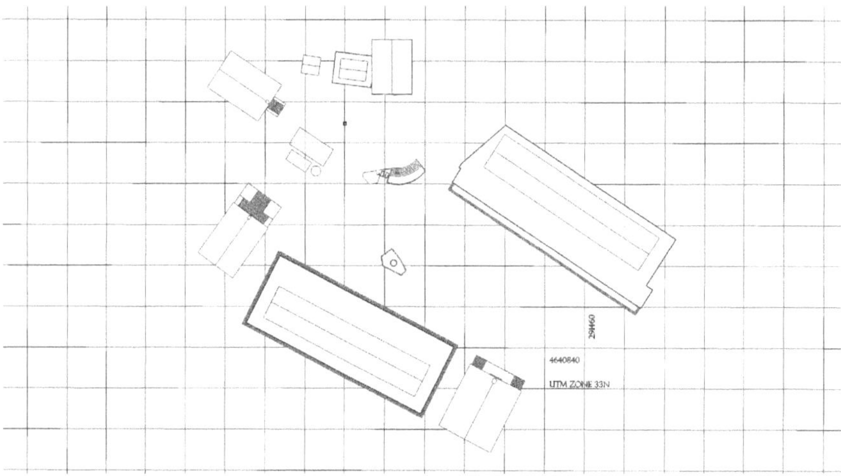

FIGURE 1.1 Injecting the coordinate system.

2. Extrude three-dimensional representations that convey, upon initial reading, the building type and possible spectator spaces. (See fig. 1.2.)

3. Represent elevations according to above-sea-level measurements. (See fig. 1.3.)

4. Skin the ground-level contours with a topographical mesh in order to deliver a multi-dimensional cartographic representation of the Forum's built form. (See fig. 1.4.)

Key elements of the funeral, the ancestors, the eulogist, the family, and the audience were inserted into this 3D model. More specifically, for this book, the monuments within the Forum were generated procedurally, that is, through a rule-based, computational system, from footprints traced within a GIS. For each monument, one should imagine a simple rectangle traced on a map that is then extruded upward to form a rectangular prism at a proportional height expected for the building, following Vitruvian rules. This form is then subdivided, pushed, pulled, and manipulated to form a 3D shape that represents a building type. These are not definitive reconstructions, but are instead abstractions, conforming in broad strokes to the topography of the land and the built environment. Critically, specific heights are derived from extant material evidence and are indicated when available, or they are approximated by planting the monumental footprint in the 3D topography and, where applicable, by estimating the number of steps needed to ascend from ground to the podium or platform above. These visualizations offer a framework within which we can explore ideas. For an elaboration of the tools and methods applied

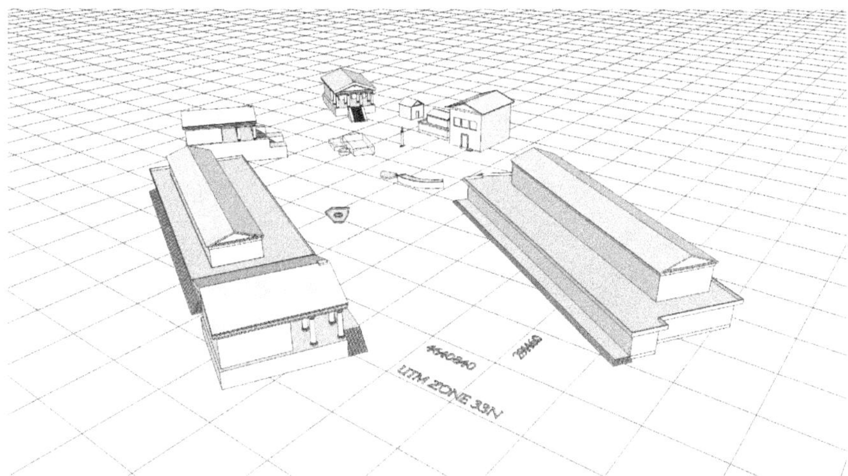

FIGURE 1.2 Extruding the built form.

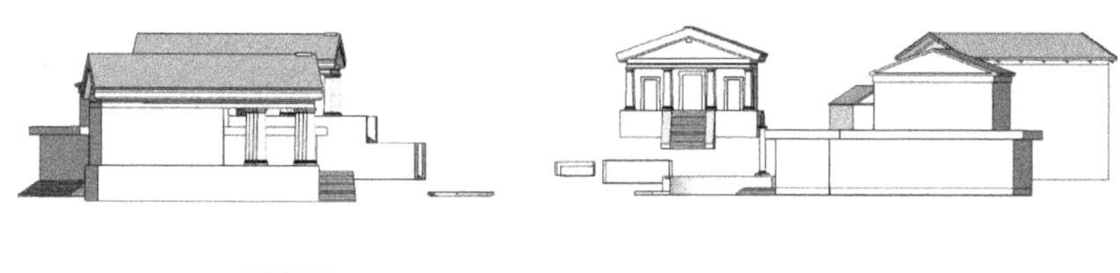

FIGURE 1.3 Building relative elevations.

and for specific documentation regarding how each monument was generated and the elevations used, see below, Appendices A and B.

This book is not a study of death ritual and it does not purport to focus on the details of Roman funerary practice.[26] Rather, as suggested above, it reads the funeral as an event that aggregated the major elements of public spectacle—oratory, procession, gladiatorial shows, and dramatic performance—within one charged landscape, the Forum. The visual argument of this book is rooted in textual source material. I pursue the various strands of testimony and contexts to find gaps in the traditional picture of the funeral. When testimony is the primary source of evidence, retrojection of later practice onto early events is difficult to avoid. Close readings of literary and spatial texts frame each visual inquiry. The ordering of

[26]The bibliography for such studies is long, a window into which can be found in Bodel 1986, Morris 1992, Toynbee 1996, Bodel 2004, Edwards 2007, Hope 2007, Hope 2011, Hope 2018, and Hope 2025.

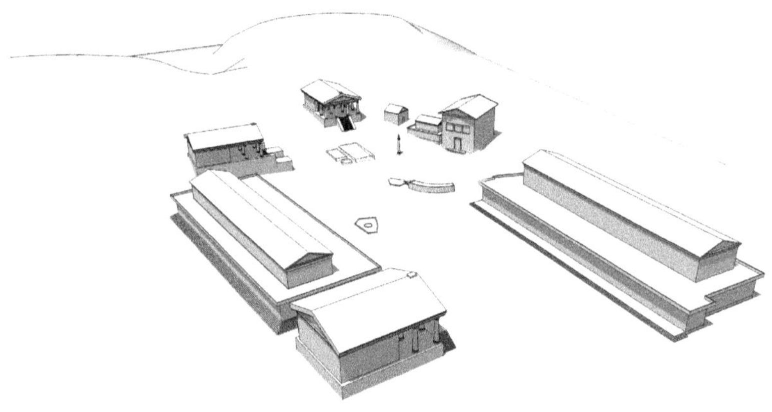

FIGURE 1.4 Representing topographical contours.

spectacular moments in the funeral directs my discussion. My argument proceeds as follows. I first follow the *pompa* from the home to the Forum (Chapter 2). I then examine the funeral eulogy (*laudatio funebris*) atop the Rostra (Chapter 3). I next explore the details of staging surrounding the *ludi funebres* and the *munera* (Chapter 4). To conclude (Chapter 5), I evaluate the consequences of understanding the funeral as a three-act, internally coherent and cohesive theatrical show that was inextricably connected to the space of the Roman Forum.

CHAPTER 2

Pompa Funebris: Visual Registers

A Roman funeral and its procession began at home. After the body of the deceased was displayed within the family's *domus*, it was then taken for a walk, perhaps directly for interment (most often following cremation), or, in the case of an aristocratic funeral, to the speaker's platform (Rostra) in the Forum. Unfortunately, in almost all cases of any known family from the Roman Republic, we will never know the specific location and appearance of their home. In addition, even the possible routes and street plans are not all well attested in the material record. Therefore, this investigation will suggest a handful of possible, albeit hypothetical locations for the home of L. Aemilius Paullus. Beginning at these hypothetical homes, it will trace the reconstructed routes of the procession as it moved toward the Roman Forum, to convey the deceased, the eulogist, the family, and the rest of the audience who might have attended the open-air funeral eulogy.

FRAMING THE DISCUSSION: THE EVIDENCE

Two sources guide modern understanding of an aristocratic funeral procession: a detailed description from the Greek historian, Polybius, dating to the first half of the second century BCE, and a relief, found at the Roman colony of Amiternum near modern day L'Aquila, that depicts an elite funeral procession of the mid-first century BCE.[1] Each source omits critical elements of the funeral. Nonetheless, text and material evidence combined provide an evidential baseline for understanding

[1] The relief was first published in Fiorelli 1879: 147. It was later extensively analyzed by Franchi 1966, who includes a series of detail photographs (pls. 5–10). Toynbee 1996: 46–47 provides a brief overview and an image (pl. 11). Bodel 1999, esp. 264–265, examines the curious spatial arrangement and partial symmetry of the depicted imagery and compares it to Polybius' description.

the overall shape and cadence for many of the events connected to an aristocratic funeral. (See fig. 2.1.)

The Textual Description: Polybius 6.53

Ὅταν γὰρ μεταλλάξῃ τις παρ᾽ αὐτοῖς τῶν ἐπιφανῶν ἀνδρῶν, συντελουμένης τῆς ἐκφορᾶς κομίζεται μετὰ τοῦ λοιποῦ κόσμου πρὸς τοὺς καλουμένους ἐμβόλους εἰς τὴν ἀγορὰν ποτὲ μὲν ἑστὼς ἐναργής, σπανίως δὲ κατακεκλιμένος. πέριξ δὲ παντὸς τοῦ δήμου στάντος, ἀναβὰς ἐπὶ τοὺς ἐμβόλους, ἂν μὲν υἱὸς ἐν ἡλικίᾳ καταλείπηται καὶ τύχῃ παρών, οὗτος, εἰ δὲ μή, τῶν ἄλλων εἴ τις ἀπὸ γένους ὑπάρχει, λέγει περὶ τοῦ τετελευτηκότος τὰς ἀρετὰς καὶ τὰς ἐπιτετευγμένας ἐν τῷ ζῆν πράξεις. δι᾽ ὧν συμβαίνει τοὺς πολλοὺς ἀναμιμνησκομένους καὶ λαμβάνοντας ὑπὸ τὴν ὄψιν τὰ γεγονότα, μὴ μόνον τοὺς κεκοινωνηκότας τῶν ἔργων, ἀλλὰ καὶ τοὺς ἐκτός, ἐπὶ τοσοῦτον γίνεσθαι συμπαθεῖς ὥστε μὴ τῶν κηδευόντων ἴδιον, ἀλλὰ κοινὸν τοῦ δήμου φαίνεσθαι τὸ σύμπτωμα. μετὰ δὲ ταῦτα θάψαντες καὶ ποιήσαντες τὰ νομιζόμενα τιθέασι τὴν εἰκόνα τοῦ μεταλλάξαντος εἰς τὸν ἐπιφανέστατον τόπον τῆς οἰκίας, ξύλινα ναΐδια περιτιθέντες. ἡ δ᾽ εἰκών ἐστι πρόσωπον εἰς ὁμοιότητα διαφερόντως ἐξειργασμένον καὶ κατὰ τὴν πλάσιν καὶ κατὰ τὴν ὑπογραφήν. ταύτας δὴ τὰς εἰκόνας ἔν τε ταῖς δημοτελέσι θυσίαις ἀνοίγοντες κοσμοῦσι φιλοτίμως, ἐπάν τε τῶν οἰκείων μεταλλάξῃ τις ἐπιφανής, ἄγουσιν εἰς τὴν ἐκφοράν, περιτιθέντες ὡς ὁμοιοτάτοις εἶναι δοκοῦσι κατά τε τὸ μέγεθος καὶ τὴν ἄλλην περικοπήν. οὗτοι δὲ προσαναλαμβάνουσιν ἐσθῆτας, ἐὰν μὲν ὕπατος ἢ στρατηγὸς ᾖ γεγονώς, περιπορφύρους, ἐὰν δὲ τιμητής, πορφυρᾶς, ἐὰν δὲ καὶ τεθριαμβευκὼς ἤ τι τοιοῦτον κατειργασμένος, διαχρύσους.

αὐτοὶ μὲν οὖν ἐφ᾽ ἁρμάτων οὗτοι πορεύονται, ῥάβδοι δὲ καὶ πελέκεις καὶ τἄλλα τὰ ταῖς ἀρχαῖς εἰωθότα συμπαρακεῖσθαι προηγεῖται κατὰ τὴν ἀξίαν ἑκάστῳ τῆς γεγενημένης κατὰ τὸν βίον ἐν τῇ πολιτείᾳ προαγωγῆς ὅταν δ᾽ ἐπὶ τοὺς ἐμβόλους ἔλθωσι, καθέζονται πάντες ἑξῆς ἐπὶ δίφρων ἐλεφαντίνων. οὗ κάλλιον οὐκ εὐμαρὲς ἰδεῖν θέαμα νέῳ φιλοδόξῳ καὶ φιλαγάθῳ· τὸ γὰρ τὰς τῶν ἐπ᾽ ἀρετῇ δεδοξασμένων ἀνδρῶν εἰκόνας ἰδεῖν ὁμοῦ πάσας οἷον εἰ ζώσας καὶ πεπνυμένας τίν᾽ οὐκ ἂν παραστῆσαι;

Whenever a distinguished Roman dies, during the funeral procession his body is conveyed with the requisite pomp to the Forum, onto the so-called Rostra, most of the time propped upright, but sometimes reclined. With the entire populace standing around him, the eulogist mounts the Rostra—a surviving son of appropriate age, if he happens to be present, but if not, someone else from the family—and he speaks about the noble works and deeds accomplished by the deceased. On account of which it happens that many recall the events and experience them vividly in their mind's eye, not only those who took part in the deeds, but also those who did not, and they all sympathize to such an extent that not only is the event a private concern for those mourning, but it is manifestly a shared concern of the populace. Afterwards, once they have performed the burial and the other customary rites, they set up a likeness (the *imago*) of the deceased in the most conspicuous place in the house, and they place it in a wooden shrine. The likeness is a mask fashioned with a great degree of verisimilitude both according to form and feature. They remove these likenesses from their cabinets on holidays and adorn them reverently, and whenever a notable citizen

FIGURE 2.1 Funerary relief from Amiternum, first century BCE, now located in the Museo Nazionale d'Abruzzo dell'Aquila. Photo Credit: Christopher Johanson.

> dies, they bring them to the procession, and they put them on those who seem to be most similar both in size and other traits. These people don a toga, if he had been a *praetor* or a *consul*, a purple-bordered toga, if he had been a *censor*, an entirely purple toga, and if he had triumphed or accomplished something similar, a golden toga.
>
> These men are then conveyed in chariots; fasces and axes and all the other paraphernalia customarily associated with the offices lead the way in accordance with the level of rank in the state achieved by each during his life. When they reach the Rostra, they all sit in a row on ivory chairs. It is not easy to see a finer spectacle than this for a youth bent on achieving glory and honor. For who would not be won over by the sight of the likenesses of men who were famed for excellence all together as if they were living and breathing?[2]

Polybius' description of a generic Roman aristocratic funeral, the lengthiest, by far, of our extant sources, is also the most detailed account of the Republican aristocratic funeral procession, the *pompa funebris*.[3] It is, however, a limited description and representative of a greater problem: it is at best generic and in no way prescriptive. Such accounts are useful because they provide a general sense of how the funeral might have been staged, and they even imply that these elements are typical. Yet we have no real sense of the degree to which Polybius' description corresponds to the event he witnessed. Did he exaggerate certain aspects for effect? Was it the case that every family participated in such an event in comparable ways? These and similar questions can never be answered with complete certitude. Nonetheless, one can assert with some confidence that Polybius witnessed events like the funerals he described and his testimony can, at the very least, serve as a scaffold for a recon-

---

[2] Polybius 6.53.

[3] Pliny *HN* 35.6 echoes Polybius' description when he reflects on how the Republican practice of carrying waxen *imagines* at funerals had ended by his time. See Morstein-Marx and Byrne 2025 for a full discussion of this passage and the use of *imagines* during the Empire.

struction of what these events might have looked like, and how they might have been experienced.[4]

Material Evidence: A Funerary Relief from Amiternum

A relief from Amiternum, dating to the late Republic, complements the text of Polybius; it also complicates an overall interpretation of the event. The relief depicts what appears to be a funeral procession of a local elite, perhaps a municipal soldier, located outside Rome. The sculptor inserted multiple registers of banding to maintain a legible scale for the figures depicted while simultaneously fitting the elements of the procession into the limited space of the stone: the single line of the participants is broken apart and the linear elements of the procession are stacked on top of each other. This visual compression potentially blurs the boundaries and order of the participants; it is not obviously clear which registers are first and last, though the specific order matters less than the representation of the constituent parts. If one reads from right to left, top to bottom, the procession plays out as follows. At the front of the procession, in the top register, are horn players. Following them are pipe players. Next come mourners, often called *praeficae*. The most dominant visual element is the funeral bier (the *feretrum* or *lectica*), which carries the funeral couch and the deceased. Eight pallbearers carry the bier. Hired workers dressed as such lead the way.[5] Those carrying the bier are similarly dressed in low-status garb. The deceased is reclined, on the double mattress of the funeral couch. The left elbow rests on a pillow and the hand props up the head. The right holds a staff or sceptre of some sort, likely not a *scipio eburneus*, which was carried by a triumphing general at Rome (and not by a municipal soldier). The *matrona* and two women, perhaps female members of the family, follow wearing long flounced skirts, with their hair undone. Another, similarly garbed, follows, accompanied by two women with their hair up. In the register below, two more women, with legs bare, possibly slaves, look to the *matrona*; one carries an oddly shaped implement, which some have argued is a fan. At the end of this procession, a figure with legs fully exposed, most likely a slave, carries a palm leaf and a *situla* that was presumably used to sprinkle on the dead.[6]

---

[4]Modern scholars have developed a funerary typology (Toynbee 1996: 44) that comprises four funeral types, the *funus militare*, the *funus publicum*, which was paid for by the state and evolved into the *funus imperatorium*, and, lastly, the so-called *funus translaticum* (*sic*), which derives from Suet. *Nero* 33 "tralaticio extulit funere." The privately sponsored Roman aristocratic funeral falls under this last classification, but it is a case where a non-technical use (that of Suetonius), when applied as a technical term, imposes a false sense of a regulated and formal event on an *ad hoc* ritual. See Green 1971: 284, whose concern over the use of *funus translaticum* has often been ignored.

[5]Richlin 2014: 286 offers a compelling description of the class consciousness apparent in the detailed depictions of the funerary garb. Carroll 2011: 130 argues that, even in a less lavish funeral such as this, attempts might have been made to convey status through depiction of hired workers, slaves, and freedmen.

[6]Franchi 1966: 26, esp. 26n25 recalls the Etruscan tradition and the reliefs that represent this practice.

Comparing Image and Text

The imagery in the relief from Amiternum and that in the written description of Polybius are radically different. Polybius highlights the propped-up body of the deceased, the *imagines* in their cabinet in the house, the chariot parade of ancestors, the accomplishments and deeds symbolized by their garb, coupled with the speeches that rehearse the *res gestae* of each ancestor. Polybius, in effect, argues that these *exempla* were inspirational for Roman youth to pursue similar deeds to achieve similar fame.

In the relief, the focus is remarkably different. There are no *imagines*, no ancestors, no chariots. In fact, apart from the representation of the deceased, one is confronted by a very different event, or, at the very least, a representation constructed with very different priorities in mind. One tends to assume that this funeral is a less lavish version of the kind described in Polybius. Further, since the relief was found outside Rome, and was perhaps removed from the use of *imagines*, the relief depicts no mechanism to promote the accomplishments of the family or those of the deceased. Instead, in an inversion of what Polybius describes, the majority of the visual space available on the relief depicts hired attendees. The elaborate, stellar imagery of the funeral canopy might reflect some accomplishment, as will the helmet at the top and the toga on the deceased. Yet, the dominant imagery, the hired attendants, is perhaps a precise indicator of how much was invested in this funeral. While there are no visible ancestors, and no visible signs of accumulated political power, there are many signs that funds were used to hire human labor to put on the show.

A GENERIC DESCRIPTION OF THE FUNERAL

These two representations, the textual excerpt from Polybius, material evidence in the relief coupled with scattered descriptions of subsequent funerals written far removed from the original time period, have led modern scholars to develop the following generalized outline of the event:

After the lying in state, which lasted as long as seven days, the public come to view the event.[7] The body of the deceased is carried out from the house to the Roman Forum in a funeral parade. Pipers, trumpeters, and horn blowers lead the way. Mourners (*praeficae)* follow. The procession is "crowded and noisy."[8] Wax masks of certain ancestors, the *imagines*, stored in wooden cabinets within the house,

[7] For the lying in state, see Serv. ad *A.* 6.218. For the attendees, see Polyb. 6.53.2: πέριξ δὲ παντὸς τοῦ δήμου στάντος ("with the entire populace standing all around"). For the modern view, see Flower 1996: 98: "Indeed a large funeral procession might take up quite a lot of space and would surely have attracted considerable crowds."

[8] Dutsch 2008: 259.

are donned by actors or family members.[9] Having evidently prepared for these funerary moments for considerable time, these embodied masks—living versions of the deceased and his forebears—imitate the actions, gait, and comportment of the *maiores* they represent.[10]

The ancestors mount chariots (ἐφ' ἁρμάτων), presumably *quadrigae*, flanked by the requisite number of lictors determined by their last magisterial rank. The oldest leads the group of ancestors, who are arrayed in chronological order, each subsequent generation lined up one behind the other. The family, including the eulogist, follows, dressed in black, their heads covered in ashes.[11] The procession moves from the house to the Rostra, winding its way through the city streets toward the Forum.[12]

The procession sets the stage for the main event, the *laudatio*.[13] Upon arrival, the ancestors mount the Rostra and sit on ivory chairs in a row. The body is then placed on or near the Rostra for all to see. Finally, the *laudator*, preferably the son of the deceased, gives the eulogy. The general public was moved to attend these events.[14] Placed within the civic, legal, and religious center of Rome, "the deceased belongs, not to the small grieving immediate family, but to the public, to the state, and to Rome."[15] The point of this event? Sumi echoes Polybius when he states, "to inculcate important social values and encourage the younger generation to aspire to great achievements in service to the state."[16]

Whenever a variety of fragmentary sources, all centuries apart, are assembled under the guidance of a few key pieces of evidence—especially for such an important civic event—the illusion of familiarity with the event emerges by consensus.[17]

---

[9] For a discussion of the people selected to wear the masks, see Flower 1996: 99–100; cf. Edwards 2007: 19, who assumes that they are family members.

[10] For the tradition of actors following the deceased throughout life, see Diod. Sic. 31.25.2 and Bettini 2005; Morstein-Marx and Byrne 2025: 334n23 question this interpretation and sees in Diodorus a reflection of a contemporary practice.

[11] On the bereaved covering their heads in ashes and wearing dark clothing such as the *toga atra* and *toga sordida*, see Bodel 2000 with numerous citations, but add Prop. 4.7.28 and Prop. 4.11.97.

[12] See Johanson 2011 for an experiential and hypothetical walk along this route; Bodel 1999: 164: "Once the funeral cortège had wound from the house through the city streets."

[13] Flower 1996: 129: "The procession with all its sounds and splendour was the essential background to the oration."

[14] Bodel 1999: 259: "Roman funerals were public events."

[15] Ochs 1993: 94.

[16] Sumi 2005: 42–43. D. W. Moore 2020: 102–106 sees Polybius' portrayal of the funeral as designed to support Polybius' overall historical program: "the role which the knowledge of the past plays in inspiring later generations remains fundamental both to history and to the aristocratic funeral. For Polybius, part of the appeal of the aristocratic funeral as an important and effective Roman custom lies in the fact that it accurately displays in practice the goals of history." Eckstein 1994: 65 also notes: "Polybius' special emphasis is on how the institutions of Roman society in the Hannibalic period produced not only honest men … but courageous men. That is the point of his description of the pomp and ceremony surrounding Roman aristocratic funerals."

[17] Beard 2007: 81 wrestles with the issue as it relates to the triumph: "In the case of the triumph, by contrast, thanks to a host of ancient references to location and context, participants and procedures, it has been possible to sketch out a richly detailed 'order of ceremonies,' from beginning to end. In fact, at

This is of course how history works. Generalizations make it possible to define themes and cultural patterns. Each historical investigation balances blind acceptance of what the ancient sources say and skepticism about their words.[18]

The tendency to overemphasize the scripting, the formulaic nature of the event, and the impact of the spectacle without engaging the problems presented by the interpreted source material is natural. This tendency often imposes rules and prescriptions onto unregulated systems. The funerary relief from Amiternum was certainly not a template to be consulted and emulated as one prepared for a funeral. The same is true of Polybius, whose insistence on the rhetorical power and cumulative cultural effect of the event convinces some modern scholars to see Polybius' account as a virtual script.[19] Of course, he was not prescribing the ritual; instead, using the funeral as an example, he engages in an unrelated argument. He presents the funeral as a cultural institution unique to the Roman world, in order to argue that this cultural practice, the funeral, was the source of Roman superiority. In fact, one overgeneralizes by referring to this section of Polybius' histories as an account of a Roman funeral; it is, instead, a specific account of the use of ancestor masks in a funerary event. Therefore, his omissions are potentially just as important as the details he includes. Attempts in the literary record to distort and to amplify are well known but not always fully considered when assessing the sources.[20] For the funeral, reasons to exaggerate the spectacle are great, but a number of factors ranging from the lack of any official sanction, the timing of the event, its comparatively small size, and the viewing and staging difficulties caused by routing, all suggest a slightly more nuanced and restrained spectacular event. The practical realities, the narrowness of the Roman streets, the uneven and worn paving stones, the dirt and filth, and the distractions of daily life directly affect interpretations of all spectacle. Recreating and simulating a historical event is impossible, but by representing certain quantifiable elements of the event, e.g., the built environment, the viewing areas, the performance spaces, and the main players, one can at least build a set of constraints within which we might better understand how funerals might unfold.

What was the true extent of the procession? How did the topographical situation in the mid-Republic affect this funeral parade and its viewing? How did the audience view and interact with this mobile form of spectacle? Who was the intended audience? Polybius presents an ideal, but the funeral procession comprised

---

the center of most modern discussions of the triumph, for all their differences in interpretation and their different theories on triumphal origins and meaning, lies a generally agreed picture of 'what happened' in the ceremony, at least in its developed form."

[18] For the full discussion, see Beard 2007: 72ff.

[19] Flower 1996: 133 expresses concern when subtle evidence on the *laudatio* differs from the Polybian view: "Polybius, however, portrays funeral speeches as moving and impressive; we should be wary about dismissing them in haste."

[20] Beard 2007: 80–81 again on the triumph: "Nostalgia, anachronism, exaggeration, creative invention, scrupulous accuracy—all these, in different combinations, determined how individual triumphs were written up by ancient authors."

a multiplicity of variables. The processional route, the number of ancestors, and the day of the event were variable parts in an extraordinarily flexible script.

In this chapter, I use the evidence surrounding the funeral of L. Aemilius Paullus to ground modern interpretations of the processional event in the temporally specific topographic and visual contexts. By modeling a case study and alternatives, I modify and expand the orthodox view by performing a visual analysis of an event that only survives in textual description. This chapter aims to assess the visual and semiotic impact of the *pompa* and proceeds as follows. I first define the spatial boundaries of the procession by representing the road system and the adjacent built environment. Within this virtual, reconstructed space, I include stylized representations of the participants and the accompanying apparatus in order to explore the potential interaction between the funeral procession and the audience. The investigation, grounded in the evidence for the funeral of L. Aemilius Paullus is therefore set in 160 BCE.

The primary goal of this chapter is to develop a more nuanced reading of the textual and material evidence through a visual, and, in part, experiential analysis of various models of Roman funerary processions. This chapter will not assert that one mode of participation and viewing predominated, rather it will offer multiple interpretations of the combined material and literary evidence in order to provide various possibilities that move the reader beyond the confines of the scenes presented by Polybius or those depicted in a single sculptural relief. The inquiry itself is just as important as its product. I explore a range of possibilities for the staging of the parade and their practical ramifications.

The current investigation proceeds as follows. First, I examine recent discussions of the *pompa funebris* with the aid of two-dimensional diagrams to establish the primary visual elements to be analyzed. I then briefly compare the *pompa funebris* to other regularly held processions. Next, I outline the evidence for the three-dimensional, topographical framework of the investigation. I present a possible set of routes for the procession to follow. I identify a handful of highly speculative possible home locations for Paullus, to then extrapolate possible routes and entryways to the Forum, and then to the Rostra. At this point I adduce comparisons to other processions to illustrate that, in Roman terms, the procession of a Roman funeral, though similar in many respects to other processions, was primarily *sui generis*. I apply an *in* virtual *situ* analysis to a hypothetical funeral roughly corresponding to that of L. Aemilius Paullus and to a series of comparable processions. The *in* virtual *situ*, visual analyses will be applied to several scenarios viewed from multiple perspectives, a birds-eye view of the event, and views on the ground. I focus on the potential audiences along the route and in the Forum; I also focus on the members of the procession, especially the young male descendant who had been selected to give the eulogy. Once I have established the limitations imposed upon the procession by the generic script of the *pompa* and by the surrounding built environment, I turn to two Roman innovations designed to circumvent these limitations. Having established the visual effect and limits of the procession, I conclude by examining its function.

THE *POMPA FUNEBRIS*: VISUALIZING THE PRINCIPAL SEMIOTIC ELEMENTS

A Roman aristocratic funeral procession might display a range of sometimes deeply contrasting elements.[21] One must assume that no funeral procession precisely mirrored another. Nonetheless, the fundamental constituent parts can be found in a combined reading of Polybius coupled with the relief from Amiternum. These elements comprised the arrangement of the *imagines*, the location of the bier, and the ordering of the parade participants, all of which were charged with meaning, and this meaning in turn had a broader cultural significance. The repetition of funerals, the overlapping, annual progression of multiple types of funeral processions filled with differing numbers of these semiotic props reinforced a series of social norms.[22] The specific visual presentation of a given funeral procession can be read as a potent event, a conveyor of cultural memory, and a visual manifestation of power and tradition. To establish the baseline semiotic elements, I will first present a two-dimensional, abstract diagram that depicts the barest constituent parts of the funeral procession removed from its topographical context.

The deceased was located in "a continuum of past, present and future."[23] The relief from Amiternum, depicting a funeral without ancestors, provides a starting point for visual analysis. The sculptor highlights the deceased in the upper register, though somewhat surprisingly, devotes significantly more space to those carrying the *feretrum*. In fact, these men, dressed as workers, not as togate elite, are also the largest figures on display. The *feretrum*, the deceased, and the eight men, each articulated individually, also present a visual division between the musicians and paid workers at the front, the deceased, followed by the family—all women—behind. The *feretrum* and pallbearers suggest a "visual symmetry" or at least a visual balance that carries over into the overall arrangement of the relief, *i.e.*, the bier itself is depicted as a symmetrical object that divides the procession into two distinct parts, thus forming a bridge between the front half and back half of the procession. In this representation, the deceased denotes a thematic transition from hired performers to the family, and a chronological turn from the funerary apparatus and the deceased to the living members of the family.

---

[21] See Sumi 2002: 578–581 on the contrasting, quasi-carnivalesque atmosphere of a Roman funeral, which, unlike the carnival (as defined by Bakhtin 1984), had a clear hierarchy with a healthy mix of praise and ridicule; and Ochs 1993: 93–94, on the tension between private grief and public celebration present in the funeral.

[22] Hölkeskamp 2004: 97-100 applies "symbolische Kapital" to the representative forms of the *imagines*, and Hölkeskamp 2023: 272–340 expands on this earlier work. Flaig 2003 and Flaig 1995 explore in greater detail the annual battles of symbolic capital on display in the Forum.

[23] Bodel 1999: 264.

Now, we will generate a new visual representation by combining the main elements from the Amiternum relief with the "ancestors." Since Polybius tells us that the eulogist recounts the deeds of the ancestors, beginning with the most distant (ἄρχεται τῶν ἄλλων ἀπὸ τοῦ προγενεστάτου τῶν παρόντων, καὶ λέγει τὰς ἐπιτυχίας ἑκάστου καὶ τὰς πράξεις), we tend to assume that the ancestors would array themselves in chronological order from oldest to youngest, followed by the *feretrum* and deceased. After the musicians who led the parade, the ancestors began a continuous symbolic transition from the eldest ancestor, to the recently deceased.[24] This arrangement of participants served as a visual means to order and connect the living and the dead. For the duration of the funeral, the chronological descent fixes the deceased in his quasi-permanent place in the familial memory. It also connects him directly to the line of successful ancestors that had gone before. The chronological thread connected the afterlife to the "liminal" figure of the recently deceased and then to the living.[25] The family members followed, and in such a chronologically defined model, they may have arranged themselves in chronological order as well, but on this last point, no evidence exists.

RECONSTRUCTING AND REPRESENTING THE ANCESTORS IN THE PROCESSION

The funeral of a local municipal elite, held over 100 kilometers removed from Rome, as represented in the relief from Amiternum, provides another reasonable lower bound to reconstruct the composition of the processional elements. According to the relief, there was a double mattress bier, carried by eight select men, perhaps comprising family and close friends.[26] The bier of L. Aemilius Paullus was famously carried by foreigners from the provinces he had conquered.[27] Horn players led the march. According to Polybius, living men donned the *imagines* of illustrious ancestors; these men were distinguished by dress according to office achieved: a *consul* or *praetor* wore the *toga praetexta*, a *censor* wore the *toga*

[24] Bettini 1991: 177 highlights this transition and ordering. Bodel 1999: 264–265 carefully analyzes how the design of the Amiternum relief uses space to order the participants. For the relief, again, see Franchi 1966.

[25] Dutsch 2008: 260: "It is tempting to conjecture that the role of the ritual performers (the *praeficae*, the musicians, and the impersonators of the dead) might have been to lure the spirits of the newly deceased by song and music, enticing them to abandon the company of the living and cross over to the realm of the dead." Thus, the arrangement situates the performers at the lead and squarely in the symbolic world of the dead.

[26] For the double mattress, again, see fig. 2.1, Toynbee 1996: 46 and note 143, and Franchi 1966: 23–32. For family members carrying the bier, see Pliny *HN* 7.142, who, if we read him literally, records that a funerary bier was carried on the shoulders of surviving sons: L. Caecilius Metellus was "a quattor filiis inlatus rogo, uno praetore, tribus consularibus (duobus triumphalibus), uno censorio" ("carried to the pyre by four sons, one *praetor*, three ex-consuls, two had triumphed, and one had achieved a censorship").

[27] Diod. Sic. 31.25.1 and Val. Max. 2.10.3.

purpurea, and a *triumphator* wore a golden-bordered toga, the *toga picta*.[28] These actors rode in chariots (ἐφ' ἁρμάτων) and were preceded by those (actors again? family members? slaves?) carrying the trappings of their past office, which would differ according to office. For every *praetor* one would expect two to six lictors, and for every ex-*consul*, presumably one would see twelve lictors.[29] Hence, there are multiple ways that one might distinguish the rank of each member of the procession.

I now turn to the ancestors present for each family. Determining precisely how many ancestors participated in the procession is not simple. Two evidentiary hurdles are impossible to overcome: 1) in almost every individual case, there is not enough evidence to reconstruct a robust family genealogy; 2) even if evidence for all Romans who ever lived might exist, *i.e.*, like a modern, state-funded, comprehensive database with birth records attested by a certifying authority, there is no way to prove with precision and accuracy which specific *imagines* might have been displayed at any one funeral.[30] In fact, one highly restrictive view holds that the semiotic power of the ancestral procession lay in its selectivity.[31] Nonetheless, we can create a conservative model, bound by specific evidentiary parameters. As we have seen, Polybius gives a short list of those who might appear: praetors, consuls, triumphators, and censors. Some have extrapolated from the appearance of these offices to argue that only those who had gained the so-called *ius imaginum* might take part in the parade.[32] Therefore, one might also expect to see curule aediles in addition to former consuls and praetors. In my view, it is hard to believe that this ritual conformed to a regulated system, however.[33] Polybius (6.53.1) is not nearly as restrictive as he is sometimes interpreted. He gives no formal rule for ancestral representations; rather, he simply lists examples. More important, he explicitly acknowledges achievements beyond the bounds of the state-recognized system of honors: ἐὰν δὲ καὶ τεθριαμβευκὼς ἤ τι τοιοῦτον κατειργασμένος ("If he had triumphed or had achieved something just as great.")[34]

Nonetheless, even within this limited subset of possibilities, there was potential for a range of ancestral representations in the funeral. We simply cannot know

[28] Walbank 1970 *ad loc.* provides the Latin translations used above.

[29] On the number of lictors for the *consul*, see Purcell 1983; for the *praetor*, Brennan 2000: 664–666.

[30] I return to a discussion of the possible *imagines* to be deployed in my discussion of the *laudatio*, in Chapter 3 below.

[31] Flaig 2003: 56–57 argues that the *agmen imaginum* was in no way analogous to a family tree.

[32] Flaig 2003: 52n15 notes that the lowest office Polybius mentions is *praetor*, but that the *ius imaginum* requires the complete curule magistracies.

[33] The argument represents a broader scholarly practice to infer formal institutions from what were probably just customary practices. See, e.g., Hölkeskamp 2023, esp. 274 and 293–295, who argues that the funeral procession for each deceased aristocratic followed a similar script that required a chronological ordering of the *imagines*. Cic. *Leg.* 2.61 notes that nearly every activity related to the *funus* is *not* governed by law, see below, p. 146. For the *ius imaginum*, Flower 1996: 53–59 reminds us that it is a modern invention and contends that the decision to create an *imago* was strictly a family affair. See also Flower 2007, who notes that the evidence does not support the existence of a regulatory system.

[34] Polyb. 6.53.7.

whether certain ancestors were omitted, or added for a given event. In fact, we also do not know how often *imagines* were fabricated, whether multiple copies were shared among houses, or when the custom of waxen *imagines* first came into use. Was it in the fifth century, or the fourth, or even in the third century?[35] For this case study, however, I focus on the ancestors who clearly fit within the definition set by Polybius. That is, I will explore representations of ancestors who had triumphed or who held the offices of *praetor*, *consul*, or *censor*, who are attested in the historical record, and who might conceivably be related to the deceased.

THE ANCESTORS OF LUCIUS AEMILIUS PAULLUS

By 160 BCE, the *gens Aemilia* was one of the most powerful and storied families in Rome. To reconstruct the funeral assemblage of Paullus, I follow a straightforward algorithmic process that produces three potential outcomes.[36] For each scenario, I only produce an assemblage of persons who are attested in the historical record. Furthermore, though I cite Broughton's *MRR* extensively, for the purposes of all visualizations, I rely on the Digital Prosopography of the Roman Republic (*DPRR*) as the authoritative record.[37] At the funeral of Lucius Aemilius Paullus, a conservative reconstruction of the Paulli branch of the family, includes *imagines* of L. Aemilius Paullus (cos. 219, 216), M. Aemilius Paullus (cos. 255), his father and grandfather. A more aggressive reconstruction might find potential ancestors who share the same *cognomen*, but are not otherwise specifically described as a direct relation. Therefore, Paullus' funeral might also include M. Aemilius L. f. L. n. Paullus (cos. 302), who shares the same *cognomen* but whose kinship relation is not specifically attested. A hyperaggressive reconstruction might look beyond shared *cognomina* to find potential ancestors of appropriate age who share only the same *nomen*, but not the same *cognomen*. By 160 BCE, the *gens Aemilia* and, most likely the Paulli branch, claimed descent from the Aemilii Mamerci/Mamercini, so in addition, this funeral assemblage might also have included (at least) *imag-*

[35] Were the *imagines* first used at public funerary events? For extended discussion on various views surrounding when funerary events were first held in the Forum, see Bodel 2024: 330n31 and 319: "The Forum did not become the main stage for aristocratic funerary celebrations before the middle of the third century."

[36] For extended discussion on the reconstruction of familial patrilines within the context of the assemblage on the Rostra, see below, p. 108.

[37] The *DPRR* (https://romanrepublic.ac.uk/) is based on "Broughton's Magistrates of the Roman Republic, which forms the backbone of the database, Rüpke's inventory of Roman priests in the *Fasti Sacerdotum*, the collection of information about family relations found in Zmeskal's *Adfinitas*, and Pina Polo's work on *repulsae*, defeated candidates." *N.b.*, when birth or death dates are unattested, the *DPPR* estimates these dates by rounding to the nearest 25-year increment. This method can naturally lead to life spans of 125 or 150 years within the database; I have made a deliberate decision to follow strictly the data within the *DPRR* with the result that some deaths may have been assigned to a 25-year period different from the actual, but unknown, date of death. For this specific investigation, this approach introduces no significant issue.

TABLE 2.1 Funerary garb of the ancestors of the Aemilii Paulli

Name	Magistracies	Triumph	Funerary Garb
L. Aemilius Mam. f. - n. Mamercus (*RE* 96)	cos. 484, 478, 473		toga praetexta
Mam. Aemilius M. f. Mamercinus (*RE* 16, 97)	dict. 437, 434, 426	426	toga picta
L. Aemilius Mam. f. M. n. Mamercinus (*RE* 93)	cos. tr. 391, 389, 387, 383, 382, 380		toga praetexta
L. Aemilius L. f. Mam. n. Mamercinus/Mamercus (*RE* 95 cf. 94)	cos. 366, 363		toga praetexta
L. Aemilius L. f. L. n. Mamercinus Privernas (*RE* 101)	cos. 341, 329	329	toga picta
M. Aemilius L. f. L. n. Paullus (*RE* 116)	cos. 302		toga praetexta
M. Aemilius M. f. L. n. Paullus (*RE* 117)	cos. 255	254	toga picta
L. Aemilius M. f. M. n. Paullus (*RE* 118)	cos. 219, 216		toga praetexta
L. Aemilius L. f. M. n. Paullus Macedonicus (*RE* 114)	cos. 182, 168, cens. 164	167	toga picta

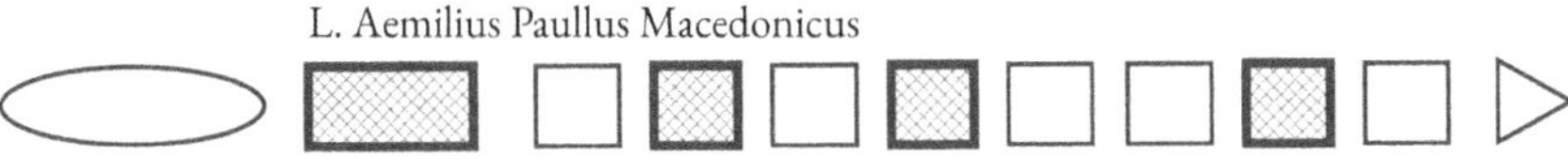

FIGURE 2.2 Funeral procession of L. Aemilius Paullus. The triangle indicates the leading elements of the procession, e.g., musicians, mourners, and the like. Plain squares indicate an ancestor who was wearing a *toga praetexta*; diagonal lines plus thickened outline, a *toga picta*. The oval indicates those that followed the deceased, who is indicated by a rectangle.

ines of L. Aemilius Mamercinus Privernas (cos. 341, 329), L. Aemilius Mamercinus/Mamercus (cos. 366, 363), L. Aemilius Mam. f. M. n. Mamercinus (cos. tr. 391, 389, 387, 383, 382, 380), Mam. Aemilius M. f. Mamercinus (dict. 437, 434, 426), and L. Aemilius Mamercus (cos. 484, 478, 473).[38] (See table 2.1 and fig. 2.2.)

If the *imagines* proceeded in chronological order, then an overarching theme of temporality and chronological kinship continuity is undeniable: the *pompa funebris* connected the past to the present *and* to the future, and it crossed boundaries from the dead to the living. The most politically successful founder of the family came first, then the parade of intervening ancestors followed. The liminal element—the deceased—marked a transition point to the realm of the living. Next, the youth designated to give the speech, and the rest of the family followed by the bier.[39] Professional mourners and presumably an additional assortment of attendees will have followed. Therefore, when viewed as a parade of symbols, the proposed chronological continuity and one's fixed place within the ancestral line-up is clearly displayed. The diagrammatic arrangement highlights a permanent ordering of internal famil-

[38] According to Plutarch in his life of Paullus, "most writers agree" that the *gens Aemilia* claim their descent from the Mamerci. Plutarch presents the origin story of the *gens Aemilia* in his life of Numa as well. See also Broughton 1968 *ad loc.* and Smith 2006: 35–36. I omit Ti. Aemilius L. f. Mam. n. Mamercus (*RE* 99) (cos. 467), since the filiation of Mam. Aemilius M. f. Mamercinus (RE 16, 97) indicates his father was a Marcus, who left no trace in the magisterial record. He was presumably the brother of this Tiberius; of course, the historicity of these early genealogical connections is dubious.

[39] Again, Bettini 1991: 167–183 focuses on the importance of the temporal continuity of the procession.

ial power.[40] The arrangement within the funeral cortege might serve as a collective memory device of a very restrictive sort: For the reader of our two-dimensional diagram, the following might seem emphatically clear: it was a precisely defined system wherein the men who had achieved a certain distinction in life, by all accounts magisterial status, would earn a spot in the ancestral line. Therefore the deeds and accomplishments of the family would be visibly articulated for a crowd. The selectivity of the procession created a visible and replicable record of familial achievement, both when read from within and without. The parade was not a walking biological family tree filled with highlights of the most successful members of the family. Rather, it was a select few ancestors who had merited commemoration for their achievements. Even if those who had not achieved an office might still have an *imago* and participate in the parade, the symbolic difference would be striking.[41] The garb of censors, consuls, and triumphators would all represent greater achievement than an unadorned toga. For families who had many successful ancestors, a clear visual judgment of the deceased could be made.[42] He has either lived up to the achievements of his ancestors or he has fallen short. It is not difficult to imagine multiple iterations of these symbolic parades accumulating over time, each reemphasizing the political accomplishment of the ancestors, often overshadowing the deceased.

The appearance of the deceased himself would have differed from that of the ancestors in significant ways. He would have been the only member of the procession who was carried, the only member who was reclined, and he would have been the only participant who was clearly immobile. It is possible that the deceased was garbed in similar fashion to that of the ancestors, but the sources are silent on the matter. If the funerary garb of the deceased followed the pattern designated by Polybius, and if the deceased had not achieved an office of note, then it would have been immediately clear how he compared to those who were being conveyed before him: the funeral parade might be the last memorial ever to occur for him; after this event, the deceased would be publicly forgotten. Even if he had achieved the office of *praetor*, for example, in many families he would have been forever marked as having not lived up to the achievements of the past. The surviving family members could have

---

[40] Flaig 2003: 52–57.

[41] A visit to the family tomb of the Scipiones reminds us that such aristocratic funerals need not be confined to those that had held magistracies. There, even young men who had never attained an office are commemorated. Cf. Flaig 2003. By the late Republic, funerals of women, replete with *imagines* were hardly rare occurrences. See Cic. *De or.* 2.225–226 and p. 120 below for an extended discussion. Presumably men who had never achieved high office, but had nonetheless lived a life of *virtus* could also receive a funeral *pompa*. Just as they received monumental commemoration in the tomb, perhaps they received the same in a wax *imago*. Polybius 6.53.1 avoids using official language to describe the deceased. They are simply illustrious men: Ὅταν γὰρ μεταλλάξῃ τις παρ᾽ αὐτοῖς τῶν ἐπιφανῶν ἀνδρῶν ("Whenever one of the illustrious men among them dies"). For τῶν ἐπιφανῶν ἀνδρῶν used as a technical term for *nobiles*, cf. Polyb. 3.40.9, where it would redefine current understanding of *nobilitas* in the second century BCE by referring to an ex-*consul and* two ex-praetors.

[42] Flaig 2003: 53.

clearly "read" the results of a life full of action in the symbols arrayed before them. There was a direct reward for civic achievement and a punishment of sorts for civic failure. Permanent glory or tacit condemnation to oblivion awaited the young aristocratic Roman male.[43] If there were no ancestors, the deceased would again stand out, this time for his success, and amongst the family his presence would indicate the possible beginning of a future ancestral parade.

Comparative diagrams offer a means of visually assessing multiple funeral parades at a time—something that could not have occurred in context, in the Roman Forum. One might recall past funerary displays, but there is no attested occurrence of explicit competitive funerals displayed side-by-side. The focus of this study remains the funeral of L. Aemilius Paullus, but throughout, I will adduce comparisons to contemporaneous families, so that we might be able to assess the symbols manifest at this one funeral compared to the competition. To this end, I will compare a family branch from the *gens Cornelia*, and a branch from the *gens Porcia*. By the mid-first century, the visual display of the Aemilii is strikingly similar to that of the Cornelii Scipiones. (See table 2.2 and fig. 2.3.) Under the present model, the Aemilii had one additional ancestor, but when examined side-by-side, these Cornelii are not far behind in the competition of colorful garb and, therefore, civic accomplishment. Achieving consulships was difficult enough in the Republic, but the additional triumphs and censorships demonstrate a family of equal merit. Compare the hypothetical funerals of both these families to the funeral put on by Cato the Elder for his son by his first wife. (See fig. 2.3.) This funeral, purportedly cheap due to Cato's poverty, would have demonstrated truncated ancestral power. Even after Cato's own death, through an honest tally, his family could never have hoped to compete with the visual prominence of the assemblage of *imagines* at funerals of the Aemilii and the Cornelii.[44] (See fig. 2.3.)

In my view, it is impossible to know precisely how many ancestors participated in a procession. Moreover, the model I follow in this investigation focuses solely on patrilineal descent. By the late Republic, there were funerary events for prominent women, and it is clearly demonstrable that patrilineal and matrilineal descent would both be used to determine which *imagines* might be held in a given house.[45]

---

[43] There is no ancient discussion surrounding the results of not receiving an *imago*, but there is, of course, clear evidence that it was considered a serious condemnation to disallow the display of specific *imagines*. An Imperial example, under very different circumstances, illustrates how the display of ancestral *imagines* or the decision not to display them, was significant: Tacitus' account of the funeral of Iunia (Tac. *A.* 3.76) "praefulgebant Cassius atque Brutus eo ipso quod effigies eorum non visebantur." ("Cassius and Brutus were conspicuous by the very fact that their *imagines* were not visible.") Of course Cassius and Brutus were a special case, but their *imagines* here highlight how display of ancestors at a funeral carried a special political weight and conveyed a narrative.

[44] On Cato's parsimonious funerary style, see Livy *Per.* 48: "M. Porcius Cato filii in praetura mortui funus tenuissimo ut potuit, nam pauper erat, sumptu fecit." ("M. Porcius Cato put on the funeral for his son, who had died during his praetorship, with the least expense as he was able, for he was poor.") As we shall see below, there were other options for visual manipulation.

[45] See below, p. 89ff. p. 120ff. esp. p.109n136.

TABLE 2.2 Funerary garb of the ancestors of the Cornelii Scipiones

Name	Magistracies	Triumph	Funerary Garb
Ser. Cornelius Maluginensis (*RE* 253)	cos. 485		toga praetexta
L. Cornelius Ser. f. P. n. Maluginensis (*RE* 256)	cos. 459	459	toga picta
P. Cornelius Scipio (*RE* 328)	Tr. Mil. c. p. 395		toga praetexta
L. Cornelius P. f. Scipio (*RE* 322)	cos. 350, cens. 340?		toga purpurea
L. Cornelius Cn. f. Scipio Barbatus (*RE* 343)	cos. 298, cens. 280?		toga purpurea
L. Cornelius L. f. Cn. n. Scipio (*RE* 323)	cos. 259, 258	259	toga picta
P. Cornelius Scipio (*RE* 330)	cos. 218		toga praetexta
P. Cornelius Scipio Africanus (*RE* 336)	cos. 205, 194; cens. 199	189	toga picta

Furthermore, it seems to have been the case that even relations outside a strict lineage might be included. Nonetheless, for the purposes of this investigation, as much as possible, the visualizations are guided by a circumscribed subset of evidence: in the case of L. Aemilius Paullus, while his marriage to Papiria (and divorce) is well documented, no evidence survives to provide the name of Paullus' mother or any of the other women in his ancestral family. Therefore, given the limits of the extant evidence, I only consider patrilineal descent and the direct patrilineal line.

Our evidence suggests that funerals of the most powerful and/or the most ambitious Roman families eventually ended up in the same place, the Roman Forum. This alone was a mark of success. An observer might compare the symbolic power on display at each funeral, and they might count triumphs or consulships. Those with more ancestors would clearly win this elite competition. A procession led by only one chariot would be demonstrably inferior to one led by fifteen or even twenty. By the time of the principate, historians deemed it important enough to record the total count, which may reflect the overall importance of this metric: the more ancestors, the more prestige, and audiences kept a tally.[46] Nonetheless, merely to have a funeral in the Forum was an accomplishment and would say much about the individual deceased and his heirs. It might indicate that this was a family on the rise or one that had already risen. For this study, the "props" on display were the heart of the competition, but it is worth underscoring the prestigious nature of the funerary event in the Forum. It remained one of the few moments where individual families might commandeer parts of this central space for matters not explicitly related to the state.

[46] Before Augustus, the greatest number of *imagines* displayed is difficult to determine. It is instructive that the funeral of Iunia Tertia, the wife of Cassius and sister of Brutus, was accompanied by twenty *imagines* ("viginti clarissimarum familiarum imagines antelatae sunt, Manlii, Quinctii aliaque eiusdem nobilitatis nomina." Tac. *A.* 3.76). It might have numbered twenty-two, were it not for the omission of Brutus and Cassius (see note 43).

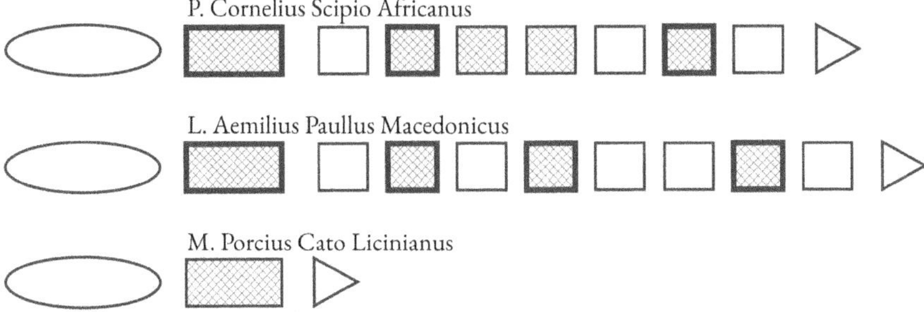

FIGURE 2.3 Hypothetical funeral processions for M. Porcius Cato Licinianus, P. Cornelius Scipio Africanus, and L. Aemilius Paullus. The triangle indicates the leading elements of the procession, e.g., musicians, mourners, and the like. Thickened outline indicates *toga praetexta*, diagonal lines indicate *toga purpurea*, diagonal lines plus thickened outline indicate *toga picta*. The oval indicates those that followed the deceased, who is indicated by a rectangle

A GENERIC PROCESSION

Processions were a quintessential element of Roman ceremony. They were employed primarily for events related to festival days. They often indicated the start of a performance or a ceremony. In the process, they conveyed the participants to stationary performance space. For a sacrifice, a procession might serve as a formal mechanism to move the participants to the altar in front of a temple where the sacrifice would occur. For theatrical performances, processions might gather less-than-human scale sculptures of gods to parade through the city before depositing them in the seating area for a performance. Circus games and later gladiatorial combat in fixed arenas would begin with a formal procession, where the participants in the race or the combat would arrive to the main event. Processions of this sort were spectacular and integral parts of ceremony, but they were also preludes and codas to performances in fixed locations. The funeral procession was similar in many ways. It moved its participants from a fixed starting location, the home of the deceased, to nodal points, where a performance would occur.

FUNUS TRIUMPHO SIMILLIMUM?

When reflecting on the funeral of Drusus the Elder in 9 BCE, Seneca calls it "a funeral most like a triumph" (*funus triumpho simillimum*).[47] Scholars have used this line to argue that a funeral was quite similar to a triumph; in fact, the funeral and the triumph display many similarities. Unlike the list of ceremonies in the preceding

[47] Sen. *Ad Marc.* 3.1. See Manning 1981 *ad loc.*

paragraph, the funeral procession also had an interesting and intertwined affinity to the triumphal procession: both processions are held specifically to honor one individual.[48] Moreover, in both events, the Forum served as a primary node, at which the participants on chariots would dismount. Strictly speaking, the pragmatic goal of a triumph was to lead the triumphing general to the Capitoline Hill, and to the Temple of Jupiter Optimus Maximus, where a culminating event might occur, but to get there, he would stop in the Forum. Similarly, the ultimate goal of the funeral procession was to reach the final place of interment, but a significant and spectacular event was first held in the Forum. Nonetheless, the funeral for Drusus was not the norm and represented a new class of funeral, one for the imperial family. The procession began in Germany, and ended with orations given by the Roman princeps in the Forum and in the Circus Flaminius. In fact, preparation for Drusus' triumph was already under way, and his long and lingering death—30 days—left enough time for Tiberius to travel to him. The merger of funeral and triumph at his death fit the circumstances, but did not necessarily resemble prior funeral practices of the Republic. The two were almost different phenomena. Nonetheless, the explicit comparison introduced by Seneca is tacitly accepted by modern scholars who discuss the triumph and the funeral procession in the same context.[49]

There are, of course, many points of intersection between the triumph and the funeral. There were chariots and triumphal regalia, the destination was the Forum, there were musicians, and ritual chanting.[50] Perhaps most striking is the shared elevation of triumphal regalia and the use of the triumphal chariot. The funeral, as presented by Polybius, highlights the triumph as a notable accomplishment that is also visually articulated in the funeral procession. In fact, the *pompa funebris* is the only instance, apart from an actual triumph, where a triumphal chariot is driven through the streets of Rome by someone wearing the triumphal toga (*toga picta*). By the time of the principate, the imperial funeral had morphed into an event that more closely replicated and even supplanted the triumph. From its display of placards and busts and statues to, in the case of the emperor, the final apotheosis, the Imperial funeral was indeed similar to the triumph. It was not the same phenomenon as that of the Republic, however.[51]

For this study, which focuses on the visual aspects of one funeral held in 160 BCE, I will primarily highlight the differences, not the similarities, between the Republican aristocratic funeral and the Republican triumph. Two factors, timing and route, define the fundamental differences between the two events. The large amount of planning, coupled with an extraordinarily lengthy and theatrically op-

---

[48] For a surprising, and perhaps controversial view suggesting that the Arch of Titus depicts simultaneously the triumph of Titus and the imperial funeral, see Östenberg 2021: 38–40.

[49] See, e.g., Flower 1996: 107, who contends that the funeral procession has absorbed elements of the triumph.

[50] Versnel 1970: 115–129 collects and analyzes many of them.

[51] Compare fig. 2.2 above to the substantial listing of participants in the "Apotheose-Prozession" in Zanker 2004: 24 fig. 6.

portunistic route, makes the triumph the most spectacular processional event in the mid-Republic. Understanding the comparative deficiency of these two elements in the funeral procession helps to situate it properly within its viewing context. The differences between funeral and triumph—some of which are specific to the Republic—inform this discussion. Since the funeral of Paullus is the ostensible focal point of this study, his triumph of 167 BCE offers a convenient point of comparison. Content and context both illustrate the fundamental visual differences.

The triumphal route was selected for optimal viewing. The triumph began, not at a home, but on the periphery of the city, where the military and stately elements of the parade could be most effectively marshaled.[52] The ultimate destination was the Capitoline Hill, where a series of ritual events ranging from the sacrifice of a bull to a private communion with the god Jupiter would occur. These last events were critical, but the entire circuitous route was an equally important theatrical element. The triumph, like the funeral, was clearly designed as spectacle, but unlike the funeral, the triumphal parade was elevated to a fundamentally different kind of street theater.[53] In fact, the city of Rome was modified to accommodate viewing the event. Bleachers were installed in the Circus Maximus and the Forum to serve as temporary seats for viewing the parade as it passed by.[54] The emphasis was placed on stationary viewing of an event in motion.[55] The general populace could gather to watch the parade of soldiers, the exotic spoils of war, the prisoners, and the general. The triumph was also long, measured both by the physical length of the procession and by the number of days devoted to it. Three days were allotted to the triumphal procession of Paullus.[56] For those who chose to sit in the circus or in the various possible locations for bleachers, it was not an event where the twists and turns of Rome might transform one's view; rather, it was designed to be viewed as theater.

In contrast, while spectacular display was obviously a motivation for the *pompa funebris*, the funerary parade was, at its core, a spectacular elaboration of pragmatic necessity. The body needed to be moved from the house to a place suitable for a public eulogy, then to the *ustrinum* or directly to the place of interment. The start and end of the procession was variable and almost entirely out of the immediate control of the family. That is, the factors that led to the location of a family's home or its tomb were likely not influenced by the potential processional route for the

[52] On the triumphal route, see Makin 1921, Künzl 1988, Favro 1994, Beard 2007: 92–105, and Popkin 2016.

[53] Beard 2003.

[54] Plut. *Aem.* 32.2: ὁ μὲν δῆμος ἔν τε τοῖς ἱππικοῖς θεάτροις, ἃ κίρκους καλοῦσι, περί τε τὴν ἀγορὰν ἰκρία πηξάμενοι, καὶ τἆλλα τῆς πόλεως μέρη καταλαβόντες, ὡς ἕκαστα παρεῖχε τῆς πομπῆς ἔποψιν, ἐθεῶντο, καθαραῖς ἐσθῆσι κεκοσμημένοι. ("The people set up scaffolding in the horse racing theaters, which they call circuses, and around the Forum. After taking over the other parts of the city, according to how each provided viewing of the procession, they spectated, clothed in white garments.")

[55] Wiles 2003: 66–67 adduces examples of processions through theatrical spaces and notes, "Ancient theatres often made the performance space a thoroughfare."

[56] Plut. *Aem.* 32.4.

funeral. Therefore, each family's processional route was potentially unique, and the overall length of the entire procession could vary dramatically depending upon building and purchasing decisions made by one's ancestors.

The funeral was also an *ad hoc* affair, governed by a number of intractable elements. The *imagines* were held ready in the atrium, the *tituli* were available as one possible source of information for the laudation, and the family tomb itself was in place. While preliminary planning was theoretically possible, the timing of the event constrained its implementation. Unlike the triumph, where the parade could be orchestrated in advance with a performance date in mind, the funeral offered very little time for preparation. In most cases, it was impossible for a family to envision an impending death. Death, of course, was the singular event that set in motion the funeral process. The canonical view gives seven days between the death and the last rites.[57] The funeral business was predicated on speed. In a culture and a time where incense was used to mask the scent of the dead body, there was not much time to lose. Doubtless, professional mourners, musicians, chariots, and spare triumphal togas were quickly acquired, but scheduling was another matter entirely.[58] Luck also played a role in staging. A number of conflicting events might interfere. The funeral of a Roman aristocrat will have conformed to a public calendar filled with religious holidays and festivals.

As it happens, the triumph of Paullus himself conflicted with two, small-scale funerary events. Four days prior to the scheduled day of the triumphal parade, his fourteen-year-old son had died. Three days after, his twelve-year-old son followed. According to Livy, Paullus was given an opportunity to discuss his accomplishments after his triumph, and in his speech, a *contio*, Livy's Paullus addressed his paradoxical fortunes:

> Quamquam, et qua felicitate rem publicam administrauerim, et <quae> duo fulmina domum meam per hos dies perculerint, non ignorare uos, Quirites, arbitror, cum *spectaculo* uobis nunc triumphus meus, nunc funera liberorum meorum fuerint, tamen paucis, quaeso, sinatis me cum publica felicitate conparare eo, quo debeo, animo priuatam meam fortunam.
>
> Citizens, although you are not unaware, I suspect, of either the happiness with which I have conducted public matters or the two lightning bolts that have struck my house—since in one moment you witnessed my triumph, in the next the funerals of my two sons—nevertheless, I ask that you let me compare in a fitting manner my private fate with the public fortune.[59]

Because of the ages of the children, we can never know the precise nature of their funerals, but there is no evidence that large funerals occurred, and scholars have

[57] Serv. ad *A.* 6.218.
[58] On the funeral business, see Bodel 1986, Bodel 2000, and Bodel 2004.
[59] Livy 45.41.1–2.

not suggested anything to indicate the contrary.[60] They were most certainly too young to have merited a funeral in the Forum. It is clear that there was no lengthy lying-in-state. The funeral for the eldest son, who had died four days prior, occurred before the triumph.[61] Livy thinks the two *funera* were known and witnessed by the people ("a source of spectacle for you"). Regardless, the triumph was not postponed, and the funerals were scheduled around it. The triumph was a spectacle of much greater scale. It was most likely the case—though no direct evidence survives—that an aristocratic funeral in the middle Republic, even a relatively lavish one, could never have overshadowed or delayed a triumph.

Lastly, timing was a crucial factor in Paullus' own funeral. One of the most memorable features of Paullus' funeral was the active and positive participation of his once conquered foes. He was so well regarded that even his former enemies were eager to attend his funeral. The description of their participation at the funeral underscores the subtle effects of chance and time.

> ὅσοι γοῦν κατὰ τύχην παρῆσαν Ἰβήρων καὶ Λιγύων καὶ Μακεδόνων, οἱ μὲν ἰσχυροὶ τὰ σώματα καὶ νέοι διαλαβόντες τὸ λέχος ὑπέδυσαν καὶ παρεκόμιζον, οἱ δὲ πρεσβύτεροι συνηκολούθουν, ἀνακαλούμενοι τὸν Αἰμίλιον εὐεργέτην καὶ σωτῆρα τῶν πατρίδων.

> For as many of the Iberians, Ligurians, and Macedonians who happened to be nearby, the young and strong accompanied the parade taking turns carrying the bier, while the older ones followed along calling Aemilius a benefactor and savior of their countries.[62]

The foreigners who lifted up his bier were said to have been present fortuitously (κατὰ τύχην). Doubtless, Paullus' surviving sons arranged to have the bier carried by the foreigners, but their presence in Rome was apparently due to chance. In fact, it seems necessary for Plutarch to explain how the foreigners happened to be in Rome, since, one assumes, it might be unreasonable for a reader to believe that conquered enemies from afar might be able to travel to Rome in time for a funeral event.

Diodorus Siculus, discussing the same event, reinforces the role of timing and articulates explicitly the distances attendees might be expected to travel to attend. He also underscores what duties might be set aside.

> Ὅτι ὁ Αἰμίλιος ὁ Περσέα καταπολεμήσας τιμητὴς ὢν καὶ σχεδὸν ἐν πᾶσι τοῖς μέρεσι τῆς ἀρετῆς πρωτεύων τῶν πολιτῶν ἐτελεύτησεν. ὡς δὲ ἡ περὶ αὐτοῦ φήμη τῆς τελευτῆς διεδόθη καὶ συνήγγιζεν ὁ τῆς ἐκφορᾶς καιρός, τοιαύτην συνέβη γενέσθαι πάσης τῆς πόλεως συμπάθειαν ὥστε μὴ μόνον τοὺς ἐργαστηριακοὺς

[60] On rites for children and the so-called *funus acerbum*, see Serv. ad *A*. 6.224, Lindsay 2000: 155, and Rawson 2002.

[61] Livy 45.41.11: "ego … ab alterius funere filii currum conscendi, rediens alterum ex Capitolio prope iam expirantem inveni." ("I mounted my chariot after the funeral of one of my sons, and, returning from the Capitoline, almost immediately I found my other son to be dying.")

[62] Plut. *Aem*. 39.8–9.

καὶ τὸν ἄλλον ὄχλον συντρέχειν, ἀλλὰ καὶ τοὺς ἄρχοντας καὶ τὴν σύγκλητον ὑπερθέσθαι τοὺς χρηματισμούς. ἀκολούθως δὲ τούτοις καὶ τῶν περιοικουσῶν τὴν Ῥώμην πόλεων ὅσαις ὁ χρόνος τὴν ἀναστροφὴν ἐδίδου ἐλθεῖν πρὸς τὸν τῆς ἐκφορᾶς καιρόν, κατήντων εἰς τὴν Ῥώμην σχεδόν τι πανδημεὶ μετὰ προθυμίας, ἅμα θεασόμενοι καὶ τιμήσοντες τὸν μετηλλαχότα.

Upon the death of Aemilius, who was the conqueror of Perseus, a censor, and who exceeded all citizens in virtue in every way, when the rumor of his passing had been spread about and the time for the funeral approached, it happened that the sympathy of all the people was such that not only did menial workers and the rest of the common people rush together, but also the magistrates and the Senate put off their duties. And in line with this, also from all the cities around Rome for which the schedule would allow for their arrival by the appointed time for the exequies, almost everyone came down to Rome with great enthusiasm both to see the spectacle and to honor the deceased.[63]

Diodorus seeks to emphasize the *size* of the crowd in attendance, but he also dwells on issues of timing, both the fixed time for the event and the influence that time had on attendance. Only those who could arrive in time attended. A day was appointed, and effort was required to attend. He underscores that Paullus was so respected that so many people came. Senators and magistrates even ceased their daily activities. Whether this actually occurred cannot be known. That Diodorus thought it merited mention *is* important. Perhaps most important of all, Polybius notes that even the presence of the eulogist—the critical player in the Forum spectacle—was governed by chance (Polyb. 6.53.2): ἂν μὲν υἱὸς ἐν ἡλικίᾳ καταλείπηται καὶ τύχῃ παρών ("if a surviving son of appropriate age happens to be present"). It is clear that Paullus' funeral was exceptional. The city of Rome did not normally stop all business to honor the dead. Magistrates and senators continued their daily tasks, and it was notable that they chose to do otherwise for Paullus. In most instances, however, the funeral had to adapt to Roman daily life, so its audience consisted almost entirely of those who happened to be in or near Rome at the time of the death.[64]

SETTING THE STAGE I: *DOMUS* TO FORUM

The funeral began at the home, but determining the precise location of a Roman magistrate's home is almost impossible. In the totality of surviving ancient source material, only four percent of Roman senators are explicitly assigned houses in Rome.[65] Specificity often ends at the neighborhood, region, or hill. The aristocratic houses cluster around the Palatine (Guilhembet cites eight in 150 BCE and by 44

[63] Diod. Sic. 31.25.1.

[64] I expand on the logistics of timing below, in chapter 4.

[65] Guilhembet 1996: 186–190.

BCE, twenty) and the Roman Forum (six in 150 BCE, fourteen in 44 BCE).[66] The areas with the most public buildings were also the most densely populated with *domus* and *insulae*.[67] Lacking a mass-transit system, the populace clustered near the center of the city in densely packed, walled-in urban spaces. Classes mingled necessarily, since they could not travel by metro to clean their masters' *domus* or bake their patrons' bread. In addition, family residences in the area were surprisingly durable. Of the houses that have been excavated, many appear to have been continuously occupied for hundreds of years.[68] In the case of L. Aemilius Paullus, we know that he owned a home *in* Rome, but its location cannot be secured. Nevertheless, it is hard to imagine circumstances that would house any member of the Aemilii Paulli—a powerful family whose origins were connected to the foundation of the city—too far away from the city center.[69] Therefore, the most probable location for the house of Paullus will have been the Palatine Hill or its slopes, adjacent to the Roman Forum.

The Domus *of Paullus*

We will never know precisely where Paullus lived. Nonetheless, the general topographical situation of elite housing on and near the Palatine Hill is clear enough, and it was this area where he most likely lived. It is certainly where many Roman magistrates owned homes, and therefore provides a useful model for us to pursue: even if Paullus himself did not live in this specific area, the general spatial arrangement of the funeral route would have corresponded, more or less, to a route like that which we discuss below.[70] Knowledge of this area has been refined by ongoing archaeological work on the slopes of the Palatine Hill, which has uncovered a series of *domus*, the footprints of which have been continuously occupied from the archaic period.[71] By 160 BCE, these *domus* flanked both the Sacra Via and the Via Nova. While we cannot know with certainty what these houses looked like, we can approximate some features. Analogs of the housing situation on the slope of the Palatine are found not in Bel-Air, or Beverly Hills, but rather on the ma-

---

[66] Guilhembet 1996: 187.

[67] Wallace-Hadrill 2003.

[68] For an overview of the continuously occupied houses on the slopes of the Palatine, see Carandini and Carafa 1995, Papi 1995a, Filippi 2004, and Carandini 2004.

[69] Eck 1995 cites Plut. *Paul.* 39.5 and Livy 45.39.14, who both give nonspecific references to Paullus' residence in Rome. Smith 2006: 35–36 gives a brief account of the genealogy and various origin myths associated with the Aemilii.

[70] The area is the subject of controversy, but the controversy does not affect our basic understanding of the processional route from the slope of the Palatine to the Forum. The topographical debate focuses on the precise route of the Sacra Via and Via Nova. See Hurst and Cirone 2003, Wiseman 2004, and Ziółkowski 2004. On the names and locations of certain temples, and whether or not the houses found were actually those of the legendary kings, see Dumser 2005, who reviews the discussion and the bibliography. For our purposes, there is no question about the existence of these houses or their general form, only who occupied them.

[71] Carandini 2004 presents a summary of the finds, though it is interspersed with lengthy arguments on the historicity of the regal period.

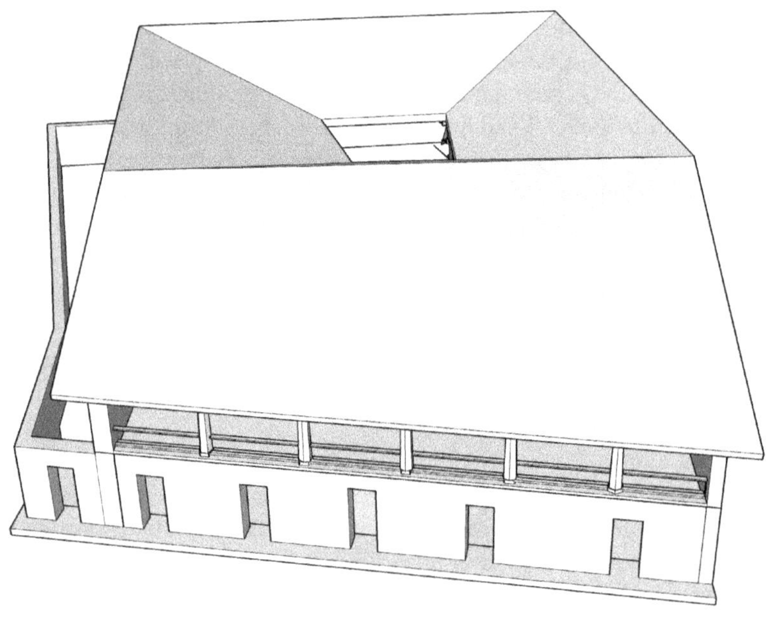

FIGURE 2.4 Domus 6.

jor thoroughfares of Herculaneum. Substantial work on housing in Pompeii and Herculaneum, in conjunction with these finds in Rome, has shaped our idea of the reconstructed form of these *domus*.[72] These houses were not strictly compounds of the wealthy.[73] (See fig. 2.4.) These large, atrium-style houses with the concomitant internal apparatus (*tablinum*, *atrium*, and continuous axial view from front-facing doorway to garden in the back of the house) contained independently accessible shops embedded in the front facade. The shops supported projecting balconies.[74] This juxtaposition of aristocratic wealth displayed within the *domus* and perhaps

[72] Wallace-Hadrill 1994: 129–130 makes the connection.

[73] Wallace-Hadrill 1994: 121–130 challenges earlier views of stately, aristocratic compounds in Pompeii that received storefronts due to moral decline during Julio-Claudian rule. The archaeological and textual evidence is compelling, but a thought experiment best frames the discussion, "Where were the shops in the early Julio-Claudian period if not along the main streets?" Wallace-Hadrill 1994: 129. Wallace-Hadrill uses the evidence from Rome to support his arguments against the then orthodox view in Pompeii and Herculaneum.

[74] Wallace-Hadrill 1994 figs. 5.9–15 summarizes the archaeological evidence and (127) lists examples of houses with shops and projecting balconies at Herculaneum: "Case del Tramezzo di Legno, del Bicentenario, del Salone Nero, and del Colonnato Tuscanico." Gros 2001: 83 shows a reconstruction of

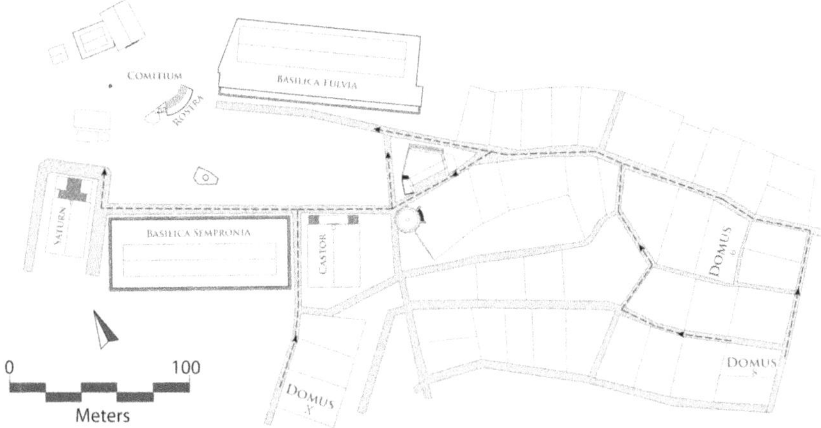

FIGURE 2.5 The Forum and the residential area on the northern slope of the Palatine. Processional routes are shown in dashed lines.

on the projecting balconies alongside a commercial district creates a productive and diverse environment for spectacle and spectator interaction. The ramifications of this interpretation of the *domus* on our understanding of spectacle in the area continue to be explored.[75] As one neared the Roman Forum, interspersed between these *domus* were, at times, temples and public buildings of relatively small scale. The Regia marked the entryway into the Forum, and the Domus Publica, the house of the Pontifex Maximus, was nearby. The road was narrow, and viewing space would be limited to those who might line the streets, and, those who could sit in the balconies of adjacent homes. (See fig. 2.5.)

3D Reconstruction of the Palatine Slope

Despite the transformative archaeological work on the slope of the Palatine, which provides a general picture of the area, reconstructing specific houses is difficult. Creating a visual representation of the streets on the northern slopes of the Palatine, connecting it to the underlying evidence, and inhabiting it with the eye of the interrogator are nontrivial matters. Only a few houses, in particular the houses labeled Domus 6 and 8 in the accompanying figure, have been unearthed and most clearly interpreted from the archaeological record. (See fig. 2.5.) These houses form the core of my facade-level visualization for the area. The rest of the area at the foot

---

Domus 6 on the Sacra Via, with the balcony applied to its front facade. Cf. Stambaugh 1988: 108 fig. 7 for a representation of the traditional view.

[75] Wallace-Hadrill 2001: 128–143 and Wallace-Hadrill 2003: 3–18 examines the social implications of broad class diversity in housing, and expands the idea of commercial and residential comingling, but no study has examined their effect on spectacle at Rome.

of the Palatine is hypothetical. The roads are extrapolated from extant pavers. Building outlines conform to the same basic footprint as Domus 6 and 8 attested in the archaeological record, but have been distributed along the hypothetical routes that enter the Forum at the foot of the Palatine. The most comprehensive plan, derived from Carandini 2003, is not designed to represent the details of the excavations or the buildings accurately. For our purposes, it is good enough.[76] For the route from the Palatine to the Forum, my focus is twofold: I will highlight that multiple routes to the forum were possible and probable, and I will illustrate the interaction between the audience and the parade. To orient and root this reconstruction in the surrounding topographical context, a GIS basemap provides an outline. There is simply not enough detailed information to represent the area with a high degree of fidelity. Moreover, even if precise and accurate evidence were available, it would not be necessary for my argument. After all, we are exploring possible homes for Paullus, and potential routes, all of which are hypothetical. Therefore, I have created abstract representations. Rather than representing the current state of the archaeological evidence, I am representing an abstraction of the state of archaeological interpretation. Within this context, we will explore multiple routes and will center our discussion on facade-level visualization and the interrelationship of approximate street width, street-level entryways, and upper-level balconies.

Establishing the Parameters: Palatine House Locations and Processional Routes

For the funeral of Aemilius Paullus, since we cannot know where his *domus* might have been located, let us first assume that the house was located within the area most densely populated by the oldest and largest aristocratic houses of the Republic, the slope of the Palatine. For exploratory purposes, I will focus on one case-study house as well as an alternate one: the case-study house lay on the western end of the slope, and the alternate, closer to the Forum on the eastern end. The Roman Forum is the intermediate destination, and there are a limited number of ways a procession might have reached it. The topographical situation for the *pompa funebris* of 160 BCE can be divided into two general spatial locations, the entry points to the Roman Forum, and the route in the Forum itself. Processional points of entry into the Forum have been most thoroughly examined in research on the triumphal procession; the eastern end of the Roman Forum, along the Sacra Via, seems to have been the preferred route suggested by modern scholars.[77] For the case-study house, the route could proceed directly to the Forum along two alternative paths. For the

[76] The explorations of Carandini are the sole source of comprehensive evidence for the area. Therefore, Carandini 2003 pl. 32 is the most inclusive cartographic representation of the area, outlining *domus* along the Palatine, the Vicus Tuscus and the Forum; it represents the archaic footprints whose general outlines persist through the middle Republic. Though the figure is attractive and apparently drawn to scale, no explicit coordinate system is cited, however. Gros 2001: 37 figs. 20–21 presents a clear interpretation of the sketched plans. See also Filippi 2004 esp. fig. 4.

[77] See Makin 1921, Favro 1994, and Popkin 2016, for full bibliography on the triumphal route. Cf. Beard 2007: 101–105 for a note of caution.

alternate case-study house, situated on the northeastern slope of the Palatine, the direct route is hardly a procession at all—consisting of a one hundred meter march along the Vicus Tuscus, followed by a short walk through the Forum. (For Paullus' house, I use Domus 6. The alternate case study is the *domus* in the southeastern corner of the plan, marked with an X, behind the Temple of Castor, see fig. 2.5.)

Mobilizing the Audience: Procession as Crowd-Gathering Strategy

A less direct path would yield a multiplicity of viable routes while simultaneously reaching a greater audience. If the procession had an ancillary function as a crowd gatherer, then there was potentially great utility in winding through the entire neighborhood, perhaps doubling back through each of the city streets. The audience might have felt compelled to participate.[78] In comparison, recall that precise scheduling of the triumphal procession allowed sufficient time for the setup of theatrical viewing spaces. For the *pompa funebris*, however, most funerals would have at most nine inclusive days between the public announcement of the funeral and the procession itself. This is perhaps time enough to prepare various viewing platforms, but in most cases, one would assume that time and resources would prohibit extensive preparation of bleachers or similar viewing platforms along the processional route. In some instances, if an announcement of the funeral had been received, those wishing to join the procession might all go to the house of the deceased at an appointed time.[79] Depending upon housing location, the room for the gathering crowd would be minimal. (See fig. 2.6.) In most instances, however, it is more likely that the day of the event carried on as normal for most Romans and when the procession moved by, bystanders would watch it pass from their houses or shops and then, if interested and able, join in the walk to the Forum. Magisterial status would also matter. While aristocratic families might remain in the *domus* during the day, the magistrates and their entourage would on most days be occupied in the Forum; funerals did not alter legislative, executive, or judicial schedules.[80] Moreover, for Paullus' funeral, if the number of attendees were so great as indicated by the textual evidence, it is hard to envision how a substantial crowd might have arrayed itself anywhere near the residential areas on the slopes of the Palatine. It certainly would have been easier to announce the *funus* to be held on a specific day, and to expect interested parties to gather in the Forum.

For those living along the processional path to the Forum, the *pompa funebris* was a highly interactive event. No matter the time of day for the funeral—another detail we cannot know—the day-to-day business of the house was surely under way. All homes in the Palatine area would at some point have a line of visiting

---

[78] Levison 2002: 247 notes that participation in processions was mandated in the Hebrew tradition and speculates that it may have been customary in Rome.

[79] On the announcement and the so-called *funus indictivum*, see p. 69. There is no evidence for a funerary announcement that includes a specific time.

[80] For a succinct treatment of elite schedules mapped to location, see Laurence 1994: 122–132, esp. 128 fig. 8.2.

FIGURE 2.6 A pedestrian's view of the procession along the Sacra Via near Domus 6.

clients. Shops in front of many of the homes would be open for business. As the procession approached, the *tibicines* and the *praeficae* would signal its imminent arrival. Those within a given house along the processional route, if so willing, could watch from the balconies above the shops, or line the streets in front of their home. (See fig. 2.7.) Space was limited. The number of people engaged in day-to-day affairs related to each individual *domus* would have been sufficient to fill the surrounding streets. For these onlookers, the view was visceral. The streets in the area barely had room for chariots. There would have been no long-distance lens nor idealized, comprehensive view of the procession as it moved by; rather, it would have been a close-up, focused view of the horn players, followed by lictors, each chariot carrying an ancestor, the deceased, and the family. (See fig. 2.8.)

Experiencing the Procession

Due to the confined space of the route through the residential area, most audience members would have been in close proximity to those walking in the procession. Therefore, the masks representing the ancestors would have been clearly visible to the audience members. They may not have been able to identify the family or the individual mask, however. Would the announcement of the funeral be known to all of the aristocracy? Would it trickle down to attendants and slaves? Was the funeral itself identifiable through internal mechanisms? If the funeral dirge, the *nenia*, was sung during the initial procession to the Forum, would the rest of the audience

FIGURE 2.7 View of the procession from a balcony on the Sacra Via.

FIGURE 2.8 View of the procession from street level.

hear enough of the life of the deceased to identify him?[81] While the *imagines* were visible, were they legible? The masks were painted and artificially shaded for veristic effect, but could anyone outside of the family of the deceased identify a *praetor* or a *consul* from one hundred years prior?

For the uninformed, and even for those who would have known their Roman history, the parade of ancestors would have been a suspenseful visual treat along the internal route from the slopes of the Palatine to the Forum. Along with certain well-known ancestors, lesser known forebears might serve as reminders of the past. The audience might be struck by the appearance of an ancestor who was not immediately associated with the family. As the parade rounded the corner, each new chariot might deliver its own cognitive reward in a crescendo culminating in the bier. (See fig. 2.9.) Not dissimilar to a parade at a theme park, where each cartoon or movie character appears in succession. Most are known to the dedicated audience, but at times, a certain character's appearance may necessitate consultation with a fellow spectator. Of course, everyone knows that the payoff of the procession comes at the end. At this point, having watched the procession move by, the audience might join along in the short walk to the Forum. In the procession of a politically successful and long-established family, however, given the circumscribed and limited viewing area for the route, the display of ancestors, doubtless, would have been impressive, but it could not have been appreciated with one synoptic view, as in figs. 2.2 and 2.3. Along the route from the *domus* to the Forum, each element of the parade would have been presented discretely and incrementally to the spectator.

Comparing Experience to Artistic Representation

These experiential views illustrate how source material such as the relief from Amiternum can potentially mislead us. The synoptic view of the procession coupled with the symmetrical presentation of the participants in the relief is dictated by artistic convention, not the exigencies of a processional route through a real city.[82] Compare the views presented above to the unobstructed image of the procession represented in the Amiternum relief. (See fig. 2.1.) The parade from the house to the entrance of the Forum offered microscopic views of the individual elements, but no opportunity to view the totality of the procession. The streets were short and narrow, and there was little opportunity for such an all-encompassing view. Space did not allow even a small funeral procession to unwrap and straighten out. An external audience could not watch it as if seated in a theater to view the full extent of the procession. Roman artists, however, often manipulated spatial relationships

---

[81] On the *nenia*, see Kierdorf 1980: 96–105, Richlin 2014 and Dutsch 2008.

[82] Bodel 1999: 264 rightly notes that "[t]he emotional articulation and spatial symmetry of the Roman cortege are captured by the limestone relief from Amiternum in the Sabine country north and east of Rome." As we shall see, however, such a view at the Roman aristocratic funeral is only visible to an audience situated in the Forum.

FIGURE 2.9 The procession rounding a corner.

in their work to achieve a desired representational aesthetic. For example, the artist who produced the Anaglypha Traiani chose to line up building facades in a row, even though they were actually situated at 90-degree angles from each other on a corner of the Roman Forum.[83] Corners are compressed, angles flattened, until what was once a jagged angular plaza has become a uniform facade. Again, on the Arch of Constantine (see fig. 2.10), the Rostra is placed in the center between the Arch of Septimius Severus on one side and (presumably) the Arch of Tiberius along with the Basilica Iulia on the other, thus uprooting the Arch of Tiberius from its true location between the Temple of Saturn and the Basilica Iulia. Instead, the artist rotates two buildings, the arch and the basilica, 90 degrees to provide a symmetrical backdrop to the representation of the Rostra.

Viewing the Procession Through the Eyes of the Eulogist

This same procession, when experienced by the eulogist, was not so much a parade of ancestors as it was a parade of onlookers. For the eulogist and the mourning family, there were only glimpses of those who had donned the *imagines* parading in front. Since the family walked directly behind the *feretrum* carrying the deceased, the eulogist's gaze forward would have focused mostly on the deceased, himself the subject of his memorized *laudatio*. If the funeral was large enough and the deceased important enough to warrant a pause in daily activities by those lining the streets or working in the houses, then the *laudator* would have seen the importance of his own family and of his father displayed as a continuous collage of spectators—their

[83] See Nash 1961: 176–177 for the images, and Richardson 1992: 292–293 for brief comment.

FIGURE 2.10 Oratio of Constantine on the northeast side of the Arch of Constantine. The buildings in the background, from left to right: Basilica Iulia, Arch of Tiberius(?), and the Arch of Septimius Severus. Photo Credit: Digitized by Wikimedia Commons user Marsyas (Public Domain). Original print source: Tyler and Pierce, L'art byzantin, Paris, 1932.

houses, and their own symbols of power—as he walked by.[84] While the parade of ancestors contained a visual display of the magisterial accomplishments and the power attained by the family over the years, for the *laudator*, this parade of his own familial power was occluded. Rather, the houses flanking the narrow streets displayed symbolic capital of another sort. Simply by their visible presence, the family members and slaves of the houses, as well as the clients and shoppers at the stores fronting the houses would have demonstrated power and status of the residents of each home. More important, the facades and fleeting views of the interiors offered their own parade of ancestral accomplishments. Long before the *suggestus* in the Forum was called the Rostra, prows of ships taken as spoils in victory—*rostra*—and other *spolia* from triumphal military accomplishments could adorn private homes.[85] It was a daily reminder for the present occupants of what the past occupants had accomplished. In comparison to the display of *imagines*, which would require knowledge of Roman ancestral history and some thought to connect the names with the waxen faces and the *tituli* with statues and legends, the *spolia* mounted on the front facade would be clearly legible as symbols of raw power and military prowess. The accomplishments of the man who had lived there before were visible daily for all to see. And for new buyers of a well-established family's home, the visual challenge of past superiority and of present mediocrity would seem to have been strong.[86] For the *laudator*, the accomplishments of Rome were displayed in front of him as he made his way to the Rostra. Like no other place in

[84] The view of these houses for the eulogist would have been not unlike the exhaustive, sequential record in Edward Ruscha's documentary photographs of Sunset Boulevard, see Ruscha 1966.

[85] E.g., Polyb. 6.39.10. On the adornment of private dwellings with *spolia*, see Wiseman 1994, and for a short analysis and a recapitulation of the ancient sources, see Roller 2010: 131, esp. n. 30. See also Gruen 1992: 70–71, who discusses the purported fragments of Cato's *de signis et tabulis*, in which Cato condemns "the display of ill-gotten gains" and those "who convert what should be state property to personal use, including statues and paintings for domestic adornment."

[86] Wiseman 1994, esp. 98–99, who lists the sources.

Rome, the entry route into the Forum, if one was able to understand the imagery, offered an overt visual performance of ancestral foundations of power.

The Entrance to the Forum

The specific location of the family's home would determine the possibilities for staging and attending the event both at the home itself and along the route. The family home located at the eastern-most end of the area under investigation was conveniently situated along the so-called Clivus Palatinus. (See fig. 2.5, Domus 6.) The parade of ancestors could have been arranged along the Clivus Palatinus before it rounded the corner to proceed along the Sacra Via to the Forum—a distance of roughly 250 meters, one of the longer marches for those living near the Palatine. Along the way, the procession would have passed only a handful of private residences before reaching the Forum. At the entrance to the Forum along these routes, one would have encountered the official home of the Pontifex Maximus, the Temple of Vesta, the nearby Atrium Vestae, and the Regia. The liminal transition from the residential area of the Palatine to the Forum was marked by the public, religious nature of the surrounding buildings. Moreover, the home of the Pontifex Maximus in particular, but also the short length of the processional route, reminds us how compact the ancient city was. To be active in politics, and religion as well, proximity to the Forum mattered. Over a century later, C. Iulius Caesar surely must have appreciated his move from the Subura to the home of the Pontifex Maximus, which would let him view all major traffic along the Sacra Via, and would provide a two-minute walk to the Curia and the Rostra.[87] In 160 BCE, during the funeral of Paullus, the Pontifex Maximus was M. Aemilius Lepidus.[88] Most scholars, modern and ancient agree that, in 160 BCE, the two *familiae*, the Aemilii Lepidi and the Aemilii Paulli, would have believed that they shared a common ancestry, which connected them to the foundation of Rome, as we have seen above. Therefore, one wonders whether there was a specific interaction between the oldest ancestors on parade and the occupants of the house of the current Pontifex Maximus. In fact, this simple question raises many more: were copies of the masks in the parade of the Aemilii Paulli also on display in the atrium of the Lepidi? Were sets of masks considered originals, and others, copies? Would certain families deny the claim of descent made by other families, and would such a denial be visible during a funeral procession, where a contested shared ancestor might turn his back on the home of another family?

Unless the family chose to deviate from a direct route, the procession to the Forum was very short. Even if the family had tried to circle through the neighborhood, not all streets would have accommodated them—to backtrack near the Palatine would require uphill climbs. If the home were located more centrally in the residential area, the preparations for the parade would have had very limited

[87] On Caesar and the Domus Publica, see Suet. *Iul.* 46 and Scott 1995.

[88] M. Aemilius (68) M. f. M. n. Lepidus, cos. 187, 175, AEMI1067 in the *DPRR*.

space. For this case-study Domus X located behind the Temple of Castor and Pollux along the Vicus Tuscus, the most direct parade route to the Forum would have been measured in minutes not hours. (See fig. 2.5.) Nonetheless, despite such short distances along major thoroughfares, comprehensive views were difficult to obtain. The route of even such an important street as the Sacra Via shifts and narrows, and the space is relatively cramped throughout, no more than the width of a standard Roman street. There was no room to take in the entirety of the procession *en route*, and there was really no opportunity for a large spectacle. The Sacra Via was not like the Circus Maximus, which could accommodate crowds that could witness more than a few meters of parade at one time. The Forum as well presented a different spatial footprint, with more opportunities for viewing a spectacular event, but not necessarily one always conducive to viewing a parade.

SETTING THE STAGE II: THE ROMAN FORUM

A Note on the Nature of the Visual Representations

The buildings surrounding the central plaza of the Roman Forum of 160 BCE were still undergoing a transition from a blend of low-lying houses peppered with more monumental temples, in the Tuscan style, to a more publicly defined, monumental space.[89] (See fig. 4.3.) This investigation into Paullus' funeral is not intended to engage directly with debates in the field of Roman topography. Much ink has been spilled over the name, location, form, or even existence of many of the buildings in the Forum at this time. I engage more directly with these arguments elsewhere.[90] The buildings I represent are meant to be abstractions that are, as much as possible, located in the most likely geographical space, oriented toward the most likely direction, and with flat areas and possible staircases illustrated.[91] These are not definitive reconstructions of actual reality; nor are they airtight visual representations of all available evidence. Instead, they are my curated interpretations of the arguments I find most convincing regarding these spaces. For some specific buildings, many possible reconstructions exist: I have decided to select the one that seems most likely to me, though in some cases, this decision involves a roll of a die more than a solid scholarly argument. Nonetheless, for the goals of this book, a slight shift in topographical interpretation has no actual effect on my underlying argument.

---

[89] Broise and David 1983 assemble the state of the scholarly debate; surprisingly little has changed since. For an axonometric drawing of the Forum in the middle Republic, see Stambaugh 1988: 108. See also Purcell 1989.

[90] See romelab.ucla.edu.

[91] For a theoretical discussion of abstraction and modeling see Johanson 2009.

An Overview of the Roman Forum, its Buildings, and its Central Plaza

A brief, counter-clockwise review of the topographical surroundings and the evidence that supports the three-dimensional representations is necessary. To the north stood the Basilica Fulvia, fronted by the Tabernae Novae. The shops are generally considered to be separate structures, which predate the basilicas. By 160 BCE their footprint and proximity to each adjacent basilica suggests that the two buildings are inextricably connected. Rather than create a completely hypothetical reconstruction of the shops and basilicas, I decided to connect the shops (*tabernae*) directly to each adjacent basilica via the upper-level balconies (*maeniana*).[92] The Comitium complex, which contained the Rostra—the speaker's platform, the archaic monuments later covered by the Lapis Niger, the Graecostasis, and the Curia Hostilia (the Senate House), occupied the northern edge of the Forum; beyond, delineating the northern extreme of the Forum, was the Carcer, the prison.[93] The Comitium requires a short comment: the Comitium has often been depicted in circular form, based on an extrapolation of the curvilinear form in the material remains of what is thought to be the speaker's platform. This view, part of a larger argument, elegantly and convincingly argued by Coarelli in multiple venues, has most recently been reassessed, the location of the Curia called into question, and the curvilinear plan which had been accepted as a hypothetical possibility is considered unsupported by material evidence.[94]

---

[92] Bauer 1993. By creating *maeniana* that extend from the basilicas to roof the shops, I am also able to depict the same *maeniana* for representations of other basilicas, like the Basilica Porcia, which had no shops, but in one narrative was the original structure upon which *maeniana* were built. Moreover, the later phase of the Basilica Aemilia, which at least one group of scholars sees as the phase extant in 160 BCE, integrates the shops into the basilica with a second-level balcony. A precise reconstruction requires extensive treatment. In the figures in this book, to convey the most important idea, that there are balconies for spectators above the shops surrounding the Forum plaza, these approximations serve. See Gerding and Dell'Unto 2022, who address the difficult chronology of the material record, and in their study of the *Basilica Sempronia* propose reconstructed phases of *Basilica Sempronia* and *Basilica Fulvia*; see Freyberger 2013 for a radical departure from prior scholarly consensus on the *Basilica Aemilia*; for a new assessment and detailed plan of the Forum and Basilica Fulvia in 168 see Bruni 2024: 16–21 and fig. 10.

[93] See Gjerstad 1941, Coarelli 1977, Coarelli 1983, Coarelli 1985, Coarelli 1998; cf. Lugli 1946, Krause 1976, Carafa 1998, and Amici 2004. The platform of the Rostra in these images stands 2.5m above the Forum pavement, which is extrapolated from the height of the stones used for the stepped area, drawn on Gjerstad's seminal plan; that is, the steps are roughly 0.31 meters tall, and, as drawn by Gjerstad, with eight risers, then the height of the platform naturally follows. It is unlikely that the platform of the Rostra was lower than this estimate, but it is possible that it may have been higher, if more steps were to have been constructed, thus leaving less room for the platform, see Morstein-Marx 2004: 51n55, who notes that Taylor 1966: 45 "reasonably guesses a height of 12 Roman feet = 3.5 meters." For the Carcer, Coarelli 1983: 62–87 and Coarelli 1993.

[94] Morstein-Marx highlights the lack of any material evidence beyond that of the speaker's platform itself. There is no evidence for a stepped viewing area surrounding the Rostra. Coarelli 2014: 48 refers to Carla Amici's work (Amici 2004–2005) on the area to the north of the Rostra, and specifically the area he previously selected for the Curia Hostilia: "Giustamente si esclude che possa trattarsi (come avevo pensato) della curia Hostilia, dal momento che esso verrebbe a trovarsi al di fuori del perimetro del Comizio, e a 10 m più in alto."

To the southwest, stood a shrine or possibly an early phase of a temple to Concord. Material evidence for a temple in 160 BCE has not been found, and the extant sources are conflicted. Therefore, for this investigation, I have created a Tuscan style temple, to give architectural shape to the slope of the Arx and to give a stepped area for spectators.[95] South of this area dedicated to Concord, the Clivus Capitolinus—the paved access road from the Forum to the Capitoline Hill—sloped upward to the Temple of Jupiter Optimus Maximus rising above the rest of the city, and, depending upon how it is reconstructed, visible to many from the streets below.[96] The Temple of Saturn, which housed the treasury—*aerarium*—of Rome, is depicted with a conservatively reconstructed stepped approach, since there are no material remains to indicate the nature of the stepped access to the podium.[97] The southern flank of the Forum plaza, just as the northern flank, was lined with shops at the ground level, the so-called Tabernae Veteres, fronting the Basilica Sempronia; here again, in my figures, the shops and the basilica are joined together by a shared second-level balcony.[98] The Temple of Castor and Pollux with its front tribunal, followed by the round Temple of Vesta, capped the southern end of the Forum.[99] The northern and southern lateral bounds of the central plaza were delineated by the combined forms of the street-level facades of the shops, with monumental basilicas rising above the second-floor balconies. The eastern end may also have been flanked by a third.[100] These basilicas, at least the visible upper levels, are depicted as light, airy structures, resembling the basilica reconstructed at Cosa.[101] The so-called *maeniana*, overhanging balconies affixed to the shops, and, in these depictions, extensions of the basilicas, were available for elevated seating and viewing of events held within the Forum.[102] In 160 BCE, statuary apparently filled the

---

[95] A temple was said to have been vowed by Camillus in 367 (Ov. *Fast.* 1.637-650, Plut. *Vit. Cam.* 42.4-6), but may never have been built. See Ferroni 1993, who suggests that material remains dating to the fourth century BCE might be present. For this model, I follow Heyworth 2011: 67, who comprehensively reviews the evidence to conclude that a Temple of Concord most likely stood on the slope of the Arx near the Comitium in the second century BCE. To generate the figures in this book, plans and elevations for a Tuscan-style temple in Stamper 2005 were used as a model for this temple and all others in the Roman Forum.

[96] For the measurements, see Dion. Hal. *Ant. Rom.* 4.61.3. For the initial reconstruction, Gjerstad 1960. Stamper 2005 presents the revised reconstruction. For a full discussion of the reconstruction problem, see Zarmakoupi 2006, Senseney 2007: 384, and J. N. Hopkins 2016: 66–125. Giuliani 1990: 16–17 reminds that in the Gjerstad reconstruction the dimensions of the Temple of Jupiter would have exceeded those of the Parthenon in its 12-meter central intercolumniation. For the possible viewsheds resulting from differing reconstructions of the Temple of Jupiter Optimus Maximus, see Favro and Johanson 2010.

[97] Richardson 1980, Pensabene 1984, and Coarelli 1999.

[98] For the Basilica Sempronia, see Iacopi 1993 and Gerding and Dell'Unto 2022.

[99] For the Temple of Castor in its earliest phases, see Nielsen et al. 1992 and Nielsen 1993.

[100] On the proposed location of the Basilica Aemilia near the later Temple of Julius Caesar, see Purcell 1989, Steinby 1993a, and Wiseman 1994.

[101] Brown 1993.

[102] Lehmann-Hartleben 1938 and Boethius 1945.

central plaza of the Forum.[103] The paved roads remained narrow; shops would have faced the processional route, and temples stood on both ends of the Forum, offering more elevated viewing spaces.

Entering the Forum

Entry into the Forum offered a dramatic, visual transition for the procession and for its audience. The Sacra Via turns slightly to the southwest just before entering the eastern corner of the Forum. The sounds—the hooves of the horses on the basalt pavers of the street, the music, the mourning songs and ululation—would have announced the arrival of the parade before the first member of the procession rounded the corner, however.[104] The playing of the *tibicines*, the mourning dirges of the *praeficae*, and the clopping of the hooves of the horses pulling the chariots set the stage. The sounds would have announced the arrival, and then the procession, occluded by the Regia, would have entered the Forum. It would have stumbled, moving in fits and starts. These cobbles were neither smooth sidewalks nor paved thoroughfares—riding in a chariot on such streets was no easy task.[105] In fact, during the time of Caesar, when wheeled traffic during the day was outlawed, the sound of one horse's hooves on the streets would have signified a special event. If an axle on Caesar's chariot could break during a triumph, which was a planned and well choreographed event (Suet. *Iul.* 37) with a primary chariot featured, one suspects that equipment malfunctions for the *ad hoc* chariots of the ancestors were more numerous than presented in the sources.[106] In 160 BCE, however, the scene was more complicated: there is no reason to think that other traffic would have ceased on the day of the funeral. Even for Paullus' funeral, it is possible that day-to-day affairs of the city did not cease. The funeral was loud, but orators could be louder.[107] They would have had to be, since their business would not stop.

Moving to the Rostra

As the procession moved through the Forum toward the Rostra, for the first time, a large portion of the funeral parade could have been viewed at a right angle—but only by a select few members of the audience in the Forum. (See fig. 2.11.) The route along the Sacra Via offered the closest approximation to an idealized view, like that presented in the relief from Amiternum. Those spectators situated on the balconies of the Basilica Sempronia would have been able to take in all of the procession at

[103] Plin. *HN* 34.30 notes that in 158 BCE the censors decided to remove all statues not authorized by the Senate. Wallace-Hadrill 1990: since most honorific monuments were privately funded, one should expect a chaotic level of visual competition in public places.

[104] On the voices of the mourners, see Hope 2025: 169–188.

[105] Was there a driver in the chariot or merely someone available to lead the four horses of each of the *quadrigae*? I omit these details from the visualization.

[106] On the bumpy ride in the chariot, see Beard 2007: 221–225.

[107] Hor. *Sat.* 1.6.42–44 jokes that one orator in particular could drown out the combined noise of three funerals and their horn sections.

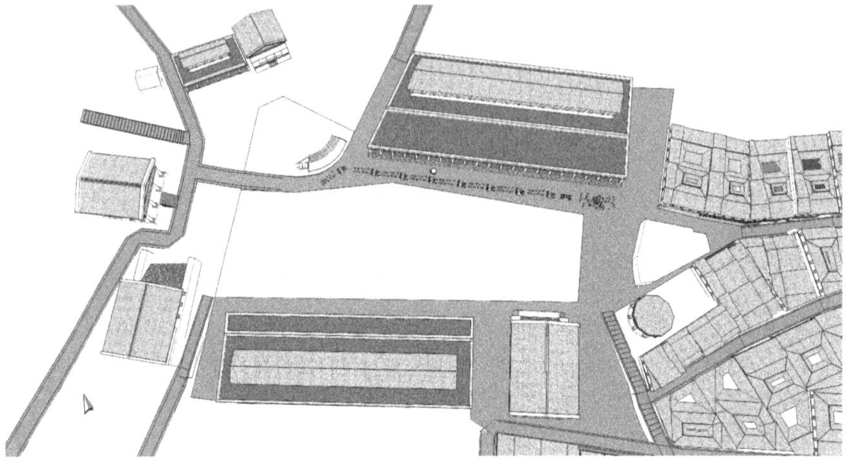

FIGURE 2.11 Overhead view of the procession in context.

once. Having the ancestors wear the dress of the highest office attained in life was a convenient visual aid for mass and distanced viewing. Those spectators on the upper levels would have had the most ideal viewing locations for more encompassing views. If a crowd lined the Sacra Via, however, it would have been difficult to pick out many of the details of the parade—except for the elevated body of the deceased. (Note the difference in visibility when the deceased is reclined, figs. 2.12, 2.13, versus standing upright, fig. 2.14.) Though such a view encompassed the entirety of the simulated procession, it also underscores a fundamental compromise for the viewer: to see everything meant that one could not see everything clearly. The up-close viewer could have seen the details of a waxen mask, but would have missed a horizontal presentation of the family's history.

The elevation of each ancestor was necessary primarily because the Forum was not designed to accommodate the viewing of processions. Recall that stands were built in the Forum for Paullus' triumph.[108] There was a reason that a triumphal procession moved through the Circus Maximus before coming to the Forum. Without stadium seating in the Forum, the triumph needed to provide gradated stands for a larger number of people than what the Forum could hold. Because we are accustomed to thinking of the Forum as performance space, it is easy to overlook the difficulties in staging performances within the area. The Forum worked well for performances on an elevated stage, or, at least, for those staged in the central plaza, but it would have least accommodated the viewing of a procession on the lateral streets, unless the procession had undergone specific visual design alterations.

---

[108] Plut. *Vit. Aem.* 32.2. See above, p. 29.

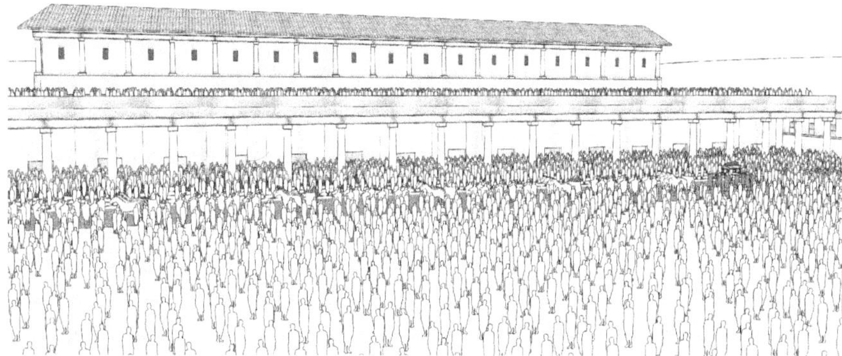

FIGURE 2.12 The procession viewed from the balcony of the Basilica Sempronia. The deceased is reclined on the bier.

FIGURE 2.13 The procession viewed from the steps of the Basilica Sempronia. The deceased is reclined on the bier.

Except for those already positioned on the upper balconies, the majority of those gathered within the Forum plaza would have been unable to see the walking members of the procession, since fellow onlookers would have blocked their views. The Sacra Via was not an elevated viewing platform, and the relatively flat central plaza was not sloped enough to provide direct sight lines to the procession. (See fig. 2.15.) While the lictors, the attendants, and the family walked along the Sacra Via to the Rostra, the ancestors rode in chariots. For the ancestors who had never triumphed, the funeral procession of their descendants would be the first time they will have ever ridden in a chariot in the Forum.[109] Chariots were essentially slow-moving el-

[109] I omit the paradox that the *pompa funebris* was most likely the lone opportunity for those *portraying* the ancestors to have ridden in chariots in the Forum. If these were family members, the opportunity

FIGURE 2.14 The procession viewed from the steps of the Basilica Sempronia. The deceased is upright on the bier.

FIGURE 2.15 An occluded view of the procession from the central plaza.

evated display platforms, like modern parade floats. Elevating their cargo above the crowd, they highlighted the most important elements of the procession and made them the most visible to those in the distance.

---

to walk in the procession might serve as motivation for future success. If they were slaves, however, then the procession might present a view even more carnivalesque than we imagine: only triumphators and slaves were conveyed through the forum on triumphal chariots.

Visible Vertical and Horizontal Registers

While the *horizontal* symmetry of the procession as presented in the Amiternum relief was difficult to see in actuality even within the Forum, the vertical arrangement presented in the relief was clearly delineated. Polybius writes that it was more common to prop the body upright when carried into the Forum. The exception was to leave the body reclined on the bier.[110] If we read him literally, as puzzling as it might seem, one would expect a fully upright body rather than even a reclined form as seen in the relief from Amiternum. Consider both options. (See figs. 2.16 and 2.17.) The body's placement was designed to be seen and to accommodate viewing spaces that were not meant to handle processional theater. The elevation of the deceased, reclined or upright, created a vertically defined symbolic hierarchy.

The neat horizontal symmetry in the Amiternum relief repays study, since it allows us to consider processions with and without the accompanying ancestors. (See fig. 2.1.) Note the deviations in visual symmetry and legibility when one compares the relief to a three-dimensional procession of ancestors accompanied by the bier. (See fig. 2.20.) There is numerical symmetry in the relief—an equal number of human elements precede and follow the bier—but the individual elements are not equally distributed spatially. The procession in the relief is somewhat front-loaded and top-heavy. Its designer emphasized the hired performers and, in turn, the spectacular elements over the mourning family. Nonetheless, it also underscores how a modest funeral with no *imagines* would present a relatively balanced funerary package. Once ancestors are added, however—something not visible in the relief—this delicate balance is tipped heavily toward the front: the parades of storied families are longer, take more time to process, and occupy significantly more physical space. The more offset the symmetrical balance due to the presence of ancestors in chariots, the more politically successful the family was. The choreography of those elements defines the viewing for those in the plaza. The deceased, coupled with his funeral couch, would have occupied the most space of the upper register, but the men in their chariots would have been the next most prominent visual element on display. There would have doubtless been variation in the heights of actors portraying the different ancestors, but the height differential would have been relatively insignificant. Their heads, their *imagines*, and their upper torsos would have risen slightly above the obstructing heads of the crowd. The deceased is clearly the focus of the relief and the procession, however. The bier fills the upper register of the relief in the same way that it would dominate the upper register of those viewing the procession in the Forum. If the body were somehow raised fully upright, as depicted in fig. 2.16, the effect would have been more exaggerated.

---

[110] Polyb. 6.53.1: ποτὲ μὲν ἑστὼς ἐναργής, σπανίως δὲ κατακεκλιμένος ("sometimes stood up to be visible, and rarely reclined").

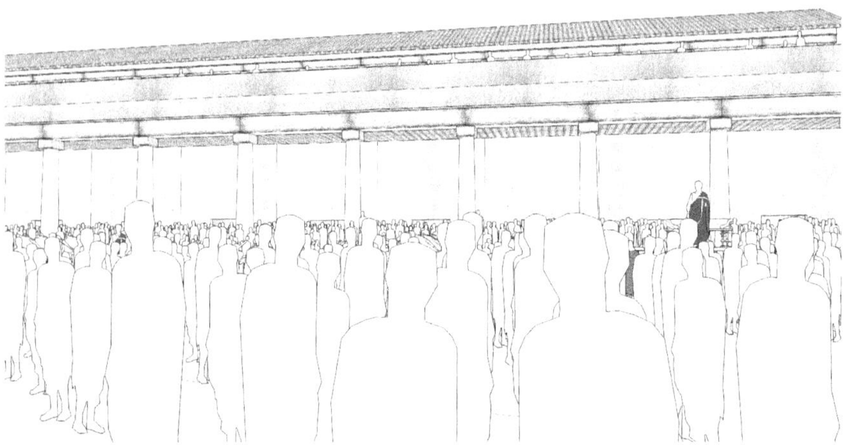

FIGURE 2.16 The deceased propped upright on the bier.

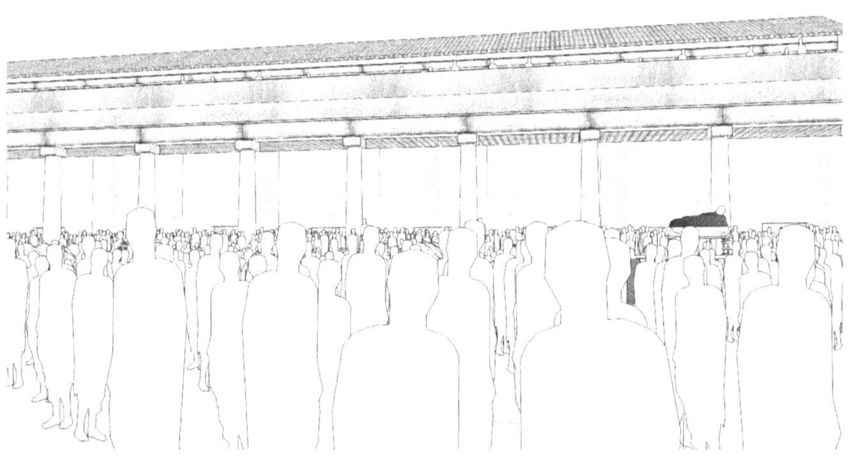

FIGURE 2.17 The deceased, reclined, as depicted in the relief from Amiternum.

Competitive Imagery

There was reason beyond an aid to the viewer for elevating the *imagines* and the deceased. There was visual competition in the Forum. By 158 BCE, it was filled with statuary. In addition, there was a tradition begun as early as the late fourth century to hang *clipeatae imagines*, portrait shields, on public buildings.[111] The *clipeatae imagines*, at the height of the balconies on the basilicas over the shops, looked down upon the pedestrians moving along the Sacra Via.[112] As the procession of ancestors moved through the Forum, those in attendance could have easily remarked on their own ancestors and compared and cross-referenced the representative statues within the Forum to the ancestors on parade. One might even imagine that the parade of ancestors was a parade of statues come to life.[113] It was certainly an opportunity to insert visual representations of one's ancestors into the Forum temporarily as quasi-statuary. For the family with only one *imago* on display, the disparity of symbolic capital will have been profound. And for the family with a long line of *imagines* and perhaps a number of statues and *clipeatae imagines* representing the same ancestors, the visual display of power as well as the deep connection to the history of Rome through its magistrates would have been difficult to ignore.

Ascending the Rostra

This vertical hierarchy in horizontal motion toward the Rostra inextricably guided the gaze of the audience to the northwestern end of the Forum. As each ancestor climbed the steps of the Rostra, the audience would observe the next ancestor in line, and when the (possibly propped-up) body of the deceased reached this part of the Forum, the culmination of the procession would have been clearly signaled. The details here cannot be known. Did the ancestors climb the steps of the Rostra serially, or did they all dismount at once from their chariots and ascend together? To manage space, perhaps each ancestor dismounted from his chariot so that the space could be freed up for the next in line. Did they always ascend in chronological order? How did the crowd react at each moment in this complex transition? At all events, following the body, the eulogist and the rest of the family, in black mourning attire, would have offered an effective visual full-stop, but only to those who could have seen them clearly through the surrounding crowd.[114] For the majority of the audience at a well-attended funeral, however, the deceased was the last element that could have clearly commanded the gaze and guided their eyes to the elevated platform of the Rostra. (See figs. 2.18 and 2.19.) Due to the surrounding crowd

[111] Winkes 1979. Plin. *HN* 35.12 notes that Appius Claudius Caecus was the first to place shield-portraits on a public building—though not one located in the Forum: "in Bellonae aede." Later (Plin. *HN* 35.13), M. Aemilius Lepidus hung them on the Basilica Aemilia in the Roman Forum.

[112] For the location of the shield-portraits on the basilica, see the reverse of a denarius of M. Aemilius Lepidus (M. H. Crawford 1974: 419 3a-b = *BMCRR* Rome 3650 and 3651).

[113] Rüpke 2006 conjectures that the *imagines* were, in fact, meant to replicate statues on parade.

[114] For black attire, see Bodel 2000.

FIGURE 2.18 Viewed from the balcony of the Basilica Fulvia, the procession approaches the Rostra.

FIGURE 2.19 The deceased arrives at the Rostra.

and monumental features of the Forum, the rest of the procession following the deceased and his bier would have been subordinated to the elevated elements that led the way.

Reassessing the Order and Arrangement of the Ancestors

I return for a moment to the two-dimensional diagrams above to underscore a larger point about the seductive nature of the evidence. (See p. 21.) Recall the ordering and visual comparisons prompted by the theoretical models of the processions for the Aemilii Paulli and the Cornelii Scipiones. (See tables 2.1 and 2.2.) In two-dimensional, diagrammatic form, with labels neatly identifying the participants, the chronological progression from eldest to youngest seems natural, acceptable, and almost like a graphical visualization of data. The *imagines*, unlike the accompanying ceremonial garb, were designed to be "read" up close, however. They were obviously not simple, abstract graphical symbols, but instead, something more complex. Either they were placed in the atrium of the home, labeled with *tituli* and near the family stemma, or they were viewed on the Rostra, verbally annotated by the eulogist during his speech. The masks were veristic portraits, with facial features and shading articulated in their design.[115] They inspired primarily through mimetic recognition.[116] Only those in close proximity to the *imagines* could have discerned the details and recognized the masks. Even then, only a few of the masks would have been identifiable. For example, how many people in the Forum of 160 BCE could have recognized M. Aemilius Paullus (a *consul* in 302 BCE) and the great-great-great-great-grandfather of L. Aemilius Paullus? The answer to this question, which we can never know, would tell us much about the overall historical and visual knowledge of the Roman populace. At this point in the funeral, it would have been extraordinarily easy to add an additional ancestor to the procession.[117] Who would know otherwise? Without a placard giving a name and without an easily identifiable face, the ancestor was simply another symbolic prop added to the overall assemblage. In addition, while it is tempting to believe that every procession followed a strict order that would have conveyed a chronological procession from the oldest to the youngest, such an ordering was not necessary. Polybius refers only to a chronological ordering within the speech, not during the procession.[118] Some families might have even found it useful that the details of each ancestor were difficult to discern. It could have given freedom to choreograph the event in ways beyond merely chronological and to highlight a visual quality or a particularly well-known ancestor. For example, one family might have chosen to display all consular ancestors (in the *toga praetexta*) first, followed by triumphators (in the *toga picta*) in order to underline more clearly the triumphal and consular achievements of the *gens*. Such an order might also mask the fact that more recent ancestors had achieved neither.

---

[115] See Hölkeskamp 2023, who highlights how important detailed representations of physical characteristics were, remarking on the veristic portrait tradition coupled with descriptive *cognomina* and *agnomina* along with the *imagines* themselves.

[116] See Flower 1996: 185–222, who examines the inspirational power of the *imagines* as reported in the sources.

[117] In Chapter 3, I discuss the manipulation of *imagines* and *tituli*.

[118] Polyb. 6.54.1: ἄρχεται τῶν ἄλλων ἀπὸ τοῦ προγενεστάτου τῶν παρόντων.

The Pompa Funebris *as Visual Manifestation of Symbolic Capital*

The procession, the *pompa funebris*, to the Rostra was not the most effective tool for waging an interfamily competition of symbolic capital, at least not that of the *imagines* alone. Visibility was limited, but so was the cumulative spectacular effect of viewing the *imagines* on their chariots. Aristocratic families of the middle Republic were a surprisingly uniform group.[119] The Cornelii Scipiones and the Aemilii Paulli are both examples of successful families, but the overall difference of their ancestral display is negligible. For example, in figure 2.20, even without topographical obstructions and the visual interference of a large crowd, the two funeral processions look remarkably similar. The purple of the *toga purpurea* and *toga picta* mark the Cornelii as a slightly more accomplished family, but only when the processions are viewed side-by-side—something that could never have happened. If a family already had six or seven ancestors, the addition of another was not easily noticed. The audience was most likely not keeping score from year to year—there is certainly no direct evidence for such counting. Aside from the decoration of the bier, which seems to have been the focus of lavish expenditure, the most discernible element that would have differentiated aristocratic processions was the mere presence of a single *imago*, and then, at a higher level, the accumulation of multiple honors.[120]

MANIPULATING THE PROCESSIONAL ROUTE

The funeral procession was open to manipulation. The location of the home and the specific path taken would have changed for each family. The *imagines* conveyed through the Forum on chariots must have been impressive, but to the casual observer, it would have been hard to recognize the deceased and his ancestors. Some families maneuvered around this limitation. By associating certain *imagines* with public spaces, they altered the approach to the Rostra and the "legibility" of their procession. In the next section, I explore the visual alteration of the funeral procession associated with two of the most influential men of the middle Republic. Both examples are later than that of the funeral of Paullus, but help to demonstrate the range of potential options available for such a funeral.

---

[119] Rosenstein 1990: 44 notes that fifty-seven percent of consuls from 249–50 BCE had sons reach the consulship or praetorship.

[120] On the adornment of the bier, see Livy *Per.* 48.11: "M. Aemilius Lepidus, qui princeps senatus sextis iam censoribus lectus erat, antequam expiraret, praecepit filiis lecto se strato linteis sine purpura efferrent, in reliquum funus ne plus quam aeris decies consumerent: imaginum specie, non sumptibus nobilitari magnorum virorum funera solere." ("Marcus Aemilius Lepidus, who had been selected *princeps senatus* by six censorships, before he died, enjoined his sons not to carry him out on a *lectica* lined with purple sheets, and not to spend more than one million asses on his funeral: the funerals of great men are made noble by the sight of *imagines*, not lavish expenditures.")

FIGURE 2.20 Views of the procession of the Aemilii (top) and the Cornelii (middle and bottom) without context.

Approaching the Rostra: the Cornelii Scipiones

The funerals of the Cornelii Scipiones are attested to have altered the usual processional route in ways specifically advantageous to the deceased and his family.[121] To the traditional cortege path discussed above, the Cornelii descended from Scipio Africanus may have added a visit to the Capitoline Hill to acquire his *imago*.[122] His waxen mask was placed in the cella of the Temple of Jupiter Optimus Maximus, in effect equating the residence of the most powerful god in the Roman pantheon

[121] The following section is loosely derived from my contribution to Favro and Johanson 2010.

[122] The primary sources are Val. Max. 8.15.1 and App. *Iber.* 23. I discuss Appian's remarks below, 60n126. It would be problematic to build an argument about the Roman funeral of the middle Republic based on famous exceptions, absent other evidence. The sources for this event are not entirely reliable. Valerius Maximus notes the retrieval of Scipio Africanus' *imago* from the Temple of Jupiter Optimus Maximus. Valerius Maximus writes "quotienscumque funus aliquod Corneliae gentis celebrandum est, inde petitur" ("Whenever the *gens Cornelia* need to hold a funeral, the *imago* is sought from there [the Temple of Jupiter Optimus Maximus].") Most likely, Valerius Maximus is ignoring the details of the *stemma* of the Cornelii. While it is possible that every branch of the Cornelii brought out the *imago* of Africanus—the Sullae did—one wonders whether the Cornelii Lentuli did the same. For an alternate view on this manipulation, see Flower 1996: 48–52, who notes (48): "Although our sources are not explicit on this point, they imply that the whole procession started at the house and continued up to the temple of Jupiter on the Capitol to pick up Africanus, before making its way to the Forum."

with the atrium of Scipio's house.[123] The Cornelii were always a special case—while the rest of Rome cremated their dead, the Cornelii continued to inter without cremation.[124] This modification might simply be an additional example of how this particular family differentiated itself from the competition. Perhaps the reason for modifying the route was pragmatic: the house of Scipio Africanus stood next to the Roman Forum behind the Tabernae Veteres, which meant, like the homes along the Vicus Tuscus, a funeral procession to the Republican Rostra would have only required a walk of less than one hundred meters—not long enough to attract a large crowd.[125] Those families whose homes were adjacent to the Forum may have been compelled to explore other ways to expand and alter the traditional procession. The use of the Capitoline Hill and the creation of an additional processional route represent another example of innovation in the ongoing visual competition in the Forum.

In the years after the *imago* of Scipio Africanus had been placed in the Temple of Jupiter Optimus Maximus, funeral processions for the family of the Cornelii Scipiones began at the house of the deceased, moved through the Forum, and then to the Rostra—the expected route. An independent segment of the cortege turned toward the Capitoline, however.[126] Most likely, the chariots and the bier remained at the Rostra, since the uphill climb and the space restrictions on the top of the Capitoline would have been difficult to overcome. Once the segment moved past the Temple of Saturn, visual contact with spectators in the low-lying Forum plaza was severed. How the *imago* was acquired has not been recorded. Presumably the event occurred in front of the south-facing Temple of Jupiter Optimus Maximus, where an actor donned the wax mask of Scipio.[127] (For the spatial relationship of the Tem-

---

[123] Ancient sources do not specify why, or when, the *imago* of Scipio Africanus was placed in the Capitoline temple. Scipio had always demonstrated a special relationship with the temple: Livy 38.51.12, 26.19.7. See Fears 1981: 44, and Vasaly 1993: 73. The similarity between the mythologies of Scipio and Alexander the Great underscore the particular difficulties of Republican evidence: legend infiltrates history, see Ruebel 1991: 17–18.

[124] On the Cornelii and the Tomb of the Scipios, see Toynbee 1996: 39–40.

[125] Livy (44.16.10–11) notes that the house, which probably stood on the Vicus Tuscus, was purchased and demolished by Tiberius Sempronius Gracchus in 170 BCE to build the Basilica Sempronia, see Richardson 1992: 134 and Papi 1995b. Therefore, the purely pragmatic need to compensate for the extremely short march to the Rostra by extending the parade to the Capitoline Hill would have been obviated within 13 years after Scipio's death.

[126] Did the main procession move up the Capitoline to retrieve the mask? Or was it a separate processional element? Appian reports that the εἰκών of Scipio was still being fetched from the Temple during his own time (καὶ νῦν ἔτι). App. *Iber.* 23. He implies that the εἰκών was incorporated into the full procession, but compares it to other *imagines* that are brought from the Forum (τὴν εἰκόνα τὴν Σκιπίωνος ἐν ταῖς πομπαῖς μόνου προφέρουσιν ἐκ τοῦ Καπιτωλίου, τῶν δ᾽ ἄλλων ἐξ ἀγορᾶς φέρονται). Rather than consider "from the Forum" an egregious error, recall that Appian was writing during the first third of the second century CE. The form of the funeral and the representation of the *imagines* had changed drastically since the Republic. See Morstein-Marx and Byrne 2025: 340–342, who argue convincingly that Appian describes "funerals of members of the imperial house" and not "the old-style aristocratic funeral parades." Nonetheless, the tradition of manipulating the conveyance of representations of ancestors and of renowned historical figures continued.

[127] The representation of the temple follows Gjerstad 1960.

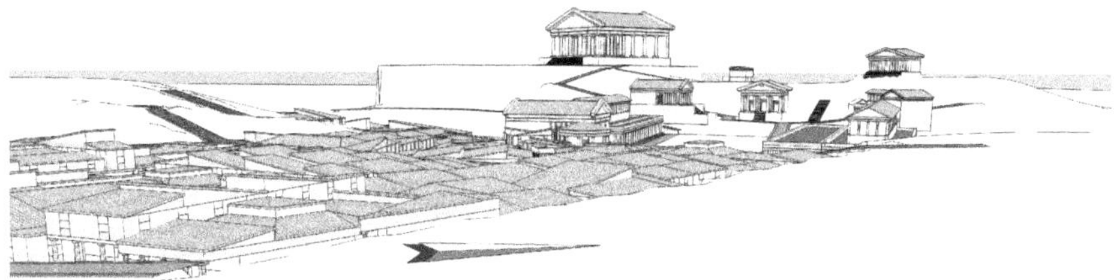

FIGURE 2.21 The Temple of Jupiter Optimus Maximus and the Forum.

ple of Jupiter Optimus Maximus to the Forum, see fig. 2.21.) How did the Cornelii interconnect this unique family custom with the more traditional program of the Republican funeral? To what degree were the symbolic connections between the funerary activities at the Rostra and those on the Capitoline magnified by spectacle? There are at least two possible models to explore. One is based on funerary practice in Ciceronian Rome; the other, on the alleged oratorical situation of the mid-Republic contemporary to that of Paullus.

Alternative I: Orators Face the Forum.

Having watched the funeral procession of the *imagines* reach the Rostra, the audience assembled in the Forum to await the *laudatio*. The ceremony occurring atop the Capitol would have been completely occluded from those in the Forum plaza. (See fig. 2.22.) Depending on the weather and ambient noise, music and chants gradually grew louder and louder, and drew their attention to the Clivus Capitolinus. The *imago* of Scipio on foot or, less likely, in a chariot rounded the corner. Adding innovation to innovation, Africanus may have worn only the *toga praetexta*; he had requested that his *imago* not exit the Temple of Jupiter Optimus Maximus with triumphal adornment.[128] He approached the Rostra to take his seat among the other ancestors. For the audience awaiting in the Forum plaza, a view of his entry into the Forum would have been momentarily obstructed. In figure 2.23, the walk from the Temple of Jupiter Optimus Maximus, passing the Temple of Saturn, to the Rostra, could not have been seen from the Forum plaza. Hence, the audience would not have observed the moment when the *imago* of Scipio emerged from the Temple of Jupiter Optimus Maximus. They would have seen his descent into the Forum, however, and it would have been particularly notable that this additional *imago* walked alone, down the Clivus Capitolinus and onto the Rostra.

[128] Livy 38.56.12: "prohibuisse ne decerneretur ut imago sua triumphali ornatu e templo Iouis optimi maximi exiret." Cf. Val. Max. 4.1.6a. See Galinsky 1966, who suggests that the *imago* of Scipio appears in Plautus' *Amphitruo*.

FIGURE 2.22 View of the Temple of Jupiter Optimus Maximus from the Forum plaza, occluded by the Temple of Saturn.

FIGURE 2.23 The descent of the *imago* of Scipio cannot be seen from the Forum plaza. The Temple of Saturn and a gathered crowd blocks the view.

Alternative II: Orators face the Curia.

The current scholarly view holds that the Forum plaza only became an oratorical theater in the late Republic. During the mid-Republic orators faced the Comitium and the Curia, not the Forum.[129] Only in 145 BCE did the orientation reverse when a tribune turned his back on the Curia to address the people directly, a populist move meant to appease the masses and annoy the magisterial classes.[130] Was the *laudatio* originally configured to face the Curia, not the Forum plaza?

The topography of the area supports a Curia-centered oration. Until ca. 184 BCE, the Cloaca Maxima, which ran through the middle of the Forum, was apparently uncovered.[131] It would have formed a natural partition between the eastern side of the Forum (a large portion of the central plaza) and the western half, occupied by the political nucleus of the Curia, the Comitium, the Senaculum, and the Graecostasis.[132] The natural topography of the area formed a self-contained cavea centered on the Rostra. The area of the Comitium lies on a small depression surrounded by gentle upward slopes on all sides save that of the Forum Plaza.[133] (See fig. 2.24.) The Temple of Concord (if one existed at this time) and the Temple of Saturn offered lengthy, stepped approaches that would have served as convenient tiered viewing areas.[134] (See fig. 2.25.) M. Porcius Cato's decision as censor to purchase land near the Curia to build the first named basilica in Rome (the Basilica Porcia) implies that the space benefited from a public, porticoed structure—another shaded viewing area.[135] (See fig. 2.26.) One assumes that those not privileged enough to merit access to the Comitium would have gathered in the Forum plaza and on the southern end of the Forum, in the space in front of the Temple of Saturn, but the elite would have filled the Comitium, and commanded the privileged views and the privilege in general of being associated with the seat of magisterial power, the *Curia Hostilia*, the Senate House. The speaker would have been elevated above many of the people. The elite were able to demonstrate their own station through prominent positions in the Comitium. Because of the naturally sloped and stepped viewing area, sight lines between the audience and the speaker were unobstructed. The privileged in the Comitium would have been close enough to hear the speech as well. Assembling in the western end of the Forum mitigates the interference caused by the open shops and the ongoing business surrounding the Forum plaza.

---

129 Plut. *C. Grach.* 5.3. For a full discussion of the evidence, see Morstein-Marx 2004: 45–47.

130 Cic. *Amic.* 25.96 and Varro, *Rust.* 1.2.9.

131 Plaut. *Curc.* 476 refers to a *canalis* in the Forum. J. N. Hopkins 2007: 9: archaeological explorations have confirmed the existence of second-century vaulting.

132 I delineate the Senaculum and Graecostasis with transparent outline in the figures. The Senaculum was the area where senators congregated before being summoned to enter the Senate House (Varro, *Ling.* 5.156). The Graecostasis was a raised tribunal for ambassadors from foreign states (Varro, *Ling.* 5.155).

133 For the general topography of the area, see Carafa 1998 and Amici 2004.

134 The actual founding date of the temple is not clear, see Ferroni 1993: 316–317.

135 On the Basilica Porcia, see Steinby 1993b; and Livy 39.44.7. On porticoed viewing at funerals during the Empire, see Dio Cass. 75.74.4.

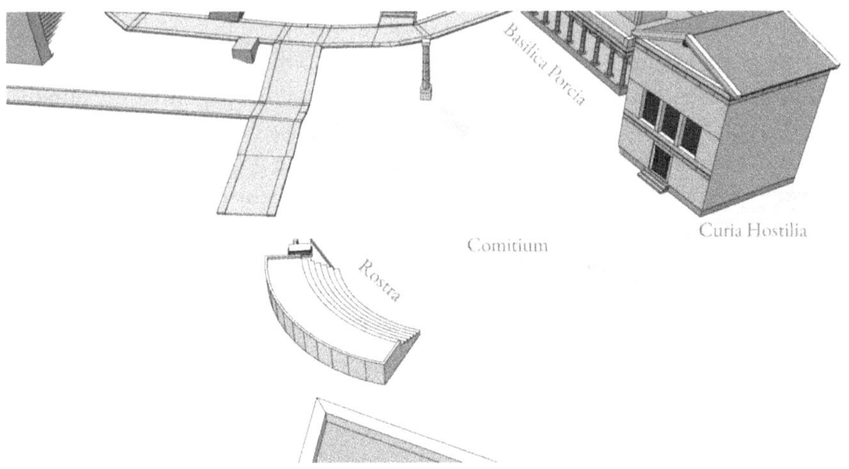

FIGURE 2.24 The Comitium.

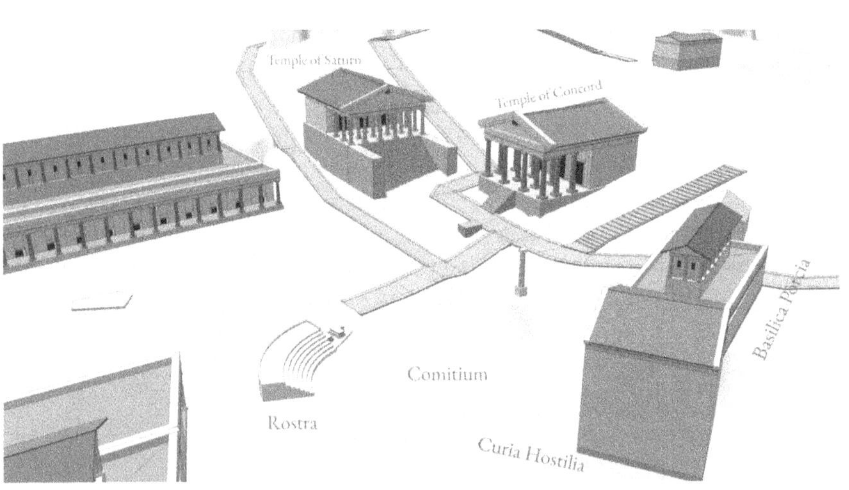

FIGURE 2.25 The Temples of Saturn and Concord as audience space.

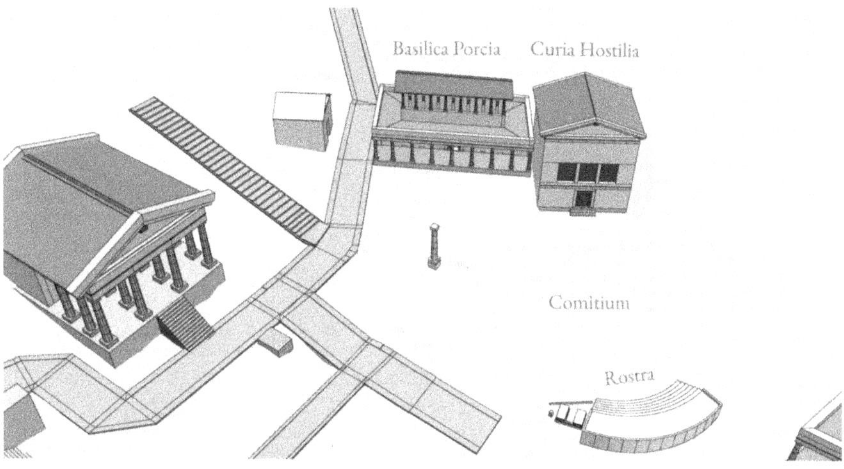

FIGURE 2.26 The Basilica Porcia flanking the Curia Hostilia.

This grouping of the spectators west of the Comitium alters the potential symbolic viewsheds, for it is precisely in this location that both the speaker and the audience could have shared in the same deictic references to the Temple of Jupiter Optimus Maximus.[136] This Curia-centered viewing configuration enabled a visual connection to the Capitoline. As the procession of the Cornelii began to fill the Comitium and the surrounding space, a branch of the parade moved up the slope of the Clivus Capitolinus, in clear view of the majority of the more privileged spectators, those in the cavea to the west of the Comitium. (See fig. 2.27.) One could have been situated favorably for the upcoming *laudatio* and still have viewed the ceremony that was occurring on top of the Capitoline *and* watched the dramatic entrance of Scipio into the Forum. Many outside the Comitium, on the sloped hillside to the west, would have been able to witness the spectacle above. Such intervisuality continues a visible connection between the ancestor of the family and the Temple of Jupiter Optimus Maximus. The uneducated (even non-Latin speakers) would have immediately understood that this ancestor had been housed in the temple of the most powerful god in the city. Most would have recognized the signal that this was a funeral of the Cornelii Scipiones, and all those of privileged status could not avoid seeing the ancestor of a potential rival emerge from the Temple of the most powerful Roman god.

These additions to the ritual approach to the Rostra drew attention to the event and helped differentiate this funeral from others—a necessary endeavor when one considers the number of ongoing distractions and the difficulty in relying on *imag-*

[136]For a discussion of Cicero's famous reference to the Capitol, see Vasaly 1993: 83–84.

FIGURE 2.27 The *imago* of Scipio descending on foot from the Capitoline.

ines alone for distinguishing one family from another. It should remind us that others might have attempted similarly innovative routes. The experiential analysis lets us consider the nature of the link thus forged between the Capitoline and the Forum. The *imago* of Scipio was housed in the "atrium" of a god. The effect of this visual connection, in turn, allows us to reevaluate the textual evidence and the configuration of the event itself. The parade route from Jupiter's temple to the Forum reflected a direct connection between Scipio Africanus—and thus all Cornelii who might try to claim affiliation—and the great god by highlighting a familial, and perhaps topographically spectacular, descent.[137] The visual connection with the Temple of Jupiter was desirable, but not essential, however. As arguably the most important temple in the Roman world its image was familiar to all spectators. They did not necessarily have to see the connection; the echoes of processional music and the directional entrance of a small cortege or even a lone *imago* were enough to forge the associations desired by the Cornelii. But when the evidence is reassessed, it is clear that in one configuration, an even more compelling visual connection reinforces the symbolic association. Our new understanding of the visual impact of the Cornelii's procession helps to clarify the event below. The oratorical stage of the mid-Republic prior to 145 BCE was different than that of the first century, and this specific configuration happens to accommodate the evidence and the practical logistics of the space better than the conventional alternative.

[137] See Farney 2023, who highlights the various connections asserted between Jupiter and Africanus as well as between this god and the Scipiones more broadly. One visible example of this connection: Scipio did not participate in business without first having visited the Temple of Jupiter on the Capitoline, see Marks 2005: 169 and 187.

Marcus Porcius Cato

In contrast to the claimed descendants of Scipio Africanus, the family of the *novus homo*, Marcus Porcius Cato, installed his *imago* in the Curia Hostilia to be retrieved during funerary events, perhaps in response to the Cornelii's bold symbolic association with the Temple of Jupiter Optimus Maximus.[138] Not merely symbolic, this tool employed in interfamily competition would have been spectacular. Rather than remain hidden from the audience by the Rostra, the *imago* of Cato would have emerged from the Curia in full view of the parting crowd. (See fig. 2.28.) Unlike the alteration of the procession initiated by the Cornelii Scipiones, the manipulation of funerary practice by the Porcii had documented (and famous) imitators. Dio Cassius writes that Augustus' body was placed in a container, but an effigy of him was manifestly visible: καὶ αὕτη μὲν ἐκ τοῦ παλατίου πρὸς τῶν ἐς νέωτα ἀρχόντων, ἑτέρα δὲ ἐκ τοῦ βουλευτηρίου χρυσῆ, καὶ ἑτέρα αὖ ἐφ' ἅρματος πομπικοῦ ἤγετο. ("And this [effigy] was carried from the Palatine by magistrates elected for the upcoming year, another, a golden one, was carried from the Senate House, and another was conveyed on a triumphal chariot.")[139] By the time of Augustus, the Forum had undergone change. A new Rostra in a new location faced the western end of the central plaza, not the Curia. The new Rostra no longer blocked the view into the Senate House. Therefore, the new configuration of the Forum offered a way for Augustus to take advantage of the same functional view that Cato had years before. His *imago* was carried down the stairs of the Senate and over to the Rostra, visible to all. Though the funeral of the first emperor was no longer the same phenomenon as that of Cato, the use of the same technique demonstrates its validity and efficacy.[140]

POMPA FUNEBRIS: CONCLUSION

In sum, funeral parades were spectacular but also a relatively common occurrence in the Forum. A Roman in the middle Republic might have experienced two or three significant funeral parades each year. The *imagines* played a significant role, but the route itself and its interaction with the surrounding environment were equally critical. Families such as the Cornelii Scipiones and the Porcii Catones created clear visual modifications to the event. Paullus could have done the same,

---

[138] The evidence is hardly clear. Immediately after his account of the *imago* of Scipio, Val. Max. 8.15.2 writes, "Tam hercule quam curia superiori Catoni, cuius effigies ad illius generis officia expromitur." ("So, by Hercules, the Curia [was used in a similar fashion as the Temple of Jupiter Optimus Maximus] for elder Cato, whose effigy was produced for *officia* of this nature.") Since Valerius Maximus makes the explicit comparison to the practice of the Scipiones, *effigies* most likely refers to an *imago*, and not merely to a statue as one might expect.

[139] Cass. Dio 56.34.2. For detailed analysis of this passage and argument for translation of εἴκων as "effigy" and not "waxen mask," see Morstein-Marx and Byrne 2025: 338 esp. n35.

[140] For detailed discussions of Imperial funerals, see Arce 1990, Davies 2000, and Favro and Johanson 2010.

FIGURE 2.28 The *imago* of Cato emerges from the Curia Hostilia in full view of the surrounding crowd.

though no direct evidence exists.[141] The additional ancestors were not acquired prior to the procession; rather, their acquisition was designed specifically to contribute to the overall visual spectacle of the funeral, timed to coincide with the arrival of the procession at the Rostra. These manipulations were entirely visual and meant to accomplish what the *imagines* alone, in a traditional parade, could not. After all, the *imagines* were never meant to function on their own. Accompanied by *tituli* in the house, and by the visible accoutrements of higher offices and honors in the *pompa*, the *imagines* required additional, explanatory aids. As demonstrated above, they would have been difficult to see in the Forum for all but those located very close to them. They were on display during the procession, but they were not the featured element. The deceased clearly dominated the upper register of the visual hierarchy. There was a limit to the visual effect the *pompa* could have, however. To compensate, one might innovate by housing an *imago* in a significant location and using these new public *atria* as a means of capturing attention and offering visual identification to the audience. Better than a connection to one's own house, which was tenuous, if the home was located anywhere but within immediate view of the Forum, the use of the Temple of Jupiter Optimus Maximus and later the Curia as a surrogate *atrium* would have attracted the attention of those in the Forum. The process of acquiring these *imagines* would have disrupted unrelated activities in the Forum. In the case of Cato the Elder, this process would have engaged directly with the Senate as the *imago* was moved from the Senate House through

[141] See chapter 5 for an exploration of hypothetical modifications made by Paullus' family.

the Comitium. This was visual theater, but of a very specific type, meant to direct attention to the critical moment at the Rostra, the subject of the next chapter.

Purposes

The announcement of the funeral directed the populace to assemble in the Forum, and in so doing, created the most potentially theatrical moment for the viewing audience. The Forum was not designed for processional theater, and choices would need to be made. As an audience member, did one await the entry of the procession in the Forum plaza or did one gather as close as possible to the Rostra? What was the spectacular draw? As all processions do, the funeral integrated its audience. Being seen by the participants of the procession was no doubt politically important. The procession *to* the Rostra was more diffuse and less focused than the subsequent, oratorical event held *on* the Rostra, however. The funeral procession to the Rostra was no triumph—it was not even, necessarily, the focal point of the larger event. In fact, far longer than the procession to the Rostra was the procession to follow the eulogy, the walk to the *ustrinum* or place of interment. The real procession, when measured in linear feet, was the walk past the walls of the city to the tomb.[142] In the case of Paullus, there would have been little practical reason to have the foreign supporters of Aemilius alternate their carrying of the bier on their walk into the Forum, but there would have been a serious need for a substantial group ready to bear the bier to the family tomb. For example, the procession to the tomb of the Scipiones would have meandered through at least 2.5 km of city streets. A slow trip, with pauses for handing off the bier might last forty minutes to an hour at slightly less than the average walking speed of 4.5 km/hr.

A One-way Perambulatory Event

The *pompa funebris* was a one-way trip.[143] It was a pilgrimage, albeit a short one. Its end goal was to deliver the body to specific points—the Forum and the pyre or place of interment—of the burial ritual. The starting point was the home, where the ancestral masks were removed from their cabinet to join the procession. The next fixed point for an aristocratic funeral was the Rostra where *laudatio funebris* would be given. We know little about how the *pompa funebris* might have reconfigured itself between each step. And we do not know how the procession's participants would have assembled or how they would have finally dispersed.

I am relatively confident in asserting that the stops of the funeral procession were ultimately more important than its motion. The *pompa* was not a round trip. Compare a modern Christian procession in Italy, for example, the annual parade in Testaccio honoring Santa Maria Liberatrice. The icon of Maria, a small statue, is carried on a bier throughout the neighborhood of Testaccio. The procession begins at the church and proceeds from block to block, sometimes doubling back on itself,

[142] See Johanson 2011.

[143] For an analysis and typology of "perambulatory events," see Marin 1987.

circling through all the internal streets of the district. The ritual is designed to expose the icon to each and every house in the neighborhood, not to carry it to a final destination.[144] As the procession moves through the district so that the icon can "see" the inhabitants, the number of participants increases. The *pompa funebris* followed a different route. It was also emphatically not a parade whose primary purpose was merely to display the ancestors. While it is possible that a secondary parade occurred in which the full procession resumed after the cremation to bring along all the masks back to the house, the sources remain silent. Questions abound, of course. Where did the actors in their masks go after riding in their chariots? Was the transformation from a "living" ancestor to a masked one accompanied by its own ceremony or did it resemble the backstage dressing room at a play? How did the ancestors act when or if they watched a cremation? Or even the funeral games? If there was a double of the deceased, how did *he* react when his corpse was burned on the funeral pyre?

Processional Leverage

The *pompa funebris* seems to have focused more on its destination, the *Rostra*, than the route. Dion. Hal. *Ant. Rom.* 9.54.5–6, who retrojects first-century practice into the fifth century, writes of the funeral of Appius Claudius in 470 BCE (*sic*)[145]:

> προενεχθέντος δὲ τοῦ σώματος εἰς τὴν ἀγορὰν ὁ μὲν υἱὸς αὐτοῦ προσιὼν τοῖς δημάρχοις καὶ τοῖς ὑπάτοις ἠξίου τὴν νόμιμον ἐκκλησίαν αὐτῷ συναγαγεῖν καὶ τὸν ἐν ἔθει Ῥωμαίοις ὄντα ἐπὶ ταῖς ταφαῖς ἀγορεύεσθαι τῶν ἀγαθῶν ἀνδρῶν λόγον ἐπιτρέψαι περὶ τοῦ πατρὸς διελθεῖν. οἱ δὲ δήμαρχοι καλουμένης ἔτι τῆς ἐκκλησίας ὑπὸ τῶν ὑπάτων ἐνίσταντο, καὶ παρήγγελλον τῷ μειρακίῳ τὸν νεκρὸν ἀποφέρειν. οὐ μὴν ὁ δῆμός γ᾽ ἠνέσχετο οὐδὲ περιεῖδε τὴν ὕβριν, ἄτιμον ἐκβληθῆναι τὸ σῶμα, ἀλλ᾽ ἐπέτρεψε τῷ μειρακίῳ τὰς νομιζομένας ἀποδοῦναι τῷ πατρὶ τιμάς. Ἄππιος μὲν οὖν τοιαύτης τελευτῆς ἔτυχεν.
>
> And after the body had been carried to the Forum, his son approached the tribunes and consuls and requested that they summon the customary assembly for him and that they let him give the speech about his father that was traditionally given at Roman funerals of great men. While the assembly was still being called by the consuls, the tribunes vetoed it and told the boy to carry away the corpse. The people, however, did

[144] See, e.g., Lajolo 2008: "Abbiamo portato [la statua della nostra Madonna] per le strade del nostro rione anche perché veda le nostre singole case, dove vivono le nostre famiglie."

[145] Modern historians agree that Appius Claudius (cos. 471) was the Decemvir of 451/450 BCE and that descriptions of his earlier death represent family meddling in the historical record. See for example, Ogilvie 1965: 2.61, who writes, "Since Ap. Claudius did not in fact die now but survived to compass his own death, detested and abhorred by *plebs* and *patres* alike, and since laudations in public were a late development … this detail must be an invention springing from some imaginatively written *laudationes* such as family historians evidently delighted to compose." The historicity of the event is of secondary concern since it is more important that the sources transmit an accurate reflection of their understanding of funerary custom.

> not accept this nor did they allow the outrage, that his body be carried away without honor, instead they ordered the boy to give the customary honors to his father.[146]

The procession arrived at the Rostra where permission was requested from the Senate that the *accensus* announce the *laudatio* to the community. Not only did the *laudatio* require permission; the tribune had the authority to prevent it. The assembly was just being summoned when the tribunes intervened. If Dionysius is correct—and there is no guarantee—then the *pompa* offered a different kind of spectacular manipulation: leverage. An oration was hardly obligatory.[147] One did not need permission to assemble, however. It would have presumably been difficult to refuse a procession with *imagines* already arrayed in the Comitium.

Pilgrimage Theater

Just as the honor for the deceased was customary, so was the choice of a young son as the eulogist. The procession was a one-way trip—a pilgrimage—for the family and for the eulogist in particular. His journey comprised two destinations: the Forum, where he mounted the Rostra for what might have been his first time, and the "grave"—in whatever form it might have taken, where he bade farewell to his father. In a useful categorization of processions, such journeys are called "pilgrimage theater [where] the spectator who matters most is the pilgrim."[148] In the next chapter, I examine the power of the *laudatio*, and how it accommodated two very different audiences, those in the Forum and the most important pilgrim in the funerary procession.

---

146 Dion. Hal. *Ant. Rom.* 9.54.5–6. See also Livy 2.61: "Haud ita multum interim temporis fuit; ante tamen quam prodicta dies veniret, morbo moritur. Cuius laudationem cum tribunus plebis impedire conaretur, plebs fraudari sollemni honore supremum diem tanti viri noluit, et laudationem tam aequis auribus mortui audivit quam vivi accusationem audierat et exsequias frequens celebravit."

147 For discussion of Cic. *de Leg.* 2.61–62, see below, p. 146.

148 Wiles 2003: 64.

CHAPTER 3

Laudatio Funebris: Reading at a Distance

A Multivariate Case Study

The *laudatio funebris* of the mid-Republic was not like other oratorical performances. While it is now generally agreed that the persuasive techniques of oratory comprised verbal (the content and delivery of the speech) and visual elements (gestures charged with meaning and explicit visual and topographic references), the degree to which the choreography of the funeral eulogy was in dialog with while simultaneously subordinating the words of the speech has not been fully examined.[1] For much of the audience, and for many funerary *laudationes* the visuality of the event might have eclipsed the aural content. Many factors contribute to this assessment. The *laudatio funebris*, like the *pompa* before it, relied on a basic set of quasi-formulaic visual cues to communicate with the audience, or to communicate *some* ideas to *some* of the audience. The *laudatio*, when viewed in its physical context, also functioned as a kind of living and breathing data visualization. In this chapter, I will analyze the event within the physical context of the surrounding Forum.[2] I will demonstrate that the *laudatio funebris* was a theatrical event, comprising two distinct elements, targeting two distinct audiences.

[1] See Beck 2018, who brilliantly explores and recreates the emotional economies of the speech.

[2] Flower 1996: 129n5: "It is notable that recent analyses of the fragments of the *laudationes* take virtually no account of the setting for the speech, and especially the *imagines*." Kierdorf 1980: 6 contends that, for the purposes of rhetorical study, the location of the *laudatio*, whether it was held in the Forum or at the tomb, is irrelevant; cf. Arce 2000, esp. 59–86, who examines the surrounding space in order to raise, rather than answer, a number of practical questions. For example, how many people attended? Could an audience hear the voice of an untrained orator unaided by devices used to amplify the voice, such as theatrical masks?

This investigation is a multivariate case-study in which I model a limited sample of variables related to the performance of the Roman funeral eulogy.[3] The combination of scriptable elements, customary rites, and forms of popular manipulation necessarily led to multiple instantiations of the *laudatio funebris*. Sweeping generalizations that describe the event are useful to delineate dramatic variations in funerary practice from Republic to Empire, but they also invite the creation of a synchronic ideal that never was. In the *ad hoc* world of the mid-Republic, years before permanent theaters and Imperial restrictions, the loose order imposed by tradition was in constant tension with the exigencies of living in a world undergoing constant change. As in the *pompa funebris*, the orchestrated event of the *laudatio* had no consistent script, only a multiplicity of interwoven scripts, tailored to individual players. Multiple variables controlled the nature of the event. Who had died and when? What had the deceased accomplished? To what family did the deceased belong? Was there a son present? Were there ancestors and *imagines*? Where exactly were the physical masks housed? Where was the body? What were the weather conditions? Were there other events taking place concurrently? Trials? Festivals? And, ultimately, who might care enough to attend? It is the goal of this investigation to tease out some of the possibilities, and to model a sample of scenarios and probabilities, all centered on the reconstructed funeral of Lucius Aemilius Paullus.

This chapter progresses from micro arguments to macro analysis. First, I focus on the words spoken during the *laudatio* by examining extant fragments and testimony of *laudationes*. I will establish, as far as the textual evidence allows, the limitations of the *laudatio funebris* as oratorical performance. I then lay the groundwork for visual exploration by delineating the topographic boundaries of the stage, the Rostra, and its surrounding environs. Having followed the procession to the Rostra, I will examine how manipulations and variations within the text of the *laudatio* have powerful visual and performance ramifications. I will then use a wider-angle lens to explore the interplay between audience, orator, and the various elements of symbolic capital spread throughout the Roman Forum. In conclusion, I will demonstrate that it is only through a combined close reading of texts and contexts, and through modeling of various possibilities, that one can fully comprehend the peculiar nature of this significant event.

THE SPEECH

The State of the Evidence

Grasping the precise nature of the speech itself is exceedingly difficult, since the evidence fails at numerous, critical points; scholarly opinion tends to migrate while

---

[3] On the method employed, see McCarty 2004, McCarty 2007, Johanson 2009, and Johanson 2015.

the sources remain more or less the same.[4] That there are no verifiably complete funeral orations extant is puzzling; that the rhetorical treatises have little to say directly about the event, even more so. To reconstruct the overall parameters for the speech given at the funeral of Paullus, I will briefly review the evidence for *laudationes*, with one qualification: I will not assemble and attempt to examine all known *laudationes*, but will instead restrict discussion to those of the Republic. Therefore, I omit (nearly) all imperial eulogies and panegyrics, and for reasons that will be made clear below, I will only touch upon two of the three epigraphic sources that are often considered *laudationes funebres*.[5] I focus primarily on the coeval evidence that might best inform a reconstruction of the specific *laudatio* that might have been given at Paullus' funeral.

My goal in reviewing the evidence is to understand as clearly as possible what was said at a funeral eulogy, based on the surviving texts. I underscore how little evidence is actually available, so we should know that we can at best hypothesize possible solutions. What will be clear in the following examples, however, is that the text of a *laudatio* tended toward the superlative, listed a set of achievements that were part of a culturally normative list of goals to be attained, and was most likely relatively short.

Cicero's Assessment of the Funeral Eulogy

According to Cicero, *laudationes funebres* at Rome, though evidently abundant, had a dismal reputation in the ancient world.[6] In the *Brutus*, a dialogue whose interlocutors include Cicero in the leading role, Atticus, and Brutus, Cicero himself provides a biographical history of oratory, which culminates in a description of his own oratorical career. He first surveys orators known for their eloquence, but whose writings had been lost (*Brut.* 52–61). Before he discusses Cato, whose speeches are the oldest extant in significant quantity, he notes:

> nec vero habeo quemquam antiquiorem [*sc.* Catone], cuius quidem scripta proferenda putem, nisi quem Appi Caeci oratio haec ipsa de Pyrrho et nonnullae mortuorum laudationes forte delectant. Et hercules eae quidem exstant: ipsae enim familiae sua quasi ornamenta ac monumenta servabant et ad usum, si quis eiusdem generis occidisset, et ad memoriam laudum domesticarum et ad illustrandam nobilitatem suam.

[4] The *laudatio* has been the subject of numerous studies. Kierdorf 1980 compiles most of the evidence, but Vollmer 1891 remains indispensable. For a brief overview, see O. C. Crawford 1941 and Durry 1950. Flower 1996: 128–158 focuses on the role of the ancestors. Arce 2000 offers a general overview and a speculative essay about the staging of the event. Ramage 2006 examines the *laudatio* as political propaganda. Beck 2018 studies the full sensory experience. Hölkeskamp 2023 brilliantly situates the *laudatio* within a comprehensive argument centered on the theatricality of Roman power during the Republic.

[5] E.g., the so-called *Laudatio Turiae* (*CIL* VI 1527), the *Laudatio Murdiae* (*CIL* VI 10230), and the fragmentary *Laudatio Matidiae* (*CIL* XIV 3579).

[6] Kierdorf 1980: 49–54 argues, instead that the *laudatio funebris* was not *a priori* "kunstlos," and that the *laudatio*, like Republican oratory, was evolving over time.

> In truth I do not know of anyone older [*sc.* than Cato] whose written work, indeed, I should think worth setting forth unless there is someone who by chance is delighted by this very speech of Appius Caecus about Pyrrhus and some *laudationes* for the dead. And *by Hercules* those indeed are extant. For the families themselves conserve these *laudationes* as something like decorations and monuments to be used if someone of the same family has died, both to recall the memory of past glories of their house and to demonstrate their own nobility.[7]

For Cicero, the *laudationes* were problematic examples of oratory and represented a genre which he purposefully chooses to overlook. He even adds that the orators of the past—Cato in particular—used an "older style of speech" ("antiquior sermo"), that was, however, hardly inferior. One need only modernize the speech, "add rhythm," "rearrange the words," and "you'll think no one better than Cato."[8] The *laudationes* did not fall into this category and were apparently irredeemable. Many survived (e.g., "Et *hercules*(!) eae quidem exstant" and "ipsae familiae servabant"), but Cicero dismisses their applicability to his discussion. The reason? Primarily, their general substance and style, but also their falsification of honors and offices.[9]

Regarding substance and style, specific features of the *laudatio* work to its detriment. In Cicero's *De Oratore*, a dialogue set in 91 BCE, leading orators Marcus Antonius, Lucius Licinius Crassus, and Quintus Lutatius Catulus, debate the requisite facets of oratorical training. Two genres, the judicial and the deliberative, are discussed at length, but the third, the epideictic, is relegated to inferior status. The *laudatio* corresponds to this latter category. Antonius explains why the third genre—and praise speech in general—does not require equivalent oratorical theorization:

> Nostrae laudationes, quibus in foro utimur, aut testimoni brevitatem habent nudam atque inornatam aut scribuntur ad funebrem contionem, quae ad orationis laudem minime accommodata est.
>
> Our *laudationes*, which we employ in the Forum, either have the bare and plain concision of courtroom testimony or are written for the funeral *contio*, which least of all accommodates praise for oratory.[10]

Though he describes two separate kinds of public speech—the testimony given as a witness in court and the funeral eulogy—he ascribes the same deficiencies to them both.[11] In testimony, the speech is plain (*nuda*) and unadorned by rhetorical

---

[7] Cic. *Brut.* 61–62.

[8] Cic. *Brut.* 68: id muta, quod tum ille non potuit, et *adde numeros* et, ut aptior sit oratio, *ipsa verba compone* et quasi coagmenta, quod ne Graeci quidem veteres factitaverunt: iam *neminem antepones Catoni.*

[9] On falsification in *laudationes*, see p. 102.

[10] Cic. *De or.* 2.341. For a discussion of the surrounding context, see Fantham 2004: 135–136.

[11] *N.b.*, Cicero consistently uses *contio* to describe the context of the eulogy, see below, p. 146; see also Suetonius *Aug.* 8.1: "[Octavius] aviam Iuliam defunctam pro contione laudavit"; and Quint. *Inst.* 11.3.153: "funebres contiones."

tropes (*inornatam*).[12] Whereas for the funeral, the event itself least of all invites praise for oratorical speech. Therefore, neither occasion is well-suited for oratorical flourish. Each type of speech is *nuda* and *inornata*. Earlier in *De oratore*, Antonius sets the stage: "Who wouldn't know what sorts of things ought to be praised about a man?"[13] Both in form and in substance, *laudationes* were classified as the sort of oratory that required no instruction. Like testimony, it was public speech where the orator was conveying information and little else. These were not speeches where orators could shine, and their written records were unable to provide even one useful example worthy of discussion in Cicero's review of the history of oratory.

Polybius Celebrates the Eulogy

Why then did Polybius place such great emphasis on the importance and influence of the *laudatio funebris*? Modern scholars have called the *laudatio* an *Antikunstprosa*—with good reason, if one believes Cicero.[14] Nonetheless, the vivid description of Polybius and the import he places on the event has led to a recent recuperation of the *laudatio*. The basic argument has, in part, focused on the extent to which one can prove that the surviving fragments are in fact *Kunstprosa*, and that the writings of Cicero on the subject do not quite mean what they purport.[15] I suggest that the confusion arises from inadequate terminology, however. When discussing the *laudatio* one can speak of a text, a speech, or an event. For Cicero, the text and the speech, judged by the standards of oratory as a genre, were disappointing. For Polybius, the event, not simply the content of the oration, was key:

> πέριξ δὲ παντὸς τοῦ δήμου στάντος, ἀναβὰς ἐπὶ τοὺς ἐμβόλους, ἂν μὲν υἱὸς ἐν ἡλικίᾳ καταλείπηται καὶ τύχῃ παρών, οὗτος, εἰ δὲ μή, τῶν ἄλλων εἴ τις ἀπὸ γένους ὑπάρχει, λέγει περὶ τοῦ τετελευτηκότος τὰς ἀρετὰς καὶ τὰς ἐπιτετευγμένας ἐν τῷ ζῆν πράξεις. δι' ὧν συμβαίνει τοὺς πολλοὺς ἀναμιμνησκομένους καὶ λαμβάνοντας ὑπὸ τὴν ὄψιν τὰ γεγονότα, μὴ μόνον τοὺς κεκοινωνηκότας τῶν ἔργων, ἀλλὰ καὶ τοὺς ἐκτός, ἐπὶ τοσοῦτον γίνεσθαι συμπαθεῖς ὥστε μὴ τῶν κηδευόντων ἴδιον, ἀλλὰ κοινὸν τοῦ δήμου φαίνεσθαι τὸ σύμπτωμα.
>
> [The ancestors line up on the Rostra.]

[12] Leeman and Pinkster 1981 *ad loc*: *testimonium* here is the testimony of good character given before a judge. For *nuda* having the sense of "empty," see Cic. *De or.* 1.218. For Cicero's explanation of *ornari orationem*, see, e.g., *Brut.* 68.

[13] Cic. *De or.* 2.45: "quis est, qui nesciat, quae sint in homine laudanda?" ("who is there who doesn't know what should be praised in a man.")

[14] Durry 1942: 114. Kennedy 1994: 106: "The traditional form seems to have been little more than a list of the accomplishments and virtues of the deceased and the deceased's ancestors. Cicero (*On the Orator* 2.341) speaks scornfully of the literary qualities of these speeches, and what little has been preserved of them seems to confirm his judgment."

[15] Kierdorf 1980: 106–111 concludes that the *laudatio* evolved, and that its Republican form reflected the rhetorical style of the time. See also Flower 1996: 133–136, who notes (133) that, "Polybius, however, portrays funeral speeches as moving and impressive; we should be wary about dismissing them in haste."

τὸ γὰρ τὰς τῶν ἐπ' ἀρετῇ δεδοξασμένων ἀνδρῶν εἰκόνας ἰδεῖν ὁμοῦ πάσας οἷον εἰ ζώσας καὶ πεπνυμένας τίν' οὐκ ἂν παραστῆσαι; τί δ' ἂν κάλλιον θέαμα τούτου φανείη; πλὴν ὅ γε λέγων ὑπὲρ τοῦ θάπτεσθαι μέλλοντος, ἐπὰν διέλθῃ τὸν περὶ τούτου λόγον, ἄρχεται τῶν ἄλλων ἀπὸ τοῦ προγενεστάτου τῶν παρόντων, καὶ λέγει τὰς ἐπιτυχίας ἑκάστου καὶ τὰς πράξεις.

With the entire populace standing all around him, the eulogist mounts the Rostra—a surviving son of appropriate age, if he happens to be present [*sc.* in Rome], but if not, someone else from the family—and he speaks about the noble works and deeds accomplished by the deceased. On account of which it happens that *many recall the events and experience them vividly in their mind's eye*, not only those who took part in the deeds, but also those who did not, and they all sympathize to such an extent that not only is the event a private concern for those mourning, but *it is manifestly a shared concern of the populace.*

[The ancestors line up on the Rostra.]

For who would not be won over by the *sight* of the likenesses of men who were famed for excellence, altogether as if they were living and breathing? What *spectacle* could be finer that this? [*Sc.* Nothing] save for when the one speaking over the body soon to be buried, after he has gone through the speech about him, starting from the oldest of all the ancestors present, recounts the successes and deeds of each.[16]

The *laudatio* was a θέαμα (6.53.10–54.1), *i.e.*, "spectacle," "a thing to be seen," and, therefore, it was also a thing to be experienced. The rhetorical brilliance of the orator alone does not paint a picture for the audience. According to Polybius, the eulogist lists deeds accomplished while the audience does the work by recalling and visualizing the events (6.53.3: τοὺς πολλοὺς ἀναμιμνησκομένους καὶ λαμβάνοντας ὑπὸ τὴν ὄψιν τὰ γεγονότα). In fact, Polybius' entire description of the *laudatio* focuses less on the details of the speech and more on the various visual aspects: the Rostra, the ivory chairs, the surrounding crowd, the ancestors lined up, their specific attire, and the eulogist standing near the body. The operative action is *seeing* (ἰδεῖν). The specific praise for the deceased, which is the section that modern scholars consider the actual *laudatio*, is not presented as the most important element of the funerary speech. Instead, Polybius considers the catalog of ancestors the highlight of the show.

Scholarly debate to date has focused on reconciling Polybius' and Cicero's descriptions of the *laudatio funebris* without fully noting that these ancient authors, armed with differing agendas, discuss two distinct subjects. For Cicero, the speech, as an example of oratorical performance, is a disappointment; for Polybius, the event, not the delivery of the text of the speech alone, is spectacular. Though Polybius' language emphasizes the visual nature of the *laudatio*, he also highlights spoken elements (e.g., λέγει περὶ τοῦ τετελευτηκότος, ὅ γε λέγων ὑπὲρ τοῦ

[16] Polyb. 6.53.2–3, 53.10–54.1.

θάπτεσθαι μέλλοντος, and λέγει τὰς ἐπιτυχίας ἑκάστου καὶ τὰς πράξεις). Polybius does not merely blend the visual and the aural, however. In order to support his argument—that the funerary event is a cultural institution critical to the success of the Roman state—he fuses multiple audiences and multiple viewing locations into one unified crowd that was uniformly affected by a monolithic event.[17] By collapsing his description of audience and purpose, he obscures the underlying concordance between his own description and that of Cicero. The textual component—the words written—of Republican *laudationes* were, in fact, relatively plain, and not simply because they reflected the rhetorical style of the time. Rather, the words of the speech and their style of delivery were not intended to reach the entirety of the audience in the same way, and the words were not meant to stand on their own. The appearance of the ancestors, historical characters from the past, alive for a moment, was itself an important and significant cultural moment. The event in its totality was a sight to behold. Its aural and visual effects worked in tandem, inextricably tied to each other and to the surrounding built environment, and they were tailored to accommodate the exigencies of daily life in the Forum and the multiple types of audiences in attendance. I first turn to the scant textual record of the speeches themselves.

EXTANT *LAUDATIONES* OF THE MIDDLE REPUBLIC

The Problematic Nature of the Evidence

No complete text of the *laudatio funebris* from the mid-Republic survives. For the time period approximately coeval with the funeral of L. Aemilius Paullus, only testimony and fragments remain. Caution is always due when fragments are considered, especially when many are preserved by the antiquarian tradition.[18] The evidence comprises a combination of possible scripts and post-event transcripts. Therefore, the correspondence between text and oral performance carries the same reservations as in any study of Roman oratory.[19] The tradition of preserving *laudationes* for commemoration or some form of reuse ought to be assurance enough that the fragments are accurate approximations of the familial record.[20] In fact, of the eight pre-Catonian speeches documented in Malcovati, three are *laudationes*.[21] Unfor-

---

[17] Polyb. 6.53.2: πέριξ δὲ παντὸς τοῦ δήμου στάντος.

[18] For a theoretically rich examination of fragmentation in the ancient world, see Čulík-Baird 2022, esp. pp. 1–29.

[19] For a brief survey concerning the degree of correspondence between "Spoken and Published Orations," see Craig 2002: 515–517, who notes, "The question remains whether, in the absence of specific evidence to the contrary, there is any general reason to assume that a speech text that we have differs substantially in content or organization from the spoken oration which it purports to represent." See also Narducci 1997: 157 ff., and Vasaly 1993: 9n11.

[20] Cic. *Brut.* 61. (See above.)

[21] See Malcovati 1976: 1–12. This was apparently already the case by the time of Cicero, when, as noted above (*Brut.* 61), there were no examples of oratory readily available save for *De Pyrrho rege* of

tunately, as the number of extant Republican speeches increased over time, so the actual survival rate of *laudationes* decreased. Less than ten more are attested by the time the young Octavian mounts the Rostra to praise his maternal grandmother Julia (Julius Caesar's sister).[22] In addition, unlike in the case of similar oratorical texts, the tradition of conservation for *laudationes* was subject to a specific type of error: motivated by a need to manipulate image and status, the family could alter the bare facts reported in the *laudatio*.[23] Therefore, the transmitted texts carry the dubious distinction of accurately reflecting an unreliable source text.

The Laudatio *for L. Caecilius Metellus (221 BCE)*

The oldest purported fragment of a *laudatio*, the funeral speech for L. Caecilius Metellus in 221 BCE (Plin. *HN* 7.139–140), represents the basic features of the surviving texts.[24] The fragment is part of the greater semantic and stylistic spheres of other *laudationes* and epitaphs. Though it happens to be one of the longest fragments in existence—not taking into consideration the epigraphic evidence—it is still barely a paragraph.

In his excursus on the nature of human happiness, which recalls the Herodotean story of Gyges, Pliny the Elder adduces the story of L. Caecilius Metellus as evidence for the vicissitudes of fortune.[25] According to Pliny, no man can be called *felix* without a final tally of the good and the bad he experienced throughout a lifetime. Pliny presents three examples of which the first two were Lucius Fulvius, who was both *hostis* and *triumphator* in the same year, and Sulla, who took on the *cognomen felix* but experienced a horrible death.[26] For his third example, he cites the funeral oration given by Q. Caecilius Metellus for his father L. Caecilius Metellus (cos. 251, 247, dict. 224):

> Q. Metellus in ea oratione, quam habuit supremis laudibus patris sui L. Metelli pontificis, bis consulis, dictatoris, magistri equitum, XVviri agris dandis, qui primus elephantos ex primo Punico bello duxit in triumpho, *scriptum reliquit* decem maximas res

Appius Claudius and a number of funeral orations. For the idea of counting fragments in Malcovati, see Goldberg 2005: 83n84.

22 Suet. *Aug.* 8.1 and Quint. *Inst.* 6.1 report the event but make no allusion to the content of the speech. It no longer survives.

23 See Cic. *Brut.* 62 and Livy 8.40.4 for the corruption of the historical record.

24 For a brief analysis of the properties found in this speech, see Vollmer 1891: 480. See Lippold 1963: 75–80 for a study of the values of *nobiles* in the language of the speech. Kierdorf 1980: 10–21 examines the factual details of this eulogy, the public language of praise, and the location of the fragment within the original oration. Flower 1996: 136–142 revisits the *laudatio* within the context of the *imagines*. Hölkeskamp 2023: 303–307 highlights how claims to be "first" or "unique" are conventions in the "media of memory": "In diesem Hinweis auf neue, beispiellose, ‹erstmalige› oder gar ‹einmalige› Errungenschaften und Erfolge taucht bezeichnenderweise genau die gleiche Semantik der Superlative auf, die sich allenthalben auch in den permanenten Medien der memoria findet, ja geradezu als typische Konvention der konservierten Erinnerung gelten darf."

25 Plin. *HN* 7.130–152.

26 Plin. *HN* 7.137: "unus hominum ad hoc aevi Felicis sibi cognomen adseruit L. Sulla." Plin. *HN* 7.138: "erodente se ipso corpore." See Beagon 2005: 334 for the details of the death.

optimasque, in quibus quaerendis sapientes aetatem exigerent, consummasse eum: voluisse enim primarium bellatorem esse, optimum oratorem, fortissimum imperatorem, auspicio suo maximas res geri, maximo honore uti, summa sapientia esse, summum senatorem haberi, pecuniam magnam bono modo invenire, multos liberos relinquere et clarissimum in civitate esse; haec contigisse ei neculli alii post Romam conditam.

Q. Metellus in that speech, which he held for the funeral eulogy of his father, a pontiff, twice *consul, dictator, magister equitum*, a *quindecemvir* for land distribution, who was the first to lead elephants in triumph during the first Punic war, left behind in writing that his father had achieved the ten greatest and best things that wise men spend their lives pursuing. For he had wished to be the chief warrior, the best orator, the strongest military commander, he wished that the greatest deeds would be accomplished under his auspices, to achieve the best honor, to be imbued with the highest wisdom, to be considered the consummate senator, to acquire a great amount of money in an honorable way, to leave many children and to be considered the most outstanding amongst the citizenry; these things happened to no one else since the founding of the city.[27]

Pliny objects that such distinction could counterbalance the misfortune Metellus suffered: "It would take a while to refute this and it would be a waste of time since just one disaster will suffice."[28] Metellus was struck blind in service of the state while rescuing the Palladium from the burning Temple of Vesta. Due to his sacrifice, he was the only man allowed to take a chariot to all meetings of the Senate. In Pliny's opinion, however, such an honor was hardly worth the cost.[29]

He notes that the speech was written down (*scriptum*). His use of *oratio obliqua* all but guarantees that he was reporting what he read with some degree of accuracy.[30] But the word forms reflect neither the third century nor epigraphic transmission.[31] Therefore, this speech, as preserved for us today, was not precisely the "earliest extant piece of Latin oratory," as it has sometimes been called.[32] Nonethe-

[27] Plin. *HN* 7.139–140.

[28] Plin. *HN* 7.141: "Longum est refellere et supervacuum abunde uno casu refutante."

[29] Plin. *HN* 7.141.

[30] On the preservation of *laudationes* in general, see Coarelli 1972: 97, who believes that there were family archives containing full *laudationes*; Kierdorf 1980: 11: "Sicher ist, daß Q. Metellus die Rede schriftlich fixierte und im Familien-archiv deponierte." Beagon 2005: 337: "The written version of the speech would have been preserved in the family archives. Whether P. used it at first hand or through an intermediate source cannot be determined." Like Horsfall 1982: 37, I suspect Pliny accessed the text through an intermediary.

[31] For example, we read *optimum* instead of *optumum*, *uti* rather than *oiti* or *utei* (see Courtney 1995: 226 for the first occurrence of *utier* in place of *oitier*), the consistent doubling of 's', where we might expect to see *ese*. For an epigraphic example, see Courtney 1999: 93ff.; again cf. Courtney 1995: 226 where inconsistent doubling is observed. If we choose to consider the listing of offices as a remnant from the speech, all archaic elements have likewise been excised (e.g., *consulis* where *consolis* would be expected, *duxit* rather than *douxit*, *maximas* and *optimas*).

[32] Flower 1996: 137: "the earliest extant piece of Latin oratory." Horsfall 1982: 37 is alarmed that Kierdorf fails to note the problems.

less, it showcases the elements of the *laudatio* in a compressed form and certainly reflects conventions preserved elsewhere.

In fact, the excerpt encapsulates the full *laudatio* for the deceased as described by Polybius (6.53.2): λέγει περὶ τοῦ τετελευτηκότος τὰς ἀρετὰς καὶ τὰς ἐπιτετευγμένας ἐν τῷ ζῆν πράξεις. Though the actual quote begins after *scriptum reliquit*, the beginning of the passage contains a brief survey of the offices achieved (*cursus honorum*), intermingled with concrete and abstract accomplishments (*res gestae*). The sampling of offices seems to follow the original source, rather than the argument Pliny wishes to make regarding happiness. The offices are scattered chronologically, not ordered by importance, and include an enigmatic addition. L. Caecilius Metellus served as *magister equitum* long before he was elected Pontifex Maximus and appointed *dictator*. The inclusion of the *quindecemviri de agris dandis* is striking.[33] It was of a certain distinctive importance in the third century, when such land commissions were few.[34] Historically, land distribution was controversial, of course. But for Pliny's audience of the first century CE it did not convey the same prestige as the preceding offices, and was not at all part of the *cursus honorum*. While it may have been important or customary for the family to approximate a comprehensive list of offices and civic duties performed, the addition of agrarian commission is an outlier. It was not a major office, and, for Pliny, who wished to demonstrate Metellus' overall accomplishments, it was not rhetorically necessary. It was surely not worth sandwiching between *pontifex*, twice *consul*, *dictator*, *magister equitum*, and *triumphator*. The last concrete accomplishment listed, that of leading elephants in triumph for the first time, is equally problematic.[35] If the text stands, Pliny contradicts himself. At *HN* 8.16, Curius Dentatus was the first to triumph with elephants.[36] One wonders whether this is a contradiction in Pliny or instead an example of the sort of familial manipulation of funerary imagery that Cicero alleges. Pliny apparently thought that Metellus was not the first to triumph with elephants, but instead reports directly. Most likely Pliny cribbed from the source text that Quintus Caecilius Metellus had left in written form.[37]

The latter half of the fragment, when understood within the context of praise-language in the mid-Republic, demonstrates the *nuda brevitas* that Cicero applied

---

[33] Gargola 1995: 105, suspecting scribal error, suggests we read "Xviri," but, nonetheless, underscores the rarity of the position.

[34] Corbett 1970 sees only two possible occasions for viritane land distributions.

[35] Horsfall 1982.

[36] Pliny (8.16) later uses "plurimos," the emendation suggested by Manuwald (see next note), to modify the number of elephants led in triumph by Metellus. See Beagon 2005: 337 and Schilling 1977 *ad loc.* for a discussion.

[37] Cf. Horsfall 1982: 37, who suggests a book such as Varro's *Imagines* as source material: "the curious conjunction of offices held and elephants led in triumph which precedes suggests a quite different origin [than a script of the *laudatio*], perhaps a book of *imagines*, conveying a cursus, but minimal biographical information." See Manuwald 2019: 32 F2 who reads *p<lu>rimos elephantos*, which would eliminate the discrepancy in Pliny but would also then deviate from the funerary custom of claiming exceptional achievements in the eulogy.

to the genre of *laudatio*. The achievement of the three, five, or "ten greatest things" was a standard topos used in the realm of aristocratic competition.[38] The language is abstract; the adjectives, superlative. The closing of the fragment is dramatic and hyperbolic. Since the founding of the city, no one had achieved such a catalog of abstract successes. When read in isolation, the claims are bold, but what if read in succession to similar speeches given in honor of other aristocrats? After all, the *laudationes* were customarily preserved *ad usum*. The cumulative effect of each hyperbolic claim of successive *laudationes* must have been commonplace. The descendants of Q. Metellus would have found it difficult to supersede their ancestor's accomplishments. Mid-Republican epitaphs illustrate the repetitive effect of what surely was a trope present in many funerary speeches.

The Scipionic Epitaphs as Funerary Eulogies

The epitaphs found in the tomb of the Scipios located on the Via Appia echo the *laudatio* of Metellus. The controversy and confusion surrounding the precise dating of the inscriptions need not concern us here; it is enough to know that the epitaphs date from the middle Republic, no later than 150 BCE.[39]

> L.] Cornelio(s) L. f. Scipio aidiles, cosol, cesor.
> honc oino(m) ploirume(i) cosentiont R[omai
> duonoro(m) optumo(m) fuise viro(m),
> Luciom Scipione(m) filio(m) Barbati.
> consol, censor, aidilis hic fuet a[pud vos,
> hec cepit Corsica(m) Aleria(m)que urbe(m),
> dedet Tempestatebus aide(m) mereto[d.

> Lucius Cornelius Scipio, son of Lucius Scipio, aedile, *consul*, *censor*.
> Most agree that this man was the best
> of the good men at Rome,
> Lucius Scipio son of Barbatus.
> *Consul*, *censor*, aedile among you,
> he captured Corsica and the city of Aleria,
> he gave a temple to the Storm gods, as was merited.[40]

Apart from its use of verse, the epitaph is practically another version of the *laudatio* for Metellus.[41] The strict chronological order of the *titulus* at the beginning is standard form for epitaphs. The later juggling of order in the verse is similar to the *laudatio*. The people agree that he was the best of the good men, just as the compounding of superlatives culminated in agreement that Metellus was *clarissimus* among the citizenry. In his discussion of the differences in Roman and

---

[38] Kierdorf 1980: 13. Plin. *HN* 7.100 cites three, Gell. 1.13.10, five.

[39] For a detailed analysis, see Kruschwitz 2002: 32–57.

[40] *CIL* VI 1287. For the Latin text used here, see Courtney 1995: 40. The subject of this epitaph is L. Cornelius Scipio (*RE* 323).

[41] Lippold 1963: 80–81 and Kruschwitz 2002: 52 discuss the semantic similarities.

Greek praise (Cic. *Fin.* 2.116), Cicero recalls the epitaph for Aulus Atilius Caiatanus: "Hunc unum plurimae consentiunt gentes populi primarium fuisse virum." ("Most families agree that this one alone was the leading man of the people.")

Again, as we turn next to the epitaph for the father, Barbatus, the blend of abstract praise and concrete accomplishment is clear:

> Cornelius Lucius Scipio Barbatus,
> Gnaivod patre prognatus, fortis vir sapiensque,
> quoius forma virtutei parisuma fuit,
> consol, censor, aidilis quei fuit apud vos,
> Taurasia(m) Cisauna(m) Samnio cepit,
> subigit omne(m) Loucanam opsidesque abdoucit.
>
> Lucius Cornelius Scipio Barbatus,
> born from his father Gnaeus, a brave and wise man,
> whose physical appearance equaled his courage,
> who was *consul*, *censor*, and aedile among you,
> he captured Taurasia, Cisauna and Samnium,
> subdued all of Lucania, and he took hostages from there.[42]

The similarities to the *laudatio* of Metellus are greater than the differences. In addition to the accomplishments Barbatus had achieved, the battles he had won and hostages he had taken, he was said to be *fortis* (but not *fortissimus* as Metellus), *sapiens* (but not possessed of *summa sapientia*), and he was as courageous as he looked. These thematic similarities have caused some to consider the epitaphs as falling in between preserved notes for a *laudatio* and the verbatim record of the actual funerary speech.[43] There are two main objections: the length and the meter. There is no compelling reason to believe that the *laudatio* in the Forum was recited in verse, so most scholars rightly assume that there is some inherent distance between the Scipionic epitaphs as written and the performed version of the related *laudatio*. In addition, if these epitaphs were delivered as speeches, even in prose form, they are exceedingly brief, and they do not always provide a comprehensive list of achievements that are otherwise known to us.[44] Nonetheless, one can imagine that not all offices were enumerated in a speech given in the Forum. Because

---

[42] *CIL* VI 1284–1285. Again, the text is from Courtney 1995: 40. The subject of this epitaph is L. Cornelius Scipio Barbatus (*RE* 343).

[43] La Regina 1968, Zevi 1970, Coarelli 1972, Van Sickle 1987, Van Sickle 1988, Wiseman 1995: 141. Cf. Goldberg 2005: 46n61: "No firm evidence supports this admittedly attractive hypothesis." While these epitaphs may not reflect the verbatim praise for the *deceased*, they must (at least) originate from the same source as the praise given to an *ancestor*.

[44] Flower 1996: 180: "Nevertheless, the *elogia* remain problematic principally because of their brevity. They omit many features which must surely have been stressed in a eulogy and which can be demonstrated to have been part of the common tradition about a family member." Van Sickle 1987 and Van Sickle 1988 argue that the *elogia* represent the arrival of Hellenistic epigram in Rome. Therefore, their form, the 6–8 line verse, was constrained by genre, not content. Flower 1996: 180n87: "As an example one may cite the omission of the triumph of Lucius, son of Barbatus, over the Carthaginians, Corsica, and Sardinia, which is mentioned in the triumphal Fasti."

of the symbolic dress of the deceased and of the ancestors—e.g., triumphal garb—the *laudatio* could have easily omitted details already conveyed through the visual display. (See below, pp. 102 and 120.)

The Shortest Extant Laudatio*: Q. Fabius Maximus (207–203 BCE)*

Before turning to the next fragment, I will dwell briefly on the brevity of the examples thus far introduced. The speech for Metellus discussed above survives in fragmentary form, but the question remains: how long was the original? Too quickly one assumes that the preserved fragments are part of substantially longer orations.[45] Recall that the short fragment—less than a paragraph—is the *longest* surviving eulogy from the middle Republic. Absent evidence to the contrary, it is worth considering that the extraordinarily brief Scipionic *elogia* and the preserved *laudatio* for Metellus may very well represent a closer approximation of the actual length of the delivered speeches in the Forum.

Now we turn to the shortest extant fragment—a speech well attested more than three centuries after its delivery—which further confirms Cicero's assessment of *laudationes*. Near the end of the third century, *ca.* 207–203 BCE, Q. Fabius Maximus Verrucosus, the famed Cunctator ("Delayer"), gave a funeral oration for his son, Quintus. Cicero refers to the speech in *De senectute*. The dramatic date of the dialogue is 150 BCE, the lead interlocutor is Cato the Elder, who imparts wisdom to the much younger Gaius Laelius and Scipio Aemilianus (the son of L. Aemilius Paullus Macedonicus, whose funeral is, of course, the subject of this book). Cato contends that old age is not a sad time, but rather a time of productivity and accomplishment. He introduces the eulogy of Fabius to advance his argument:

> Multa in eo viro praeclara cognovi; sed nihil admirabilius, quam quo modo ille mortem fili tulit clari viri et consularis. Est in manibus laudatio, quam cum legimus, quem philosophum non contemnimus?
>
> I know many distinguished things about that man; but there is nothing more admirable than the way which he bore the death of his son, an outstanding man who had achieved the consulship. His *laudatio* is in general circulation, which when we read, what philosopher do we not scorn?[46]

There is no doubt that funeral orations were preserved and circulated. This speech was apparently "well known" (*in manibus*). Thus it was relatively accessible to the broader reading public.[47] Only three words survive today: "Fabius Maximus: *amitti*

[45] For example, Ramage 2006: 48 calls Dio's version of Antony's speech "a mini *laudatio funebris*." Dio's Antony notes, however, that his speech for Caesar would be long, in comparison to a more customary speech for a private citizen. On the *laudatio* for Caesar, see below.

[46] Cic. *Sen.* 4.12.

[47] In reference to Naevius' *Bellum Poenicum*, Brink 1981: 102–103 argues that Horace's use of the term indicates that it "was much read at the time." See also *TLL* 8.363.41 ff. Cf. Powell 1988: 128 *ad loc.*, who understands *in manibus omnium*, but within the current context is also sympathetic to "in my possession."

quam apisci, passive omnia sunt prolata." ("Fabius Maximus: *to be lost rather than to be gained*, each is produced passively.")[48] Priscian, the late-antique grammarian who preserves these three words, focuses only on the grammatical discussion. He comments that the normally deponent form *apisci* is in a passive use, but offers no additional details about the content of the speech.

The testimony surrounding this eulogy alludes to its nature, content, and style. While this particular speech was *in manibus* at the time of Cicero, the rest of Fabius' speeches did not fare so well. In the *Brutus*, Cicero considers Fabius among the bulk of pre-Catonian orators whose works had already perished.[49] Cicero had to rely on the testimony of others to categorize Fabius Maximus as a skilled orator.[50] In fact, by the end of the first century CE, the only extant speech of Fabius Maximus was this funeral oration; for Plutarch, it was the sole proof that Fabius Maximus had an unadorned style, replete with aphorisms.[51] This same speech was one of the extant *laudationes*, mentioned above, that Cicero disdained.[52] Nonetheless, by following the strands of the testimony, we find a speech that was plain, lacking in rhetorical tropes, *gravis*, and somewhat reminiscent of Thucydides. Of course, this description would just as readily apply to the use of asyndeton in funerary contexts.[53]

Cicero's Cato admires the content of this speech, but not its style.[54] The *De senectute* is, itself, a *consolatio* composed during a time when grief and consolation were

[48] Prisc. *Inst.* 8.4.16.

[49] Cic. *Brut.* 52–57, which begins (52), "veniamus ad nostros, de quibus difficile est plus intellegere quam quantum ex monumentis suspicari licet." ("Let us now come to our orators about whom it is difficult to know more than what we can infer from historical records.")

[50] Cic. *Brut.* 57: "Q. etiam Maximus Verrucosus orator habitus est temporibus illis" ("Q. Maximus Verrucosus was considered an orator in those times"). In the very next sentence, Cicero remarks that M. Cornelius Cethegus was the first to be considered a good orator and whose works survived to prove it. "Quem vero exstet et de quo sit memoriae proditum eloquentem fuisse et ita esse habitum, primus est M. Cornelius Cethegus"

[51] Plut. *Fab. Max.* 1.8: οὐ γὰρ ἐπῆν ὡραϊσμὸς οὐδὲ κενὴ καὶ ἀγοραῖος χάρις, ἀλλὰ νοῦς ἴδιον καὶ περιττὸν ἐν γνωμολογίαις σχῆμα καὶ βάθος ἔχων, ἃς μάλιστα ταῖς Θουκυδίδου προσεοικέναι λέγουσι. διασῴζεται γὰρ αὐτοῦ λόγος ὃν εἶπεν ἐν τῷ δήμῳ, τοῦ παιδὸς αὐτοῦ μεθ' ὑπατείαν ἀποθανόντος ἐγκώμιον. ("His oratory lacked ornament, and there was no empty forensic grace, but he had a cast of mind that possessed a particular dignity and seriousness and was replete with maxims, which they say resemble those of Thucydides especially. [We know this] because a speech of his survives, which he gave in the Forum, a eulogy for his son who had died after holding a consulship.")

[52] Cic. *Brut.* 62.

[53] Dufallo 2007: 54–55 and 141n3 notes that the "economy of expression" (142n3) in Cicero's praise of Caesar (Cic. *Phil.* 2.116) resembles the same practice found in the eulogy of Metellus and the Scipionic Epitaphs.

[54] I will only briefly comment on Cato's famous remark regarding philosophers, which is otherwise beyond the scope of the current discussion. For a general overview of the tradition, see Astin 1978: 169–177. In 155 BCE, Athens sent a group of philosophers on embassy to Rome to appeal an unfavorable arbitration. For a detailed analysis of the event, see Gruen 1990: 169–179. In addition to their appeal, the philosophers held a series of lectures. One of the philosophers, Carneades of the New Academy, spoke to a crowd of enthusiastic youth, first in defense of justice and the next day against it. Cato took umbrage at the blatant disregard for the truth masked by what he thought was rhetoric. See Plin. *HN* 7.112, Plut. *Cat. Mai.* 22.4–5, and Quint. *Inst.* 12.1.35.

very much on Cicero's mind.[55] He seems to have been particularly impressed with the way that Cato endured his own son's death.[56] The character of Cato shares similar feelings about this speech. Fabius must have alluded to how he was dealing with his grief, and it was this quality that Cicero admired. He makes no comment regarding its rhetorical technique, however. Far from purple prose, the speech seems to have been compressed and unadorned. Therefore, this text, which was known to Cicero, was clearly an example of the type of *laudatio* that Cicero omits from his catalog of early oratorical skill. It was not stylistically impressive enough to merit inclusion in the *Brutus* as evidence of Fabius Maximus' oratorical skill. It was, in short, like most other funeral orations, save that it may have been shorter and even less florid.

Eulogy for P. Scipio Aemilianus (129 BCE)

While the number of surviving fragmentary examples of oratory increases dramatically in the mid-second century, conversely, only one additional fragment of a *laudatio* is extant. In 129 BCE, Q. Fabius Maximus Allobrogicus—ostensibly a member of the *gens Fabia*, but a direct descendant from L. Aemilius Paullus, his grandfather by blood—delivered a funeral eulogy for his uncle, P. Scipio Aemilianus, *i.e.* the son of Paullus. C. Laelius Sapiens, one of the best orators of the time and a famously good friend, wrote the speech. A fragment from the end survives:

> Super eius laudibus extat oratio C. Laeli Sapientis, qua usus videtur Q. Fabius Maximus in laudatione mortui Scipionis, in cuius extrema parte haec verba sunt: quiapropter neque tanta diis inmortalibus gratia haberi potest, quanta habenda est, quod is cum illo animo atque ingenio hac e civitate potissimum natus est, neque moleste atque aegre ferri quam ferundum, cum isto modo mortem obiit et in eodem tempore periit cum et vobis et omnibus qui hanc rem p. salvam volunt maxime vivo opus est, Quirites.
>
> Concerning his praises, a speech of C. Laelius Sapiens survives, which Q. Fabius Maximus seems to have used in the *laudatio* of the dead Scipio. These words are in the last part of the speech: therefore, not enough thanks can be given to the immortal gods, as there should be, because with that spirit and innate ability in *this* city in particular *he* was born, nor can the death be borne with burden and pain as it should, because he died in that way and he passed away at that time when, both for you and everyone who wants to preserve the state, there was the greatest need for him to be alive, Citizens.[57]

Both Plutarch (*Mor.* 202A and *Mor.* 201F) and Cicero's *Pro Murena* 75 refer to this exact section of the speech. A disconcerting pattern emerges, however: all surviving testimony refer to this section of the speech.[58]

[55] Powell 1988: 1–4. The use of *amittere* in the preserved speech suggests that there was some mention of the loss suffered. See Kierdorf 1980: 83–85.

[56] Cic. *Amic.* 2.9: "Quo modo … mortem fili tulit [Cato]!" ("How he bore the death of his son!")

[57] Schol. Bob. *Mil.* 16. I use the updated text supplied by Manuwald 2019: 116, F 22.

[58] Cf. Kierdorf 1980: 25, who cites the concurring examples as proof of the veracity of the Scholiast.

> [Aemilianum] cum supremo eius die[59] Maximus laudaret, gratias egit dis immortalibus quod ille vir in hac re publica potissimum natus esset; necesse enim fuisse ibi esse terrarum imperium ubi ille esset.
>
> When he praised Aemilianus during his funeral, he gave thanks to the immortal gods because that man had been born in this state in particular; for it was necessary that, wherever he might be, there be an empire.[60]

The elaborate parallelism made an impression. Perhaps this passage was preserved because it differed so radically from other *laudationes*? Only this passage is reflected in multiple sources. The full text may never have been available.[61] Moreover, the speech was exceptional. It had been written by a skilled orator, not the eulogist or someone from his family. After Cicero (*De or.* 2.341) remarks that *laudationes* were ill-suited to rhetorical display, he grudgingly admits that, sometimes, an orator might be called upon to write one.[62] This was likely not the norm, however. His example was this very speech written by Laelius for the nephew of Scipio Aemilianus.[63] He needed to reach back nearly four decades from the dramatic date of the dialogue to find a well-known example. In this case, it is highly likely that Laelius was enlisted to write the speech not because he was a skilled orator, but because he was a very close friend of the deceased. While the fragment of the speech represents an elevated style, its genre seems to have otherwise constrained the writer and the orator to standard elements of a *laudatio*. Later in the same work, with this speech fresh in his mind, Cicero's Antonius lists the basic techniques to employ in a *laudatio*: one praises outstanding and unprecedented deeds, passes over the commonplace, and compares the deceased to other outstanding men.[64]

Elsewhere, without explicit citation, Cicero potentially channels a different section from this speech:

> Cum illo vero quis neget actum esse praeclare? Nisi enim, quod ille minime putabat, inmortalitatem optare vellet, quid non adeptus est, quod homini fas esset optare? qui

---

[59] For a similar use of *supremus dies* to mean the day of the funeral, see Livy 2.61, p. 71n146 above.

[60] Cic. *Mur.* 75.

[61] Of course, "in cuius extrema parte" implies the existence of a longer speech, but even this note could simply have been transmitted along with the fragment; testimonies report that the excerpt comes from the end of the speech but none of our sources have apparently seen the entirety of the speech.

[62] As Cicero himself did for Serranus Domesticus. Cic. *QFr.* 3.8.5: "Serrani Domestici filii funus perluctuosum fuit a. d. VIII. Kal. Decembr.: laudavit pater scripto meo."

[63] Cic. *De or.* 2.341: "Sed tamen, quoniam est utendum aliquando, non numquam etiam scribendum, vel ut Q. Tuberoni Africanum avunculum laudanti scripsit C. Laelius" ("Nevertheless, since sometimes *laudationes* need to be employed and sometimes even written out, as C. Laelius wrote for Q. Tubero, who was eulogizing his uncle Africanus"). Cicero confuses the nephews but knows better, as shown at Cic. *Mur.* 75 where "Maximus" gives the speech; Tubero handles the *epulum*, but mismanages the task. Tubero covered the funeral couches with skins that would have befit a funeral for Diogenes the Cynic, but not the "divine Africanus." Kierdorf 1980: 21–22 sees through the murk.

[64] Cic. *De or.* 2.347–348: "Sumendae autem res erunt aut magnitudine praestabiles aut novitate primae aut genere ipso singulares; neque enim parvae neque usitatae neque vulgares admiratione aut omnino laude dignae videri solent. Est etiam cum ceteris praestantibus viris comparatio in laudatione praeclara."

> summam spem civium, quam de eo iam puero habuerant, continuo adulescens incredibili virtute superavit, qui consulatum petivit numquam, factus consul est bis, primum ante tempus, iterum sibi suo tempore, rei publicae paene sero, qui duabus urbibus eversis inimicissimis huic imperio non modo praesentia, verum etiam futura bella delevit. Quid dicam de moribus facillimis, de pietate in matrem, liberalitate in sorores, bonitate in suos, iustitia in omnes? nota sunt vobis.

> In truth, who would deny that it had gone admirably for him? For unless he had wished to obtain immortality, which least of all was on his mind, what did he not achieve which would have been right for a man to desire? As a young man, he continually surpassed, with unbelievable virtue, the greatest hope of the populace which they had for him since he was a boy. He never sought the consulship, but was made *consul* twice, first before the legal time, again in his own proper time—nearly too late for the state. He averted not only present but also future wars by overthrowing two cities that were the most hostile to this empire. What shall I say about his pleasant manners, about his *pietas* towards his mother, his generosity towards his sisters, his beneficence towards his own, his justice toward all? These are known to you.[65]

The style and content of a *laudatio* emerge in the midst of a *consolatio* concerning the grief that Laelius felt toward Aemilianus.[66] Cicero clearly had this speech on his mind in more than one context. Since the language adheres closely to the content and compressed style one expects from a *laudatio*, why should it not be considered representative of the general outline of the speech? Again, the eulogy was given not by Laelius, but by a young politician who had just risen to the level of quaestor, Q. Fabius Maximus Allobrogicus. The content, if it is represented in the passage above, presented a few notable accomplishments, described with superlatives, and selected offices held by the deceased. There was no need to be comprehensive, since the lesser offices would have been obvious, and some of the more important accomplishments would have been transmitted through visual means, such as magisterial garb and triumphal monuments. (See below, p. 102.) Through *praeteritio*, he notes that Aemilianus was, in general, a good man in the domestic sphere as well. Finally, he closes with a rhetorical flourish, the lone fragment that survives today. Just as in the speech for Metellus, or in the Scipionic epitaphs, hyperbolic generalities pervade. The repetition, funeral after funeral, must have influenced Cicero's opinion of the genre. Just as the novelty of reading formulaic epitaphs in succession quickly fades, so delight in the text of the *laudatio* must have been tempered by its similarity to other eulogies.

---

[65] Cic. *Amic.* 11.

[66] Kierdorf 1980: 27–32 contends that the surrounding context resembles a *consolatio* and should, therefore, not be considered part of the original *laudatio*. Nothing precludes a hybrid, however. Cicero could have decorated the original praise of the *laudatio* with words intended to mollify grief.

Laudationes *for Women (102 BCE–54 BCE)*

During the next eighty years, the extant record of *laudationes* takes a surprising turn: surviving testimony primarily concerns funeral speeches for women.[67] In 102 BCE, Q. Lutatius Catulus gave the eulogy for his mother, Popilia, purportedly the first *laudatio funebris* ever delivered in the Forum for a woman.[68] Thereafter, funeral eulogies held for women merited no special attention.[69] Three subsequent funeral orations were connected to Julius Caesar, the first two in 69 for his aunt Julia and later his wife Cornelia, the last of my examples, as well as in 54 for his daughter Julia.[70]

Caesar's Innovation: Laudationes *for Julia and Cornelia (69 BCE)*

The speeches in 69 are intriguing, in that they represent Caesar's bold attempt to utilize a death to take control of the oratorical stage, and to use the entire funerary apparatus for political gain. The first oration was for his aunt, the widow of Marius. He used the occasion to proclaim his political allegiance by parading the *imagines* of Marius for the first time.[71] Some in the audience objected. The crowd shouted down dissenters and greeted Caesar with applause, acting more like the audience of a political *contio* than a *laudatio funebris*.[72] For his wife, he broke precedent anew. While praise for older women was common, according to Plutarch, *laudationes* for the relatively young were not. Indeed, Caesar was the first to give a eulogy for such

[67] For expanded analysis of *laudationes funebres* for women, see Pepe 2018 and Östenberg 2023.

[68] Cic. *De or.* 2.44: "scio et me, et omnes qui adfuerunt, delectatos esse vehementer, cum abs te est Popilia, mater vestra, laudata, cui primum mulieri hunc honorem in nostra civitate tributum puto." ("I know that I along with everyone who attended were very much delighted when you praised your mother Popilia, the first time, I believe, that a woman was given this honor in our state.") The character of Antonius, not Cicero, enjoyed the speech. It is the presence in the dialogue of Catulus that gives rise to the aside. Given the full context of Cicero's description the joy stems not from the skill demonstrated in the oration, but from the seminal event: this was the first time a woman was given such an honor. Cf. Dugan 2001: 39–40, who suggests that Cicero would not have admired the *laudatio*, since he was a *novus homo* and lacked the "image technology." Antonius, however, as a *nobilis*, "would have reason to resist any assault on the integrity of this mainstay of aristocratic image-production."

[69] In Cic. *De or.* 2.225–226, during a trial held in the Forum, L. Licinius Crassus points out the *imagines* of a passing funeral procession for a woman. She happened to be the aunt of Crassus' opponent, the defendant in the case. See below, p. 120, and see further note 73 below.

[70] For his aunt Julia and Cornelia: Suet. *Iul.* 6.1, Plut. *Caes.* 5.1–6; for his daughter: Cass. Dio 39.64.

[71] Plut. *Caes.* 5.2.

[72] Plut. *Caes.* 5.3: ἐπὶ τούτῳ γὰρ ἐνίων καταβοησάντων τοῦ Καίσαρος, ὁ δῆμος ἀντήχησε, λαμπρῷ δεξάμενος κρότῳ καὶ θαυμάσας ὥσπερ ἐξ Ἅιδου διὰ χρόνων πολλῶν ἀνάγοντα τὰς Μαρίου τιμὰς εἰς τὴν πόλιν. ("When some shouted down Caesar, the people responded by greeting him with a vigorous cheer, and marveling that he was as bringing back to the city after so many years, as if up from Hades, the honors of Marius.")

a young wife.[73] He met again with approval from the crowd.[74] Of the three funeral orations cited above, only the fragment of the eulogy for his aunt Julia survives:

> Quaestor Iuliam amitam uxoremque Corneliam defunctas laudavit e more pro rostris. et in amitae quidem laudatione de eius ac patris sui utraque origine sic refert: Amitae meae Iuliae maternum genus ab regibus ortum, paternum cum diis inmortalibus coniunctum est. nam ab Anco Marcio sunt Marcii Reges, quo nomine fuit mater; a Venere Iulii, cuius gentis familia est nostra. est ergo in genere et sanctitas regum, qui plurimum inter homines pollent, et caerimonia deorum, quorum ipsi in potestate sunt reges.
>
> As quaestor he gave the funeral oration for his aunt Julia and his wife Cornelia in the traditional manner at the Rostra.[75] In fact, during the praise (*laudatio*) of his aunt he spoke about her and his father's lineage in this way: the maternal family of my aunt Julia came from kingly stock, the paternal side was connected to the immortal gods. For the Marcii Reges, from which family my mother came, are descended from Ancus Martius, and from Venus come the Iulii, our *gens*. There is, therefore, in our stock both the virtue of kings, who are most influential among men, and the sacred status of the gods, in whose power are the kings themselves.[76]

Suetonius cites the speech as part of his chronological narrative of Caesar's early career. He highlights only this section of the eulogy, presumably to use Caesar's own words in the description of his divine and legendary genealogical origins. Caesar addresses the practical difficulty of praising a Roman woman, for, unlike a man, she could not have attained offices or made the same civic contributions. His explicit connection to the divine was an innovation in surviving funerary evidence, but it was not the focal point of the speech.[77] It is true that a *laudatio* for a woman would have differed from a *laudatio* for a magistrate. Genealogical origins may be read as functional equivalents to magistracies, though such an *origo* would equally apply to a man. Based on audience reaction, however, the innovation was not in the speech itself, but in the manipulation of the event. The words in praise of Caesar's wife were not as significant as simply holding the event. Likewise, the praise for his aunt was subordinated to the visual presentation of the *imago* of Marius.

Despite the lack of a *cursus* and *res gestae*, *laudationes* for women still mirrored those for men in fundamental ways. Each had its own semantic award system. The

---

[73] Plut. *Caes.* 5.4–5: τὸ μὲν οὖν ἐπὶ γυναιξὶ πρεσβυτέραις λόγους ἐπιταφίους διεξιέναι πάτριον ἦν Ῥωμαίοις, <ἐπὶ> νέαις δ᾽ οὐκ ὂν ἐν ἔθει, πρῶτος εἶπε Καῖσαρ ἐπὶ τῆς ἑαυτοῦ γυναικὸς ἀποθανούσης. ("While it was customary for the Romans to go through funeral orations for older women, it was not so for young women; Caesar was the first to speak on behalf of his own deceased wife.")

[74] Plut. *Caes.* 5.5: καὶ τοῦτ᾽ ἤνεγκεν αὐτῷ χάριν τινα καὶ συνεδημαγώγησε τῷ πάθει τοὺς πολλοὺς ὡς ἥμερον ἄνδρα καὶ περίμεστον ἤθους ἀγαπᾶν. ("For this he won some favor and with his passion he helped persuade many to regard him fondly as a kind man, full of character.")

[75] On *pro rostris* see below, p. 110n139.

[76] Suet. *Iul.* 6.

[77] Weinstock 1971: 18: "What he said was probably traditional on such occasions and did not mean much by itself: it did not concern his own person. He was thirty-two and still far away from mastery of the world: the highest office he had attained was that of quaestor."

evidence is difficult to assess fully, however. Apart from the extant fragment of the oration given by Caesar, three other *laudationes* are preserved—only two of which are in a legible state. All are epitaphs. Hence their purpose and method of distribution are intrinsically different from those of spoken orations. Most modern scholars believe that these *laudationes* were held at the tomb, their content being unsuitable for a *laudatio* in the Forum, but some doubt whether they were ever performed as written.[78] I pass over very briefly two of these three epitaphs. In comparison to the rest of the surviving evidence adduced above, the *Laudatio Turiae* is *sui generis*.[79] It dwells excessively on matters of inheritance, provides a detailed explanation of how the deceased maintained her husband's property during the civil wars, and pleaded with Mark Antony on his behalf, and it inverts the feminine and masculine spheres of praise.[80] The *Laudatio Matidiae* is barely legible, dates to the second century CE, and was given by Hadrian.[81] The third, the *Laudatio Murdiae*, also addresses issues of inheritance and may also have been representative of a private *laudatio* designed for a private audience. Nonetheless, its brevity and the way it handles praise of womanly virtues parallel similar features in *laudationes* for men:

> quom omnium bonarum feminarum *simplex similisque* esse laudatio soleat, quod naturalia bona propria custodia servata varietates verborum non desiderent, satisque sit eadem omnes bona fama digna fecisse, et quia adquirere novas laudes mulieri sit arduom, quom minoribus varietatibus vita iactetur, necessario communia esse colenda, ne quod amissum ex iustis praecepteis cetera turpet. Eo maiorem laudem omnium carissima mihi mater meruit, quod modestia probitate pudicitia opsequio lanificio diligentia fide par similisque cetereis probeis feminis fuit, neque ulli cessit virtutis laboris sapientiae.
>
> since praise for all good women ought to be simple and similar, because the natural good traits preserved by their own care do not require variations of words, and because it is enough to have done the same things worthy of good repute, because finding new praises for a woman would be difficult, since her life is disturbed with lesser variations, by necessity the common things must be tended, lest something omitted from just standards foul the rest. Therefore my mother, dearest of all to me, has earned praise that is all the greater because in modesty, honesty, chastity, obedience, wool work, attentiveness, and trust, she was similar and equal to the rest of virtuous women, and neither does she yield to any in virtue, diligence, and wisdom.[82]

The end of the surviving fragment of the *Laudatio Murdiae* summarizes the virtues all Roman women might aspire to attain. According to the eulogist, the *laudatio* of a woman was "simple" and "similar" to all the rest. While no prescribed rule existed, there were bound to have been a finite number of traits and actions

---

[78] Flower 1996: 132. Kierdorf 1980: 112–116. See Butler 2009: 23–26 for a brief but full discussion of the transmission of *laudationes* in their various written forms.

[79] *CIL* VI 1527. See Durry 1950, Wistrand 1976, Horsfall 1983, and Osgood 2014.

[80] Hemelrijk 2004.

[81] *CIL* XIV 3579.

[82] *CIL* VI 10230. The final surviving words after "sapientiae" are not understood.

that composed the definition of a *bona femina*. Such reasoning applies equally well to *laudationes* for men, however. It was not because females lacked a means of differentiating themselves that their *laudationes* revisited the same themes and made the same claims. Rather, most *laudationes*, regardless of the gender of the subject, would have done the same. The text lists a range of attainable virtues within the female sphere.[83] Compare this enumeration of virtues to that of Metellus in the first *laudatio* examined above. Metellus is said to have achieved *decem maximas res optimasque*. Others will have striven for the same. Funerary praise of virtues calls to mind Garrison Keillor's Lake Wobegon.[84] There are different spheres of virtues for men and women, but the best men, like the best women, will have accomplished very similar achievements. The resulting praise of one great man, just as one virtuous woman, would have exhibited little variation.

The Laudatio *for C. Iulius Caesar (44 BCE)*

The last *laudatio* of the Republic is also informative, despite its unique nature. The *laudatio* given by Antony at the funeral of Caesar in 44 BCE is a fraught but useful source for detailed information about the length of the eulogy and its use of the deceased as a prop.[85] Paradoxically, though this evidence is deeply illuminating for this investigation, it is also the least historically accurate. Multiple versions of the narrative are preserved. The details are controversial, but for the present discussion, a solution to the controversy is unnecessary.[86] The general order of events was as follows. Antony gave a customary funeral oration, adding a few words (*perpauca verba*) amidst readings of senatorial decrees.[87] He roused the crowd by using Caesar's body and his bloodied clothing as props. The crowd rioted.[88] Cicero registers his disgust when he reads "de tanto viro" and "de clarissimo civi" in the *contio* of Antony.[89] Cassius Dio tells an entirely different story.

Cassius Dio presents the most complete *laudatio* purported to date from the Republic; it is, however, a creative fabrication.[90] It is also a useful fiction: Dio's narrative ought to reflect a certain familiarity with Republican funerary tradition ac-

---

[83] Hemelrijk 2004: 188–190.

[84] Keillor 1999: 71: "And that's the news from Lake Wobegon, where all the women are strong, the men are good looking, and all the children are above average."

[85] On explicit testimony of the use of the body as prop, exploited first by the followers of Clodius and then by those of Caesar, see Hall 2014: 133–140.

[86] The primary sources are Suet. *Iul.* 84.2; App. *BC* 2.144–147; Cass. Dio 44.36–49; Plut. *Ant.* 14.6; and Cic. *Att.* 14.10.1, 11.1. Weinstock 1971: 351–352 assembles the evidence and contends that Appian's version is the most reliable; Ramage 2006: 48–51 seems to trust Suetonius.

[87] Suet. *Iul.* 84.2: "perpauca verba." Plut. *Ant.* 14.6: ὥσπερ ἔθος ἦν ἐν ἀγορᾷ διεξιὼν ἐγκώμιον ("giving the *laudatio* in the Forum as was customary").

[88] App. *BC* 2.147, Plut. *Ant.* 14.6.

[89] Cic. *Att.* 14.10.1.

[90] Ramsey 2003: 213, on Cicero's reference to "tua illa pulchra laudatio" in *Phil.* 2.91.2 notes, "the version in Dio 44.36–49 is pure invention." Kierdorf 1980: 150–158 remarks that it is a rhetorical whole, but accepts that it is a fictitious speech. Cf. Vollmer 1891: 483, who insists that, though Cassius Dio has created a work of fiction, it still gives us a "bonam laudationum imaginem." I omit Dio's rendition of

quired during the years of his research on early Rome.[91] The structure of the speech is similar to that of the *laudationes* listed above. The family lineage is introduced, including references to divinity; an abstract and lengthy *praeteritio* lists inherent qualities, education, intelligence, military, and civic accomplishments. Antony uses both comparison and hyperbole in his praise.[92]

Dio's Antony demonstrates the flexible nature of the address in a *laudatio*. In the beginning, the speaker addresses the Roman people as *Quirites*, a clear use of contional language from atop the Rostra (*pro rostris*).[93] For most of the oration, he refers to the deceased in the third person. At the end, however, he addresses the body of Caesar directly.

> ποῦ δῆτά σοι, Καῖσαρ, ἡ φιλανθρωπία, ποῦ δὲ ἡ ἀσυλία, ποῦ δὲ οἱ νόμοι; ἀλλὰ σὺ μέν, ὅπως μηδ' ὑπὸ τῶν ἐχθρῶν τις φονεύηται, πολλὰ ἐνομοθέτησας, σὲ δὲ οὕτως οἰκτρῶς ἀπέκτειναν οἱ φίλοι, καὶ νῦν ἔν τε τῇ ἀγορᾷ πρόκεισαι ἐσφαγμένος, δι' ἧς πολλάκις ἐπόμπευσας ἐστεφανωμένος, καὶ ἐπὶ τοῦ βήματος ἔρριψαι κατατετρωμένος, ἀφ' οὗ πολλάκις ἐδημηγόρησας.

> Indeed, Caesar, where was your humanity, where was your inviolability, where were the laws? While you promulgated many laws that ensured that no one would be killed by his enemies, you were thus struck down pitilessly by friends. Now you lie bloody in the Forum, through which you were often conveyed in triumphal procession; stabbed to death, you were cast down on the Rostra, from which you often addressed the people.[94]

The shift to the second person must have been dramatic.[95] The body lay before Antony, positioned to become part of the speech. His visual interaction with the deceased incited revolution, but the act of interacting with the dead need not have resulted in violence and was not an innovation.

The second person address of the dead is common in the funerary sphere.[96] It is evidenced in epitaphs, and appears in the Scipionic corpus.[97] Further confirmation comes from the Fayum, where a fragment of Augustus' funeral oration for Agrippa survived on papyrus:

> nam tribunicia tibi potestas in quinque annos ex senatus consulto Lentulis consulibus data est et rursus eadem in alterum lustrum consulibus Ti. Nerone et Quintilio Varo

---

Tiberius' funeral oration for Augustus, since the gap between praise for an emperor, made *by an emperor*, and a mid-Republican oration is too vast to overcome.

91 Swan 2004: 326, on the funeral oration Dio contrived for Augustus: "Historically irrelevant as Tiberius' long fictional address has seemed to many ... one end that Dio wanted to achieve through it, I suggest, was to transport his readers to a living theater of Roman and world history"

92 Ramage 2006: 50n39 examines the rhetorical structure.

93 Cass. Dio 44.36.1. As in the speech of Q. Fabius Maximus Allobrogicus, above (Schol. Bob. *Mil.* 16). On *Quirites* and the Roman crowd, see Connolly 2006: 86–89. On *pro rostris*, see below, p. 110n139.

94 Cass. Dio 44.49.3

95 App. *BC* 2.146 uses the second person as well.

96 See Feldherr 2000 on Catull. 101.

97 Courtney 1995: 41–42: "qua re lubens te in gremiu(m), Scipio, recipit terra, Publi, prognatum Publio, Corneli."

> generis tuis addita est. et quascumque te in provincias res publica Romana adhibuisset, nullius in eis ut esset imperium maius tuo per legem sanctum est. sed tu in summum fastigium et nostro studio et virtutibus propriis per consensum universorum hominum evectus.
>
> For you were granted *tribunicia potestas* for five years by decree of the senate during the consulships of the Lentuli (18 BCE) and the same was added for another five years during the consulships of your sons-in-law Tiberius Nero and Quintilius Varus (13 BCE). In addition, it was sanctioned by law that, no matter what province the Roman state called you into, there would be no one with greater *imperium* than you. You have been raised to the highest honor by our zeal and by your very own virtues, through the agreement of all men.[98]

Short and concise, the fragment belongs to the left column, with all of the right column of text lost.[99] Again, the last line invites comparison to the hyperbolic end of the speech for Metellus. Obviously, the second person address, on this occasion, was not used to incite a riot. Rather, it represents a flexible element of the *laudatio*. At some point during the speech, the speaker could have chosen to interact directly with the deceased. Such a shift also offered an opportunity to communicate visually with the audience.[100] The entire audience could have seen the transition in the speech and reacted accordingly. It may have even served as a visual time marker, where a turn to the body signaled that the end of the praise for the deceased was near, or that it was time for outward signs of mourning. Below, I explore how this visual interaction may have worked in practice. (See p. 110.)

Conclusion: "I would not have needed many words"

I have reviewed every major surviving fragment of the mid-Republican *laudatio funebris*.[101] So few remain. What little survives reflects Cicero's assessment of the genre: the content of these speeches tend to range between specific lists of accomplishments and attribution of positive generic personal and professional characteristics. To recapitulate, I return briefly to Antony's speech for Caesar. Insofar as the literary versions of that speech resemble the original, its utility for my investigation lessens. After all, the events surrounding Caesar's death, the reading of the will, and the subsequent tumult, make it clear that this was no customary speech.

98 The fragment survives in Greek. For details and interpretation, see Koenen 1970, Badian 1980, Haslam 1980, and Gronewald 1983. I follow the convenient back-translation of Haslam 1980, combined with the three-line addition of Gronewald 1983 to underscore the similarities between the other Latin *laudationes* reviewed above.

99 Swan 2004: 326 remarks that "[T]he fragment records grants of *imperium* to Agrippa with fastidious precision as to term, scope, date, and source in law."

100 Of course, the shifts were ways to include the audience *and* use the rhetorical topos *mortuos ab inferis excitare*. See Flower 1996: 142–143 and Dufallo 2007: 14–16.

101 I have omitted two. The *laudatio* of Sulla (App. *BC* 1.106) was delivered by "the best speaker of the time" (ὁ κράτιστος εἰπεῖν τῶν τότε) at a state sponsored funeral (*funus publicum*). The second, the *laudatio* of M. Claudius Marcellus (208 BCE), I discuss on p. 102.

Fortunately, Dio, in the voice of Antony, explains what one might have expected given a different context:

> εἰ μὲν οὗτος ἰδιωτεύων ἐτεθνήκει κἀγὼ ἐν ἰδιωτείᾳ ὢν ἐτύγχανον, οὔτ᾽ ἂν πολλῶν, ὦ Κυιρῖται, λόγων ἐδεήθην, οὔτ᾽ ἂν πᾶσι τοῖς ὑπ᾽ αὐτοῦ πεπραγμένοις ἐπεξῆλθον, ἀλλ᾽ ὀλίγα ἂν περί τε τοῦ γένους καὶ περὶ τῆς παιδείας τῶν τε τρόπων αὐτοῦ εἰπών, καί πῃ καὶ τῶν ἐς τὸ κοινὸν αὐτῷ πεπολιτευμένων μνησθείς, ἠρκέσθην, ἵνα μὴ καὶ δι᾽ ὄχλου τοῖς οὐδέν οἱ προσήκουσι γένωμαι.

> If he had died a private citizen, and if I happened to be speaking in a private capacity, Quirites, I would not have needed many words, nor would I have covered in detail all his deeds. After saying a few words about his family, his education, and his character traits, and, at some point, having recalled his civic accomplishments for the state, I would have been content, lest I annoy those not related to him.[102]

The beginning of the speech sets up a contrast between a traditional, private *laudatio*, where a family member gave the speech, and a state-sponsored *funus publicum*, where a current magistrate delivered the eulogy.[103] Dio's Antony sums up precisely Cicero's assessment of *laudationes*. Very little in the extant *laudationes* prove him wrong. One might imagine a lengthy oration that included great biographical detail similar to, for example, Tacitus' *Agricola*.[104] But the evidence suggests otherwise. In the speech, the eulogist adduced some, but not all of the deeds of the deceased. He provided a general family lineage. Most likely, he gave more detail when his family had famous and powerful ancestors. He listed the virtues of the deceased, and, in no particular order, surveyed his important civic accomplishments. Above all, as the fictitious Antony notes, the eulogist kept it short.

VISUALIZING THE *LAUDATIO*: VISUAL INDICATORS IN POLYBIUS

I now turn to the physical space of the Forum—the most important stage of the Roman Republic—to investigate the visual elements of the *laudatio funebris*. To set the visual stage, Polybius (6.53–54) remains the most detailed source for the spatial configuration of the eulogy. I have already translated and summarized the entire passage in Chapter 2 (see above, p. 13). Since the precise language Polybius uses to describe the speech is so critical, however, I will briefly highlight the specific visual indicators that will serve as the foundation for the experimental visualizations that follow.

---

[102] Cass. Dio 44.36.1.

[103] Kierdorf 1980: 151n1 rightly concludes, "Das gedachte Gegenbild ist wohl kaum eine private Leichenrede am Grabe, sondern die normale gentilizische *laudatio pro rostris*." On the *funus publicum*, see Morstein-Marx and Byrne 2025: 331n6, Wesch-Klein 1993 and the comprehensive treatment by Blasi 2012.

[104] O. C. Crawford 1941: 26: "*Laudationes* were sometimes published as political pamphlets and it was probably from this practice that the literary biography developed. For this reason it has often been suggested that Tacitus' *Agricola* is closely akin to the funeral oration."

Visualizing the Funeral Assemblage

Polybius describes the funerary assemblage as follows. Men of a similar stature to that of the ancestors, whose masks they wear, ascend the Rostra to sit on ivory chairs arranged in a row (ὅταν δ᾽ ἐπὶ τοὺς ἐμβόλους ἔλθωσι, καθέζονται πάντες ἑξῆς ἐπὶ δίφρων ἐλεφαντίνων).[105] The body of the deceased, "stood-up to be visible" (ἑστὼς ἐναργής), is conveyed into the Forum to the Rostra (πρὸς τοὺς καλουμένους ἐμβόλους).[106] If a son survives who is old enough to give a speech (ἐν ἡλικίᾳ), he ascends the Rostra (ἀναβὰς ἐπὶ τοὺς ἐμβόλους).[107] The *entire city* ("all the populace"), gathered around (πέριξ δὲ παντὸς τοῦ δήμου στάντος), hears the speech, recalls the events it evokes and reconstructs them in the mind's eye.[108]

According to Polybius, our only contemporaneous source, we have now reached the critical motivational moment in the performance. He asks, "What more than this could be as inspirational to see for a young man pursuing honor and virtue? What could be more noble than seeing all the ancestors living and breathing together?"[109] He answers his own rhetorical question: not the praise of the recently deceased, but the moment when the orator renews the fame of each ancestor, as he recites their deeds.[110] The result is that young men are motivated to do anything for the public good in order to attain fame for bravery.[111] Therefore, for Polybius, the most important elements of the *laudatio* of the mid-Republic were the visual presence of the ancestors and their individual moments of recognition. What one might consider the *laudatio* proper, that is, the funeral eulogy for the recently deceased, is subordinated in this expanded *contio funebris*, even though the praise for the ancestors may have been less aurally exciting than the praise of the dead that came before.[112] Each of these mini-addresses may have resembled the original *laudatio* given upon death, but was surely much abbreviated. Therefore, the most powerful element for Polybius was likely the most *nuda* and *inornata* of the *contio*. Polybius asks what *spectacle* could be better motivation for youth set on attaining greatness. He did not ask what *words* or what *speech* could motivate more.[113] That

---

105 Polyb. 6.53.8–9.

106 Polyb. 6.53.1. Cf. Walbank 1970 *ad loc.*: "probably sitting erect."

107 Polyb. 6.53.2.

108 Polyb. 6.53.3: δι᾽ ὧν συμβαίνει τοὺς πολλοὺς ἀναμιμνησκομένους καὶ λαμβάνοντας ὑπὸ τὴν ὄψιν τὰ γεγονότα. See Feldherr 1998: 16, esp. 16n43, who discusses the meaning of the phrase. Elsewhere, Polybius (6.15.8) uses ὑπὸ τὴν ὄψιν to describe the effect of *enargia* in narrative (1.4.1), where the reader can picture the event in the mind's eye; cf. 6.15.8 where the triumphing general uses actual props placed ὑπὸ τὴν ὄψιν of the audience so that his deeds can be seen.

109 Polyb. 6.53.9–54.1.

110 Polyb. 6.54.1: ἄρχεται τῶν ἄλλων ἀπὸ τοῦ προγενεστάτου τῶν παρόντων, καὶ λέγει τὰς ἐπιτυχίας ἑκάστου καὶ τὰς πράξεις.

111 Polyb. 6.54.3: οἱ νέοι παρορμῶνται πρὸς τὸ πᾶν ὑπομένειν ὑπὲρ τῶν κοινῶν πραγμάτων χάριν τοῦ τυχεῖν τῆς συνακολουθούσης τοῖς ἀγαθοῖς τῶν ἀνδρῶν εὐκλείας. ("The youth are incited to endure everything for the sake of the country in the pursuit of glory that attends the brave.")

112 For "*laudatio* proper," see Walbank 1970: 6.53.2 *ad loc.*

113 For what Polybius might have written, if he had meant to emphasize the aural component of the *laudatio*, see Xen. *Symp.* 2.2: θεάματα καὶ ἀκροάματα ἥδιστα παρέχεις.

young men are motivated to fight and die for their country is a direct result of the most spectacular visual moment, but, from a technical standpoint, the weakest part of the delivered speech. Now that the stage has been set, it is time to examine the *contio funebris* in its surrounding context.

VISUALIZING THE *LAUDATIO*: THE TOPOGRAPHICAL CONTEXT

In 160 BCE, at the time of the funeral of Lucius Aemilius Paullus, the civic heart of the Forum lay *in Comitio*.[114] Mass oratory, for the most part, took place on the Rostra.[115] (See fig. 3.1.) Literary tradition holds that the speaker in a *contio* would still have faced the Curia when he addressed the audience, but one assumes that he could have easily turned to face the Forum plaza if the opportunity arose.[116] The central space of the Comitium itself, separated from the Forum plaza by the Rostra, was located within a slight depression surrounded by a slope that offered a natural viewing area.[117] (See fig. 3.2.) The steps and podium of the Temple of Saturn would have provided elevated viewing opportunities to the southwest of the Rostra; and to the northwest, either the natural slope of the hill, or the steps and podium of a Temple of Concord would have offered the same.[118] The relatively recent additions of the Basilica Porcia (184 BCE), Basilica Fulvia (179 BCE), and Basilica Sempronia (170 BCE) along with their frontage shops and upper-level balconies (*maeniana*), presented additional viewing spaces.[119] (See fig. 3.3.) Rather than wade into the

---

114 See p. 47 for my initial discussion of the topographical situation of the Forum in 160 BCE. Coarelli's seminal reconstruction of a rounded Comitium is most familiar to the broader scholarly audience. See Gjerstad 1941, Coarelli 1977, Coarelli 1983, Coarelli 1985, Coarelli 1998; cf. Lugli 1946, Krause 1976, but more recently, the prevailing view, visible in plans published in recent scholarship, has eliminated the surrounding terraced, circular steps, see Carafa 1998, and Amici 2004.

115 Morstein-Marx 2004: 34–67 surveys the locations for the *contio*. Amici 2004 provides a CAD-based approach to the Rostra. The plans and elevations in Gjerstad 1941 remain indispensable for understanding the space.

116 Arce 2000: 64 asserts that this viewing situation must have applied during the funeral as well. The Forum was apparently not used as a primary audience space until after 145, when C. Licinius Crassus "instituit in Forum versus agere cum populo" (Cic. *Amic.* 96); see also Varro *Rust.* 1.2.9; Morstein-Marx 2004: 45–47 examines the sources, but notes that the "graceful arc" of Gjerstad's Suggestus J, which Morstein-Marx dates to the middle of the second century, might have better accommodated an audience in the Forum. Nonetheless, the rostrated facade seems to have always faced southeast, away from the Curia, and maintained a convex shape toward the Forum even prior to Suggestus J. It is likely that C. Licinius Crassus' turn-about represents a deviation from custom, but not a rule. At times, the Rostra must have been used to address an audience in the Forum plaza as well.

117 For the natural topography of the area, see Ammerman 1996 and Alvarez et al. 1996.

118 Stamper 2005 reconstructs both monuments according to the Tuscan standards of the time.

119 On *maeniana*, see Lehmann-Hartleben 1938, Boethius 1945, Festus 120L, Vitruvius 5.1.2 and Isid. *Etym.* 15.3.11. For the shops, see Livy 1.35.10 and Dion. Hal. *Ant. Rom.* 3.67.4. Cato built the Basilica Porcia during his censorship of 184: Livy 39.44.7, *De vir. ill.* 47, and Plut. *Cat. Mai.* 19.2; for its location and proximity to the Curia Hostilia, see Asc. *Mil.* 29 and Coarelli 1985: 59–63. Livy 40.51.5: M. Fulvius Nobilior during his censorship in 179 BCE built his eponymous basilica *post argentarias novas*, *i.e.*, on the north side of the Forum. Livy 44.16.10–11: Ti. Sempronius Gracchus built the Basilica Sempronia

debate surrounding the precise and accurate reconstruction of the *basilicae* and the *tabernae*, I have instead created simple representations of colonnaded *basilicae* with the shops represented as independent foundations, connected to the basilica via their balconies (*maeniana*).

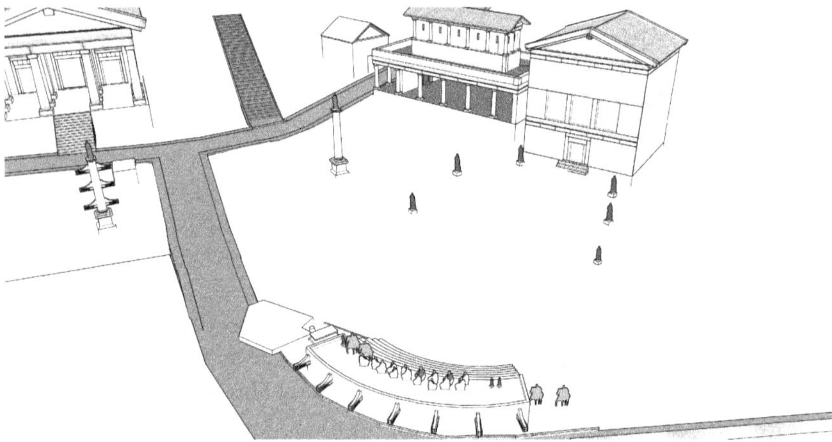

FIGURE 3.1 The Comitium in 160 BCE, depicted here as a paved area surrounded by a sloping landscape.

VISUALIZING THE *LAUDATIO*: POPULATING THE SPACE

It is not easy to grasp the scale and internal sight lines of the Roman Forum without recourse to visual aids. In order to help the reader comprehend the massive scale of the space and of its potential audience locations, I randomly planted 20,000 virtual scale figures on temple podia, basilica balconies (*maeniana*), and in the Forum plaza.[120] If we believe ancient testimony, Paullus' funeral might have had even more spectators in attendance; it is highly unlikely that most funeral orations would have ever commanded the full attention of such a large number of people spread throughout the Forum, however.[121] Nevertheless, the populated spaces increase scale legibility and aid the modeling process. Without recourse to scale indicators, one might imagine that a spectator could have easily viewed an oration from the

in 170 BCE; see also Coarelli 1985: 138–140. For the Basilica Sempronia and basilicas surrounding the Forum see Gerding and Dell'Unto 2022, which masterfully analyzes recent scholarship through the lens of a 3D reconstruction of the most recent archaeological project centered on the Basilica Sempronia.

[120] Millar 1998: 224 speculates that the Forum might hold 20,000; Arce 2000: 64 agrees. In fact, as figure 3.5 demonstrates, there is room to spare. The scale figures are derived from the outline of generic togate statues.

[121] E.g., Polyb. 6.53.1 and Diod. Sic. 31.25.1.

FIGURE 3.2 The Comitium as audience space.

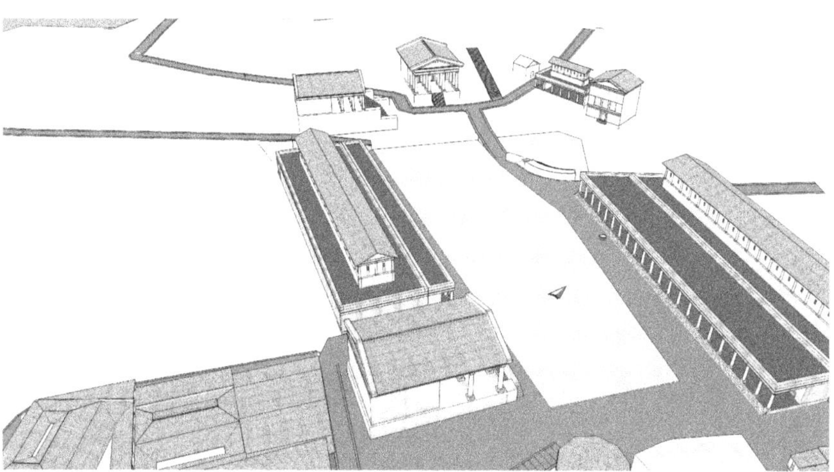

FIGURE 3.3 A bird's-eye view of the Forum in 160 BCE.

eastern end of the Forum. In contrast, with scale markers at hand, the reader can ascertain the size of the Forum plaza at a glance: it is larger than an American football field. The reader is also able to assess viewing difficulties that such a space might impose. (See figs. 3.4 and 3.5.) Modeling events within a virtually populated space also reveals potential sight-line obstructions. (See figs. 3.6 and 3.7.)

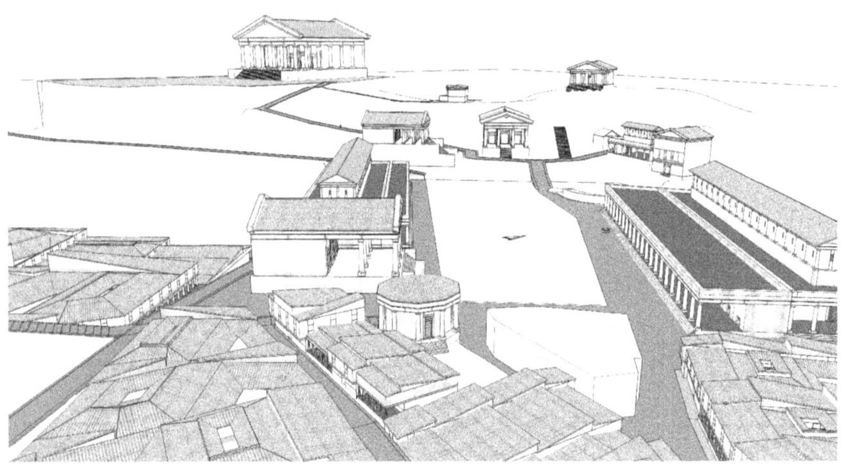

FIGURE 3.4 The Forum without scale figures.

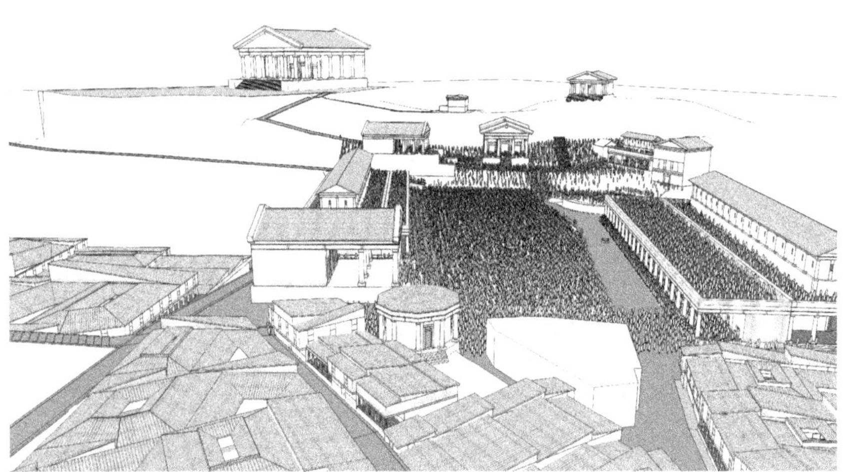

FIGURE 3.5 Populating the Forum for scale comprehension.

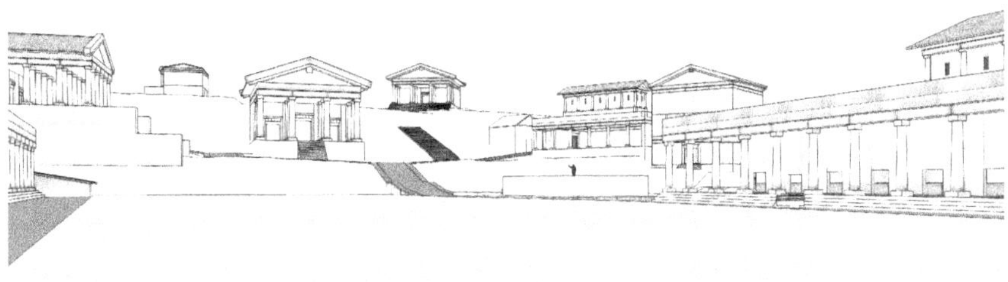

FIGURE 3.6 View of the Rostra from the eastern end of the Forum.

FIGURE 3.7 View toward the Rostra from the eastern end of the populated Forum.

TABLE 3.1 Funerary garb of the ancestors of the Aemilii Paulli

Name	Magistracies	Triumph	Funerary Garb
L. Aemilius Mam. f. - n. Mamercus (*RE* 96)	cos. 484, 478, 473		toga praetexta
Mam. Aemilius M. f. Mamercinus (*RE* 16, 97)	dict. 437, 434, 426	426	toga picta
L. Aemilius Mam. f. M. n. Mamercinus (*RE* 93)	cos. tr. 391, 389, 387, 383, 382, 380		toga praetexta
L. Aemilius L. f. Mam. n. Mamercinus/Mamercus (*RE* 95 cf. 94)	cos. 366, 363		toga praetexta
L. Aemilius L. f. L. n. Mamercinus Privernas (*RE* 101)	cos. 341, 329	329	toga picta
M. Aemilius L. f. L. n. Paullus (*RE* 116)	cos. 302		toga praetexta
M. Aemilius M. f. L. n. Paullus (*RE* 117)	cos. 255	254	toga picta
L. Aemilius M. f. M. n. Paullus (*RE* 118)	cos. 219, 216		toga praetexta
L. Aemilius L. f. M. n. Paullus Macedonicus (*RE* 114)	cos. 182, 168, cens. 164	167	toga picta

VISUALIZING THE *LAUDATIO*: THE EULOGIST AND THE ANCESTORS

To borrow terminology from the theatrical stage, blocking for the *Rostra* was potentially complicated. The inclusion of ancestors on the stage altered the visual reception and frame of the eulogist. He would have worn mourning garb, in dark contrast to the colorful attire of the triumphators, censors and consuls, thus shining a metaphorical spotlight on the stars of the show. Paullus' youngest son would have been nineteen at the time, had he not died an untimely death 4 years prior.[122] Two sons remained. His oldest, Q. Fabius Maximus Aemilianus was twenty-nine. If we continue to follow Polybius' description, the youngest surviving son, in this case, twenty-five year old P. Cornelius Scipio Aemilianus, in all probability, delivered the speech instead. At the time, he was already a seasoned soldier, having fought alongside his father at Pydna, but he was still relatively new to the world of political electioneering and the oratorical performances that would have accompanied the process. Under these circumstances, when a younger man addresses the city, perhaps less practiced in performances of this scale, the ancestors may have been even better positioned to steal the show. As for the *imagines*, the Aemilii Paulli were a successful family, and would have counted at least eight ancestors, based only on claimed agnatic descent, who had triumphed or held the office of *consul*.[123] (See table 3.1) These ancestors seated in a row would have constituted the most visually dominating elements on the Rostra, commanding the audience's field of view. The eye naturally focuses on the contrast between the ceremonial garb of the ancestors and the mourning clothes of the young man standing before them. (See fig. 3.8.)

Manufacturing History

The lineup of the ancestors highlights the practical ramifications of ancestral manipulation of family history in the *laudatio funebris*. In my examination of the speeches, I omitted the attested oration for M. Claudius Marcellus (208 BCE); its associated testimony reveals nothing of the speech itself.[124] Marcellus was an ex-

[122] Polyb. 31.28.2; see Walbank *ad loc.* for a full discussion.
[123] See above, p. 24, for the algorithm I used to reconstruct the assemblage of L. Aemilius Paullus.
[124] Kierdorf 1980: 108.

FIGURE 3.8 The eulogist standing amidst the ancestors of the Aemilii. The audience near the Rostra are represented in dark, mourning attire.

traordinarily successful politician and general, who was ambushed and killed after zealously pursuing confrontation with Hannibal.[125] According to Livy, his source, Coelius Antipater, outlined three conflicting reports about the nature of Marcellus' death: one came from an account handed down by tradition, another, from the funeral eulogy given by his son, and a third was the result of Coelius' own research.[126] As Pliny warns in his discussion of Metellus and the vicissitudes of fortune, the end matters, but so does the story that follows. *Laudationes* could challenge the historical record, and they could reframe the presentation of accomplishments. It is not clear how the account in the eulogy given by Marcellus' son differed from the others, since it seems to have acknowledged the ambush.[127] Nonetheless, it also differed from other accounts. It may have depicted the circumstances that led up to the event in a more favorable light. Though defeat in battle had surprisingly little effect on later political success, I suspect that the *laudatio* was not the occasion for a family to glorify a death that resulted from a foolhardy strategy.[128] Instead, a family might choose to modify history through the *laudatio*.[129]

---

[125] Livy 27.25.6–28.2.

[126] Livy 27.27.13: "Coelius triplicem gestae rei memoriam edit, unam traditam fama, alteram scriptam in laudatione fili, qui rei gestae interfuerit, tertiam, quam ipse pro inquisita ac sibi conperta adfert." See Carawan 1984: 140–141 and Steele 1904: 57.

[127] Livy 27.27.14: "omnes insidiis circumventum tradant."

[128] For successful politicians who had experienced defeat in battle, see Rosenstein 1990: 9–53, and for Marcellus, 25 and 104 *ff.*

[129] See Wiseman 1996 for a detailed treatment of the Minucii, another family guilty of manipulating the funerary record.

Laudationes could also directly change the appearance and arrangement of ancestors on the stage:

> vitiatam memoriam funebribus laudibus reor falsisque imaginum titulis, dum familiae ad se quaeque famam rerum gestarum honorumque fallente mendacio trahunt; inde certe et singulorum gesta et publica monumenta rerum confusa.
>
> I attest that the historic record has been corrupted by funerary praises and false *tituli* for the *imagines*, when all families appropriate for themselves with deceptive lies the fame of honors and deeds accomplished; wherefore, of course, both the deeds of every individual and the public record of the works have been confounded.[130]

Families might attribute unearned accomplishments to their forebears, which would change the garb of one of the ancestors on the Rostra. Or a family might even claim false ancestors thus adding to the props, as it were, on the stage. Dio was not the only one guilty of writing a fictitious *laudatio*, the family or possibly the larger *gens* might contrive a *laudatio*, not to be performed, but only to circulate new familial propaganda.[131] Over the years additional offices might be alleged. After Cicero disparages *laudationes* in the *Brutus*,[132] he lists the methods employed by such families:

> quamquam his laudationibus historia rerum nostrarum est facta mendosior. *multa enim scripta sunt in eis quae facta non sunt*: falsi triumphi, plures consulatus, genera etiam falsa et ad plebem transitiones, cum homines humiliores in alienum eiusdem nominis infunderentur genus; ut si ego me a M'. Tullio esse dicerem, qui patricius cum Ser. Sulpicio consul anno x post exactos reges fuit.
>
> Our history is made more mendacious by these *laudationes*. For, many things have been written in them that were never accomplished: false triumphs, more consulships, even fake claims of family and transitions to the plebs, when men of lower status are inserted into a family of the same name; as if I were to say that I was descended from Manius Tullius, who was a patrician and *consul* with Servius Sulpicius ten years after the kings were expelled.[133]

Altering the *laudatio* reconfigured the visual components of the entire funeral. The falsification of one consulship in the remote past would have given a family an additional *imago* and an additional participant in the funeral. This alteration would have resulted in more fasces and lictors, an extra chariot, and an extra chair on the Rostra. Further, if a *triumphator* were claimed, then he would have worn the *toga*

---

[130] Livy 8.40.

[131] For example, consider the purported funeral oration for Appius Claudius, who died on Euboea in 48 BCE (Val. Max. 1.8.3). The fourth century grammarian, Diomedes, writes, (Diom. 1.367.27) "amicio amicui, ut Brutus laudatione Appi Claudii, 'Qui te toga praetexta amicuit.'" This *laudatio* was never delivered in the Forum. On this *oratio scripta*, see Kierdorf 1980: 138 and Vollmer 1891: 482, who writes, "haec laudatio non habita, modo scripta est … Appius in Euboea insula mortuus est." See Val. Max. 1.8.10.

[132] See above, p.74 for quotation and translation of the preceding passage.

[133] Cic. *Brut.* 62.

FIGURE 3.9 View of an orator unaccompanied by ancestors.

FIGURE 3.10 View of an orator accompanied by one additional ancestor.

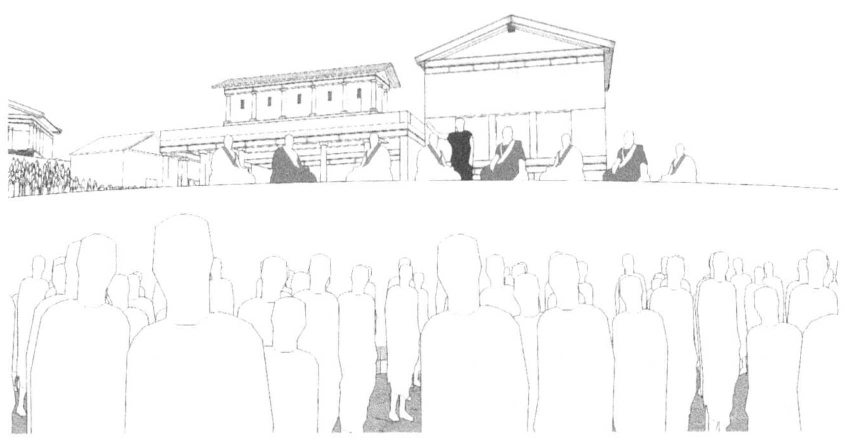

FIGURE 3.11 The ancestors of the Aemilii viewed from the Forum.

picta and would have brought additional visual capital to the family. Also, falsifications of this sort constituted manipulation of the part of the eulogy that Polybius claims mattered most. The consequences were visibly manifest. For some with less glorious ancestry, such claims may have meant the difference between showcasing an empty stage on the Rostra or showcasing a single, triumphal ancestor. (See figs. 3.9 and 3.10.) A lone orator in a *toga atria* would not have necessarily aroused the curiosity of others in the Forum, whereas the presence of even one ancestor would have signified that something special was happening on the Rostra: a historical figure was now in their midst. Passersby might want to approach the Rostra for a better look. Nowadays, one could easily imagine this moment as an opportunity for a photograph. In so doing, they might inadvertently hear the first major public speech of a young aristocrat, given specifically to celebrate his family.

The Funerary Assemblage as Data Visualization

Unlike the *pompa funebris*, the *laudatio* offered the opportunity to read the family's symbolic capital at a glance. When dispersed along the triumphal route, the overall display was impressive but not easily legible. On the *Rostra*, however, the ancestors were arrayed in a row, constrained by a limited space. When grouped together, the ancestors functioned almost like a modern, visualized data abstraction of familial accomplishments. The ranks of the ancestors on display in figure 3.11 are more visible and more readily understood than when the same group of ancestors is on parade, as depicted in Chapter 2, figure 2.20. A cursory glance at the ancestors of the Aemilii and Cornelii depicted in figures 3.13 and 3.14 demonstrates the manifestly visible superiority on display in comparison to that of an oration for a

FIGURE 3.12 The ancestors of the Cornelii viewed from the Forum.

FIGURE 3.13 The ancestors of the Aemilii viewed from the Curia.

novus homo as depicted in figure 3.9. As shown in figure 3.13, a spectator could have clearly discerned the visible manifestation of ancestral accomplishment, even when standing on the upper steps of the Curia Hostilia, at some distance from the Rostra.

FIGURE 3.14 The ancestors of the Cornelii viewed from the Curia.

Calculating the Maximum Count of Imagines

The Aemilii would have presented a formidable family. Their ancestral lineup in 160 BCE could have easily comprised eight *imagines*. This was more or less the maximum one could attain through an agnatic lineage dating to the founding of the Republic. In fact, by chance, one family has a patriline, attested by textual evidence, from the founding of the city: the agnatic line descended from P. Valerius Poplicola, who was *consul suffectus* in 509 BCE. This founding father produced a continuous family tree that is attested in the textual record through the first century BCE. A descendant of this Poplicola, C. Valerius Laevinus, was born ca. 219, a year after the birth of Paullus. When this Valerius died, his family could have displayed seven ancestors on the Rostra.[134] (See table 3.2.) Each man from the entire patriline—*i.e.*, Poplicola, his son, his son's son, and so on—had achieved the office of *consul*, so the ancestral display would have been the maximum possible for that family. Practically speaking, unless a family were to have included uncles, brothers, or relatives through matrilineal descent, by 160 BCE, ten *imagines* are probably a realistic upper bound.[135] In comparison, if the family of Paullus chose to display the ancestors I propose, they would have presented one of the largest assemblages of ancestors of the time. Their superior numbers, as depicted in figure

[134] C. Valerius (RE 208) M. f. P. n. Laevinus.

[135] A theoretical, though unrealistic maximum is closer to fifteen, however: If a *consul*—let us artificially apply the *lex Villia annalis* of 180 BCE that a man must be 42 when entering office—has a twenty-year-old son when he assumes the consulship, and that son later achieves the consulship under the same conditions, then it is theoretically possible that the family might have had a consular ancestor every twenty-two years. For a general over view of the law and custom regarding age limits for magistracies, see Astin 1957.

TABLE 3.2 Funerary garb of the ancestors of the Valerii Laevini

Name	Magistracies	Triumph	Funerary Garb
P. Valerius Volus. f. — n. Poplicola (RE 302)	cos. 509, cos. 508, cos. 507, 506?, 504	509, 504	toga picta
P. Valerius P. f. Volus. n. Poplicola (RE 301)	cos. 475, cos. 460	475	toga picta
L. Valerius P. f. P. n. Poplicola Potitus (RE 304)	cos. 449	449	toga picta
L. Valerius L. f. P. n. Potitus (RE 307)	cos. 392, cos. 391	392	toga picta
C. Valerius L. f. L. n. Potitus (RE 306)	cos. 331		toga praetexta
P. Valerius Laevinus (RE 213)	cos. 280		toga praetexta
M. Valerius P. f. P. n. Laevinus (RE 211)	cos. 220, cos. 210		toga praetexta
C. Valerius M. f. P. n. Laevinus (RE 208)	pr. 179		toga praetexta

3.11, perhaps yielded to the slightly more colorful array of accomplishments on display by the Cornelii as shown in 3.12. The colored garb of the four censors and triumphators of the Cornelii, clustered together chronologically, stand out more clearly, especially when viewed from a distance, as a comparison of figures 3.13 and 3.14 demonstrates. Such a diachronic comparison can only be made with the aid of modern technology, however. For many Romans milling about in the Forum, the ancestral lineup of the Aemilii in 160 would have distinguished itself from other, smaller ancestral displays held in recent memory, but most likely failed to call up direct comparisons to other families with similar accomplishments to their name. Of course, their numbers set them apart from families with only one or two ancestors. Since the Aemilii Paulli might have a funeral in the family every twenty years, however, their display must have been virtually indistinguishable from the earlier ones of the Cornelii. Could those among the general audience of the Forum have recalled a funeral ten or fifteen years prior in which a family had displayed eight or more ancestors? I will return to this question near the end of this chapter.

Looking beyond these comparisons, we should briefly consider the broader funerary context. While each aristocratic clan might hold a major funerary event every decade at most, the collective aristocracy could have put on a fairly regular display of funerals every year. In fact, based solely on attested magistrates, it is possible to estimate how often such funerals might have occurred. For example, according to the *DPRR* there are 47 aristocratic men who could have conceivably died between 175–151 BCE and who might have claimed more than two ancestors who had triumphed or held the office of *consul* or *censor*.[136] Therefore, based on evidence for attested magistrates, over a twenty-five year time period, there could have been, on average, two funerals with *imagines* staged in the Forum every year. (See fig. 3.15.) If we stipulate that this number is a baseline to calculate the regu-

[136] See Östenberg 2023 "[Extant testimonies do not prove that a] public funeral *cum laudatione* was staged on the Forum, but they do at least tell us that female funerals were a cause for public debate, rumours and celebration earlier than 100 BCE." During this time period there is no evidence for the display of matrilineal ancestors or funerals of prominent women, but if either were to occur, as it does in the late Republic, then one might imagine funerals held with more regularity and populated with more ancestors. Data gathered from the Digital Prosopography of the Roman Republic, see Bradley 2017. The death dates in the *DPRR* are often estimates, so the number above should be considered an approximation.

larity of spectacular aristocratic funerals, we can imagine that, by the time a child of an aristocratic family had reached age 25, they could have potentially witnessed fifty funerals of some note. Following Polybius' assertion that the display of ancestors is meant to provide models for behavior and achievement, the repetitive effect of these funerals, coupled with the clear variation in length and constituent parts, would have revealed quantifiable achievement within one family and comparanda across families. These funerals were visual, living data representations of the competition for symbolic capital. The rules of the game were established by the *cursus honorum*, but interfamilial competition was built upon these yearly occurrences.[137]

VISUALIZING THE *LAUDATIO*: THE BODY

The body of the deceased was a functional prop that affected both the delivery method of the orator and the visual balance of the event. Direct address of the deceased, as seen in the *laudationes* for Agrippa and Caesar, provided an opportunity for visual interaction with the body. The action need not have been as dramatic as Antony's use of Caesar's bloody clothes to have an impact on the audience. For example, Polybius reports that the orator speaks "over" the body (Polyb. 6.54.1: λέγων ὑπὲρ τοῦ θάπτεσθαι μέλλοντος). Jerome cites an old custom whereby sons ("liberi") once spoke "super cadavera."[138] The degree of visceral interaction depended upon its placement in relation to the orator, however. It is common to assume that the body was carried onto the Rostra, but the evidence is imprecise; by the Empire, in Latin *pro rostris*, "on the Rostra," is the norm when the funeral event of the past is discussed, but during the time of Paullus, the evidence is less clear.[139] Polybius gives us πρὸς τοὺς καλουμένους ἐμβόλους, which delivers the body *to* the Rostra but not necessarily on top of it.[140]

---

[137] Hölkeskamp 2004: 97–102 and Hölkeskamp 2023: 272–340 for the yearly competition of symbolic capital. Flaig 2003: 54–55 examines the reactivation of ancestral performance at each procession.

[138] Jer. *Ep.* 60.1.3: "moris quondam fuit ut super cadavera defunctorum in contione pro rostris laudes liberi dicerent et instar lugubrium carminum ad fletus et gemitus audientium pectora concitarent." ("It was once custom that sons would speak over the bodies of the deceased in a *contio* on the *Rostra* (*pro rostris*) and equivalent to songs of mourning they would stir up the spirits of the audience to weeping and moaning.")

[139] For example, Bodel 1999: 264: "the exhibition of the body, usually upright, on the Rostra." For the Latin usage: *pro* had an unambiguous meaning according to Festus, who defines *pro* to mean "on": "pro significat in, ut pro rostris, pro aede, pro tribunali." See Frank 1925, who comments on Festus' view but proposes that 'pro' in each case evolved from a standard meaning of "before," each for reasons that are *sui generis*. Cass. Dio 44.49.3 puts the body of Caesar ἐπὶ τοῦ βήματος, *i.e.* on the Rostra of the late Republic—which was a completely different monument than its mid-Republican counterpart. For the radically different *laudationes* of emperors, see Cass. Dio 75.4, in which he describes a wooden platform erected next to the Rostra to elevate the effigy of Pertinax.

[140] Paton 1975, Shuckburgh 1962, and Scott-Kilvert 1979, each retain the slight ambiguity of πρὸς + acc. in their translations.

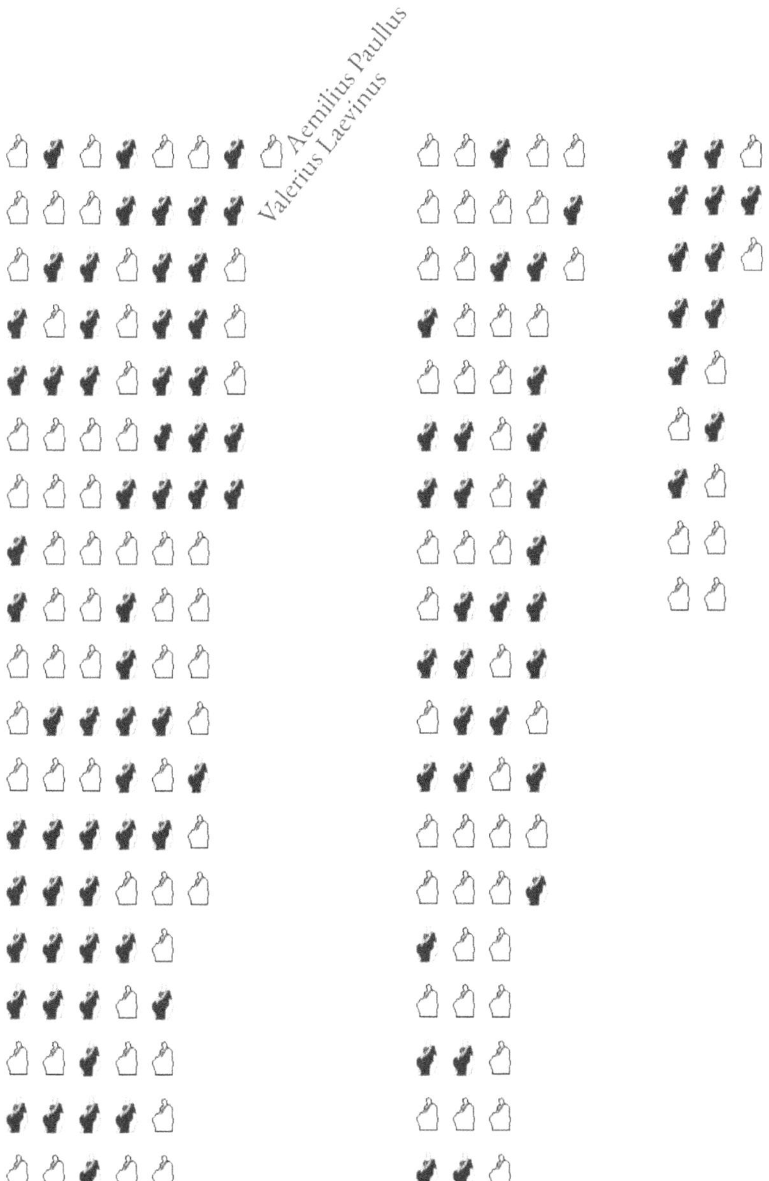

FIGURE 3.15 Computationally reconstructed ancestral assemblages for funerals, 175 BCE–151 BCE. The assemblage for Aemilius Paullus appears at the top, in the first column, followed by the funeral assemblage for Valerius Laevinus.

The position of the body *on* the bier is also ambiguously defined. According to Polybius, the body was rarely reclined (κατακεκλιμένος); it was "propped up" most of the time. Guided by the relief from Amiternum (fig. 2.1), scholars are reluctant to interpret ἑστὼς as "stood up."[141] The contrast might have been between a fully prone body and a body "propped up" as in the relief; κατακεκλιμένος can equally mean reclining to sleep *or* reclining on a couch to eat—a similar position to that depicted on the relief. Therefore, ἑστὼς might mean exactly what it implies when read without influence from the few visual depictions that survive: the body of the deceased was standing fully upright.[142] These variables—placement on the bier and position in relation to the Rostra—produce alternative readings of the visual interaction on display. We will now explore alternative locations for the bier and alternative configurations for the body.

The Bier Was Placed Before the Rostra.

If the bier were placed below the Rostra, pragmatic concerns about ascending the Rostra with a bier carrying the deceased would have been allayed. There is no actual evidence from the historical record to guide us, but one might argue that it would have been wise to avoid an accidental misstep that would lead to pallbearers and the body of the deceased falling atop each other. If the body was fully upright, so as to be conspicuous (Polyb. 6.53.1: ἑστὼς ἐναργής), it would have partly mitigated the effect of being rooted on the ground; it would have risen slightly above the Rostra, only just visible to the audience, but on a lower register than the orator and the ancestors. Those on the *maeniana* (fig. 3.16) could have had a clear view, but the audience in the rest of the Forum would have had to strain to catch a glimpse of the body. Conversely, if it was reclined, it would have been nearly invisible to the rest of the audience. The bier in fig. 3.17 is obscured by the crowd. The visual hierarchy of the procession examined in Chapter 2 will have shifted. In the procession, the body and the bier were the focal points. They rose higher than the ancestors to dominate the gaze both vertically and horizontally. But if the bier was placed in front of the Rostra, it took on a secondary role to the speaker and the ancestors, the main protagonists of the *laudatio*. If the count of ancestors was low, the visual focal point of the spectacle would have been the orator, who clearly occupied the upper visual register. Polybius underscores the kinetic ascent of the orator onto the Rostra (ἀναβὰς ἐπὶ τοὺς ἐμβόλους), and supports this shift in visual hierarchy. As the eulogist ascended, he met his ancestors and looked down on the crowd. In the meantime, in this model, the body would have lowered as the pallbearers set

[141] E.g., Walbank 1970 *ad loc.*: "probably sitting erect."

[142] Swan 2004: 321n191: "But why not rather standing, the literal sense?" How this might have been achieved is beyond the scope of this book and outside this author's expertise. To my knowledge there is no ancient testimony that describes the embalming process and structural support, including cephalic support, necessary to stand up the recently deceased. Nonetheless, there are modern parallels, see, e.g., Robertson and Robles 2014 on posed cadavers as well as Salvador-Amores 2018, esp. 13 fig. 8, on the use of a funerary chair for the deceased.

FIGURE 3.16 Deceased propped up before the Rostra, viewed from the Basilica Fulvia.

the bier on the ground, effectively situating the deceased in a visually liminal stage. The orator would have stood above the body (*super cadavera*). At that moment, the place of the deceased was no longer one of power and authority. It fell to his son to assume that role. Nor had he yet joined his ancestors, who also sat above him. All except the recently deceased were active participants in the event. If a family displayed even two or three ancestors, however, the orator would have no longer commanded the same presence. His visual role in the event would have diminished with each additional ancestor.

Placement of the body at the foot of the Rostra, rather than atop it, would have divided the audience into two groups: those in the Forum plaza and those in or near the Comitium. Those closest to the deceased would have had the only unobstructed view. Because the body was on the Forum floor, a few members of the audience, not the eulogist, would have had the most intimate view. The location of the body would have forced the eulogist to look down to address it. Hence, the action would have offered a visual cue that the eulogist was incorporating the deceased into the speech. If the body was placed within the Comitium, the entire Forum would have been effectively excluded from part of the event. The eulogist would have needed to abandon the body and turn to the Forum to interact with his audience positioned behind him, as shown in figure 3.18. For the audience on the Comitium side, however, the body would have played a more visible role. As shown in figure 3.19, the audience on the elevated steps of the Curia and the nearby slopes of the *Arx* had relatively unobstructed views. When the body was propped up, the orator would have maintained his dominant visual position, and the deceased below would have

FIGURE 3.17 Deceased, reclined in front of the Rostra on the Forum side, is invisible to the audience in the central plaza.

been more visible to the rest of the audience. Hence, in this configuration, the body could not have been reclined while still considered ἐναργής.

The Bier was Placed on the Rostra

Placing the body atop the Rostra would have altered the entire visual display. The orator would have had to maneuver around the bier, within the limited space available. (See figs. 3.20 and 3.21.) Speaking *super cadavera* would have been more intimate and visceral if the body were to have been reclined. The final moment of the speech, the second person address of the deceased, could have been spoken in a whisper, for dramatic effect, rather than a shout. Yet, all in the audience—on both the Comitium and Forum side—could have seen the body. If the entire populace had somehow managed to attend, it could have surrounded the Rostra to view the event (Polyb. 6.53.1: πέριξ δὲ παντὸς τοῦ δήμου στάντος).

Propping the body fully upright would have fundamentally altered a visual reading of the event even more. It would have been difficult for the eulogist to speak "over" (*super* or ὑπὲρ) the deceased, since the propped up body would have, conversely, towered over the orator and the ancestors. (See fig. 3.22.) Nonetheless, the vertical hierarchy of the procession would have been maintained. In fact, the decision to seat the ancestors reinforced a clear division within this vertical hierarchy. The deceased would have been the focal point in this configuration, then the orator, and finally the seated ancestors. For those at a distance from the Rostra, the elevated body of the deceased dominated the rest of the imagery, as shown in 3.23. In such a configuration, the event no longer would have presented merely a visual transition

FIGURE 3.18 Deceased, reclined before the Rostra on the Comitium side, as viewed from the steps of the Curia Hostilia.

FIGURE 3.19 Deceased stood fully upright before the Rostra, on the Comitium side.

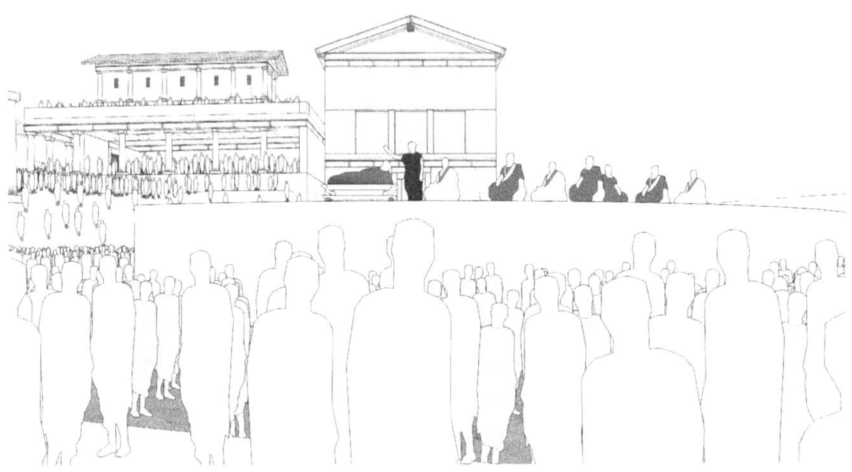

FIGURE 3.20 Deceased reclined atop the Rostra, as viewed from the Forum.

FIGURE 3.21 Deceased reclined atop the Rostra, as viewed from the Comitium.

FIGURE 3.22 Deceased propped up, as viewed from the Comitium.

FIGURE 3.23 Deceased propped up, as viewed from the Forum.

of power. Instead, by elevating the deceased above the surrounding ancestors and *laudator*, it would have visually represented the last time the deceased would have ever been prominently featured in this specific position on the oratorical stage of the Rostra, elevated above all his ancestral peers.

VISUALIZING THE *LAUDATIO*: HEARING THE SPEECH

Of course, it was not simply the seductive power of images that outweighed the verbal component of the *laudatio*. Physics played a role as well. Studies on gesture in the Roman world have shown that a grammar of body language both complemented the verbal delivery of the speech and conveyed meaning to spectators who were unable to hear the orator.[143] These gestures were as important a skill to the orator as his ability to project his voice and speak with rhetorical flourish. But how important? Over a century later, Pliny, when taking part in a trial in the Basilica Iulia during the early principate, observes that those on the second level of the basilica "zealously struggled to hear (something that is difficult) and to see (something that is easy)" the court case below.[144] Pliny points out that an audience could expect to see more easily than hear the speeches of skilled orators at a trial. A more unseasoned orator would have been even more difficult to hear. As testimony asserts, according to custom, the best orators of the day did not perform the *laudatio*. Instead, a surviving son of a relatively young age was preferred. At a time when he had just lost his father, the eulogist would have delivered what might have been his first speech in front of a crowd of this scale, from the most important stage in the city. He had to maintain his composure even amidst a spectacle that contained elements designed to elicit outward displays of grief.[145] For the funeral of Paullus, one suspects that his twenty-five year old son could have handled the pressure, but one wonders how younger, less experienced teenagers might have fared.

It would have been difficult to hear even an experienced voice in an open-air environment. Sound itself has limited effective range. One could expect sound wave attenuation in a conical shape surrounding the orator. He could have been heard in a radius of roughly 42 meters by those directly in front of him, but only within a zone of 30 meters on the sides, and 17 meters from behind.[146] (See figs. 3.24 and 3.25.) The voice of the orator who faced the Forum would have reached a smaller

[143] E.g., Aldrete 1999: 73–84 and Hall 2004.

[144] Plin. *Ep.* 6.33: "Ad hoc stipatum tribunal, atque etiam ex superiore basilicae parte qua feminae qua viri et audiendi (quod difficile) et (quod facile) visendi studio imminebant." The MS tradition diverges here; some preserve *quod facile* or *facile* before *visendi*; others omit the parentheticals entirely. See Mynors 1963 *ad loc.*; cf. Döring 1843 *ad loc.*, who suspects a gloss.

[145] MacMullen 1980, who reviews specific evidence of tears in the Roman world.

[146] This estimate is a simple application of the inverse square law in acoustics to estimate sound attenuation. For work on the audibility of *contiones* given on the first century BCE Rostra and the podium of the Temple of Castor, see Kopij and Pilch 2019. For a detailed sound cone analysis applied to ancient performance spaces, see Rose 2005. For a ground-breaking methodology that focuses on the visibility of hand gestures in Roman oratory, see Kopij, Głomb, and Popławski 2023. Though many of the speeches cited were delivered by men in their mid-twenties, modern scholars view the funeral through the lens of Polybius, who implies that the eulogists were much younger; e.g., Bodel 1999: 264: "When a young man was called upon to deliver the oration, sometimes as his first public speech." See as well Kondratieff 2009: 348–352, for a detailed discussion on the degree to which ambient noise may have affected performance at the tribunals in the Forum. Among other things, Kondratieff notes that a surprising amount of ambient noise can be ignored if one is within 5 meters of a speaker. Conversely, a shouting crowd at over 100 meters from a speaker is barely discernible if their backs are turned toward you.

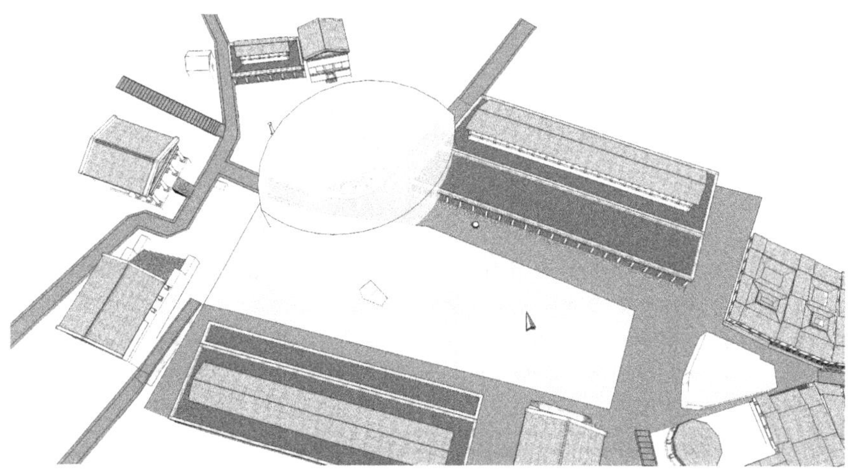

FIGURE 3.24 Sound attenuation cone: speaker facing the Curia.

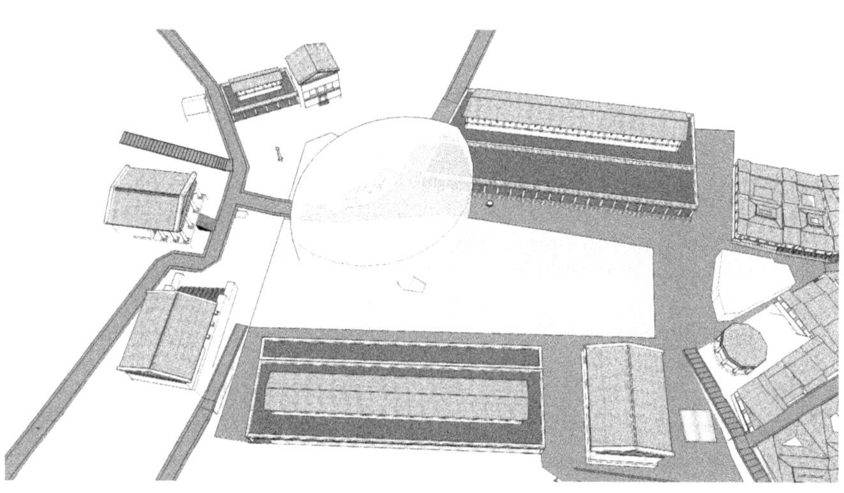

FIGURE 3.25 Sound attenuation cone: speaker facing the Forum.

part of the entire Forum plaza. Although the natural slope that surrounded the Comitium, and the enclosing facades of the Curia Hostilia and Temple of Concord would have helped to contain and reflect sound, only those within the immediate area could have heard the *laudatio* on a clear, windless day if the orator faced the Comitium. It follows, therefore, that only a limited subset of the spectators could have actually heard the speech.

THE DISTRACTIONS OF THE FORUM

The Forum was filled with myriad distractions. In general, daily life in Rome did not cease upon the death of a Roman aristocrat. The *laudatio* may even have been one of many concurrent public orations. One could choose to ignore the surroundings, or incorporate them into the delivery. L. Licinius Crassus, the well-regarded orator of the late second/early first century BCE, was famous for his masterful use of the surrounding environment in his forensic orations. In the second book of Cicero's *De oratore*, we find Crassus in the Forum, defending a client against the prosecution of M. Iunius Brutus, a notoriously active litigant and son of the famed second-century jurist.[147] In the middle of his oration, Crassus applied his skill for improvisation to an improbably perfect opportunity. By chance, the funeral procession of Brutus' aunt was passing by. Crassus confronted Brutus directly:

> Brute, quid sedes? Quid illam anum patri nuntiare vis tuo? Quid illis omnibus, quorum imagines duci vides? Quid maioribus tuis? Quid L. Bruto, qui hunc populum dominatu regio liberavit? Quid te agere? Cui rei, cui gloriae, cui virtuti studere? Patrimonione augendo? At id non est nobilitatis. ... Tu illam mortuam, tu imagines ipsas non perhorrescis? Quibus non modo imitandis, sed ne conlocandis quidem tibi locum ullum reliquisti.
>
> Brutus, why do you sit? What do you want that old woman to announce to your uncle? To all of those whose *imagines* you see being led? To your ancestors? To Lucius Brutus, who freed our people from regal domination? What should she say you are doing? What deed, what glory, what virtue do you pursue? Adding to your inheritance? But this is not worthy of nobility. ... Do you not shrink away from that dead woman and the *imagines* themselves? You haven't left for yourself a place for emulating them or even setting them up.[148]

Crassus' response underscores both his ability to think on his feet and the impromptu nature of the funeral procession. Deaths could not be predicted, and trial dates could not easily be moved. There was no tradition of embalming. No more than seven days would elapse between the time of death and the procession.[149]

---

[147] Cic. *De or.* 2.225–226.
[148] Cic. *De or.* 2.225–226.
[149] Servius Ad *A.* 5.64.

Therefore, Iunius Brutus found himself litigating on the same day of his aunt's funeral procession in the Forum. Daily life at Rome continued without interruption. Rescheduling civic life was no trivial matter.

Horace reminds us that the Roman Forum of his time was a loud place:

> at hic, si plostra ducenta
> concurrantque foro tria funera magna, sonabit,
> cornua quod vincatque tubas
>
> even if two hundred wagons and three great funerals
> run together in the Forum, this guy will make such a racket
> that bests the horns and the trumpets.[150]

While obviously an exaggeration, satire is most effective when tightly connected to daily life.[151] Not only does Horace emphasize the volume of a funeral, he introduces the very real possibility that the noise of a funeral was a distraction a trained orator would have had to overcome. There were many occasions where a funeral would have interfered with other activities in the Forum. Shops would no doubt have remained open. Official business and holidays seem not to have been canceled. Within the crowded daily routines conducted in the Forum, the eulogist needed to compete for an audience.

Imagery and Narrative in the Forum

The use of ancestors as props engages with the greater milieu of visual propaganda in the Forum. Again, Cicero records how a skilled orator incorporated the surrounding environment into his presentation: in what may have been a civil case, C. Iulius Caesar Strabo was asked his opinion of Helvius Mancius. He replied by pointing to a painted shield, a trophy hung by Marius in front of the New Shops, on the north side of the Forum. It depicted "A Gaul, twisted, with tongue sticking out and cheeks puffing," which must have been an obvious reference to the famous T. Manlius who earned his *cognomen Torquatus* by wearing the torque of the Gaul he defeated in one-on-one combat.[152] Another example of the presence of imagery in oratory: we also know of a German legate who was asked to judge the value of a

---

[150] Hor. *Serm.* 2.6.42–44.

[151] As K. Hopkins 1983: 23 notes on Juv. 6.102 ff.: "Satire certainly, and exaggerated, but pointless unless it was also based to some extent in reality."

[152] Cic. *De or.* 2.266: "pictum Gallum in Mariano scuto Cimbrico sub Novis, distortum, eiecta lingua, buccis fluentibus." ("a Gaul, twisted, with tongue sticking out and cheeks puffing, painted on a Cimbrian shield of Marius under the New Shops.") Plin. *HN* 35.25 attributes the remark to Licinius Crassus, and places the Gaul in front of the Old Shops. By Pliny's time, the connection to Marius had disappeared. All that remained was the Gaul, which must have been an allusion to the fight with the Gaul that earned Tarquatus his *cognomen*. A version that described the Gaul's unseemly gesture was found in Claudius Quadrigarius (Aul. Gell. *NA* 9.13.7–19). Livy 7.10.2–14 omits this detail, though it must have been widely known, if the painting in the Forum was still present in the late first century. Cic. *De or.* 2.266 records that it was C. Iulius Caesar Strabo who pointed to the Gaul. Interaction with imagery in the Forum was common, see Vasaly 1993: 34n33 for a brief discussion of this passage and Cicero's use of a similar technique.

painting displayed in the Forum that depicted an old shepherd with a staff.[153] It is clear that imagery in the Forum was brought to bear in oral argument.

Props Used to Bolster Arguments

The standards of truth in visual arguments were low, however. For example, L. Hostilius Mancinus, the first man to break through the walls at Carthage, employed an image-based campaign technique. He commissioned a painting that portrayed his momentous breach of the Carthaginian walls. He used this painting as a prop to recount the event to all passers-by in the Forum; he also omitted the aftermath, when his commanding general was forced to save Mancinus, since his reckless advance allowed him to be surrounded by the enemy.[154] Nonetheless, Mancinus decided to use an image as a foundation for his campaign; it served as proof of an action that words and oratory alone could not make. Moreover, the prop proved critical and was effective in propelling him into a consulship. Such a use of props added to the vividness of the account, and achieved nearly the same effect as that which Polybius attributes to the spectacle of the *laudatio*: the audio-visual effect helped the audience visualize the events.[155] They also provided a visual form of communication in a context where hearing might not be possible for the majority of the audience.

The Other Imagines *in the Forum*

Romans were acutely aware of the need for visual aids in their public presentations. In the funeral eulogy, the props—the men wearing the *imagines*—stole the show. By the first century BCE, the *imagines* of twenty or more magistrates of varying ranks would have presented an overwhelming show of familial power and the role of the family in Roman history. Such displays would become natural points of comparison for the families of a *novus homo* such as Cicero, C. Maenius, or even M. Porcius Cato, when faced with the task of presenting the *laudatio*. In addition to the temporary *imagines* on display on the Rostra, more permanent *imagines*—statuary of Roman magistrates, legendary founders, and other celebrated personages from myth and history—dotted the Forum with potential, visual referents. In fact, by 158 BCE, there were so many statues in the Forum that the Senate ordered all those un-

---

[153] Plin. *HN* 35.25.

[154] For the story, see Plin. *HN* 35.23. The display angered Aemilianus, who saved Mancinus shortly after he had breached the walls, when he and his troops were cornered by the Carthaginians. Scipio sent Mancinus back to Rome. Brennan 2000: 216 sorts out the historical background for the display. Cf. Broughton 1968: 462n3, who states that Mancinus "had some independence of action and could [have] succeeded, yet he went home at Scipio's command." For a recent discussion of this "unconventional" campaign effort, see Farney 2007: 15. Cf. Gruen 1992: 118, who contends (rightly, I believe) that the use of imagery for aristocratic self-promotion was "an extended continuity in utilization of the arts to further the ends of Roman leaders and the *res publica*." Horsfall 2003: 91 describes the "accidental museum" of the Forum, and uses this example to note that some imagery required explanation, however.

[155] Polyb. 6.53.3: ὑπὸ τὴν ὄψιν.

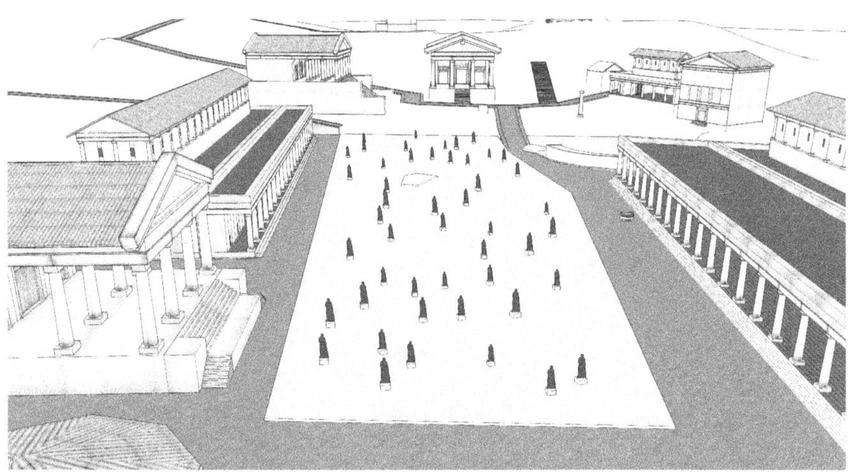

FIGURE 3.26 Hypothetical statuary in the Forum.

approved removed.[156] To help us imagine how the Forum looked at the time of Paullus' funeral, I present a hypothetical distribution of statues in the Forum and the Comitium, see figs. 3.26 and 3.27.) During the middle Republic, the Forum abounded with visual representations. The family of a *novus homo* was, in effect, fighting an uphill symbolic battle against the *imagines* of more established families. Sallust demonstrates the sensitivity to ancestral display when he presents Marius' recruitment rally before he assumes command in Africa:

> Non possum fidei causa imagines neque triumphos aut consulatus maiorum meorum ostentare, at, si res postulet, hastas, uexillum, phaleras, alia militaria dona, praeterea cicatrices aduerso corpore. Hae sunt meae imagines, haec nobilitas, non hereditate relicta, ut illa illis, sed quae ego meis plurimis laboribus et periculis quaesiui. Non sunt composita verba mea: parvi id facio. Ipsa se virtus satis ostendit.
>
> I cannot show as evidence *imagines*, triumphs or consulships of my ancestors, but, if the situation demands it, I [can show] spears, the standard, martial decorations, and other gifts from combat, chiefly the scars on my chest. These are my *imagines*, this is my *nobilitas*, not gained through inheritance, as it is for them, but that which I sought through my many labors and risks. I have not contrived a speech: I don't consider that worth much. My *virtus* stands out on its own.[157]

The visual competition was real: Sallust elevates the visual language and highlights the *necessity* of imagery. For Sallust's Marius, words alone could not demonstrate his *virtus*; it was not enough to mention his success in battle, instead he needed

---

156 Plin. *HN* 34.30.

157 Sall. *Iug.* 85. Flower 1996: 16–23 discusses the historical problems of the speech.

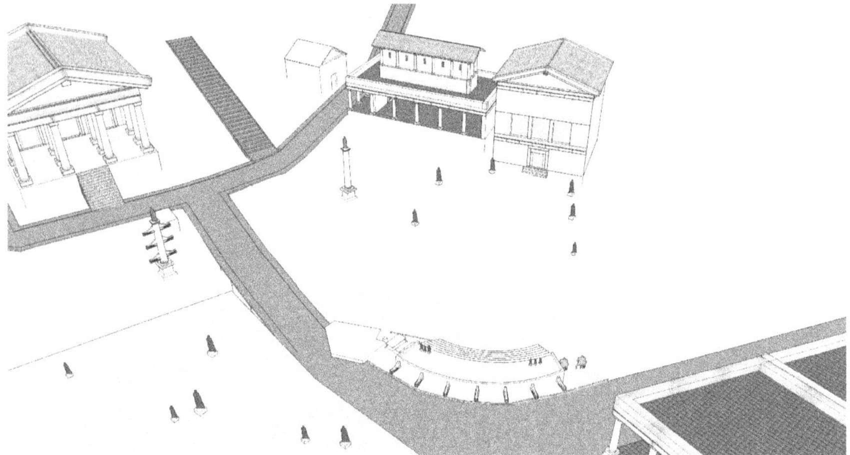

FIGURE 3.27 After Sehlmeyer 1999: 318. Hypothetical statuary on the Comitium. Equestrian statues of C. Maenius and Camillus were set up on or near the Rostra. At least four half-sized pedestrian statues of men who had died on embassy also stood on the Rostra. Statues of Marsyas, Attus Navius, Horatius Cocles, and Hermodorus were in the Comitium. Statues of Alcibiades and Pythagoras were closely tied to the Curia Hostilia.

to use physical scars as props. The visual tradition of aristocratic families and their explicit relationship to the topographical context of the Forum demanded that competitors use visual evidence as well. Mere words were not an adequate substitute for aristocratic imagery. Sallust's Marius felt compelled to point to military gear and spoils, and, in an overtly dramatic gesture, to his own scars. Specific references and gestures to visible elements connected to a broader audience than the words of any speech could address. The *novus homo* knew well his ultimate fate: his *laudator* would one day stand alone on the Rostra, the sole focus of attention, lost amidst the surrounding *imagines* of other families.

As the speech of Marius suggests, however, works and deeds could indeed function as *imagines*, so long as they could be reified. The installation of more permanent visual symbols in the Forum created worthy surrogates. For example, in 338 BCE, C. Maenius redefined the physical setting of the political stage to create a permanent and far more powerful proxy for the *laudatio* in its role as cultural mnemonic device. Two bold moves, one less secure in the sources than the other, defined his revolutionary visual manipulation. The Maenii were not a powerful family.[158] C. Maenius was the only one to achieve the consulship. Nevertheless, by redefining the Comitium, Maenius was able to attain permanent renown for his

[158] C. Maenius (*RE* 9) P. f. P. n. See Broughton 1968: 584.

family. After the naval victory at Antium in 338 BCE, C. Maenius affixed the beaks (*rostra*) of the defeated ships to the speaker's platform in the Forum. As a result, the monument came to be known as the Rostra. By his action, Maenius effectively appropriated public space to transform it into private honorific.[159]

As the first *triumphator* to mount his *spolia* on a monument in the Forum, Maenius stood to gain the complex set of associations inherent in such a move.[160] The speaker's platform became an extension of the private sphere. Its connection to Maenius served as a constant reminder of his deeds. Although there would have been no ancestors at his funeral, his son could have pointed down to the Rostra to remind the audience of his triumph. One bold move was not enough for Maenius, however. In the same year, he erected an honorary column. Its prominence in the funeral landscape is noteworthy. When viewed from any vantage point, monumental columns stand out and fill the highest visual register in the Forum. (See fig. 3.28.) Such appropriation of the public sphere continued. In 260 BCE, C. Duilius installed a rostrated column on or near the Rostra.[161] A statue of Alcibiades stood next to the Senate House, ready to be highlighted by the Aemilii as part of their legendary origins.[162] In 184 BCE, M. Porcius Cato expanded this concept: rather than augmenting a public monument with private *spolia*, he built a new public monument, and gave it his name, the *Basilica Porcia*.[163]

The visual hierarchy of the *laudatio* must be viewed within this context. Potential mnemonic devices—symbols of familial power and Roman history—were spread throughout the Forum. The spatial configuration of the event—the number of ancestors, the location of the orator, and placement of the deceased—directly affects the way the visual form of the *laudatio* competed with these other displays of symbolic capital. Quite simply, elevated imagery in the Forum was more easily visible and more effectively referenced. Elevating the ancestors *and* the deceased placed them in dialog and in direct visual competition with these monumental statements of individual and familial power.[164] Figures 3.29 and 3.30 demonstrate how placing the deceased on the Rostra and propping him up enabled entry into the vertical register of the Forum.

---

159 See Wallace-Hadrill 1990, who notes that Republican monuments, even in public spaces, were primarily privately sponsored.

160 The ownership of *spolia* is the subject of some controversy. Shatzman 1972 was the first to contend that *spolia* fell under the sole purview of the triumphing general. Churchill 1999 argues for state ownership. At all events, some *spolia* had a permanent place on private homes. See Plin. *HN* 35.6: "aliae foris et circa limina animorum ingentium imagines erant adfixis hostium spoliis, quae nec emptori refigere liceret, triumphabantque etiam dominis mutatis aeternae domus." Wiseman 1994: 98–100 connects the display of *spolia* on temples to a similar display on private homes.

161 Plin. *HN* 34.20, Quint. *Inst.* 1.7.12.

162 Smith 2006: 35–36.

163 For the sources, see above, p. 97.

164 Following the theoretical discussion in Roller 2013, the ancestors were temporarily in dialog with the "intersignification" of Republic monuments.

FIGURE 3.28 The Columna Maenia stands on the left, and the rostrated Column of Duilius to the right.

FIGURE 3.29 Reclined atop the Rostra, the deceased is subordinated to the surrounding imagery.

FIGURE 3.30 The propped up deceased participates directly in the vertical competition in the Forum.

The Mime

Thus far I have overlooked a potentially critical player at Paullus' funeral: his double. Diodorus Siculus, when writing about the funeral of Lucius Aemilius Paullus, explains a custom where *mimetai* would study men, notable due to noble birth or noted ancestry, throughout their lives. Upon the death of a man like Paullus, these *mimetai* would take the place of the ancestors and march in the funeral. Diodorus must have confused source material in some way, since it was impossible for such a process to play out over generations within the context of a Roman family's funerary tradition. After all, one could not study the mannerisms of a long-deceased founder of the city. Nonetheless, the further implication is that the tradition later attested during the Empire also held at Paullus' funeral: a man who had observed Paullus during his life portrayed him at the funeral. There is no evidence to tell us how this actor (for lack of a better word) participated in the funeral of the deceased.[165] Did he walk alongside the bier with the mourning family? Did he ride in a chariot of his own? Did he sit in a curule chair on the Rostra? Did he interact with the eulogist? Rather than dismiss this phenomenon entirely, let us briefly consider the experiential ramifications if an actor portrayed Paullus on the Rostra. He either roved about the stage (while possibly offering some form of comic relief), or he sat in a chair with the other ancestors. For the former, the possible visual interpretations are manifold: he might have interacted directly with the body, he might have stood alongside the eulogist to cement the relationship between the two, or

[165] Morstein-Marx and Byrne 2025: 334–335 esp. n24 are convincingly skeptical about a "reanimated" deceased attending "his own funeral."

to provide a guiding hand, or to demonstrate that the family continues. If at some point he were to sit in a curule chair, then the eulogy would also have visually depicted a kind of passage for the deceased, where he would visibly join the specific collection of ancestors who had *imagines* made for them and who would participate in funerals of the family for generations to come. This would have provided satisfying continuity for the audience. It would also have demonstrated a literal transition from living Roman patriarch to actor-portrayed ancestor. The moment the actor sat in the curule chair, he would have established a new role for the deceased: his body was still to be interred, but the man had now joined the group of fellow ancestors; he was, in fact, indistinguishable from those on the stage apart from his specific waxen mask and attire. He would do so in perpetuity. Evidence for the mime is difficult to represent with certainty, and any reconstruction must remain highly speculative.

The Funeral Eulogy as Visual Theater

It should by now be clear that the *laudatio* functioned as visual theater and participated in the ongoing visual competition in the Forum.[166] For the bulk of the audience, the *laudatio* was primarily a multi-sensory experience, not simply an oration where rhetorical flair prevailed on its own. Cicero's disregard of *laudationes* focused entirely on the rhetorical weakness of the speeches, not the overall spectacular effect of the event. Nonetheless, it is absurd to suggest that the content of the speech was irrelevant to the institution. Romans cared about the words in the *laudatio*—they would also serve as the foundation for the recurring praise of ancestors for subsequent generations—but the audience who could actually discern these words was limited. I now return to Polybius' interpretation of audience experience at an aristocratic funeral like that of Paullus.

AUDIENCE(S)

It is hardly surprising that the vast majority of scholars reflect a Polybian analysis of the funeral: these were culturally important, memory-making events. If managed carefully as part of a cultural tradition, one can imagine the emotional effect of a lineup of one's ancestors, living and breathing. These were the heroes that formed Rome; the men who fought in battle; some legendary; these are the men whose names were used to refer to the past, to public buildings, to the years, and to statues. Moreover, these were icons who were visible in paintings, in statuary, and in stories. When icons come to life, in costume, there is a certain power and attraction. Visitors who stand in line at theme parks around the world to take photographs, to greet and interact with their favorite characters, and to cheer them on as they pass by in parade would understand Polybius' basic argument: living, representational

[166] This view aligns well with the overall thesis of Hölkeskamp 2023.

icons have intrinsic power. They draw an audience and are inherently spectacular. When presented in such general terms, the observation of this Greek ethnographer seems sound.[167] Polybius does not stop with his rhetorical question, however. He precisely defines the inspirational effect of the Roman funeral and the *imagines*. Roman youth observed the funeral and wished to attain similar glory, to be sure. More specifically, the institution of the Roman funeral inculcated courage in these same youths to such an extent that Romans would accept challenges of one-on-one combat to decide the fate of an entire army.[168]

Polybius gives evidence to prove that his assertion is true, but the evidence is problematic. He uses the story of Horatius Cocles to illustrate the bravery of Romans inspired by the funerary tradition.[169] When the Etruscan general Lars Porsenna approached Rome with his army, Horatius Cocles stood alone on the Pons Sublicius. As he fought off the Etruscan army, the Roman army destroyed the bridge behind him. Once Rome was safe, Horatius Cocles jumped into the Tiber River, only to drown before he reached the other side. So says Polybius.

Livy tells a different tale.[170] Horatius Cocles survived the swim and was rewarded with the farmland equivalent of a shopping spree. For his courage he was allotted as much land as he could plow around in one day. Livy's variation is troubling, since it indicates that Polybius was not sensitive to the legendary status of his example.[171] Why reach so far back in time to find such an example? And why select an example that had multiple traditions and multiple outcomes? We can ascertain with high confidence that he intentionally used a story of a Roman citizen who had *died* for his country in single combat, rather than an example of one who had fought heroically and lived; in fact, there were many such examples of this latter case.[172]

The logic of Polybius' argument is further complicated when viewed within the context of the funeral assemblage. For a comic but poignant analysis of the underly-

---

[167]Flaig 2003: 51: Polybius was a non-Roman who had sufficient "ethnologische Distanz" to comment on the unusual elements of the funeral. As an educated Greek he could also offer a sophisticated classificatory vocabulary.

[168]On single combat in the Roman world see Oakley 1985, who notes (292): "Modern scholars, however, have taken little notice of this remark and some have tried to belittle the importance of single combat at Rome." Fries 1985 gives a comprehensive treatment of the episodes of single combat in Livy.

[169]Polyb. 6.55.1–4.

[170]Livy 2.10.11.

[171]Walbank 1970: 740: "In contrast to Livy (ii. 10. 11, 'rem ausus plus famae habituram ad posteros quam fidei') P. treats it as wholly historical."

[172]His example is exceedingly strange. The *spolia opima* awarded to Roman generals who had defeated the opposing leader in single combat had a highly visible record. They were dedicated in the shrine of Jupiter Feretrius. Before his death, M. Claudius Marcellus had been awarded the *spolia opima* for his duel in Gaul. (E.g., Livy 4.20.5–11 and Plut *Marc.* 8 give the details and Harrison 1989 treats the apparent Augustan modifications.) Its absence is conspicuous here and in Polybius' earlier account of the Roman victory (Polyb. 2.34). Gruen 1990: 94 notes the omission without comment. A statue of Horatius Cocles stood in the Comitium (Livy 2.10.12 and Gell. *NA* 4.5.1). Sehlmeyer 1999: 92–96 examines the evidence. Was this statue Polybius' inspiration?

ing issue in a different context, John Hodgman reflects on the famous choice given to Achilles—to die young but receive immortal fame, or to live a long life in relative seclusion:

> [I]t was always Achilles' choice that made the story seem as remote as the moon. A choice between a long life that goes unsung and an early death that is remembered forever? Unless you are 19, this is a no-brainer. But Achilles, of course, chases glory.[173]

Though he writes in jest, Hodgman highlights the logical result of such a decision. If Achilles were a Roman, his dramatic death might have been the stuff of legend, but would it have earned him an *imago*? Reading Polybius with no evident skepticism, Dupont notes, "Si le guerrier accepte la mort, c'est qu'il est certain de connaître l'immortalité grâce au rituel funéraire."[174] If, however, a spectacular aristocratic funeral of the mid-Republic was predicated on the deceased's acquisition of a magistracy, then fighting and dying for one's country on the field of battle was the wrong way to achieve a place amongst the ancestors on the Rostra. Edwards rightly notes:

> The men whose *imagines* appear in the funeral processions of their descendants are men who have achieved senior magistracies, as praetors and consuls. These are not men killed in battle in the flower of their youth.[175]

Doubtless there is middle ground in this discussion. The Roman historical tradition records many examples of one-on-one combat, where a Roman magistrate wins. The essence of Polybius' argument holds: based on the historical tradition, it is undeniable that Roman men, some of whom achieved the highest offices, would be motivated by displays of ancestors to emulate their achievements, even to the point of giving their life for their country.

There is another element to consider: Polybius has compressed distinct subsections of the audience. Just as the use of *Quirites* in an address creates a unified whole out of an audience of disparate parts, so Polybius creates a monolithic *populus* who watched the event. There was no such thing. It is possible that Aemilius Paullus' funeral and that of a few other extraordinarily powerful and popular Roman aristocrats attracted a larger proportion of the populace. The funerary sphere invites embellishment and distortion for familial propaganda, however. Polybius was taking part in a similar game. Rather than distort the record of the deceased, Polybius distorted the record of an event. Though the funerary event was a critical element of Roman political life, Polybius amplified its effect on the Romans and struggled to find an example to demonstrate his more narrow argument, namely that this event made Romans superior in battle.

One should always be skeptical when the Roman crowd is described as wholly intent on any subject.[176] The Forum could not have looked like the figures I have

---

173 Hodgman 2008.
174 Dupont 1987: 169.
175 Edwards 2007: 22–23.
176 Connolly 2006: 89.

created. Daily life abided. A significant number of audience members could not have heard the event. Still more might have been intent on their own business. A more subtle reading of Polybius provides clues to the nature of the event. The content of the speech was not directed entirely toward the audience. The speaker did not take the stage to entertain and impress. He did not necessarily have the experience to command a large audience in a setting such as the Forum. Instead, the visual imagery dominated the event. The visual spectacle was designed for the audience. The controllable elements of the spectacle—the ancestral masks, the ceremonial garb, the permanent monuments in and around the Comitium, and the deceased—ensured that a predefined message would be conveyed. Like a theme park parade or even a short performance, few remember what the characters say; it is enough to have seen whatever themed character happened to be present, or even the mascot at a sporting event. The audience could see the symbolic capital, which had been designed in advance and stored away for the family. The words were not as important to certain audience members. But the sight of a bier, with a body propped upright—either fully or reclined—flanked by an array of masked men wearing the regalia of Roman power, was something to see, to note, and to comprehend, even from a distance. The speaker was a small part of a larger, elevated visual display.

The words were not irrelevant, of course. The eulogy was part of a transitional ceremony, and the words of the speech could circulate in written form for years after the event.[177] Some young men were surely inspired to equal the exemplary ancestors sitting before them, and to die for glory. Only some of those ancestral representations on the Rostra were men who fought to the death for Rome. Instead, most were the commanders of armies and the civic leaders of the state. For many, the recited history of Paullus' family on display might have been relatively meaningless, but the parade of prominent and successful Romans might have been awe-inspiring. The story of the family, ultimately, mattered most to the family members themselves, and especially to the eulogist. Lost in the spectacle of the event is the personal view of the orator. He saw the entire Forum from atop the Rostra and may have been experiencing his first opportunity to speak on the Rostra in a sympathetic environment. He alone had the best view of the ancestors. (See figs. 3.31 and 3.32.) *He* could know the words of the speech, since he had himself memorized them. The speaker, more than anyone in the audience, benefitted from the full audio-visual experience. He rehearsed the deeds and accomplishments of his father, as he looked out at the crowd and as he looked directly at the dead body, which had been carefully positioned for one last show. If there was ever a situation for *imagines* to inspire, this was it.[178]

---

[177] Ochs 1993: 90–95, Scheid 1984, Flower 1996: 130–131, and Feldherr 2000: 211, who provides a brief summary of the transitional elements.

[178] Flower 1996: 143 wrestles with the problem: "It is hard to determine whether the section on the careers of the ancestors would have been addressed to them or to the audience. Perhaps they were directly spoken to in a construction parallel to that frequently used for the dead person."

FIGURE 3.31 The eulogist's view, facing the Temple of Saturn.

eius te suscitat
imago, cuius effigia, quo gnatu's patre.

His *imago* stirs you,
the portrait of the father from whom you were born.[179]

The combined power of the spectacle *and* the details of the speech itself was aimed directly at the eulogist.

The *laudatio funebris* was the final stop before the culminating moment for the deceased, but it was not the culmination of the funerary event for the rest of Rome. After the funeral, the procession resumed, heading beyond the city walls to cremate the deceased, in the case of Paullus, but in some cases to inter without cremation in a private setting. Those who happened to be on the Via Appia would have encountered the parade. We do not know whether the chariots, ancestors, and a mime accompanied the procession; in fact we know very little about this particular aspect of an aristocratic funeral. Polybius only writes θάψαντες καὶ ποιήσαντες τὰ νομιζόμενα ("after burying and performing the usual rites"). For the funeral of L. Aemilius Paullus, however, the final act of *his* funeral was *not* the *laudatio* or even the interment. In fact, for many Romans, the *pompa funebris* and the *laudatio* were not even the most spectacular elements of Paullus' funeral, since they could easily have been overshadowed by the final and most critical act, the funeral games (*ludi funebres*).

[179] L. Afranius *Vopiscus* 12.364–365 = Nonius 790L. Context here is elusive, however. The fragment might come from a recognition scene. See Flower 1996: 282.

FIGURE 3.32 The eulogist's view, facing the Curia Hostilia.

CHAPTER 4

Ludi Funebres: A Visual Argument

GLADIATORS, ANCESTORS, AND FUNERALS

This chapter will test the evidence and hypotheses for the staging of gladiatorial matches at the funeral of L. Aemilius Paullus. Gladiatorial combat and its stagecraft have been extensively studied, but no scholarly work to date has assessed how and why these combats were staged within the context of an aristocratic funeral, held within the Roman Forum.

Because this book focuses primarily on one funeral, broader questions related to diverse funerary practices at different times and on different scales are sometimes overlooked. Not all funerals contained all elements discussed thus far. It is by no means clear, for example, that every funeral that could have paraded *imagines* would have done so. It is certainly not the case that all funerals would have included the added expense of *ludi funebres* afterward. These various funerary expenses are similar to the expenditure one might dedicate to a tomb, to a grave marker, a funerary urn, or a sarcophagus. Money mattered and limited what could be done. This book proposes that the aristocratic funeral could be interpreted as a three-act play of spectacle, consisting of the procession, the eulogy, and the subsequent funeral games. A more precise way of wording this statement would be to add that this view applies more specifically to the funeral of Lucius Aemilius Paullus.

I contend that the funeral of Paullus was a three-act event. The first act, the *pompa funebris* performed the practical function of transporting the body to the Roman Forum. It also participated directly in the symbolic landscape of perambulatory spectacle at Rome. Its mode of spectacle resembles major, state-authorized events. The funerary procession operated in a similar sphere as processions for public games and triumphal processions: it was in dialog with state-sponsored activities. The second act, the *laudatio funebris* followed a culturally defined script as reflected in Polybius' discussion of the aristocratic funeral. There was room for experimentation and creativity, to be sure, but the use of *imagines* and the nature of praise for a Roman aristocrat was constrained by custom. This custom elevated the importance of patrilineal power and generational success of the family. It was an event that interacted directly with the foundation of Rome and the competition of symbolic capital ongoing in the Roman Forum. The final act, the funeral games, was something different. It was not a state-sponsored activity and it was not in dialog with the political past of Rome. Instead, it was a clear manifestation and celebration of the living family. Ostensibly put on to honor the deceased, it was an opportunity for the survivors to hold an event that celebrated the present and the future. It no longer centered visually on the deceased but instead was an event to advertise the continuing potential of those who were staging the games, most often the surviving children.

This chapter focuses on Paullus' funeral, but not before we attempt to understand the overall chronological and spatial context for *ludi funebres*. When did gladiators first fight in Rome? When did the Romans of the second century BCE think this happened? Were gladiatorial fights common at funerals? Were they regularly held in Rome at all? How do gladiatorial games and the use of ancestor masks relate to each other? I suggest that the three-act nature of this funeral supplies one answer to that question.

TEMPORARY STAGING, AND *AD HOC* EVENTS

The *ad hoc* nature of a Roman funeral in the middle Republic helps inform our understanding of the staging of the games that followed. The particular form of funeral games held at Rome and their method of staging illustrate both the necessity for a flexible staging apparatus and the overwhelming effect the topographical and symbolic features of the Roman Forum had on the entire funerary spectacle. The Forum was not designed as a theater; and the Republican Forum never had a coherent and logical design. Yet a combination of symbolic and practical advantages outweighed the inconvenience of staging games in such a cluttered and irregular space.

Roman funeral games arose from a Mediterranean tradition of games and combats held at the grave site.[1] These games were apparently a blend of Greek-style athletic competitions, acrobatics, boxing matches, and armed combats. For the Romans, according to our textual evidence, the most well-known element of Roman funeral games were gladiatorial shows. In fact, the evidence used to debate whether gladiatorial games originated in Etruria or Campania is almost entirely funerary

[1] See K. Hopkins 1983 esp. 3–13. Kyle 2001: 45 summarizes the evidence and notes: "The origin of gladiatorial and beast combats is probably not a historical question answerable in terms of a single original location (e.g., sacrifice, contests, vengeance, scapegoats), and a simple linear transmission (e.g., Etruria to Rome). Combats, sacrifices, and blood sports were simply too widespread in antiquity."

in nature or context.[2] The Romans may have initially held all funeral rites at the tomb, like their Etruscan neighbors to the north or their Campanian neighbors to the south. Indeed, the grave site continued to serve as the location of the *laudatio* for those unable or unwilling to use the Rostra.[3] The ancient sources offer only glimpses into the aristocratic innovation that transferred the staging location from the tomb to the city center, however. In Rome, the first recorded funeral games were held in 264 BCE in the Forum Boarium for Decimus Iunius Brutus.[4] After 264 BCE, all documented occurrences of funeral games at Rome before the first century BCE were apparently held in the Roman Forum.

At some point in the third century, Roman aristocrats amplified the spectacle of the event and overtly politicized it by translating the games from the tomb to the central civic and political space.[5] A similar decision must have been made when Roman elites chose to move the *laudatio* to the Forum, most likely to take full advantage of the benefits of such a politically charged space. Regardless of when such moves took place, by the end of the third century BCE, the *laudatio funebris* and the *ludi funebres* were tightly coupled. *Ludi* for the funeral differed substantially from other Roman *ludi*, however. For one, staging in the Forum precluded certain kinds of games. One could not hold Greek-style athletic contests in the Forum. There was neither room nor a smooth and level tract of land available.[6] Instead, events of a more portable variety were required. Gladiatorial combats fit the bill perfectly. Their traditional staging had to be flexible. If they were held at the family tomb, then their early staging occurred at the boundaries of the city, wherever space could be had adjacent to the tomb. In this way they resembled Roman dramatic performances of the Republic, which often had to adapt to specific spaces, since the association with a religious cult was of primary importance to the festival celebration.[7] The need to be held in a specific location not designed for the show superseded the practical needs of accommodating the audience. In central Italy,

[2] Tert. *De spect.* 12 claims that gladiatorial games arose from human sacrifice performed *in exequiis*. Tomb paintings from sixth–fifth-century Tarquinia display some form of violent games used to commemorate the dead, and late fourth-century tomb paintings from Campania seem to show funeral games consisting of chariot races, boxers, and armed combatants. For an overview see Vismara 2001: 20–21, K. Hopkins 1983: 3–13, and Kyle 2001: 64n64.

[3] Flower 1996: 132. Kierdorf 1980: 112–116.

[4] Val. Max. 2.4.7, Livy *Per.* 16.6, and Auson. *Griphus* 36–37. Its location, a public space and a popular entryway into the city, defined the southwestern boundary of the Romulean Pomerium (Tac. *Ann.* 12.24). The sources seem to reflect this liminality. While Valerius Maximus gives the Forum Boarium as the location, Ausonius records that the games were held at the tomb. The location might represent an initial transition in which the gladiatorial combats moved from the tomb to the closest public space in Rome.

[5] K. Hopkins 1983: 14–19.

[6] Furthermore, according to Livy (39.22), Greek-style games were not introduced to Rome until the triumph of Fulvius Nobilior in 186 BCE: "athletarum quoque certamen tum primo Romanis spectaculo fuit." Köhne 2000b: 10 notes: "Their performances do not seem to have been to the public taste—or at least, the sources show that the next athletic contest was not held in Rome until 80 BC."

[7] I argue below that staging considerations for gladiatorial games resembled (*mutatis mutandis*) the staging practices proposed in Goldberg 1998 and expanded upon in Goldberg 2018, who contends that

armed combats always had a funerary association, but their inherent portability allowed them to follow the funeral and to be staged rapidly in places not necessarily designed for their production.

GLADIATORS AT THE FUNERAL

While textual evidence strongly suggests that gladiators appeared at Rome only within the context of a funeral, such a view by no means represents the scholarly consensus. Nowhere is the overwhelming effect of Polybius' account on the scholarly record more apparent than in the general disregard of the games that followed the *pompa* and the *laudatio*. The broad dissemination of the relief from Amiternum (see Chapter 2), by chance, parallels the scholarly treatment of the Polybian story. The relief is a nearly complete depiction of an aristocratic funeral procession, lacking only a representation of the ancestors. And yet, it is almost always discussed separately from what was very likely a companion piece from the same tomb: a relief that depicts a pair of warriors engaged in combat, brandishing spears and rectangular shields, and flanked by two attendants.[8] (See fig. 4.1.) After their initial publication, these two reliefs have not since been cited adjacent to each other, in the same scholarly work, even though for years they were displayed side-by-side in the Museo Nazionale d'Abruzzo.

Modern scholarship has compartmentalized the study of the funeral. Inquiry into the spectacle of the funerary ritual focuses almost exclusively on the *pompa*, the *laudatio*, and the interment. Likewise, studies of gladiatorial shows examine the practicalities of staging the games without taking into account the greater funerary context. Scholars are hardly unaware of the connection—prior to the late Republic, the literary sources *only* record gladiatorial games associated with a funeral commemoration.[9] Rather, firmly rooted preconceptions coupled with evidentiary lacunae have resulted in a redirection of research priorities. Research has bifurcated in such a way that the games are a footnote to Roman funerary studies, and the funeral a footnote to the history of gladiatorial combat.

The later prevalence of monumental amphitheaters throughout the Roman Empire has focused scholarly conversation. The Colosseum attracts tourists and scholars. It was the first monumental building type dedicated to showcasing gladiatorial games, and it represents a material separation between the privately-sponsored fu-

---

Roman stagecraft of the middle Republic required only a constructed stage, not an entire theater. The audience took care of itself.

[8] The relief was first published in Fiorelli 1879: 147. Franchi 1966: 30 considers them *bustuarii*—gladiators who fought at the tomb—garbed as Sabines or Samnites. The connection must remain speculative. The reliefs were found in close proximity to one another, but not in their original context. There are, of course, other examples of gladiatorial imagery found in funerary contexts, see, e.g., Papini 2004: 115–148. There are also numerous Etruscan and Oscan examples, see, e.g., Torelli 1999.

[9] On the gladiatorial games as an exclusively funerary event until the late Republic, see, e.g., Ville 1981: 42–51, Bodel 1999: 260, Futrell 2000: 18–24, Coarelli 2001, Welch 2007: 18–22.

FIGURE 4.1 The gladiatorial relief from Amiternum, now located in the Museo Nazionale d'Abruzzo dell'Aquila. Image created by Christopher Johanson and derived from Guidi 2015, an interactive 3D model of the relief.

nerary practice of the Republic and the later, state-sponsored performances of the Empire. By *ca.* 70 BCE, permanent monumental amphitheaters had been erected in Italy.[10] The first attested stone amphitheater in Rome was not built until 29 BCE, however.[11] In fact, based solely on extant textual evidence, it was only near the end of the Republic that gladiatorial games in Rome were staged without a stated connection to a funerary event.[12] Before then, the games at Rome were, with one exception, *always* held in the Roman Forum and, according to the literary sources, *always* associated with a Roman aristocratic funeral.[13] Nonetheless, studies of the

[10] See Welch 2007: 179–263 for a complete catalog of the 18 extant Republican amphitheaters.

[11] On the amphitheater of Statilius Taurus, see Cass. Dio 51.23.1 and Coarelli 2001.

[12] In the Cerealia of 42 BCE, the aediles seem to have put on gladiatorial games in lieu of horse races. See Cass. Dio 47.40.6: οἱ ἀγορανόμοι τοῦ πλήθους ὁπλομαχίας ἀγῶνας ἀντὶ τῆς ἱπποδρομίας τῇ Δήμητρι ἐπετέλεσαν."

[13] See Bodel 2024: 320, who comments on the move of eulogy and games to the Forum: "for the rest of the Republican period, the Forum became the standard venue both for funerary orations for élite men and for gladiatorial combats, all of which that we know of were offered as funerary games." The evidentiary picture is far from complete, and there is reason for caution: by 44 BCE, municipally sponsored gladiatorial combats were clearly attested in the amphitheaters outside of Rome. See Welch 2007: 77–79, who notes, among other things, that the existence of Sullan *tesserae* could suggest "the possibility of official organization" of the combats. See as well Purcell 2022: 183: "The newly transformed Forum of the early third century was already the stage for elite funerals, however, an important and very long-lasting aspect of its public role, which intersected with the life of the people through the long-lasting tradition of the funerary laudation and the games staged to honour the deceased."

early form and structure of gladiatorial combat retroject, to some degree, the later, more elaborate spectacles into the earlier Forum context. How we arrived at this point is understandable and a natural consequence of two overlapping theories put into practice. The first is that later monumental amphitheaters derived from earlier, wholly enclosed wooden bleacher systems that resembled the later amphitheaters made of stone and concrete. The second is that, once games are staged in an enclosed, purpose-built space, they become literally and figuratively self-contained. Once one engages with this kind of reconstruction, it is simple enough to imagine that the Republican games held within those self-contained spaces, for which we have little direct evidence, were equally as elaborate as the games that would be staged in the Imperial period. It is challenging to envision the Imperial version of gladiatorial contests staged within the significant constraints caused by a more direct association with the death of an aristocratic. When one envisions the construction of large, temporary amphitheaters, wooden theaters for dramatic performances, and circus contests, the scale of these events could easily exceed the possibilities allowed by the limited time frame of the funeral. After all, apart from exceptional circumstances, for the funeral events to have included games, the games would have had to occur within a few days of the death. To offer games within days of the unexpected death of a Roman aristocrat would have allowed very little time to organize an overly elaborate staging apparatus.[14] Research on the gladiatorial games tends to treat them as separate, stand-alone events, with their own scheduling and staging concerns. By the time of the first century, this is a valid approach, but in the third and second centuries, the situation differed.

Polybius never mentions the games in his lengthy description of the funeral, but he mentions them elsewhere and in such a way as to indicate that the games were a common feature of a funeral. Therefore, though Polybius is aware of the custom of *munera* at a funeral, the description of Republican funerary practice—the longest extant—culminates in the *laudatio*. Guided by this passage in Polybius, modern scholars tend to view the *pompa* and the *laudatio* as the primary and spectacular events of a Roman funeral in the middle Republic.[15] A simple and plausible reason for this omission is that *ludi funebres* were uncommon events. It is striking to consider that our understanding of the funeral would be quite different had Polybius continued his reflection on the funeral by describing the games. Instead, he mentions the burial and alludes to other customs: "θάψαντες καὶ ποιήσαντες τὰ νομιζόμενα" ("after burying and performing the usual rites"). Much later in his *Histories* he notes that the sons of Aemilius wished to stage games for their father on the occasion of his death—and curiously, in this context, he does not assert that staging games at a funeral was peculiar or a rarity, only that they were expensive. In fact, he is familiar enough with the cost structure of such games that he is able

---

[14] Gilula 1989: 285: "Things were not done so quickly in those days."

[15] Bodel 1999: 16: "The principal attractions of the aristocratic funeral during the Republic were in any case the cortège (*pompa*) and the public eulogy in the Forum (*laudatio*)."

to give a price.[16] Granted, this price is extraordinary, and only the most wealthy at Rome could afford such a sum. The fundamental question, which is beyond the scope of this book, is how many families could have afforded such an expense. If only a handful of families possessed the wealth to hold games, then that was the limiting factor, but if the elite in Rome of the second century BCE generally possessed such extraordinary wealth, then one might expect games to be held more regularly. Extant evidence is hardly decisive. For example, Plutarch discusses the funeral of Paullus, but, like Polybius, he also omits the games. Why? Most likely, because his narrative highlights how the modest celebration of virtue rather than lavish expenditure was the distinguishing mark of Paullus' funeral.[17] In my view, Polybius' omission of the games in his earlier discussion of the funeral is far from rock-solid proof that games were a rarity. If anything, the evidence from Polybius is unambiguous: a funeral for an aristocrat comprised a procession, a eulogy, and, when children wished to do so and had the means, gladiatorial games. Nonetheless, the absence of the games in Polybius' description of the funeral contributes to a tension in modern scholarship: the games are always vaguely considered a part of the funeral, but the details are never explicitly addressed. Questions such as when and how often the games occurred, what they comprised, and how they were staged in relation to the rest of the funeral are ignored, or assessed within the context of the first century rather than the second.

Did Every Funeral Have Gladiatorial Games?

One assumes that not every aristocratic funeral had gladiatorial games, but this assumption requires scrutiny. In contrast to studies of Roman funerary practice, where the games are generally an afterthought in comparison to the *pompa* and *laudatio*, studies of gladiatorial combat are emphatic: gladiators *only* fought within a funerary context until the late Republic.[18] Therefore, it appears that the lens through which one views these historical phenomena conditions one's conclusions, but when viewed through both lenses—funerary and gladiatorial—there is a relatively clear path of convergence. Instead of asking whether gladiatorial games were regularly staged at Roman funerals, one should first ask: how often were gladiatorial games staged at Rome? One might then juxtapose a similar question: how often do we think significant Roman aristocratic funerals, replete with *imagines*, were likely to have been held in Rome? Finally, we might conclude: if all gladiatorial

---

[16] Polyb. 31.28.6: "The whole sum is not less than 30 talents, if someone does it at a lavish scale." ἔστι δ' οὐκ ἐλάττων ἡ σύμπασα τριάκοντα ταλάντων, ἐάν τις μεγαλομερῶς ποιῇ.

[17] Plut. *Aem.* 39.7–8: ταῦτα δ' ἦν οὐ χρυσὸς οὐδ' ἐλέφας οὐδ' ἡ λοιπὴ πολυτέλεια καὶ φιλοτιμία τῆς παρασκευῆς, ἀλλ' εὔνοια καὶ τιμὴ καὶ χάρις.

[18] Dodge 2011: 22: "Over the next two centuries the scale and frequency of gladiatorial shows steadily increased; they were still staged within a funerary context, but became an increasingly significant part of more general aristocratic status display." Carter 2009: 302: "During the mid Republic especially, when gladiatorial spectacles were directly associated with aristocratic funerals, the loss of such important men—the civic and military leaders—was felt not simply by the family of the deceased, but by the entire community."

games were staged within a funerary context, and if there were a limited but regular number of funerals, *and* if evidence suggests that gladiatorial games occurred on a regular basis in Rome, then, for every funeral whose family had means, there is a likely chance that funeral games with gladiators were held. It might have been the case that funerals with *imagines* on parade were more likely to host gladiatorial games, since those families would have had more wealth, but one might equally imagine that a paucity of *imagines* could also lead a family to sponsor games to compensate for this deficiency. Regardless of any larger conclusion, it is certainly the case that *ludi funebres* were held at the funeral of L. Aemilius Paullus.

Ephemeral Games

I contend that the transitory and ephemeral nature of the games underscores the *ad hoc* nature of funerary activity and spectacle in the Forum of the middle Republic. The Forum space was used for spectacular performances of disparate kinds, but it was not designed with this purpose in mind—in fact, it was hardly designed at all.[19] Instead, the multi-use nature of the space and the overlapping activities occurring therein simultaneously constrained and augmented spectacle in the Forum. Commemorating the death of a family member within the Forum required that all the events occur immediately. A death apparently offered the only legitimate means for a family to hold a multi-day celebration within the Forum, but this was only possible, in part, because the celebration did not unduly disrupt day-to-day activity and did not alter the built environment of the area.

So far I have laid the groundwork for studying the funeral games within the context of the funerary celebration of the middle Republic. I argue that the *ludi funebres* were the capstone of a multi-day spectacle, the purpose of which, in part, was to offer a continuous showcase of generations of continuous familial power within the Forum. The display of symbolic capital did not end with the *laudatio*, only to be continued at a later date with games. Rather, the display of the deceased and the ancestors was also the beginning of the *ludi funebres*, a multi-day series of events that were *sui generis* due, in part, to their staging location, the Roman Forum. Reconnecting the games to the funeral requires a reexamination of the source material—primarily textual—a reevaluation of accepted hypotheses, and a recombination of arguments that have been artificially separated. I first establish the explicit spatial and temporal connection between the games and the funeral. Next, I force current hypotheses on the staging of various components of the *ludi funebres* to confront the textual and visual evidence of the middle Republic. Having established the primary difficulties in staging the games in the Forum, I argue that portability and adaptability were the defining traits of activities at mid-Republican funeral games. To conclude, I contend that the funeral games of the middle Republic were, simultaneously, the most important spectacular element of the funerary

---

[19] Only later would Vitruvius make such a claim (Vitr. 5.1.1–2). See p. 158.

apparatus for surviving family, *and* that they were staged so as to exploit the surrounding environment. Like the rest of the funeral, the key to their performance was the opportunity for the family to engage with the Forum space: the speed and relative ease of their staging was critical.

TIMING

As was the case for the *pompa funebris* and the *laudatio*, the evidence from the first century BCE for gladiatorial games can potentially mislead studies focused on earlier time periods. By the first century BCE, funeral games did not always occur immediately after burial. Most often cited are the games given by Caesar in 65 BCE for his father, twenty years after the funeral, and for his daughter in 46 BCE, eight years after her death.[20] The funeral games of Agrippa were delayed five years, and those for Drusus the Elder, fourteen.[21] Similar examples are difficult to find prior to the late Republic. Nonetheless, this later practice distorts the record for earlier funerals.

A Roman aristocrat had to balance innovation with tradition. The symbolic capital inherent in a Roman funeral was not easy to employ, however. A funeral presented an opportunity to hold a *contio* for familial self-advertisement. It also let the family temporarily dedicate a section of the Forum to a celebration of its historical power. At the time of Julia's death, it was still apparently the *only* occasion to call for gladiatorial games. There were many possible avenues for a family to fund public spectacle, even in the Forum, but if a Roman aristocrat wished to demonstrate public largesse through an event of massive scale *in the Forum*, put on solely to celebrate his family, he needed a death in that family.[22] During Caesar's aedileship in 65, while fully realizing the power of gladiatorial games, he did not attempt to hold them as independent celebrations.[23] The connection between the games and the funerary tradition was too strong to break for political expedience. Instead, he had to claim that they commemorated his father.[24] It is possible that these funerary games were the first to be held at Rome years after the death of the

[20] For the games dedicated to Caesar's father in 65 BCE, see Cass. Dio 37.8 and Plin. *HN* 33.53. For those dedicated to Julia held in 46 BCE, see Suet. *Iul.* 26.2 and Cass. Dio 43.22.3.

[21] For the funerals of Agrippa and Drusus the Elder, see Swan 2004: 77, who notes, "To hold funeral games five years after a death was not unusual."

[22] Futrell 2000: 30: "The *munera* had much to offer as an implement of public persuasion, and one could not count on a death occurring at the optimal moment. The temporal connection between the death of a noted individual and the production of *munera* was therefore stretched quite thin."

[23] On the commemorative nature of the games, see Cass. Dio 37.8 and Plin. *HN* 33.53: "in aedilitate munere patris funebri." The same was apparently the case for Q. Gallius during his campaign for the praetorship in 66 BCE. Among various irregularities associated with his candidacy, he held gladiatorial games in honor of his father (Asc. *Tog. cand.* 88): "Q. Gallium, quem postea reum ambitus defendit, significare videtur. Hic enim cum esset praeturae candidatus, quod in aedilitate quam ante annum gesserat bestias non habuerat, dedit gladiatorium munus sub titulo patri se id dare."

[24] Futrell 2000: 238n97 details the argument surrounding a possible institutionalization of gladiatorial games in 105 BCE, and Edmondson 1996: 79n39 expands upon the bibliography. Before the official

deceased, but there is no evidence to guide us. One should take care not to apply the exceptions of the late Republic—especially those attached to Caesar—to earlier times.

Notwithstanding this anomaly and the rapidly changing political landscape of the first century BCE, our admittedly limited extant sources reveal that the games in the second century BCE were expected to occur soon after the obsequies. In general, due to the nature of evidence in the middle Republic, it is impossible to know with any degree of certainty the time comprising the lying in state, the *pompa*, the eulogy, and the games. In the case of the games, direct evidence has eluded us, but clues remain.

Tradition held that funeral games were to be staged on the ninth day following the death. According to the fourth-century CE grammarian, Servius, the body of the deceased remained in the home for seven days. On the eighth, it was cremated, and on the ninth, it was buried:

> Apud maiores ubiubi quis fuisset extinctus, ad domum suam referebatur ... et illic septem erat diebus, octavo incendebatur, nono sepeliebatur. unde Horatius novendiales dissipare pulveres; inde etiam ludi qui in honorem mortuorum celebrabantur novendiales dicuntur.
>
> Among our ancestors, wherever someone died, he was carried back to his own home ... and he remained there for seven days. On the eighth he was cremated, and on the ninth, he was interred. Whence Horace writes *novendiales dissipare pulveres*; also, for this reason, the *ludi* that were celebrated in honor of the dead are called *novendiales*.[25]

It is elsewhere attested that the ninth day had a certain funerary significance, but it is only here that we are given a time frame for the *ludi funebres*.[26] One proceeds with caution; the days of this custom had long since passed.[27] Nonetheless, Servius seems to have read Virgil correctly.

In Book Five of the *Aeneid*, Aeneas returns to Sicily, the final resting place of his father, Anchises, whom he had buried in haste. A year to the day had passed since Anchises' death. Aeneas calls for funeral games:

---

institutionalization of the games in 42 BCE, Caesar was party to an earlier innovation. Among the large number of honors given to him in early 44 was the setting aside of one day per year for gladiatorial games in Rome and in all of Italy. Cass. Dio 44.6.2: κἀν ταῖς ὁπλομαχίαις μίαν τινὰ ἀεὶ ἡμέραν καὶ ἐν τῇ Ῥώμῃ καὶ ἐν τῇ ἄλλῃ Ἰταλίᾳ ἀνέθεσαν. Edmondson 1996: 79n39 reminds us that "since this was part of a set of sycophantic honors voted to Caesar just before his assassination, it is unlikely to have been put into practice."

[25] Serv. ad *A.* 5.64.

[26] Servius and Horace are but two of the voices to connect the ninth day to interment. Porphyr. ad Hor. *Epod.* 17.49 notes, "novendiale dicitur sacrificium quod mortuo fit nona die qua sepultus est." Mankin 1995 *ad loc.* discusses most of the sources related to the *ludi novendiales*, but acknowledges that the evidence is "scanty." See also August. *Quaest. in Heptat.* 1.172. Libations and a funeral banquet, the *novendialis cena*, would also take place on the ninth day; see Petron. *Sat.* 64–65 and Tac. *Ann.* 6.5.

[27] Servius ad *A.* 5.64 undermines his credibility when he adds that "[pulveres] etiam domi suae sepeliebantur, unde orta est consuetudo, ut dii penates colantur in domibus." ("Ashes were also buried in their own home, from whence arose the custom that the *penates* are worshiped at home.")

si nona diem mortalibus almum
Aurora extulerit radiisque retexerit orbem.

If the ninth dawn has brought forth a nurturing day for man
and covered the world with its rays.[28]

Aeneas, true to Virgil's Homeric model, presents Greek-style games—not gladiatorial shows—but adheres to the Roman tradition that they be held on the symbolic ninth day after the death.[29]

Silius Italicus, writing a century later, puts forth a similar sequence of events. In 211 BCE, P. and Cn. Cornelius Scipio, the father and uncle of Scipio Africanus, were killed in Spain. In 206 BCE, Africanus returned to New Carthage to fulfill his vow to commemorate their deaths.[30] Evidently, due to the exigencies of the war, he was unable to offer proper funerary rites prior to victory. Again, according to Silius, efforts were made to replicate the entire ceremony of a more traditional funeral, which included funerary games:

Iamque dies praedicta aderat, coetuque sonabat
innumero campus, simulatasque ordine iusto
exequias rector lacrimis ducebat obortis.
omnis Hiber, omnis Latio sub nomine miles
dona ferunt tumulisque super flagrantibus addunt.
ipse, tenens nunc lacte, sacro nunc plena Lyaeo
pocula, odoriferis aspergit floribus aras.
tum manis uocat excitos laudesque uirorum
cum fletu canit et ueneratur facta iacentum.
Inde refert sese circo et certamina prima
incohat ac rapidos cursus proponit equorum.

Now the established day had arrived, and the plain
resounded with the gathering of a huge assemblage. The director led
a surrogate funeral procession with proper rites and tears overflowing.
Every Iberian soldier and every soldier under the Latian name
bore gifts, and added them above the burning tumulus.
Scipio himself, holding cups of milk and cups filled with sacred wine,
sprinkled the altars with sweet-smelling flowers.
Then he called on their *manes* to rise, and he sang tearful
praises for them, and he honored the deeds of those who had fallen.
From there, he brought himself back to the circus, began the
first contests, and exhibited the fast race courses of the steeds.[31]

---

[28] Verg. *Aen.* 5.64–65.

[29] Kehoe 1989: 251–252 notes that Virgil neatly combines an aetiological story of the *parentalia*, which lasted nine days, with Roman funerary custom for the games.

[30] For the deaths of P. and Cn. Cornelius Scipio: Livy 25.32.1–34.14 and 25.35.1–36.16. The return: Livy 28.1 and Sil. *Pun.* 16.304*ff.*

[31] Sil. *Pun.* 16.304–312. For a persuasive reevaluation of the Roman views toward the *manes* and their relationship to the funeral, see King 2020, esp. 128–146.

Since the games are *certamina*, they represent a reconciliation of Greek epic tradition and Roman custom.[32] Nonetheless, these games begin with a compressed funerary ritual. On the appointed day the *rector*, Scipio, led a "surrogate funeral procession" (*simulatas exequias*) to the burial mound. There, Scipio sang praises for the men (*laudes virorum*) and "honored their deeds" (*ueneratur facta*). Thereupon, he returned to the circus for the games. Therefore, Silius Italicus envisions a simulated funeral procession, complete with a *laudatio* at the tomb, followed immediately by the games.

As a final example of games presented as a necessary part of the funeral, I adduce Viriathus, the Lusitanian leader who received a funeral in 140 BCE that paralleled Roman funerary custom.[33] This legendary figure received an "extraordinary funeral that befit a great man."[34] There was a pyre, and paeans were sung in his honor. All sat around until the fire had died down. They then organized gladiatorial games, where two hundred pairs of gladiators fought at his tomb.[35] Though the activities described were explicitly not Roman (e.g., βαρβαρικῶς), the model for the funeral reflects the Roman practice of tightly coupling the exequies and the subsequent ludic celebration: the army staged gladiatorial combats at the tomb without even a delay to build temporary bleachers.

For the specific timing of the event, one must accept that multiple hypotheses rather than one final conclusion will result. Either the games were held on the day of the interment, or they were delayed for an indeterminate length of time. Each hypothesis rests on substantially different assumptions. For the games to have been held so soon after the death means that they had to be relatively easy to assemble, whereas holding the games at a fixed point, weeks or months after the funeral, implies more complicated performances and more elaborate spectacle. Most important, the body and the funeral pomp would not have accompanied games that were delayed weeks or months after the death.

LUDI FUNEBRES: DEFINITIONS AND DURATION

Knowledge about the funeral games in the middle Republic hinges upon informed speculation. Edmondson notes: "It is often forgotten that we have evidence for only a tiny percentage of all the *munera* that were staged in Rome."[36] Sweeping generalizations about the games during this time period are problematic. In many ways, even less is known about the funerary games of the middle Republic than the *lau-*

---

[32] See above, note 6.

[33] App. *Iber.* 75 and Diod. Sic. 33.21a.

[34] Diod. Sic. 33.21a: "ταφῆς παραδόξου καὶ μεγαλοπρεποῦς."

[35] App. *Iber.* "περιθέοντες αὐτὸν ἔνοπλοι βαρβαρικῶς ἐπῄνουν μέχρι τε σβεσθῆναι τὸ πῦρ παρεκάθηντο πάντες ἀμφ' αὐτό. καὶ τῆς ταφῆς ἐκτελεσθείσης ἀγῶνα μονομάχων ἀνδρῶν ἤγαγον ἐπὶ τοῦ τάφου." For the two hundred pairs: Diod. Sic. 33.21a: "διακοσίοις ζεύγεσι μονομάχων ἀγῶνα πρὸς τῷ τάφῳ συνετέλεσαν."

[36] Edmondson 1996: 75. Ville 1981: 42–51 discusses the sources.

datio or the *pompa*. Therefore, basic assumptions must be questioned. First among them: the definition, duration, and content of the games.

In modern scholarship, Roman funeral games are called two different names: *ludi* and *munera*. Bodel presents the orthodox and generally applicable view:

> Already in the second century BCE gladiatorial combats were regarded as the special "gift" (*munus*) of the heirs to the people at the funeral of a great man, and other forms of entertainment—theatrical performances, *ludi scaenici*, and "funeral games," *ludi funebres* (probably combat sports, such as boxing, and chariot races)—were sometimes provided as well.[37]

Strictly speaking, no firm regulations and no technical terminology governed the word choice in antiquity. For the games of L. Aemilius Paullus, such strict delineation is difficult to detect in the sources. Only in authors who wrote after Cicero does the unqualified use of *munera*, the plural form of *munus*, generally signify "gladiatorial games."[38] Earlier, one reads *munus gladiatorium* and *munus gladiatorum*.[39] But there might also be *munera ludorum* or *munera venationum*.[40] In Cic. *Off.* 2.57, the *magnificentissima munera* held by Pompey at the inauguration of his theater complex in 55 BCE included dramatic and athletic performances, as well as a *venatio*, but most likely did not include gladiatorial combats.[41]

In Cicero's discussion of funerary law and custom in the Twelve Tables, he alludes to a *de facto* rule concerning *ludi funebres*:

> Reliqua sunt in more: funus ut indicatur *si quid ludorum*, dominusque funeris utatur accenso atque lictoribus, honoratorum virorum laudes in contione memorentur, easque etiam ut cantus ad tibicinem prosequatur.
>
> The remaining [activities] are dictated by custom: that a funeral be announced if there are to be any *ludi*, and that the funeral director employ an attendant and lictors, that the *laudes* for the honored men be recalled in a *contio*, and also that a song sung to the pipe follow these.[42]

Dyck concludes, "The announcement is thus de rigueur if games are to be held."[43] The presence of games was apparently the deciding factor as to whether a funeral should be formally announced. The implication is that the most important funerary events—those with *ludi*—would have required some form of official sanction. Following this interpretation, one could not commandeer part of the Forum for a

---

[37] Bodel 1999: 260.

[38] Ville 1981: 72–78 discusses the variation in usage.

[39] Cic. *Har. resp.* 26.56 and Cic. *Off.* 2.55.

[40] Cic. *Off.* 2.55: "gladiatorum muneribus ludorum venationumque."

[41] Cic. *Off.* 2.57: "magnificentissima vero nostri Pompei munera secundo consulatu." As Jory 1986: 539 correctly notes, neither Cass. Dio 39.38 nor Plut. *Pomp.* 52 mentions gladiators, and Cicero (*Fam.* 7.1.3: "Nam quid ego te athletas putem desiderare, qui gladiatores contempseris?") refers only to Marius' earlier disdain of gladiators.

[42] Cic. *Leg.* 2.61–62.

[43] Dyck 2003: 409.

major spectacle without making a formal declaration.[44] It seems that one could not hold a *contio* at the Rostra without first reserving the space either. Cicero refers to *ludi* specifically, but one wonders whether even here it is a blanket term covering all possible "games." To assume otherwise would mean that there would have been a very specific custom that pertained only to *ludi* strictly defined—*i.e.*, circus games and boxing matches—or are *scaenici* included as well?—and not to *munera*.[45] Furthermore, it would be striking that such a custom would only apply to *ludi* as strictly defined but not to *munera*, since all activities of this nature would require defined space in the Forum. Depending on context, *munera* and *ludi funebres* might refer to a range of funerary events.

I suspect that *ludi funebres* encompass the entire set of celebratory activities that accompanied the funeral, because there is surprisingly little evidence detailing what, specifically, the *ludi* comprised. In fact, within the Roman context, the English translation, "games," may miss the underlying definition of *ludi*. For example, one of the most famous and certainly the longest *ludi* at Rome were the *Ludi Romani*. These state-sanctioned *ludi* comprised processions, sacrifices, and shows of various kinds. I suggest that "festival" or even "celebrations" is a better translation in modern English to describe events that span multiple days. Such an interpretation can also help us understand the meaning of *ludi funebres*. Yes, they are conventionally called "games," and I will continue to use that translation throughout this book, but they are much more. I suggest that one should consider *ludi funebres* as analogous to *Ludi Romani* or *Ludi Megalenses*: *ludi funebres* are funerary celebrations, whose most critical, practical component is that they reserve public space and time. They consisted primarily of gladiatorial games. Only writers of epic, who inserted Roman custom into a Greek framework, include circus contests. Therefore, aside from gladiatorial combats, the *only* other documented events associated repeatedly with *ludi funebres* were dramatic performances. For example, the *didascaliae* of Terence's *Adelphoe* and *Hecyra* note that these plays took place at the *ludi funebres* of L. Aemilius Paullus.[46] Furthermore, in Plautus' *Mostellaria*, the clever slave, Tranio, plays on the double-meaning of *ludos*, 'tricks' and 'funeral games':

> ludos ego hodie vivo praesenti hic seni
> faciam, quod credo mortuo numquam fore.

---

[44] Varro *Ling.* 6: "indixit funus."

[45] Edmondson 1996: 69–70n1: "The term [*munera*] distinguishes them [gladiatorial combats] quite clearly from *ludi*, *i.e.*, such entertainments as chariot races or stage plays put on by the community to honor the gods at religious festivals." Cf. Ville 1981: 353, who asserts that the semantic range of *ludi* would necessarily include gladiators, "ajoutons que ce texte concerne sans aucun doute, outre les *ludi*, le *munus* funèbre."

[46] Gruen 1992: 210n124 briefly discusses the veracity of the *didascaliae* and cites additional bibliography. Ter. *Hec.* didasc.: "relata est iterum L. Aemilio Paulo *ludis funeralibus*;" Ter. *Ad.* didasc.: "Acta ludis funebribus L. Aemelio Paulo, quos fecere Q. Fabius Maximus P. Cornelius Africanus." Cf. Donatus praef. *Ad.* 1.6: "haec sane acta est ludis scaenicis funebribus L. Aemili Pauli."

I shall put on *ludi* here today for the old man while he's alive,
a thing which I believe will never happen once he's dead.[47]

For Tranio, the *ludi funebres* of Theopropides included dramatic performances.[48]

Evidence for Gladiatorial Games in Rome

The most remarked upon elements of funerary celebrations in the middle Republic were the gladiatorial games. They receive lengthier, but still relatively slight treatment in the sources. If one highlights the similarities in the reports and follows the testimony rigorously, a uniform set of features arises, which I will now summarize before we review the evidence. Gladiatorial games were held in the Forum and always at a funeral. They were part of the *ludi funebres*. These *ludi* would primarily comprise gladiatorial combat as well as dramatic performances, and they might be accompanied by a banquet of some sort. Gladiators always fought in pairs, and a typical day with combats might see a maximum of twelve pairs fight. If more gladiators were desired, then more days were added to the event. Under this model, if one wanted to hold an event with thirty pairs of gladiators, one would expect to see ten combats per day. In order to situate Paullus' funeral within the greater context of Republican gladiatorial games, I will now briefly review the textual evidence available for mid-Republican gladiatorial games to establish the patterns I have just summarized.

The first *munus gladiatorum* was given in the Forum Boarium in 264 BCE. Marcus and Decimus, the sons of Brutus Pera, gave them at their father's funeral.[49] Ausonius (*Griphus* 36–37), writing six centuries later, claims that three pairs of gladiators fought at the tomb:

Tris primas Thraecum pugnas tribus ordine bellis
Iuniadae patrio inferias misere sepulcro.

The sons of Iunius offered the first funerary [gladiatorial] combats
of Thracians, with three fights in order at the tomb of their father.[50]

Livy records the next five gladiatorial performances, four of which were held in Rome. Though his reports included specific details, they are not uniform in what

[47] Plaut. *Mostell.* 427–428; the joke is, of course, that no one will want to pay for his actual funeral games.

[48] If this play, the *Mostellaria*, were staged at funeral games, the joke would carry additional weight. Not coincidence, but meta-theater may be the reason why we read a deictic *hic* following *vivo praesenti*.

[49] Val. Max. 2.4.7: "Nam gladiatorium munus primum Romae datum est in Foro Boario App. Claudio Q. Fulvio consulibus. Dederunt Marcus et Decimus filii Bruti Perae funebri memoria patris cineres honorando" ("For the first *munus gladiatorium* held at Rome was given in the Forum Boarium during the consulships of Appius Claudius and Quintus Fulvius. Marcus and Decimus, the sons of Brutus Pera, gave them as a memorial by honoring his ashes."); see also Livy *Per.* 16.6: Decimus Iunius Brutus munus gladiatorium in honorem defuncti patris primus edidit. ("Decimus Iunius Brutus was the first to hold a *munus gladiatorium* in honor of his deceased father.")

[50] Auson. *Griphus* 36–37.

they describe and are, at times, frustratingly imprecise. Nonetheless, a careful reading reveals the average length of the funeral games, their composition, and their staging location.

> (216 BCE) M. Aemilio Lepido, qui bis consul augurque fuerat, filii tres, Lucius, Marcus, Quintus, ludos funebres per triduum et gladiatorum paria duo et viginti in foro dederunt.
>
> Lucius, Marcus, and Quintus gave their father, Marcus Aemilius Lepidus, who was an *augur* and was twice elected *consul*, *ludi funebres*, which lasted three days, and they exhibited twenty-two pairs of gladiators in the Forum.[51]

Here the Latin is somewhat ambiguous. This much is known: an event termed *ludi funebres* lasted for three days and twenty-two pairs of gladiators fought *in the Forum*. It seems likely that the gladiators fought during those three days dedicated to *ludi funebres*, but it is not entirely clear from this passage whether the combats should be considered separate events, related to the funeral but not circumscribed by the term *ludi*. Compare the previous passage to the following:

> (206 BCE) Scipio Carthaginem ad uota soluenda dis munusque gladiatorium, quod mortis causa patris patruique parauerat, edendum rediit. ... Huic gladiatorum spectaculo ludi funebres additi pro copia provinciali et castrensi apparatu.
>
> Scipio returned to Carthage to fulfill his vow to the gods by giving a *munus gladiatorium*, which he provided in commemoration of his father's and uncle's deaths. ... To this spectacle of gladiators, *ludi funebres* were added in proportion to the provincial funds and military camp infrastructure.[52]

Here, at first glance, Livy seems to differentiate between the "spectacle of gladiators" and the *ludi funebres*. His language implies that these *ludi* were something other than gladiatorial games, but the overall context complicates even this interpretation. He devotes considerable time in this passage to describing how the combatants who fought at this event were not the typical kind who one might hire from a *lanista*. Instead they were local volunteers, and, in one case, there were two cousins who were both vying to be chief of a local town and wished to use the occasion to determine by combat who should prevail. Livy had just referred to this particular match as a *spectaculum*. Therefore, *huic spectaculo* refers in part to this particular spectacle rather than the generic concept of a larger gladiatorial show. One might better translate this section as: "The funeral celebrations were added to this spectacle of combatants in proportion to the available provincial infrastructure."

Livy's description for the year 200 BCE again lacks disambiguating details, but also conforms to my reading:

---

[51] Livy 23.30.15.
[52] Livy 28.21.2,10.

> (200 BCE) Et ludi funebres eo anno per quadriduum in Foro mortis causa M. Valeri Laevini a Publio et Marco filiis eius facti, et munus gladiatorium datum ab iis; paria quinque et viginti pugnarunt.
>
> *Ludi funebres*, which lasted four days, were put on in the Forum in that year by Publius and Marcus, on account of the death of their father Marcus Valerius Laevinus, and a *munus gladiatorium* was given by them. Twenty-five pairs fought.[53]

Livy writes that the *ludi funebres*, held in the Forum, lasted four days. He lists the *munus* gladiatorium separately (*et munus*). He provides the duration of the *ludi*, but he elides how the *munus* is related to the *ludi* and he does not explicitly reveal whether the gladiatorial games occurred for a specified number of additional days or whether they were instead held during the four-day *ludi*. Most likely there was no need for Livy to specify a distinction. The correct reading in my view is that the funerary celebration lasted four days, and among the various aspects and rituals of funerary *ludi*, there were gladiatorial games, which Livy highlighted. Therefore, it is reasonable to conclude that twenty-five pairs of gladiators fought over the course of four days: roughly six pairs per day, or possibly eight pairs per day if, as in past listings by Livy, gladiators fought for three days, one day less than the days allotted to the overall celebration of *ludi funebres*. Moreover, Livy states that the *ludi funebres* were held *in Foro*. Therefore, the type of activity was limited. The space did not allow for chariot races or for contests that involved a track. Instead, the most well-attested events held in the Forum were, without exception, gladiatorial games and dramatic performances. Moreover, the *munus gladiatorium* is the one spectacular event consistently and exclusively staged *in Foro*.

> (183 BCE) P. Licinii funeris causa visceratio data, et gladiatores centum viginti pugnaverunt, et ludi funebres per triduum facti, post ludos epulum.
>
> *Visceratio* were given out for the funeral of Publius Licinius, and one hundred twenty gladiators fought, and the *ludi funebres* lasted three days; after the games there was a feast.[54]

The *ludi funebres* for Licinius were only three days long. If *ludi funebres* contained events wholly distinct, then one must consider the following questions. Did 120 gladiators—60 pairs—fight first? For how many days? Or instead should we understand that 20 pairs fought per day for three days? If they had followed previous standards and fought 7–10 pairs per day, the event would have lasted more than eight days. With regard to the location, though Livy doesn't overtly state the location of the *ludi funebres*, it is clearly expected that these funerary activities were held in the Forum. This particular funeral was noteworthy because the dinner that followed was disrupted by a strong and portentous wind; Livy continues his description from above by adding that the wind arose "[in this *epulum*] once the

---

[53] Livy 31.50.4.

[54] Livy 39.46.2.

triclinia were set up throughout the entire Forum"[55] The locus for funeral games was the Forum.

The next report on gladiatorial games in Livy reveals a tantalizing hint that there were perhaps regularly more games occurring than those Livy mentions. In addition, this report also helps further clarify the relationship between *ludi* and *munera.*

> (174 BCE) Munera gladiatorum eo anno aliquot, parva alia, data; unum ante cetera insigne fuit T. Flaminini quod mortis causa patris sui cum visceratione epuloque et ludis scaenicis quadriduum dedit. Magni tum muneris ea summa fuit ut per triduum quattuor et septuaginta homines pugnarint.
>
> A few *munera gladiatorum* were given in that year, some were small; one marked beyond the rest was that of Titus Flamininus, on the occasion of the death of his father, which, along with a *visceratio*, an *epulum*, and *ludi scaenici*, he gave for four days. The expenditure for the *munus*—big for that time—was such that seventy-four men fought for three days.[56]

Though he makes no mention of *ludi funebres* explicitly, Livy cannot mean that there were no *ludi funebres* at the funeral, only *ludi scaenici* and *munera gladiatorum.* Instead, the *ludi scaenici* and gladiatorial shows must form the constituent parts of what one might normally call *ludi funebres*, though this time Livy elides those words. This four-day event included a dinner and dramatic performances. The expenditure was sufficient to support 37 pairs of gladiators who fought over three days, approximately 12 per day. While it is possible that the dramatic performances and the dinner were staged independently for an unstated period of time, my reading, within the context of other reports from Livy, is that the *ludi funebres* lasted four days, and during three of those days, a particularly large number of gladiators fought for three consecutive days. Of course, the first of those days might also have included a gladiatorial fight along with the dramatic performances and some form of outdoor dining. Similarly, dramatic performances may have been held on one of the days otherwise dedicated to larger displays of gladiatorial games. If, however, the *ludi funebres* were to be considered an entirely separate event from the *munus gladiatorium*, then what might they comprise? If these *ludi* were to have been held in the Forum as those of 200 BCE, there would have been few possibilities. The most well-known were gladiatorial combats. In my view the term *ludi funebres* appears to encompass the collection of activities, which include *munera* held after the funeral. Moreover, in this example, Livy begins his description of *munera gladiatorum* but then, with a relative clause, slips into a broader description of related funerary events. Therefore, one should consider carefully whether Livy's

[55] Livy 39.46.3: "in quo cum toto foro strata triclinia essent." This feast gained notoriety because a large storm arose, which forced many to erect *tabernacula* ("tents") to shield themselves from the rain, thus fulfilling an earlier prophecy that tents would be erected in the Forum.

[56] Livy 41.28.11. It is now believed that Livy used the wrong praenomen, and that he should have written Lucius Quinctius Flamininus (L. Quinctius (*RE* 43) T. f. L. n. Flamininus).

use of these terms is as consistent and so tightly delineated as a modern scholarly textbook might demand.

Frequency, Regularity, and Scale of the Gladiatorial Munera

Building on the evidence above, we will turn to the last example of funerary games at Rome during the mid-second century BCE, to help us determine the duration and scale of the combats at this time. One view, which is often repeated in scholarly conversation, is that the games steadily increased in size:

> The relative completeness of Livy's account of the period 218–167 BC allows us to trace how, over this period, the competitiveness of Roman public life meant that on each occasion the spectacle presented—like the number of ancestral masks—had to improve on what had gone before."[57]

> The *munera* continue to appear sporadically in the literary sources, revealing great advances in terms of scale and, presumably, elaborateness of the production.[58]

Such conclusions are plausible based on a strict interpretation of the evidence. They are perhaps influenced by hindsight, since at the later games of Caesar and others in the first century BCE, gladiators might number in the hundreds or thousands. It is undeniable that gladiatorial combats would eventually increase in scope and scale to such an extent that Imperial games were substantially more lavish than those staged centuries before. For the second century BCE, however, the evidence is extremely limited. We must acknowledge that Livy's record is incomplete both because books of his history have been lost and because his work is not a comprehensive database of ancient spectacle. Livy does not purport to provide an accounting of all events that occurred, he is instead highly selective. Bearing this in mind, one finds that amidst the totality of evidence a consistency in gladiatorial stagecraft emerges contrary to conventional thought. After all, Livy records only games that congregated a large number of participants, those that could be characterized as extravagant, or simply those held in honor of a particularly famous aristocrat. Recall that in his review of 174 BCE, he notes that a few small gladiatorial shows were given but provides no additional details: *munera gladiatorum eo anno aliquot, parva alia, data.* Only the funerary celebration for Flamininus was given space in Livy's annalistic report.[59] He considered the others minor, which strongly implies that there are many others missing from his reports on other years. In fact, how one chooses to interpret Livy's note has significant ramifications for our understanding

---

[57] Wiedemann 1992: 6.

[58] Futrell 2000: 24.

[59] The family tree of Lucius and Titus Quinctius Flamininus has been the subject of much debate and is beyond the scope of this book, e.g., see Badian 1971. Nonetheless, it is still worth noting that L. Quinctius Flamininus, who died in 170 BCE, may not have displayed any *imagines*, or perhaps only three or four. Would such a situation merit compensation through gladiatorial display? Of course, the Quinctii were an old Roman clan, and any branch may have chosen to display legendary figures like the famous L. Quinctius Cincinnatus.

of this formative stage of gladiatorial combat. When Livy writes that some *munera* were given in 174, is this evidence that no *munera* were given in years when Livy makes no mention of them? I contend that the phrase here is meant to contextualize the larger event, the games for Flamininus, and is not stating that in 174, unlike all other years, there were a few small games given as well. In my view, Livy's statement implies that every year one might expect *aliquot munera parva gladiatorum* to have been given. After all, given the training infrastructure required to stage gladiatorial combats, one assumes that gladiatorial combats were offered on a regular basis at Rome, certainly at least one a year. Furthermore, if one believes that gladiatorial events were only offered at funerals, and that there were a handful of significant funerals a year, it is no small stretch to assume that gladiatorial matches were held at *ludi funebres* annually in Rome, and at least a few times per year. Another way to view Livy's remark is that *munera gladiatorum eo anno aliquot* is also clear evidence for frequency of aristocratic funerals, since each of those smaller gladiatorial shows were necessarily part of a funeral.

Testimony from Pliny, often omitted from similar lists of early gladiatorial games due to uncertain dating, sheds additional light:

> Pingi autem gladiatoria munera atque in publico exponi coepta a C. Terentio Lucano. is avo suo, a quo adoptatus fuerat, triginta paria in Foro per triduum dedit tabulamque pictam in nemore Dianae posuit.

> C. Terentius Lucanus began the practice of commissioning a painting of gladiatorial games and showing it in public. He gave 30 pairs in the Forum over three days for his grandfather, who had adopted him. He set up the painting in the grove of Diana.[60]

There is debate whether C. Terentius Lucanus was a moneyer of *ca.* 135 or a senator of *ca.* 170, but the details are not relevant to this discussion. Most important is that in the mid-second century BCE, he showed 30 pairs of gladiators in the Forum over a three-day period.[61] This dating contradicts the claim that gladiatorial games, as a rule, increased in complexity during the middle Republic. Instead, there is only one extravagant outlier, the funeral of 183, where 60 pairs fought. One might better assert that, over time, the most extravagant gladiatorial shows became increasingly lavish, but, for the most part, most shows held at Rome were staged in the same place, the Forum, and followed a similar playbill and schedule. This example also serves as a reminder that such small sample sizes can yield artificially robust conclusions.

Games at Rome and Beyond During the Republic

In fact, when the totality of the evidence is assessed and compared with games in other locales, one senses a relative stability, rather than a transformation in scale.

---

[60] Plin. *HN* 35.52.

[61] Wiseman 1964: 125 discusses the identity of a Terentius Lucanus (senator *ca.* 170) who manumitted the slave and playwright P. Terentius Afer.

TABLE 4.1 Gladiatorial games over time

Gladiatorial games held at Rome				
Date	Days	Pairs	Per day	Sources
264	1	3	3	Val. Max. 2.4.7 *et al.*
216	3	22	7	Livy 23.30.15
200	4	25	6	Livy 31.50.4
183	3	60	20	Livy 39.46.2
174	3	37	12	Livy 41.28.11
170/130	3	30	10	Plin. *HN* 35.52
Comparative sample of games outside Rome				
166	30	240	8	Polyb. 30.25.5, 26.1
Late 1 C BCE	4	20	5	*CIL* IV 9979–9981a, Tumolesi 1980: 23–24
1 C CE	4	20	5	*CIL* IV 3882, Tumolesi 1980: 91–92
55/56 CE	3	30	10	*CIL* IV 1179, Tumolesi 1980: 36

In table 4.1, I lay out the elements at play in each of the reported gladiatorial events: the length (in days) of the event, the number (in pairs) of combatants showcased, and the daily average number of fights. With the exception of one example, the games of 183 BCE, all games average between six and twelve fights per day and last for three to four days.[62] This average is striking, for it approximates the number of combats to be held later at Pompeii. Even the gladiatorial games that Antiochus IV introduced to the east counted only eight pairs per day when averaged over the entire thirty-day ceremony.

Although the games were *ad hoc*, the scheduling and pairs of fighters per day varied little. An apparent adherence to the custom of showing pairs of gladiators in sequence meant that munificence was constrained by intractable factors. An emperor in the second century CE could have commanded thousands of men to fight in group combat, whereas a mid-Republican aristocrat, according to the scant evidence we have, could have only shown a limited number of pairs per day. Unless there were multiple combats occurring at the same time in different venues, or unless some of the gladiators were encouraged to end their matches quickly, the only way for an aristocrat to outdo and to outspend visibly another was to extend the *length* of the games, in part, by increasing the number of gladiators.[63] Moreover, the physical arena that could serve three gladiatorial combats in one day, as in the first combats of 264 BCE, differed little in practical terms from one that could accommodate ten per day, as in 170 BCE. In other words, the setup of a "stage" for gladiators for one match was the exact same as the setup for thirty: only two com-

[62] Ville 1981: 395–398 proposes 12–13 combats per day. Potter 1999: 313 notes: "It appears that at a festival where gladiators would take up the whole afternoon (this was not true in all places) there would be between ten and thirteen pairs."

[63] On conspicuous consumption in the arena, see Plass 1995: 46–55.

batants took to the arena at any one time. To be clear, there was clearly sufficient space for multiple pairs to have fought at the same time in different parts of the Forum, but frequent use of *paria* to describe the contests and the uniform depiction in reliefs and paintings of two combatants fighting alone suggests the contrary.[64] Therefore, the accommodations for the games held in 264, which many assume involved nothing more than gathering round in a circle to watch the fights, would have sufficed for the shows of the second century BCE.[65]

LUDI SCAENICI IN FORO

In general, staging spectacles of all kinds in the Republic required flexibility, but the *ludi funebres* were a special case. As we have seen, the gladiatorial games were not necessarily the only shows at funeral celebrations. *Ludi funebres* apparently encompassed a variety of funeral festivities, ranging from the public distribution of meat (*visceratio*) to a public feast (*epulum*), as well as various sorts of combats and contests. Athletic competitions were well-established in the Greek and Etruscan funeral traditions, but references to many lesser events associated with Roman funeral games have not survived. In consequence, the use of the term *ludi* calls to mind the most prominent Roman festival events, *ludi circenses* and *ludi scaenici*. *Ludi circenses* were a common component of other public *ludi*, but no written testimony survives that explicitly associates *ludi circenses* with the funeral.[66] Hardly surprising, considering the funeral took place in the Forum. In fact, the testimony that details other *ludi* at the funeral describe only the addition of dramatic performances, *ludi scaenici*.

Dramatic performances were sometimes held at the funeral games, but their frequency cannot be known. Livy attributes the source of Roman drama to the Etruscans, who may have included dramatic performances at their funeral games, but the evidence is problematic.[67] The written sources describe two occasions. In 174 BCE at the funeral of T. Flamininus, *ludi scaenici* were part of the celebration.[68]

[64] Ville 1981: 395–399 assumes that the pairs fought in sequence in his discussion of the duration of the combats. Potter 1999: 313–314 agrees. The famous mural depicting the riots at the amphitheater at Pompeii (for the image, see, e.g., Gabucci and Coarelli 2001: 82) is often thought to show that brawlers spilled over into the arena, not multiple combatants engaged in gladiatorial combat (Wiedemann 1992: 119–120).

[65] As Welch 2007: 30 suggests regarding the first gladiatorial combats: "The arena [at the funeral of Brutus Pera] may have been formed either by wooden benches or simply by the people watching the show."

[66] Cf. Pascal 1894, who uses the depiction of chariots on funeral monuments to argue that *ludi circenses* were a common component of the funerary *ludi*.

[67] Livy 7.2.4–13. Edwards 1993: 100–101 notes that Livy is obviously "overemphasizing" the Etruscan influence. Oakley 1998: 40–72 examines the sources and historicity of the passage to conclude that, despite various incongruities in Livy's account, Etruria clearly played a role in the early development of drama in the Roman world. Mere 1982 suggests that a terracotta relief depicting a dramatic performance might carry funerary connotations.

[68] Livy 41.28.11.

Later, in 160 BCE, Terence's *Adelphoe* and *Hecyra* were staged at the *ludi funebres* held in honor of L. Aemilius Paullus.[69] An apparent eyewitness account highlights the overriding effect of the funeral apparatus on the staging of *ludi*.

The prologue of the *Hecyra* purports to explain what happened at the event:

> Hecyram ad vos refero, quam mihi per silentium
> numquam agere licitum est; ita eam oppressit calamitas.
> Eam calamitatem vestra intelligentia
> sedabit, si erit adiutrix nostrae industriae.
> Cum primum eam agere coepi, pugilum gloria,
> funambuli eodem accessit expectatio:
> comitum conventus, strepitus, clamor mulierum
> fecere ut ante tempus exirem foras.
> Vetere in nova coepi uti consuetudine,
> in experiendo ut essem: refero denuo.
> Primo actu placeo; cum interea rumor venit
> datum iri gladiatores; populus convolat:
> tumultuantur, clamant, pugnant de loco:
> ego interea meum non potui tutari locum
> nunc turba nulla est: otium et silentium est:
> agendi tempus mihi datum est: vobis datur
> potestas condecorandi ludos scaenicos.

> I give to you the *Hecyra*, which I have never been allowed
> to present in peace; disaster has fallen upon it thus.
> Your understanding will allay that disaster, if it will help our effort.
> When I first began to put on the play, the boasting of boxers,
> (a gathering awaiting a tight-rope walker had come to the same place)
> the milling about of attendants, the noise, and the shouting of women
> made it such that I needed to leave before it was time.
> I undertook to employ an old custom afresh
> that I might learn by experience; I presented anew.
> I meet favor with the first act; meanwhile, when word came
> that gladiators were to be given, the people flocked together;
> they were in an uproar, they shouted, and they fought for the space:
> I, however, could not protect my place.
> Now there is no mob: only peace and quiet:
> The opportunity for putting on the show has been given to me;
> for you remains the power of adorning the performance.[70]

The circumstances surrounding the staging of the *Hecyra* as depicted in the prologue are clear enough.[71] The first performance ended early due to several distractions: boxers, a tightrope walker, the "shouting of women," and the general din. Five

[69] See above, note 46.

[70] Ter. *Hec.* 29–45

[71] See Gilula 1981, Jory 1986, Sandbach 1982, Parker 1996, Bravo 2006, Sharrock 2009: 244–248, and Goldberg 2018.

years later, the *Hecyra* was staged again at the funeral games of L. Aemilius Paullus. It was a hit at first, we are told. Rumor spread that gladiators would arrive soon. Evidently, eager fans interrupted the performance. Tumult followed, and the fans of the gladiatorial show took over. Those already in attendance lost their places. In the case of both performances of the *Hecyra*, a crowd of some sort interfered with the production; the excitement surrounding these other events somehow spilled over into the "theater."[72]

Two key points emerge: the gladiatorial games and the performance of the *Hecyra* were to be held in the same general area, and the staging of both events could have overlapped. To understand how such a disruption might have been possible requires brief engagement with the study of stagecraft for Roman dramatic performances.

Much work has already been done to reconstruct the temporary stage at Rome. Traditionally, the stone theater has been translated into wooden form and imposed upon its topographical context.[73] Recent discussions have abandoned this belief. They favor more *ad hoc* structures, adapted to the staging area.[74] According to these arguments, there was no fixed location for dramatic performances in ancient Rome. The theater—insofar as there *was* a theater—moved from place to place. In the first half of the second century BCE, the viewing space was variable. The topographic and built environment dictated the seating arrangement. The seating area—the *cavea*—referred more to the space where the audience gathered than to a physical structure. Some sat on benches (*subsellia*), some stood. If a temple with a suitable approach were available, some of the audience could have sat there.[75] There was most likely a small stage, built of wood. In reference to documenting the location for scenic performances, Saunders sums up the situation best: "Our evidence is too slight and the period of time involved is too long for us to believe that it was marked by a perfectly uniform practice."[76]

While there was no permanent location for staging theatrical performances, it is clear that *ludi funebres* for the most prominent Roman citizens were consistently held in one place: the Roman Forum. For all documented cases of *munera gladiatorum* held at Rome, aside from the first show, the gladiators fought *in Foro*.

[72] Parker 1996: 596–598. Gruen 1992: 214 questions the veracity of the prologue, given the unlikelihood that enthusiastic fans of gladiatorial games could have interrupted a play commissioned by the two sons of L. Aemilius Paullus, at substantial expense, on the occasion of an aristocratic Roman funeral. Sharrock 2009: 244–248 suggests that the prologue reflects Terence's opportunistic retelling of the events.

[73] E.g., Sandbach 1982: 134–135: "[The theater] would be a temporary wooden structure, erected for the occasion, of uncertain form, but providing a stage and seating for spectators;" and Millar 1998: 147: "For theatrical *ludi* … an actual temporary wooden theater might be constructed)."

[74] E.g., T. J. Moore 1991, Goldberg 1998: 14n47, and Marshall 2006: 31–48. Goldberg 2018 argues that only a stage was necessary.

[75] Goldberg 1998.

[76] Saunders 1913: 22.

Therefore, the second staging of the *Hecyra*, performed at the funeral of L. Aemilius Paullus, was most likely held in the Forum as well.[77]

Holding funeral events in the Forum demanded a flexible staging apparatus. The failed second staging of the *Hecyra* is exceedingly difficult to understand if one retrojects later architecture forms. Though it is *possible* that a wooden theater, resembling later incarnations of monumental stone theaters, stood next to a wooden amphitheater erected in the Forum, such a configuration complicates a reading of the text. Fans intent on watching gladiatorial games would have had no reason nor means to disrupt a performance staged within a self-contained, wooden theater with wooden bleachers. Instead, the stage was a highly portable structure, and the audience had to adapt to the surrounding space.

SPECTACULA IN FORO

Having established the scheduling parameters for the games and the basic script for scheduling pairs of gladiators, I now turn to the spectators to determine how they might have attended and viewed the totality of *ludi funebres*. Imagining the staging of gladiatorial games and dramatic performances in such an irregular space as the Forum challenges preconceptions of Roman spectacle. One imagines large stone theaters and amphitheaters, venues like the Theater of Pompey or the Flavian Amphitheater. In the following section I will introduce a rather conservative reconstruction of spectacular stagecraft, one that uses the Forum itself as the "bleachers" for the audience, and a simple fence as the ring for gladiators.

To understand how gladiatorial games were staged in the middle Republic, the material remains within the Roman Forum are of little direct help: no explicit evidence is visible for purpose-built or even temporarily constructed theater-like spaces, seats, or grandstands. Instead, one must seek evidence in the admittedly problematic textual record. In modern scholarship, at the end of the previous century, a new theory had begun to take hold: though permanent amphitheaters were first built outside Rome, the form and layout of the amphitheater originated in temporary structures built at Rome.[78] The argument makes two fundamental conjectures. First, it suggests that the oblong shape of Roman *fora*, derived from the initial form at Rome, was specifically designed to accommodate gladiatorial games.[79] Second, although there were no permanent amphitheaters in Rome before Augustus,

[77] Recall that in 200 BCE, at the funeral of M. Valerius Laevinus, funeral games lasting four days were held entirely *in Foro*. Livy 31.50.4: "ludi funebres eo anno per quadriduum in foro … facti."

[78] Coleman 2003: 61: "It has recently emerged that the amphitheatre as a permanent fixture was a feature of Roman colonies at least one hundred and fifty years before the Colosseum was built, and that the design appears to have been predicated on the temporary structures erected in the Forum Romanum at Rome." For the theory itself, see Golvin 1988, Welch 1994, and Welch 2007: 30–71, but cf. Holleran 2003: 48–49, who insists on Campanian origins.

[79] Golvin 1988 first presents the hypothesis, and Welch 2007: 30–71 expands the argument. The representations of the amphitheater in my figures, e.g., fig. 4.2, are derived from Welch 1994.

this initial oblong form created boundaries for audience seating within which temporary amphitheaters, formed by connecting wooden bleachers, were constructed in the Forum. These facilities took on a circular or ovoid form, and magistrates charged for access.[80] The temporary stands were bounded by the semi-rectangular shape of the Roman Forum's central plaza, and they surrounded a central oblong arena. (See fig. 4.2.[81])

Scholarly Communication Through Reconstructed Space and Imagery

Thus far, I have generated imagery as a means to create hypothetical models of ancient funerary phenomena related to the funeral of L. Aemilius Paullus. For this chapter, I will first employ a slightly different modality that focuses on existing reconstructions and the related scholarly conversations. To this end, I will briefly outline this modified approach and argue that the stakes are particularly high when one uses imagery to make an argument.

Arguments presented graphically and rooted in three-dimensional space are compelling. A well-wrought reconstruction drawing contains a complex web of interpretation and represents interlocking forms of source material. A reader can quickly take in the image without a rich understanding of the spatial context. These images are arguments and they all operate at insidious cognitive levels. Once a convincing reconstruction is presented, the idea reifies. The peculiar nature of the way humans and all animals interact with space amplifies the strength of an image-based argument rooted in three dimensions. For example, when a human visits a physical space, they construct a cognitive map of the landscape through experience of the physical space. This map becomes the mental territory. It can even be augmented by secondary sources, such as maps, plans, axonometric drawings, and the like.

> An allocentric model (like a map) of the environment appears to be built up as a derivative of physical travel through the environment. As the animal's route-based knowledge increases, an allocentric map composed of survey-based information is inferred. While this process is the normal "organic" process by which an allocentric model develops, the presence of an external or secondary source (such as an actual map, aerial photograph or other resource) can lead to the instant formation of an allocentric representation (albeit relatively impoverished) without the need for travel in the environment.[82]

Since the Republican Forum is largely hidden from modern, experiential view, secondary resources become the primary mode for building a spatial understand-

---

[80] On the confusion surrounding magistrates, see below for my extended assessment, p. 164ff.

[81] These representations are based on the well-executed plans and sketches by P. Stinson in Welch 2007: 49–55, figs. 21–26. They are designed as abstractions within which we can perform a three-dimensional interrogation of the evidence. For the methodology, see Johanson 2009.

[82] Roche et al. 2005: 625.

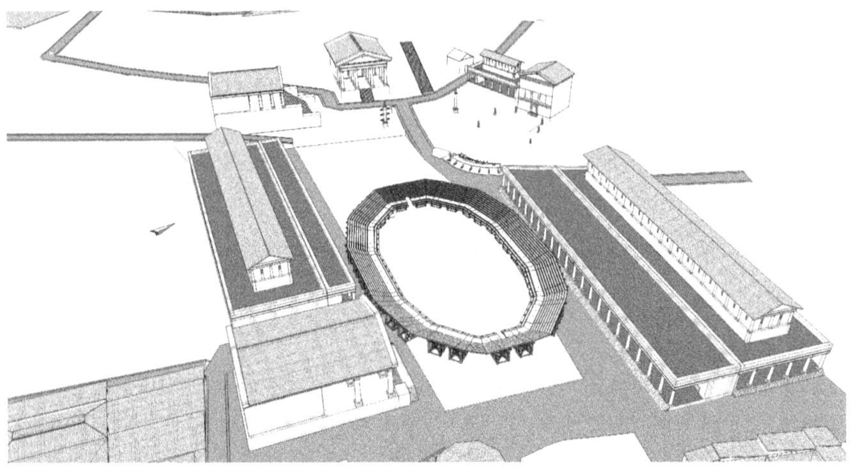

FIGURE 4.2 View of a conjectural temporary wooden amphitheater in the Forum of 160 BCE.

ing of this civic, religious, and cultural center of Republican Rome. It is impossible to walk through the Republican Forum today. Therefore, the "impoverished" model—created through plans and hypothetical reconstructions—is the only one scholars have within which to work. The cognitive, allocentric map might be augmented by visits to the actual Forum of today, but, ultimately, the imagery of the reconstructed forms that is accessible in scholarly literature serves as both map *and* territory. In short, once you see a few images of these reconstructed spaces, they become fixed as part of your own internal map of the space. They are particularly convincing and compelling when they stand alone, unchallenged by other imagery, and strongly influence one's internal map.

In the case of the proposed temporary amphitheater in the Forum, the imagery constitutes a significant portion of the argument, and the images themselves are so well executed that the reconstructed amphitheater's reified form is extraordinarily convincing. To analyze, refute, or, as I will do, modify the proposed solution, a similar, image-based analysis is required. To expand a scholarly conversation rooted in imagery most effectively, images must be brought to bear. We will now return to our study of the evidence for Republican gladiatorial stagecraft by first reassessing the proposed reconstructions for temporary amphitheaters in the Forum.[83]

[83] On the debate surrounding visual argumentation and refutation, see Birdsell and Groarke 1996, Lake and Pickering 1998, and Roque 2012.

Rome as Unique Venue for Spectacle

It is tempting to look for analogies in the archaeological record beyond Rome that presuppose a Roman source. *Capitolia, comitia, templa,* and now amphitheaters have all been implicated as originating first in Rome and then replicated in cities beyond. There are several problems with this scenario. To derive the architectural form of these buildings and the amphitheater from a Roman origin is to ascribe to a controversial theory of colonial development, in which Rome led, and the colonies followed.[84] Others have objected to this concept at greater length than space here allows.[85] In what follows, I briefly detail the pitfalls in applying this theory to the Roman Forum and *fora* outside Rome.

The colonies reflected, at best, a circus-mirror image of the Eternal City. There were, of course, many similarly *named* features. One might find a Capitolium, a Curia, a Comitium, a Temple of Jupiter Optimus Maximus, and a Forum in many urban areas throughout the Roman world. One would also find many features that did not exist initially at Rome, e.g., a *cardo*, a *decumanus maximus*, a monumental theater, and, by the first century BCE, an amphitheater. The grid plan alone would have reminded visitors at the time, and should remind scholars now, that these cities were unlike Rome. The curved streets and haphazard planning of the mother city were obviously not evident in cities and towns built, from the start, by design with a rigidly conceived urban plan.[86]

Capitolia outside Rome were more often the products of architecture and the built environment than they were naturally formed hills; they were also rectilinear, unlike the Capitoline Hill at Rome. *Curiae* maintained a uniform tripartite structure whose central building had similar proportions to the Curia Hostilia, but differed in that these *curiae* were flanked by two smaller chambers.[87] These *curiae* also faced a square structure that enclosed circular, stepped assembly places—in some ways shaped like the later Ludus Magnus (*mutatis mutandis*) that comprised a stepped, ovoid form embedded into surrounding, rectangular architecture.[88] One theory holds that the Comitium at Rome formed the model for these *comitia*.[89] It is curious, however, that at Rome the Rostra, which is thought to form one section of this rounded assembly space, had a curvilinear facade that faced the Forum. Therefore, the external architectural form was circular, unlike the square form with a circular interior found at the colonies. The repetition of this form throughout the

---

[84] The theory is not new: see Brown 1980 and Stambaugh 1988: 109.

[85] Fentress 2000: 11–24 explores the architectural differences between Cosa and Rome.

[86] It is important to note that these cities were rarely the result of a single master urban plan. The coloniae developed over time, but in so doing, more often than not, adhered to a grid system. See Anderson 1997: 183–203 for a brief survey of town planning and layout.

[87] For a full visual review of *curiae*, see the comprehensive collection of plans in Bonnefond-Coudry 1989.

[88] E.g., the *comitia* at Cosa, Paestum, and Fregellae. For a concise list accompanied by plans of the major square *comitia* outside of Rome, see Coarelli 1998.

[89] The argument is Coarelli's, and varies little since first proposed in Coarelli 1977.

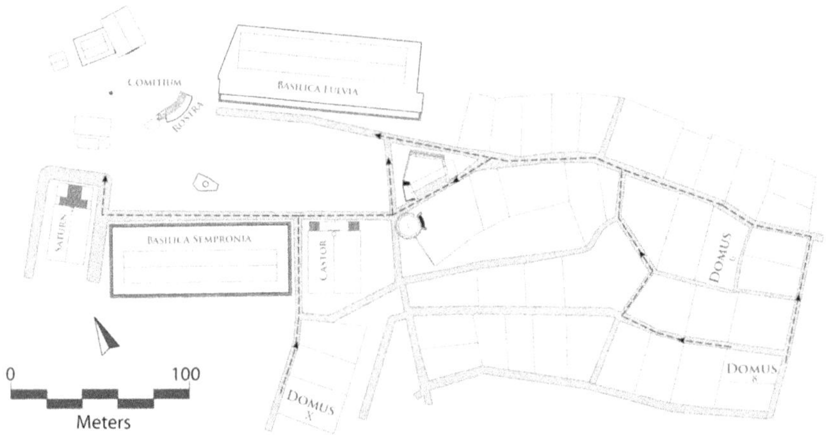

FIGURE 4.3 The Roman Forum in 160 BCE. Note the irregular plan, especially on the western end of the plaza.

cities and towns of Italy results from the consistent, regular plan found outside of Rome. These *fora* were self-contained rectangular forms that resembled other Roman cities and towns, but differed quite drastically from Rome itself. Many buildings shared walls, and all shared alignment. In contrast, the highly irregular layout of the Roman Forum did not evolve according to a symmetrical grid. (Note the irregular plan of the Republican Forum visible in fig. 4.3.) In most reconstructions, the Curia faces due south, whereas the Forum plaza runs northwest to southeast. The Regia to the east was trapezoidal and formed part of a jumble of monuments that each aligned to slightly different axes on that side of the Forum. The Lacus Curtius inconveniently lay—from a design standpoint, inexplicably—in the middle of everything. An aetiological myth was most likely developed to explain why a monument of this type was constructed, seemingly at random, on such prime real estate.[90]

Finding Space to Build in the Roman Forum

In fact, the Lacus Curtius illustrates an additional problem that monumental construction of any kind at Rome, even if temporary, always faced: *religio*. The following oft-quoted assertion given by Livy's Camillus merits another citation here:

[90] There were conflicting stories. According to one version of the legend (Livy 1.13.5), the Lacus Curtius marked the place where Mettius Curtius emerged from the swamp where he had been mired to renew the battle with the Sabines. In an alternate version (Livy 7.6.1–6), the earth had opened up spontaneously and, according to soothsayers, only Rome's greatest treasure could fill it. M. Curtius, the "treasure," rode his horse into the hole, and that depression was known afterward as the Curtian Lake (Lacus Curtius).

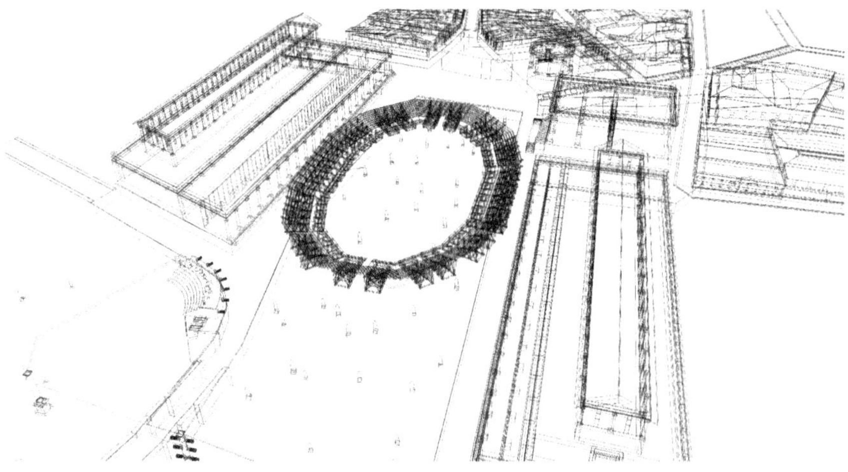

FIGURE 4.4 A conjectural wooden amphitheater, statuary, and the Lacus Curtius (obscured) in the Forum of 160 BCE.

> Vrbem auspicato inauguratoque conditam habemus; nullus locus in ea non religionum deorumque est plenus; sacrificiis sollemnibus non dies magis stati quam loca sunt in quibus fiant.
>
> We have a city founded in auspication and augury. There is no place within the city that is not full of religion and gods. Neither are there more days fit for solemn sacrifices than there are places within which these rituals might take place.[91]

The city of Rome in the mid-Republic held monuments that had been standing in the same place in some cases for at least 300 years. Some had undergone significant modification, but the basic footprints had remained virtually unchanged. Ritually defined boundaries limited construction opportunities.[92] The profane similarly would have introduced insurmountable impediments for would-be builders of a temporary amphitheater. Fierce political competition left its symbolic and monumental mark on the city. Statuary also dotted the Forum plaza. Any temporary amphitheater must also account for these literal, monumental hurdles. (See fig. 4.4.)

[91] Livy 5.52.

[92] Caesar removed an altar in the Lacus Curtius for the last games he sponsored in the Forum. Plin. *HN* 15.20.78: "ara inde (*sc.* the Lacus Curtius) sublata gladiatorio munere divi Iuli quod novissme pugnavit in Foro." ("An altar was removed from [the Lacus Curtius] in the gladiatorial *munus* of the divine Julius, the last one he staged in the Forum.") Might this be the first occasion where significant alterations were made to the built environment of the Forum to accommodate the games?

Seating the Audience in the Forum

The evidence for audience-designated spaces in the Forum is complex and ambiguous. So-called *maeniana*, the balconies connected to shops and basilicas in the Forum were the most attested means for audiences to view spectacular events. Constructed bleachers or platforms of some kind were used at Rome for some public events by the late first century BCE, but their systematic use is much harder to determine. As I will argue below, events in the Roman Forum, especially those associated with a funeral, were *sui generis*, unlike those held in the Italian peninsula, and more likely to have used a sparse apparatus for all aspects of the games. The arena was fenced in with a portable, commonly used and well-attested system of stanchions (*cancelli*); the audience would use the monumental features of the Forum itself as their viewing areas.

In fact, for the time period contemporary with that of the funeral of Paullus, Welch, whose insightful, highly visual work has expanded our understanding of possible bleacher systems in Rome, notes that the second-century *munera* differed dramatically from the later incarnation: "Beyond the existence of *maeniana*, we can only guess as to what other physical arrangements were made in the Forum."[93] Many of the same difficulties found in the sources describing games at Rome pertain to later time periods. Welch's overall thesis, however, that the amphitheater only spread to Campania upon the arrival of the Roman military, need not rely on the creation of a temporary wooden amphitheater in the Roman Forum. Just as *comitia*, the grid system, and *fora* all developed unique forms that represented a blend of current practice in military camps and the architectural influence of Rome, so the amphitheater. One wonders whether only the oblong form of the *arena* should be traced to Rome, whereas the surrounding seating should derive from an innovation pursued outside the city. For example, the first amphitheaters were built around excavated arenas, *i.e.*, man-made oblong pits. The earliest example is found at Pompeii, where the central arena was excavated and the removed earth was used to build up the surrounding support structure for the *cavea*.[94] The architectural form would naturally follow. Free-standing Roman theaters claim a similar origin. Their precursors were built into hillsides, but the topography of Rome prohibited such constructions. The form of the theater was then adapted to fit the city, not the other way around, as could happen in urban areas outside Rome.

Explicit testimony that mentions gladiatorial games using a bleacher-like system at Rome is only found in one oft-cited passage of Plutarch, who was writing in the first century CE, over 200 years after the death of Lucius Aemilius Paullus. Plutarch describes Gaius Gracchus' actions as tribune, 38 years after the death of Paullus.

> ἔμελλεν ὁ δῆμος θεᾶσθαι μονομάχους ἐν ἀγορᾷ, καὶ τῶν συναρχόντων οἱ πλεῖστοι θεωρητήρια κύκλῳ κατασκευάσαντες ἐξεμίσθουν. ταῦθ' ὁ Γάιος ἐκέλευεν

[93] Welch 2007: 35.

[94] On the construction techniques employed, see Richardson 1988: 134–135 and Welch 2007: 74–76.

αὐτοὺς καθαιρεῖν, ὅπως οἱ πένητες ἐκ τῶν τόπων ἐκείνων ἀμισθὶ θεάσασθαι δύνωνται· μηδενὸς δὲ προσέχοντος, ἀναμείνας τὴν πρὸ τῆς θέας νύκτα, καὶ τῶν τεχνιτῶν ὅσους εἶχεν ἐργολάβους ὑφ' ἑαυτῷ παραλαβών, τὰ θεωρητήρια καθεῖλε καὶ τῷ δήμῳ σχολάζοντα μεθ' ἡμέραν ἀπέδειξε τὸν τόπον.

The people were getting ready to watch gladiatorial combats in the Forum, and most of the magistrates, after they had set up bleachers in a circle, were charging a fee for their use. Gaius ordered them to tear down the stands so that the poor could watch from those places without paying. But when no one obeyed, he waited until the night before the show, took with him as many contractors as there were from the skilled workmen, and tore down the stands. On the next day he showed forth a vacated space for the people.[95]

In other words, according to Plutarch, a *munus gladiatorium* had been appointed for a certain day. At an indeterminate number of days in advance, magistrates began to construct bleachers, which were arranged in a circle. These magistrates were in effect selling tickets to the event, by charging individuals to use these bleachers. The stands were small enough to be torn down in one night, but complex enough that they required the use of skilled laborers to carry out the task. Gracchus was moved to action because these seats blocked the view of the poor, who could not pay and would not have been able to see. After the bleachers were removed, the audience would watch the gladiatorial events for free (ἀμισθὶ), with a view unobstructed by bleachers. In this instance, the passage confirms that bleachers were not necessary for the combats, since Gracchus expected the games to be held without them.

This passage is also deeply problematic. If gladiatorial combat in the 120s was still only celebrated at a funeral, it seems unlikely that magistrates unrelated to the host family might build a separate seating apparatus to charge for attendance.[96] It is also difficult to understand how the timeline for the construction of these bleachers might coincide with that of the funeral procession and eulogy. Plutarch implies that the bleachers were built at least one day prior to the event; if that were the case, should we imagine that bleachers were under construction or even set up at the funeral itself? Or are we to imagine that these games were also innovative and were the first to have no overt funerary connection?

All we can conclude with certainty from this passage in my view is that, at some time in the Republic, perhaps around 123 BCE, bleachers were a possible feature

[95] Plut. *C. Gracch.* 12.3.

[96] Edmondson 1996: 87n78, who observes that it had to be the deceased's family, not the magistrates, who were blocking the view of the poor. "Plut. *C. Gr.* anachronistically claims that it was 'the magistrates' who had set up the temporary seating." I should add that it is of course possible that a price for admission to gladiatorial shows was an accepted innovation by those who put on the games; if bleachers were desired, doubtless someone needed to be paid to install the seating; gladiators were already an expensive investment. It is not impossible to imagine that an arrangement was made between the sponsor of the games and those managing the bleacher system. In addition, if one imagines that aediles or other magistrates more formally managed space in the Forum, then perhaps that might explain Plutarch's account. Of course, he may simply have made an educated guess.

of gladiatorial matches but were by no means a requirement. This passage does not necessarily imply that gladiatorial games were regularly viewed from a temporary wooden amphitheater. Rather, it reveals that the Forum itself without the aid of bleachers would have accommodated the general populace, who did not pay to attend. These events were integral to the Republic. Talking about a later time (56 BCE), Cicero claims that they were the optimal occasions for the voice of the people to be heard.[97] Livy calls these events *munera* with good reason: they were gifts to the people that accompanied a funeral. In 160 BCE, they were most likely free to attend. To disallow the attendance of the poor seems counterproductive.[98] Everyone could see the games regardless of their social class. Gracchus did not merely object to the charge; he reacted to these newly constructed seats that encircled the arena and that would have left no space for those to watch the combats who could not afford to pay. Of course, there was also no practical need to build reserved seating, save that temporary bleachers would allow those who built them to charge admission. The Forum was already equipped with a different type of more permanent "box seats," but profit from offering access to the *maeniana* might be more difficult to manage.[99]

While I contend that it is risky to retroject customs of the Empire into that of the Republic, it is also the case that some practices of the mid- to late first century BCE were continuations of what came before. For example, textual evidence surrounding Julius Caesar's manipulation of the space for the staging of gladiatorial games suggests a similar viewing apparatus. Pliny writes (amidst an extensive discussion of the various uses of linen in ancient Rome):

> Caesar dictator totum Forum Romanum intexit viamque sacram ab domo sua et clivum usque in Capitolium, quod munere ipso gladiatorio mirabilius visum tradunt.

> Caesar, when dictator, covered the entire Roman Forum, the Sacred Way beginning from his house (the Domus Publica), and the *clivus* all the way up to the Capitoline, a thing which they say seemed more marvelous than the gladiatorial *munus* itself.[100]

For these games, Caesar did not limit the span of the awnings to the boundaries of the central plaza of the Forum, instead he covered an area that reached well beyond. There would have been no real need to shade the western slope of the Capitoline Hill or the eastern end of the Forum in front of the Regia during gladiatorial com-

---

[97] Cic. *Sest.* 124: "Maximum vero populi Romani iudicium universi consessu gladiatorio declaratum est."

[98] Later, it could be dangerous to withhold games. See Suet. *Tib.* 37: "Cum Pollentina plebs funus cuiusdam primipilaris non prius ex foro misisset quam extorta pecunia per uim heredibus ad gladiatorium munus." ("The plebs in Pollenta refused to let the funeral procession of a certain high-ranking soldier leave the forum before they had extorted funds from his heirs through force to dedicate to a gladiatorial show [*sc.* in honor of his father].")

[99] See below and Vitr. 5.1.1.

[100] Plin. *HN* 19.23.

bats, unless the spectators customarily situated themselves in those places. To view the combats from those places required unobstructed sightlines.

Even by the time of Augustus, evidence suggests that the gladiatorial arena in the Roman Forum might still have been an open space with a crowd gathered round, rather than a structured wooden amphitheater. Dio writes regarding the funeral of Agrippa in 12 BCE:

> κἀν τούτῳ καὶ αἱ ἐπιτάφιοι ἐπὶ τῷ Ἀγρίππᾳ ὁπλομαχίαι, φαιὰν ἐσθῆτα τῶν τε ἄλλων πλὴν τοῦ Αὐγούστου καὶ αὐτῶν τῶν υἱέων αὐτοῦ λαβόντων, καὶ ἑνὸς πρὸς ἕνα καὶ πλειόνων πρὸς ἴσους, ἐν τοῖς σέπτοις διά τε τὴν ἐς τὸν Ἀγρίππαν τιμὴν καὶ διὰ τὸ πολλὰ τῶν περὶ τὴν ἀγορὰν οἰκοδομημάτων κεκαῦσθαι, ἐγένοντο.
>
> At this time there were also armed funerary combats for Agrippa, consisting of one-on-one and group matches. Everyone attended wearing white, except Augustus and his sons. The games were held in the Saepta Iulia, both to honor Agrippa and because many of the buildings surrounding the Forum had burned.[101]

The gladiatorial games Augustus held in honor of Agrippa, five years after his death, were moved to the Saepta Iulia. Dio knew only the gladiatorial games held within stone amphitheaters. By his time, the games were structured events in their own right. One might expect that he would have imagined a temporary amphitheater into the Forum space. Yet, he reports that damage to buildings surrounding the Forum forced the move. The buildings, not necessarily the bleachers, were apparently critical for viewing the event.[102]

Cicero, writing at the height of Republican spectacle provides critical evidence for reconstructing space when he describes the crowds reaction to the appearance of P. Sestius at gladiatorial games held in the Forum in honor of Q. Caecilius Metellus Pius (cos. 80 BCE):

> [P. Sestius tribunus plebis] venit, ut scitis, a columna Maenia: tantus est ex omnibus spectaculis usque a Capitolio, tantus ex fori cancellis plausus excitatus, ut numquam maior consensio aut apertior populi Romani universi fuisse ulla in causa diceretur.

[101] Cass. Dio 55.8.5. The selection of the Saepta Iulia illuminates what must have been one of the most important factors behind the continued use of the Roman Forum as the customary location for gladiatorial games—it was a memory bank for symbolic capital and a container for physical and imaginary *lieux de mémoire*, whereas monolithic structures with individual names attached were something entirely different. Statilius Taurus had already dedicated his amphitheater in 29 BCE, which would have served as the obvious location to hold subsequent gladiatorial games. Instead, it was apparently never considered. The Forum, the traditional choice, was the first option. The second was the Saepta, most likely because it was a sufficiently large space and because Agrippa himself had dedicated it in 26 BCE (Cass. Dio 53.23). One presumes that a Roman aristocratic family would not have desired to commemorate the deceased in a monument dedicated by another. Such reasoning must have also played a role in the general senatorial animosity toward the construction of permanent entertainment spaces in Rome: the sponsor of the event would have avoided sharing credit with the dedicator of the monument. More detailed argument is required, but extends beyond the scope of this chapter.

[102] Purcell 1995a: "A poorly attested devastation by fire in the latter part of 9 BCE is a strong candidate for a catalyst for a major change in function." Of course, it is also possible that the buildings surrounding the Forum were a critical part of the bleacher system.

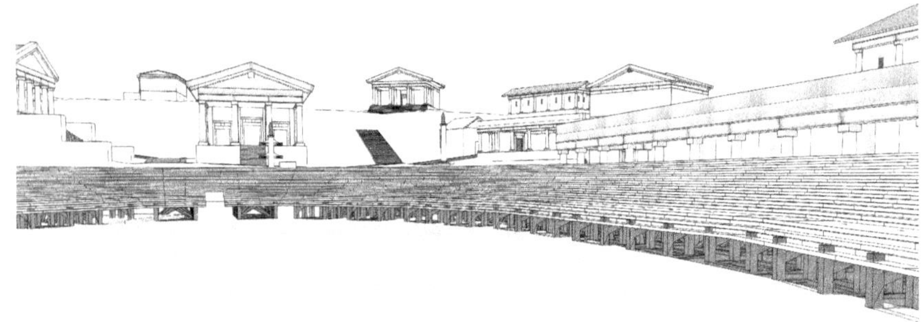

FIGURE 4.5 A view toward the western end of the Forum from within a hypothetical amphitheater.

> [Publius Sestius, tribune of the plebs,] came, as you know, from the Maenian Column: the applause from all the viewing locations right up to the Capitoline and down to the barriers of the Forum was so great that never could it have been said that there was a greater and more open agreement of all the Roman people on any subject matter. [103]

In the Republic, *spectacula* need not signify "seats" and should here be translated as "viewing locations."[104] According to Cicero's description, Sestius walked along the sloped base of the Capitoline near the Comitium. The crowd saw him from vantage points all along the Capitoline down to the fences (*cancelli*), which presumably cordoned off the arena in the central plaza of the Forum.[105] A fully enclosed wooden amphitheater would have occluded the sight lines that Cicero describes. In figure 4.5, the hypothetical amphitheater would have blocked views of Sestius' dramatic entrance. In figure 4.6, the exterior walls of the amphitheater, in turn, would have blocked the views of the audience along the lower slopes of the Capitoline.

---

[103] Cic. *Sest.* 124.

[104] *Spectacula* was, of course, the term used to refer to the first amphitheater at Pompeii in its dedicatory inscription (*CIL* X 852).

[105] Kaster 2006 remarks on this passage, "The games themselves were held in the forum, but spectators climbed the Capitoline to look down on the venues from a height. The 'barriers' here are not the *saepta* set up for voting ... but lattice-work railings (*cancelli*) used to mark off temporary arenas for the contests.

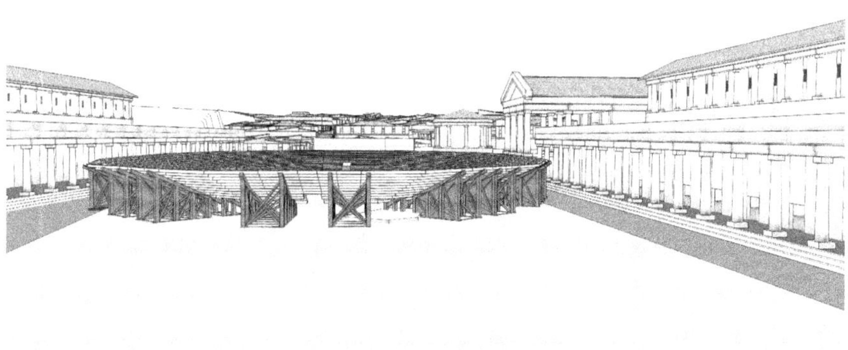

FIGURE 4.6 A view from the slopes of the Capitoline toward the reconstructed amphitheater. The enormous construction dominates the Forum and blocks many potential, ground-level *ad hoc* vantage points.

The Forum as Spectacula

I contend that the textual evidence suggests that the Forum itself, its surrounding porticoes, its sloping hills, and its balconies served as the *spectacula* for *ludi funebres*. Piecemeal bleachers may have been added at times, but they were not a regular feature. When Vitruvius writes at length on the generic characteristics of Roman *fora*, he highlights the key elements of a Roman forum that make it particularly well-suited for games.

> Graeci in quadrato amplissimis et duplicibus porticibus fora constituunt crebrisque columnis et lapideis aut marmoreis epistyliis adornant et supra ambulationes in contignationibus faciunt. Italiae vero urbibus non eadem est ratione faciendum, ideo quod a maioribus consuetudo tradita est gladiatoria munera in foro dari. Igitur circum spectacula spatiosiora intercolumnia distribuantur circaque in porticibus argentariae tabernae maenianaque superioribus coaxationibus conlocentur, quae et ad usum et ad vectigalia publica recte erunt disposita. Magnitudines autem ad copiam hominum oportet fieri, ne parvum spatium sit ad usum aut ne propter inopiam populi vastum Forum videatur. Latitudo autem ita finiatur uti longitudo in tres partes cum divisa fuerit, ex his duae partes ei dentur. Ita enim erit oblonga eius formatio et ad spectaculorum rationem utilis dispositio.

> The Greeks build square *fora* with broad, double porticoes, and they decorate these *fora* with thick columns and stone or marble architraves. Above, they make walkways on the second story. In fact, it is not done with the same reasoning by the cities of

> Italy, because the custom handed down by the ancestors is that *gladiatoria munera* are given in the *Forum*. Therefore, wider intercolumniations are distributed *circum spectacula* and all around, the banks and shops are set up in the porticoes, and on the upper floors, balconies (*maeniana*), which are arranged for general use or profit. The dimensions, however, ought to fit the number of people lest there be a space too small for its function or lest, on account of the paucity of the populace, the Forum appear too vast. The width should be defined in such a way that, when the length is divided into three parts, two parts of these constitute the width. For its form will thus be oblong and fit for the arrangement (*ratio*[106]) of the *spectacula*.[107]

Vitruvius first highlights that it was a custom handed down by the ancestors that *gladiatoria munera* were given in the Forum. Within this context, he highlights the differences between Greek and Roman central plazas. While the oblong form of the Forum is important, the primary element in Vitruvius' argument is his comparison of the overall structure of the surrounding porticoes.[108] The intercolumniations of Roman *fora* were wider "around the *spectacula*" (*circum spectacula*). *Spectacula* is an ambiguous term that is best translated as "viewing places" for the audience. Because of this primary meaning, the semantic range of *spectacula* includes various kinds of bleachers, platforms, and elevated spaces; hence when the first amphitheater at Pompeii was built, the dedicators called the seats they had constructed *spectacula*. The term could even suggest spectacular performances themselves. Vitruvius makes explicit (*igitur*) that the purpose of the extra wide intercolumniations was to serve the gladiatorial games. The increased space between the columns was meant to accommodate the spectators. The wider space would have allowed easier access to shops housed within the porticoes, *and* the narrower columns would have been less obtrusive for the audience standing in the shade of the colonnade. An enclosed, wooden amphitheater obviates this benefit: the wooden construction of the bleachers blocks access to the surrounding porticoes. (See fig. 4.2.)

Vitruvius notes that the shops below and the *maeniana* above, the projecting balconies on the upper levels of basilicas and shops, were designed for use, *i.e.* in this context viewing gladiatorial games, and as a general profit-making venture for the state (*vectigalia*). It is now time to reflect more carefully on the *maeniana* in the Roman Forum at the time of Paullus' funeral. The origin of the term *maeniana* is transmitted through disparate historical traditions—the details of which need not be elaborated here—but these origins coalesce around the area adjacent to the Comitium.[109] There are two strands that can help us understand their relationship

---

106 *Ratio* can mean many things in Vitruvius. Here, the term refers to the "système de relations" of the viewing places, see Callebat and Fleury 1995: 71.

107 Vitr. 5.1.1–2.

108 E.g., Welch 2007: 32: "Vitruvius' explanation for the fact that Italian *fora* are oblong is that gladiatorial games had traditionally been held inside them, suggesting that the oblong space of a forum was considered a natural one for displaying and watching gladiators. Vitruvius also tells us that the space inside *fora*, in which gladiatorial combat took place, was called a '*spectacula*' (that is, 'showplace,' or 'looking place')."

109 Welch 2007: 32–35 reviews the texts.

to gladiatorial shows: either C. Maenius, the fourth-century *consul*, built a platform for viewing games that extended from the top of his own free-standing column in the Forum, or a certain Maenius of the second century who sold one of the *atria* that flanked the Curia Hostilia, to make way for the Basilica Porcia, reserved a column on the newly built basilica to demarcate his own privileged seat for games.[110] Over time, the *maeniana* came to refer to cantilevered balconies in general, but even from an early date, columns were located in an area adjacent to the Comitium, and they were used as markers to reserve a section of a connected, cantilevered balcony.

The proximity of the Columna Maenia to the Basilica Porcia, coupled with the later proximity of *maeniana* to the larger basilicas flanking the Forum, indicates that one of the functions of basilicas in the second century BCE was to provide elevated viewing places for spectacle. An intriguing pattern emerges when one studies chronological development of basilicas in the Forum. The first named basilica in Rome was the aforementioned Basilica Porcia.[111] It was nearly attached to the Curia Hostilia, the approximate location of which is more or less known.[112] It offers an excellent view of the northwestern end of the Forum and the Rostra below. The free-standing Columna Maenia must have also stood nearby.[113] Therefore, the origin of the term *maeniana*, the cantilevered balconies—here designated for privileged viewers—suggests that they originated in the northwest corner of the Forum.

The first basilica in Rome and the first *named* basilica were two different buildings. A basilica appears in Plautus' *Curculio* that antedates the construction of the Basilica Porcia.[114] Most likely, the remains of the first, unnamed basilica lay below the later Basilica Fulvia, to the west of the Cloaca Maxima.[115] Again, this basilica was adjacent to the Rostra, in the area cited as the origin of the *maeniana*. The location of this first basilica extends the elevated views available surrounding the Comitium. It would have been well-situated to view the Rostra and the events that

110 C. Maenius (*RE* 9) P. f. P. n. Lehmann-Hartleben 1938 and Boethius 1945 sketch out the conflicting texts. Coarelli 1985: 39–53 contends that two separate Maenii have confused the matter. Wilskman 2024 finds a path to align both traditions.

111 *De vir. ill.* 47: "Basilicam suo nomine primus fecit." Plut. *Cat. Mai.* 19.

112 Asc. *Mil.* 33: "Porcia basilica ... erat [Curiae] iuncta." Though the reconstruction of the Comitium is controversial, most accept Coarelli's placement of the Curia. See Coarelli 1983: 138–143, 154–160 and Coarelli 1985: 33–36. Cf. the objections of Amici 1995 and Amici 2004, who contends that the archaeology cannot support the current interpretation of the space. Since I do not wish to make a topographical argument in this book, I follow Coarelli for the location of the Curia Hostilia, but have omitted the circular form of the Comitium, which I represent as an open, paved area in the figures of this book.

113 Plin. *HN* 7.212 describes the use of the Maenian Column as a solar marker visible from the Curia Hostilia.

114 Plaut. *Curc.* 472. See Duckworth 1955 for the initial discussion and Hanses 2020 for an extended analysis of the passage.

115 T. J. Moore 1991: 343n2: "several plausible cases have been made for a building which Plautus could have called a basilica at the site of the Basilica Aemilia in the earliest years of the second century B.C., and topographers have begun to take the existence of such a building for granted." E.g., see Welch 2003: 19 and 29. For an alternate location of the Basilica Aemilia, however, see Steinby 1993a. Gerding and Dell'Unto 2022: 183 fig. 19 assembles the material evidence.

took place directly in front of the it, on the Forum side, yet quite a distance removed from the space on the other side of the Cloaca.[116]

The Rostra as Reserved Seating

The basilica mentioned in Plautus may have stood from at least 210 BCE until 179 BCE, to be replaced by the substantially larger Basilica Fulvia. The Basilica Porcia was built in 184 BCE. Therefore, the first two *maeniana* attached to basilicas clustered in the northwestern end of the Forum, bounded to the east by the open canal of the Cloaca Maxima. At the center of the basilicas lay the Rostra, which, by the time of the late Republic, also offered potential space for privileged seating. To honor Ser. Sulpicius Rufus, who had died on embassy, Cicero proposed the following:

> Quas ob res ita censeo ... senatui placere Ser. Sulpicio statuam pedestrem aeneam in rostris ex huius ordinis sententia statui circumque eam statuam locum ludis gladiatoribusque liberos posterosque eius quoquo versus pedes quinque habere.

> Therefore, I recommend that the Senate decree to set up a bronze pedestrian statue for Servius Sulpicius on the Rostra, and his children and descendants would also have a place, five feet surrounding that statue, for [*sc.* watching] games and gladiators.[117]

Cicero refers to an already established tradition, in which honorific columns on the Rostra were dedicated to men who had died while working in service to Rome on foreign embassy.[118] Cicero adds that this statue be used to reserve seating for watching gladiators and *ludi*, which in this context might also mean dramatic performances.[119] He apparently wished to apply an old custom to the new Rostra, recently constructed by Caesar, that capped off the western end of the Forum plaza. Nonetheless, since his proposal is not presented as particularly innovative, and since the principle—to use a statue as a marker for privileged seating like the original Maenian Column—is attested, it seems likely that he references a long-standing tradition. Therefore, as I contend above, the northwest corner of the Forum functions as a principal, privileged viewing space.

At the funeral of L. Aemilius Paullus in 160 BCE, the built-in *maeniana* had expanded significantly. The massive Basilica Sempronia and Basilica Fulvia, fronted by shops and *maeniana*, lined the northern and southern sides of the Forum. The area surrounding the Comitium and Rostra remained a place for privileged views. As Cicero reminds us in the passage quoted above, the Rostra offered privileged

[116] Gerding and Dell'Unto 2022: 183 fig. 19 shows the original basilica mapped onto the material remains.

[117] Cic. *Phil.* 9.15–16. See above, p. 155.

[118] Pliny *HN* 34.22–25.

[119] As Robert Morstein-Marx suggested to me, Cicero also mentions that a Vestal Virgin could have potentially had a seat at the games to lend to others (Cic. *Mur.* 72–73: "si virgo Vestalis ... locum suum gladiatorium concessit huic," "if a Vestal Virgin gave her place at the gladiatorial games to Murena"); by the time of Cicero, was this reserved seat on the Rostra?

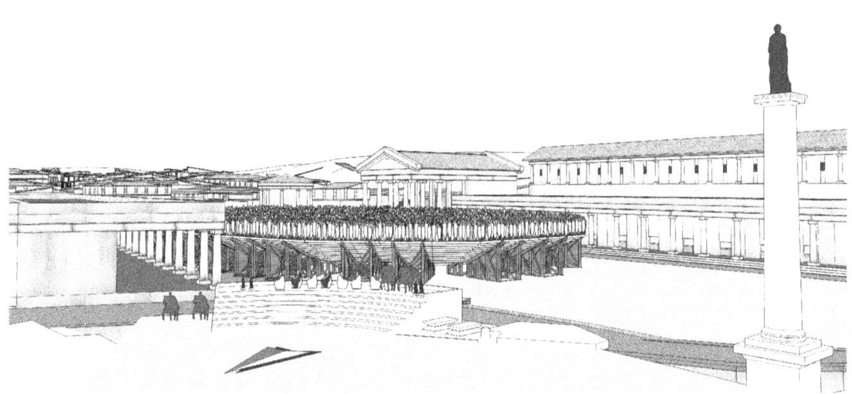

FIGURE 4.7 View from the Basilica Porcia blocked by the walls of an amphitheater.

spectacula for gladiatorial games into the late Republic. The gladiatorial combats staged for the funeral of Paullus would have accommodated viewers from all these distinct, elevated areas. A complex, fully enclosed bleacher system in this space would have had to open up its western end to the audience on the Rostra. (See fig. 4.7.)

COMPARATIVE IMAGERY AS EVIDENCE: TEMPORARY ARENAS

I will now briefly digress to introduce an additional image from an analogous event to help us consider what simple staging options might have been possible and plausible in 160 BCE at the funeral of Paullus. In 1860, in a field near the village of Farnborough, two of the greatest living fighters met in what is now considered the first international championship match in boxing.[120] The stakes were high, upwards of 200 quid, and the reputations of two countries were on the line. John Heenan, from California, represented America, and Tom Sayers, England. These were bare-knuckle brawlers of the highest caliber fighting in a tradition of dockside battles that had been popping up on the sly and illegally for a century throughout the vicinity of 19th century London.

[120] I have attempted to summarize various accounts of the event, see Malakoff 1860, *The Annual Register* 1861: 49–52, Mee 2001: 140–162, and Keating 2010.

FIGURE 4.8 "Championship of England and America." By Jem Ward (Copy of the original painting) [Public domain], via Wikimedia Commons.

The match was preserved in images derived from photographs. Though the art of photography was in its infancy, local talent was keen to put it to creative use. The photographs of the event were not distributed, however. Instead, artists were commissioned to paint stylized versions of the event. Photographs were used to record close-ups of over 400 attendees, each of whom was then incorporated individually into a painting to commemorate the event and to highlight attendees. As evidenced by these commemorative techniques, it was truly a spectacle where being seen was equally important as witnessing the event. To commemorate attendance as a member of the audience was crucial.

The stagecraft and performance context are also illustrative. The fights were illegal, but enormously popular. Lacking state sanction, the event sponsors had to set up quickly. The boxers often fought by a river just in case the authorities were to show, they would have time to dive in and swim to the safety of the neighboring county on the opposite bank. Bare-knuckle fights were conveniently simple. They required little space and, at most, a few hours. Sayers and Heenan lasted 40 rounds—more than two hours—before the fight was stopped and declared a draw. (See fig. 4.8 and 4.9.)

London had become a mega-city by 1860, already teeming with over three million residents. Sport was in its infancy: what had been known as mob football a century before would soon, in 1863, receive its own rules. Spectator sport was, in many ways, even less sophisticated than that of Rome before the advent of the am-

FIGURE 4.9 "The International Contest Between Heenan and Sayers at Farnborough, on the 17th of April 1860." Lithograph with tintstone on paper by W. L. Walton. National Portrait Gallery, Smithsonian Institution. Creative Commons Zero (CC0) license.

phitheater, and before the full monumentalization of the Circus Maximus. People wanted sport, but large, bleacher-based stadiums were only beginning to be used. Tradition instead ruled, but tradition circumscribed by law. Boxing was highly popular but illegal. If there were boxing rings and seating available, Londoners could not have used them. Yet, these were big money shows. They were events that attracted the elite and commoners alike. The attendance at the Sayers versus Heenan international prize fight is estimated to have been somewhere between 12,000 and 30,000. The venue for such numbers? By necessity, a bare field, with a river on one side, a ring of stanchions and a sloping hill on the other.

What could the vast majority of the attendees see? Probably little more than what a modern fan of the Los Angeles Lakers sees from the top row in a modern arena, and most likely, substantially less. Absent replay and instantaneous mass media, physical attendance at an event was the only way to experience the spectacle. Did it matter that you could have barely seen the fighters unless you were in the first few rows? Not necessarily. Most important was the entire show—the pop-up food stands, the crowd, and, of course, the prestige of attendance, preserved for posterity. The paintings and drawings created to commemorate the event can help us think more carefully about the basic requirements of spectacle centered on single combat. We can see a ring composed of stanchions delineated the boxing space from the crowd. The surrounding crowd could stand or sit. One might have sat on the ground, or on a chair, presumably provided at one's own labor. A sloping hill gave some a better vantage point. A select few climbed trees to watch from above.

The line between bare-knuckle boxing and gladiatorial fighting is both fine and broad. They are similar professions, but separated by years and cultural differences that render comparison almost impossible. In terms of stagecraft and overall organization, there are perhaps more similarities between gladiators and bare-knuckle boxers than there were between gladiators of different time periods, however. The gladiator of the arena in the 40s BCE, in the newly repaved Forum plaza, was not quite the same as the one who fought in 79 CE in the Flavian Amphitheater or even as those of the first century BCE who fought in both *fora* and amphitheaters in all towns *except* Rome. In the early second century, the differences were greater: there were no amphitheaters, and no canonical gear; there were simply two men battling in front of a crowd. The men were not even fighting for a purse. We have no clear documentation on the gambling that may have surrounded the event of the early second century. We know only one thing: the men fought because a wealthy family paid for a show in honor of a deceased member of the family. The most extravagant way to do so was to feature, at a funeral, gladiatorial performances lasting a day or more.

Cancelli *and the Arena at the Funeral of Paullus*

So much emphasis on the later development of the monumental amphitheater overshadows the fundamental point made by Vitruvius and the crucial element of gladiatorial performances of the Republic: *fora*—not amphitheaters or bleacher systems—provided the *spectacula*. The Roman Forum was a quintessential multi-use space, and this feature was critical to the nature of public life at Rome. Millar explains the underlying importance of such an adaptable space:

> It was a crucially important characteristic of Roman public life that a wide variety of events took place, on no clearly regulated timetable, in the same physical space, the Forum. It was in this space that the *populus Romanus* played a variety of roles, from idle spectating to the exercise of their sovereign rights as voters. To convert the Forum for a gladiatorial *munus*, all that was needed was to line it with barriers, *cancelli* (for theatrical *ludi*, in contrast, an actual temporary wooden theater might be constructed).[121]

A large-scale bleacher system or even a wooden amphitheater-like structure, no matter how temporary, would have been a monumental imposition in the Forum. Rather than inject an enormous structure into the irregular space of the Forum, I will first expand upon Millar's suggestion to produce a simpler solution that also

---

[121] Millar 1998: 147 first highlights the use of *cancelli* as the only necessary addition to support gladiatorial shows. Goldberg 2013: 17 reviews the evidence within the context of Roman drama.

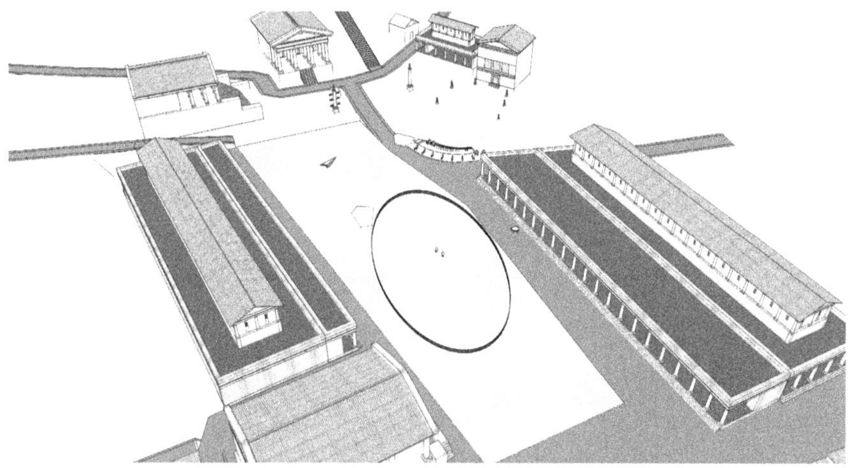

FIGURE 4.10 A simple arena defined by *cancelli*.

better accommodates the evidence for the funeral of 160 BCE: *cancelli*.[122] (See fig. 4.10.)

A representation that delineates the arena space with temporary fencing satisfies the demands of the textual evidence we have reviewed so far. The Rostra can then function as privileged seating with an appropriate view of the events. (See fig. 4.11.) These were not modern box seats, however. Part of the privilege of sitting on the Rostra will have been the opportunity to *be seen*. Without the additional apparatus of a complex bleacher structure, the Rostra remains the "most visible place" in the Forum.[123] The gaze of the audience surrounding the *cancelli* would have been drawn to the Rostra where the visible honor conferred upon a family granted such a seating location would be readily understood. (See fig. 4.12.) In this configuration, the dramatic entrance of the Tribune P. Sestius is no longer occluded, for example. (See fig. 4.13.) And the easy access to the surrounding shops and porticoes is preserved.

This truly *ad hoc* arena demonstrates the effective intrinsic arrangement of *spectacula*, "viewing places," in the Forum. By fencing in such a large space in the central plaza, the obstruction of the surrounding crowd was minimized and unobstructed

[122] The size of extant Republican arenas did not vary by a great amount. Welch 2007: 190 gives the following measurements for the length of each arena: "Pompeii (67 m), Telesia (ca. 68 m), Puteoli (69 m), Nola (ca. 68 m), Cales (ca. 70 m), Cumae (probably ca. 65 m), Carmo (ca. 60 m), Paestum (57 m), Sutrium (50 m)." The *cancelli* in the figures conform to the measurements of the arena at Pompeii: 67 × 35 meters (Welch 2007: 74).

[123] Plin. *HN* 34.24: "senatus statuam poni iussit quam oculatissimo loco, eaque est in Rostris." Dionys. Hal. *Ant. Rom.* 1.87: ἐν τῷ κρατίστῳ χωρίῳ παρὰ τοῖς ἐμβόλοις.

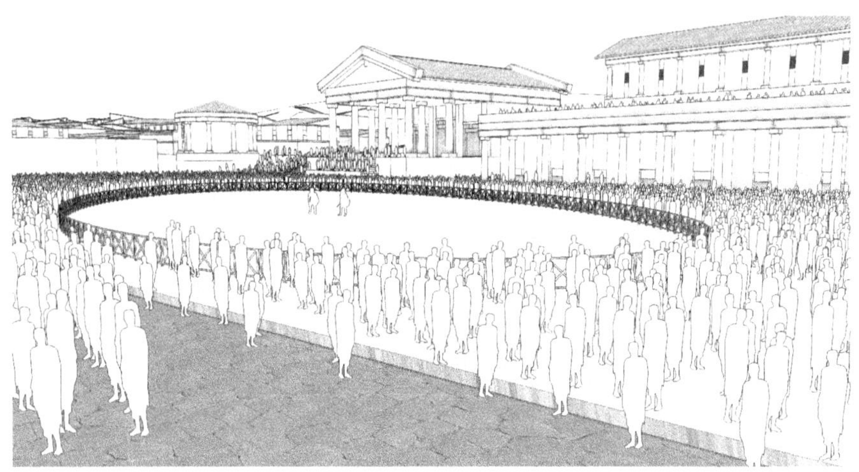

FIGURE 4.11 View of the *ad hoc* arena from the Rostra.

FIGURE 4.12 View from the arena of the Rostra.

FIGURE 4.13 A clear view toward the Columna Maenia and the slope of the Capitoline Hill.

viewsheds were enhanced. As can be seen in the following figures, an arena floor of similar size to those of early amphitheaters also maximizes viewsheds: the larger space allocated to single combat makes it easier for a larger group of audience members to see because there are fewer obstructions near the central performers. In addition, a larger arena produces a longer perimeter that can accommodate more front-row audience members. One obviously could have watched the event from the Forum plaza. (See fig. 4.14.) In addition, excellent views were available from the *maeniana* over the shops in front of the Basilica Fulvia. (See fig. 4.15.) In fact, most of the elevated space in the Forum offered surprisingly effective *spectacula*. For example, moving clockwise, there were clear views of the event from the podium of the Temple of Castor (fig. 4.16), the *maeniana* over the shops in front of the Basilica Sempronia (fig. 4.17), the podium of the Temple of Saturn (fig. 4.18), the slope of the Capitoline (fig. 4.19), the stepped area of Concord (fig. 4.20), and the *maeniana* of the Basilica Porcia (fig. 4.21). This configuration was not merely a practical and efficient solution for rapidly staging games without blocking the Forum with temporary architecture; it may have accommodated a larger audience than a purpose-built bleacher system.

This *ad hoc* seating arrangement calls to mind the arrangement of a number of irregular public spaces forced to accommodate spectacle in the modern world, such as concerts held in parks, closed streets, or central plazas of major cities. Gladiatorial shows in the Roman Forum *were* different from elsewhere. The combats may have had a certain homogenized feel in the rest of Italy, once regularized structures

FIGURE 4.14 View of the gladiators from the Forum plaza.

became the norm. Spectacle held in those arenas also needed to acknowledge the patron of the monument, which, in Rome, would undermine the point of a funerary performance meant to honor the deceased. When held in an *ad hoc* unobtrusive arena, the shows could have capitalized on the full weight of the symbolic capital of the space. A temporary amphitheater homogenizes the viewing locations, thus minimizing the potential loci available to be seen—this was a desired effect in the Empire. In the Republic, however, a simple arena, demarcated by *cancelli* avoided the isolating effect of a large-scale bleacher system and instead facilitated interaction with the surrounding space and maintained continuity with the rest of the funerary activities.

THE CULMINATING EVENT

Ludi funebres contained more than gladiatorial combats. The evidence for the staging of plays and gladiatorial games at the *ludi funebres* of L. Aemilius Paullus is irrefutable. The "theater" at those games should be conceived of in only the loosest

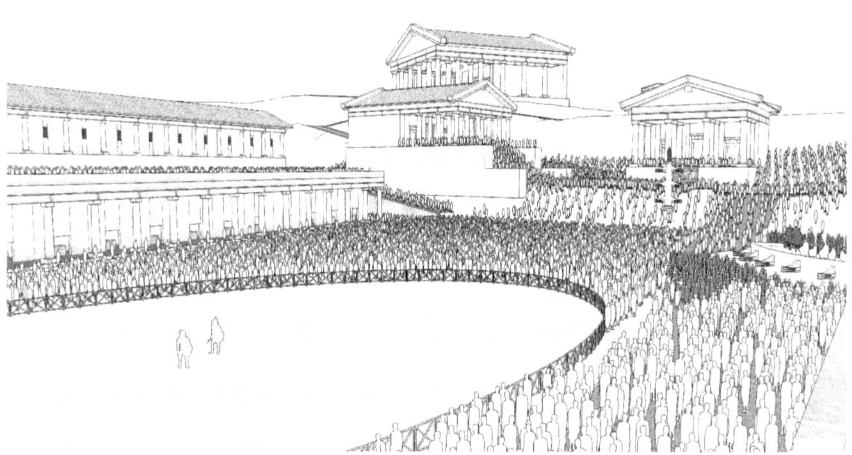

FIGURE 4.15 View of the gladiators from the *maeniana* of the Basilica Fulvia.

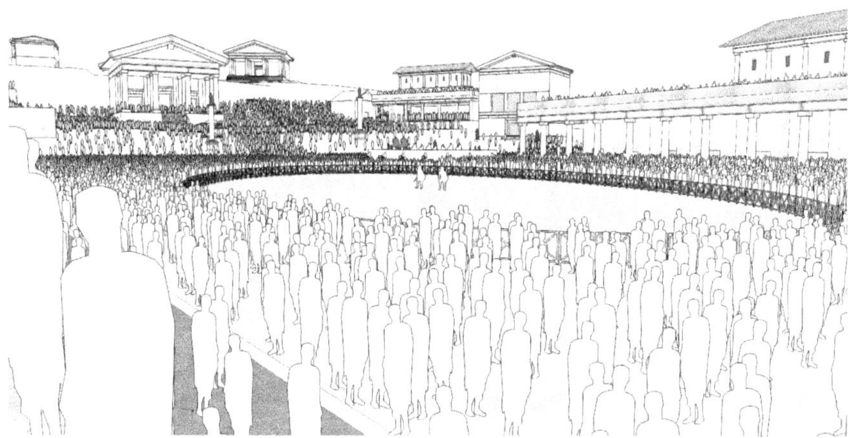

FIGURE 4.16 View of the gladiators from the Temple of Castor.

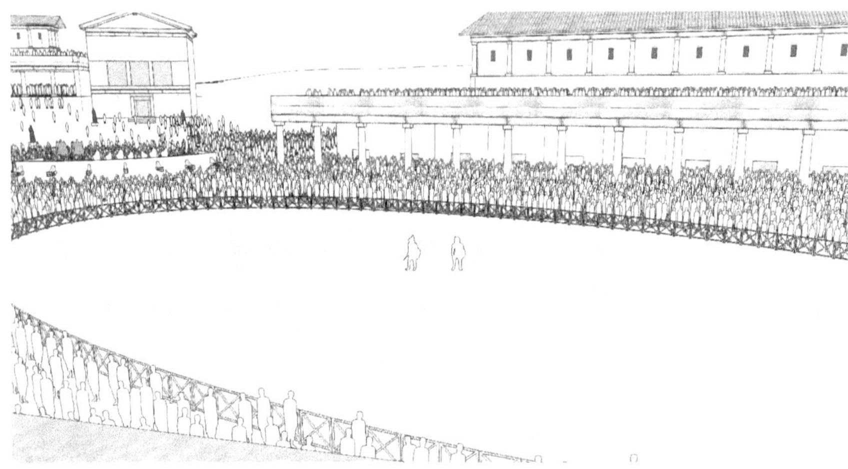

FIGURE 4.17 View of the gladiators from the Basilica Sempronia.

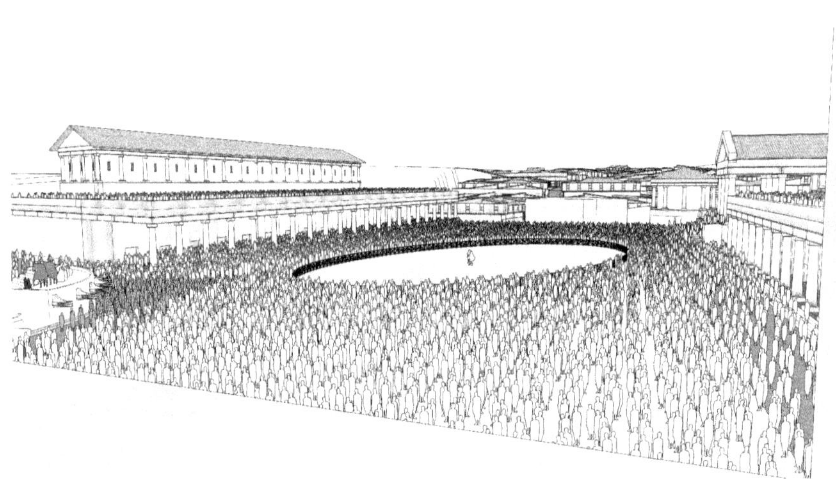

FIGURE 4.18 View of the gladiators from the Temple of Saturn.

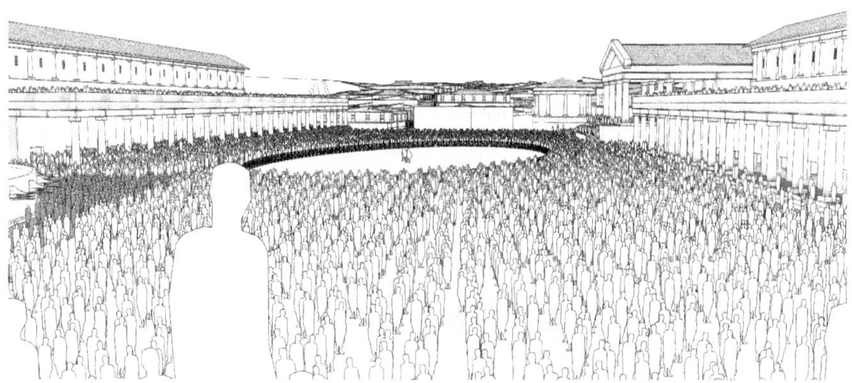

FIGURE 4.19 View of the gladiators from the slope of the Capitoline.

FIGURE 4.20 View of the gladiators from the Temple of Concord.

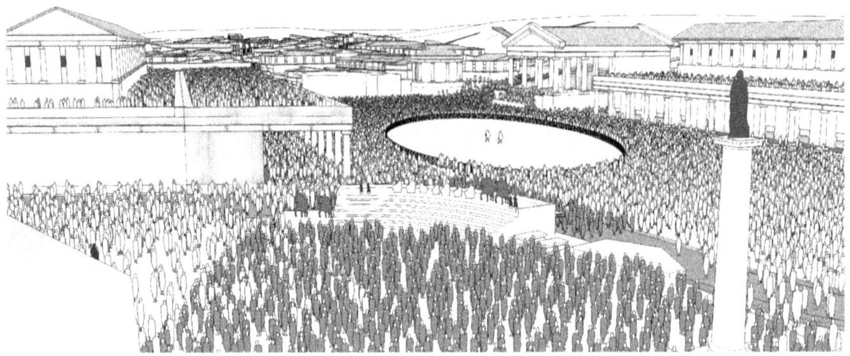

FIGURE 4.21 View of the gladiators from the *maeniana* of the Basilica Porcia.

sense.[124] The combats and performances shared the same space. Spectators for one event *might* intrude on spectators for another. The possible options are:

- A temporary stage was built within the arena of a temporary amphitheater. The audience used the *cavea* of the amphitheater to watch the theatrical performances. The stage was dismantled prior to the start of the gladiatorial games. (See fig. 4.22.)
- A temporary "theater" was erected *alongside* the temporary amphitheater. (See fig. 4.22.)
- There was no theater building, only an *ad hoc* stage and benches. Likewise, there was no wooden amphitheater, only a central *arena* demarcated by *cancelli.* (See fig. 4.23.)

[124] In the following examples, I construct a temporary stage according to Beacham 1992 and Hughes 1996. The visualized stage is hypothetical and problematic. Beacham 1992: 56–85 relies on wall paintings to reconstruct the stage. Hughes 1996 focuses on vases. Cf. Marshall 2006: 32–33, who finds multiple problems with both types of evidence. Marshall critiques the use of wall paintings as evidence for Roman stagecraft (32): "The combination of imperial wall painting, incorporating features found on temporary South Italian stages, and employing Greek *trompe l'oeil* painting techniques is too complex a combination to posit without corroboration." And the use of vases (33): "As the influence of fifth-century Athenian comedy on these illustrations becomes increasingly apparent, there exists less reason to assume that any Italian traditions used such stages, to say nothing of the chronological disparities." Marshall also objects to the notion of an elevated stage and argues that the steps implied two levels of performance space. See Goldberg 2018 for a related, experimental exploration of the Forum.

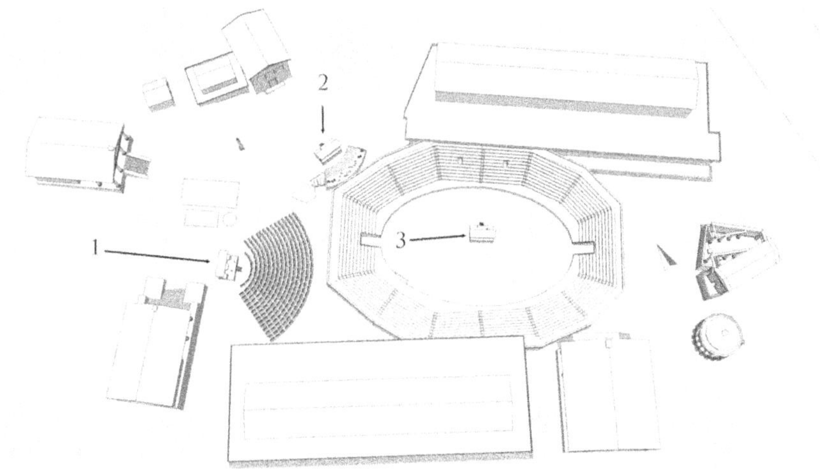

FIGURE 4.22 Multiple stage configurations and the temporary amphitheater. 1. Hypothetical stage placed next to the Temple of Saturn. 2. Hypothetical stage located in the Comitium. 3. Hypothetical stage located in the arena.

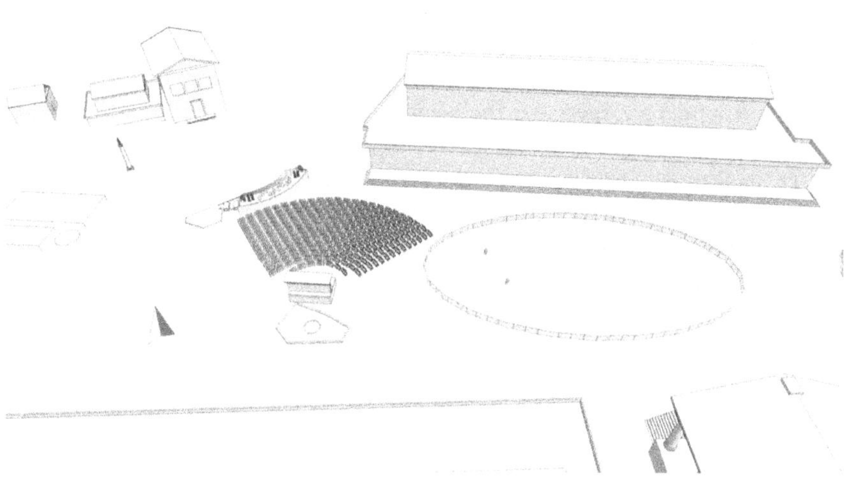

FIGURE 4.23 The *ad hoc arena* and a hypothetical stage.

Timing was critical. If the games were staged on the day after the exequies, then the construction of wooden seating would have interfered with the *pompa* and the *laudatio*. A temporary wooden amphitheater, built in the center of the Forum, and braced by timbers connecting to the surrounding basilicas would have blocked the processional pathways. The visual impact of the procession as it entered the Forum would have been greatly diminished if forced to move *under* the bleachers of the amphitheater. The procession might have moved *through* the amphitheater, however. (See fig. 4.22.) Under this model, it would have used a spectacular mechanism similar to the triumph, which marched through the circuses of the city. The large wooden amphitheater would have partitioned the *pompa* into two clearly distinct phases of viewing, however. The audience would have first gathered in the wooden amphitheater to watch the procession as it entered the Forum. Afterward, everyone would have headed to the Rostra to await the *laudatio*. In this scenario, the temporary amphitheater interferes with the staging of the funeral. The construction process for such elaborate seating could have shut down the Forum for days. Not impossible, but improbable. Unless, of course, the family wished to turn its back on the Forum and its symbolic capital. Perhaps up-and-coming families with no ancestors to show might wish to subordinate the parade of *imagines* and the *laudatio funebris* in favor of the gladiatorial show.

Why should there have been a temporary amphitheater or bleacher system in the Forum of 160 BCE? Unlike in the rest of Italy, where, according to Vitruvius, the design of central *fora* was rectilinear and meant to accommodate public shows, at Rome the games adapted to the Roman Forum. The Roman Forum was not designed to host games. The buildings of the Forum did not follow a standardized plan. Though it was not an ideal spectator space, it was the hub of the city. In place of symmetrical seating, the Forum offered a flexible environment that could incorporate surrounding imagery into the event. Its location in the civic heart of the city guaranteed an audience. As noted above, it is quite possible that the first attempt to charge for seating in the Forum plaza was in 123 BCE. Previously, the poor could have watched the games unobstructed, on the Forum floor.

Spectator accommodations influence understanding of attendance habits. The model of a fixed amphitheater presupposes an audience who attended for the duration of the event solely to observe the combats, as in the case of a modern-day football game. For gladiatorial matches held over multiple days, six to seven per day, it is equally likely that attendance was sporadic. An audience member might have watched the show for an hour, before leaving to manage the rest of the day's affairs. It might even be the case that an audience member would have attended the beginning of a dramatic performance only to be pulled away by the lure of the arena. The games themselves were disruptive, but their monumental facilities need not have been.

Little infrastructure was required to show *ludi funebres*. To hold funeral games on the ninth day after death, the organization of the event had to be tractable. The

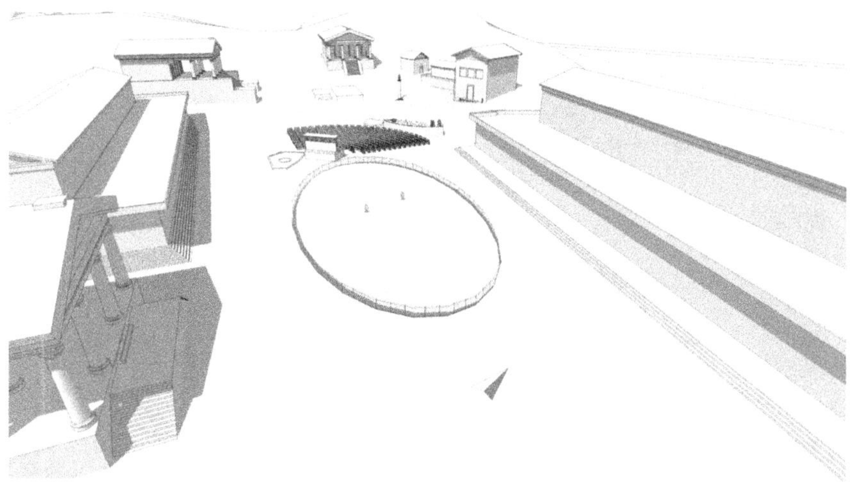

FIGURE 4.24 A hypothetical temporary stage and the *cancelli* of the arena.

principal expense of staging a Roman funeral was the hiring of performers.[125] It was, therefore, a simple matter to install some benches, if needed, on one side of the Forum to accommodate plays on the first day; then, to install small barriers to demarcate the arena in the central plaza. (See fig. 4.24.) It might have been the case that benches were not necessary. Those who owned their own chairs could have carried them to the show themselves. The gladiatorial games, which depended more on sights than sounds, could have drawn and accommodated a large audience—potentially much larger than a hypothetical amphitheater in the Forum could have contained. In contrast to viewing the *pompa* and the *laudatio*, to watch the gladiatorial games the audience could have lined the entire Forum, stood on the steps of the basilicas, marked out places on the *maeniana*, stood on temple podia, and even, as Cicero suggests, used the slope of the Capitoline as *spectacula*. As we have seen, the views provided by all these locations would have been very good. If the *cancelli* kept the central arena clear, the Forum, for all of its irregularity, could well have transformed into an effective staging area for gladiatorial combat. (See fig. 4.25.)

The Forum as Adaptable Stage

The funeral of Paullus showcased the Forum. The *pompa* and the *laudatio* were the opening events. The *ludi funebres* followed. Dramatic performances, gladiatorial combats, and a host of activities were staged entirely within the Forum. In some cases, the dinner (*epulum*) would have followed. After removing the *cancelli* for the

[125] As later expenditures attest, skilled gladiators were expensive to hire. See, e.g., Carter 2003.

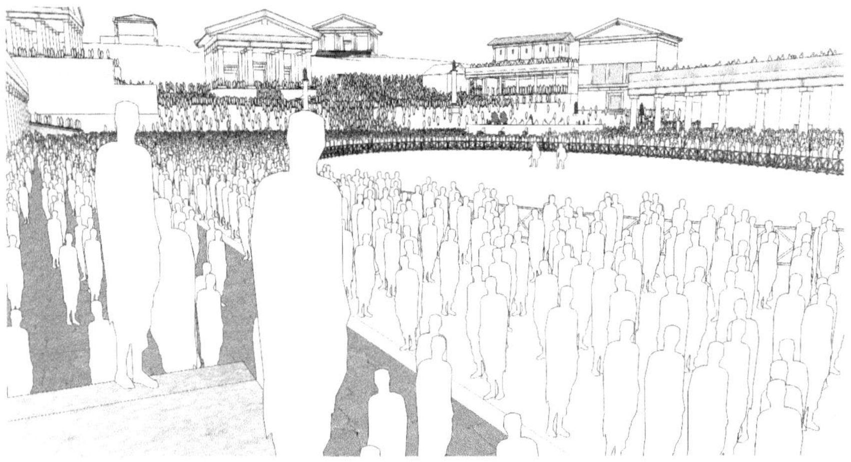

FIGURE 4.25 The *ad hoc spectacula* in the Forum. Note the spectators on the slope of the Capitoline, the Rostra, and on the surrounding *maeniana*.

arena, workers would have needed to transport hundreds of dining couches to the Forum. In each case, the key to staging the event was the ability to rapidly implement the staging apparatus to let the family take full advantage of the opportunity to hold an extended event in the Forum. And in each case, interaction with the Forum space was facilitated by the staged event. The Forum could have still accommodated day-to-day activities despite the intrusion of the *ludi funebres*. Meanwhile, the imagery of the Forum would not have been obstructed by the staging apparatus.

The Roman funeral games of Paullus were spectacular, they were events to see and be seen, but they were not monumental. They did not require a sophisticated production apparatus. Spectator accommodations were never the cause for later acclaim. In the extant sources, funeral games were recorded based on the number of pairs put on display. Each pair represented a quantifiable expenditure. Development of distinct seating arrangements makes no similar mark in the record. Lengthy preparation need not have delayed the games. Nonetheless, these performances were still, by far, the most expensive component of the funeral and would have served as a clear example of conspicuous consumption for the family of the deceased.[126] Those who knew the costs, and Polybius counted among them, could have estimated accurately how much was spent on Paullus' funeral games simply by counting pairs of gladiators. Polybius argued that the *laudatio* and the *pompa* were the principal elements of an aristocratic funeral, but his failure to mention

[126] Polyb. 31.28.5–7: the games for Paullus cost 30 talents.

the games has colored modern interpretations. The evidence indicates the contrary. The games in the second century were an integral part of the funeral, used as a capstone to the entire sequence of events. As Cicero reminds us (*Leg.* 2.61–62), it was considered custom by the late Republic that the funerals of import, *i.e.*, those that had *ludi*, were the ones that should be publicized. In consequence, the *ludi funebres*, not the *pompa* and not the *laudatio*, constituted the most spectator-friendly, the most easily accessible, and, for many in the audience, the most memorable spectacular elements of a Roman aristocratic funeral.

CHAPTER 5

Conclusion

A FUNERAL IN THE FORUM

The funeral of Lucius Aemilius Paullus reshapes our understanding of the Roman spectacular triad of procession, oration, and games. Throughout the course of my argument, the individual elements of this triad diverged from expectations raised by their independent generic forms. An aristocratic funeral presented disparate themes, with spatial tendrils reaching from home to Forum to tomb outside the city. The deceased and the ancestral *imagines* represent primary themes for study of the aristocratic funeral. As we have seen, each played extraordinarily important cultural roles. I contend, however, that the central organizing principle of the aristocratic funeral at Rome—one that makes it differ from all other funerals—is its setting, the Roman Forum. The Forum offered an integrated backdrop of continuity. It influenced all aspects of each "script." For all the individual narratives that might have developed in each family, and for all the processional paths that might have been taken from home to tomb, the Forum ensured that each funeral was in dialog with funerals past and future. The influence of the funerary context and the space of the Forum itself modifies our interpretations of each component of the funeral and fundamentally reshapes our understanding of the complete event.

The Toolkit of Spectacle for an Aristocratic Funeral

The *pompa funebris* was a procession *sui generis*. It resembled and was in dialog with processions at state-sponsored or state-approved events. Comparisons to the triumph that were explicitly made in the ancient texts need to be qualified, however. From the routing, to the preparation time, to the management of theatrical moments, a triumph was a far more complex and well-planned affair than a funeral *pompa*. The funeral did not benefit from a traditionally prescribed and lengthy entry route—the procession always began at a different house, whereas a triumph tended to begin in one location. There was little time to plan and a large audience was difficult to assemble. The purpose of the triumph was not only to deliver the general to the Capitoline Hill, but it was also to showcase the spectacle of the parade. For the funeral, however, the procession was the conveyance mechanism for the ritual and not so well-suited for displays of familial power. Families could innovate by altering the route in order to promote visual connections to symbolic capital.

The *laudatio* deviated from more traditional forms of oratory due to its set of unique props—the body of the deceased and a parade of storied ancestors. The event was clearly the visual highlight of the initial stage of the funeral. The ancestors and the deceased, rising relatively high above the rest of the Forum, drew the attention of the nearby crowd. The size of the crowd is debatable, but the highly visual nature of the oration is not. It was designed to be legible from a distance. Innovations such as those of the Cornelii and the Porcii further worked to guide the eye to the Rostra. These were all visual suggestions not commands, however. Those in the Forum were not compelled to look, and they certainly were not compelled to listen. It was unlikely that the majority of the audience could have heard much at all. Instead, the visual elements facilitated understanding of the event. Subtle manipulations of spatial relationships, such as the placement of the body *vis-à-vis* the eulogist, could have a profound effect on the reception of the *laudatio*. For many, it was possible that the speech was secondary to the visual display. The constraints imposed on the speech by tradition and occasion potentially limited its ability to impress the vast majority of those in the Forum. The relative youth and inexperience of the orator and the rather mundane genre of praise worked against it. Therefore, the words of the *laudatio* seem to have been designed to accommodate the eulogist and the family, who stood close to the Rostra, while the visuals were designed to reach the rest of the Forum.

Polybius found meaning in the *laudatio* that did not coincide with the system of reward displayed by the *imagines*. For him, the speech and the display of the ancestors inspired young Roman versions of Achilles—men ready to die young for their country—rather than would-be consuls and censors. Few would have achieved a triumph by spending one's youth engaging in single combat. Yet Polybius saw the speech through Greek eyes. As Dio's Antony reminds us by suggesting that most *laudationes* were short so as not to lose the audience, the rest of the Forum was not necessarily concerned with or inspired by the details. Only the youth, the family, and close friends, such as Polybius, were predisposed to listen and could have stood close enough to hear. Roman aristocrats might have hoped for "a shared sympathy" from "all of the people," as Polybius describes the reception of the speech, but that was not the principal reason why most Romans came to the Forum. There were shops, and courts, magisterial business, religious functions, and festivals.

Room for exaggeration in the funerary sphere was great. Polybius selected the funeral as his example of Roman institutional superiority to the Carthaginians. It made little sense for him to focus on the problematic aspects of the display that might be more difficult to explain to his Greek audience. He omitted the strange and histrionic mourning customs of the Romans, the carnivalesque atmosphere, and the gladiators.

His most conspicuous omission, gladiatorial combat, would have also been the most appropriate to include. Centuries after the death of Paullus, Pliny writes on gladiators at the shows of Trajan:

> Visum est spectaculum inde non enerve, nec fluxum, nec quod animos virorum molliret et frangeret, sed quod ad pulchra vulnera contemptumque mortis *accenderet.*
>
> A spectacle was seen which was not weak and limp, and which would not soften and break the spirits of men, rather it would inflame them toward beautiful wounds and a contempt of death.[1]

Using similar language, Sallust reflects on his reasons for retelling the deeds of great men:

> Nam saepe ego audivi Q. Maximum, P. Scipionem, praeterea civitatis nostrae praeclaros viros solitos ita dicere, cum maiorum imagines intuerentur, vehementissime sibi animum ad virtutem *accendi.*
>
> For I have often heard Quintus Fabius Maximus and Publius Scipio Africanus—and in addition, outstanding men of our citizenry—say that their spirits were vigorously inflamed toward virtue, whenever they contemplated the *imagines* of their ancestors.[2]

According to Sallust the *imagines* could inflame a Roman toward the pursuit of *virtus*. For Pliny the Younger, gladiatorial games could kindle a desire that recalls the motivational capacity of the funeral that Polybius observes. Some consider the didactic character of gladiatorial games paramount.[3] The games seem not to have impressed Polybius, however.

He wished to focus on institutions that made the Romans a dominant military force, but overlooked their institutionalized, public combats that were held in the heart of the civic center of the city. Modern studies that take seriously the notion

---

[1] Plin. *Pan.* 33.

[2] Sall. *Iug.* 4.

[3] Cic. *Tusc.* 2.17.41: "cum vero sontes ferro depugnabant, auribus fortasse multae, oculis quidem nulla poterat esse fortior contra dolorem et mortem disciplina." ("when criminals fought with swords, for the ears there were perhaps many ways, but for the eyes, indeed, nothing could have been a stronger lesson against pain and death.") Wiedemann 1992: 35–38 adduces the funeral speech for L. Caecilius Metellus discussed in Chapter 2 as evidence that Roman aristocrats wished to become *primarium bellatorem* and prided themselves on skill at single combat. Futrell 2000: 50: "The public in the stands was expected to emulate and surpass the gladiator in qualities highly appropriate to the imperialistic goal." As Coleman 2006: 233–234 notes, however, Gellius *NA* 12.5.13–14 considers a gladiator's contempt for death *contra naturam*, not *virtus*.

that Roman military commanders actively sought out monomachy during battle refer to the games as influential.[4] Yet Polybius fails to mention an event that would have served, at the very least, to demonstrate the Romans' enthusiasm for violent combat, even in peace.

The games are the key to understanding the *ad hoc* nature of the funeral production. Their staging originated at the tomb, and the simplicity of the viewing situation persisted until the late Republic. At some unknown point in time, an aristocrat chose to hold a *laudatio* for his father in the Forum. The practical benefits of such a choice were obvious: a public oration on the Rostra could command the attention of an audience who might have come to the Forum for other business. The Forum was the heart of mid-Republican Rome and it was located in close proximity to the homes of the most powerful and storied aristocratic families.[5] To commandeer this space was a means of demonstrating familial status and honor.[6]

A question remains frustratingly unanswered. While the events surrounding the funeral of Paullus clearly dominated the Forum and affected the entire city, was explicit permission required to perform the three acts of a funeral? More specifically, was permission required to parade through the Forum, to give a speech on the Rostra, and/or to hold games? By the late Republic, Sulla received a *funus publicum*, and it is this funeral that is the first attested to have been accompanied by the proclamation of a *iustitium*, which resulted in a formal cessation of all official activity in the Forum and at Rome. For Paullus, and those like him, it is impossible to determine whether a similar declaration occurred. While it is clear that a *funus publicum* would occur with a *iustitium* declared, there is no evidence to indicate that such official proclamations were necessary for a large-scale funeral during the middle Republic.[7] One might assume that some formal mechanism was required to parade into the Forum and to occupy the Rostra, but I am not aware of evidence to indicate such a mechanism was specifically required. Perhaps the evidence has been lost. Or perhaps the process was organic and built around custom. Diodorus Siculus' description of the funeral of Paullus, for example, implies that the interest generated to show support for the deceased led to a gradual cessation of activity, culminating in magistrates ceasing to perform their duties without mention of a formal decree.[8] The images I present in this book depict a Forum full of attendees who focus on the various funerary events, and the testimony regarding Paullus' fu-

---

[4] Oakley 1987: 35: "It is obvious that there are many similarities between a single combat fought with both armies watching and a gladiatorial show." Rich 1999 explores the claim that Drusus the Elder was exceedingly zealous in his pursuit of one-on-one combat on the battlefield.

[5] Purcell 1995b discusses the early tension between the public and private sphere manifest in the Forum.

[6] Control of the Forum and the Rostra in particular became increasingly important until the end of the Republic. See Arce 2000: 64. See also Millar 1998: 41: "When violence became a regular feature of *contiones* and of meetings of the *comitia tributa*, physical control and occupation of the Rostra became a crucial objective."

[7] On the categories of funerals and the *funus publicum*, see above, pp. 16n4 and 95n103.

[8] See above, p. 33.

neral implies that all focused on him. Nonetheless, were shops required to close? Were law courts officially shut down for large-scale funerals? Possibly, but these were also temporary installations, whose *tribunalia* and *subsellia* were apparently easily moved.[9] I personally think the death itself and its public commemoration were the metaphorical key that opened the door, as deaths often do, to activities that in other circumstances might require more formal approval. If one possessed *imagines*, that might be enough to allow for a parade into the Forum and a eulogy on the Rostra. If one were wealthy enough, the tradition of funeral games in Rome, in Italy, and in the Mediterranean might be so overwhelming that, if one wished to host games in the Forum, there was no mechanism to deny it, nor any mechanism to seek approval. For the moment at least, in my view, it is simply impossible to reach an evidence-based conclusion on this point.

It remains the case that the Forum provided potent symbolic context. The tacit acceptance that the games were often delayed has led directly to a retrojection of later evidence and an accidental diminishing of the significance of *ad hoc* spectacle. Wooden theaters and amphitheaters, which have been reconstructed by blending evidence from different time periods, would have altered the symbolic effect of the surrounding built environment.[10] The gladiators were on display, but so was the rest of the symbolic capital in the surrounding Forum. The primary advantage of having "box seats" on raised platforms like the Rostra was the elevation of status bestowed upon the family, not necessarily a better view of the event. The space was well-equipped to house a number of different *ad hoc* spectacles. It was also neutral. Aristocrats were vying to put their names on individual monuments, but no one had his name attached to the Roman Forum. The arena and the theater remained outside of the sphere of competitive architecture. By staging events in the Forum, an aristocratic family could have demonstrated its wealth and power through the number of theatrical performances and gladiatorial combats it sponsored. There was no need to build a more sophisticated architectural form, and there was little time available for such a project. Speed was fundamental to staging these events. The deterioration of the recently deceased demanded fast action, and the funerary preparations could not obstruct the Forum for long.

The simple arrangement of *cancelli*, *sellae*, and *subsellia* was an efficient and effective means of staging *ludi funebres*. The flexibility of such portable infrastructure satisfies the textual evidence and the exigencies of the Forum. Such a simple apparatus highlights how the topographical arrangement, varied as it was, accommodated spectacle. To hold oratorical or theatrical events in all corners of the Forum re-

---

[9] Asc. *Mil.* 29 and Suet. *Iul.* 84.3. both report that tribunals were movable; in both examples they are used as kindling.

[10] There are also less quantifiable benefits. A temporary bleacher system provides better sight lines to the majority of an audience, but it compromises overall aesthetics and comfort. For example, Olsen 1979: 48–52, writing on musical performances of colonial Philadelphia, notes that the temporary theaters of the time were rarely as architecturally or aesthetically impressive as the major public buildings that were sometimes used as performance spaces.

quired an elevated stage, whereas a gladiatorial contest could have been performed in the central plaza. The result? The *pompa* and the *laudatio* lay the groundwork for the final and most important demonstration of individual and familial power and largess, the *ludi funebres*. Perhaps it is no accident that the only surviving testimony that mentions explicitly a formal announcement of a funeral states that this occurs when *ludi* are planned.

The entire funerary spectacle in the Forum was continuous, multi-day street theater. For many in Rome, the *pompa* and the *laudatio* were not the culmination of the event, but instead the public announcement of things to come: the parade and the *imagines* in the Forum were also visible indicators that, if the public were so lucky, the *ludi funebres* would be next.[11] The carnivalesque atmosphere surrounding the funeral procession and the treatment of the deceased may strike the modern reader as odd, but only if viewed without broader context. The carnivalesque was a primary element of the funeral, in part because the public space within which it was held was a shared concern of all Romans; hierarchies were visible but they were also subverted; reserved seating was the exception not the rule; and all took place in the location where the fundamental and public events were held, the Forum.[12] The Roman funeral was a source of continuous spectacle. Not merely a solemn occasion for the commemoration of the deceased, but a blend of mourning ritual, commemoration, and political manipulation. During the second century BCE, the games were not stand-alone events, separated by weeks or months from the *laudatio* and *pompa*. Rather, they formed an integral part of the public spectacle of the funeral—an event that capitalized on the integration of the Forum space into the entire production.

The Role of the Forum

Nearly every element of Paullus' funeral would have been engineered to interact with the Forum. In fact, his funeral and its games would have been presented in front of his own contributions to the built environment. In 168, so the story goes, at the conclusion of the battle of Pydna, the Dioscuri appeared near Rome to announce the Roman victory and were later seen in the Forum, watering their horses at the Lacus Iuturnae.[13] Four years later, when Paullus was appointed censor, he commissioned the construction of statues of Castor and Pollux to be placed in the Lacus Iuturnae, adjacent to the Temple of Castor and Pollux. In addition, though the textual record is silent, the archaeological record tells us that a modification to the Temple of Castor and Pollux occurred around this time. Its front row of columns was removed and an elevated platform was added. Due to his overt affil-

[11] Cic. *Leg.* 2.61: "funus ut indicatur *si quid ludorum*."

[12] On the carnival, see Bakhtin 1984. As it happens, the events occur in front of the Temple of Saturn, whose own festival, the *Saturnalia* famously subverted hierarchies and norms.

[13] For an in-depth investigation of the Dioscuri as symbols of Roman victory, see Sumi 2009, esp. 175n40 where he surveys the sources regarding the appearance of the Dioscuri in the Forum following the battle at Pydna.

iation with these gods, it is often hypothesized that this modification was carried out by Paullus.[14]

From the time of the Twelve Tables, a funeral with *ludi*, which was the maximal instantiation of an aristocratic funeral, needed to be announced publicly. This provided an opportunity to insert the deceased and the deceased's immediate family into the fabric of the Forum. It allowed opportunity for the children of the deceased to hold a simulacrum of a triumph to celebrate their family and to place it on par with the elite who had come before. The line-up of ancestors reinforced Roman history told through the lens of one group's agnatic genealogy. It also placed these ancestors on the principal stage in the Forum, in dialog with the commemorative monuments that surrounded them. The *ludi* capped off the event by temporarily inserting the family into a calendar and a city's festival days and public spaces that were otherwise reserved for traditional celebrations related to the divine or to the Roman state. The ancestors on stage bore the names used to refer to specific years in the historical record; these same names were associated with buildings, with cults, with statuary, and paintings, all visible in the Forum. An aristocratic funeral at Rome was inextricably connected to the Roman Forum, and it is evident that each family used this connection in advantageous and innovative ways.

CONCLUSIONS: THREE ACTS

Three Acts: Increasing Visual Registers

The spectacle of the funeral consisted not of three disparate parts, but of a three-act theatrical performance that used the same semiotic system, the same principles of stagecraft, and the same setting throughout.[15] The visible presence of the family and its deposited symbolic capital are the most important elements of the display. The degree of their presence determined the specific aspects of each element of the funeral. When assessed within a vertical hierarchy, the family's position moves upward, step-by-step, from *pompa* to *ludi*, with a transference from dead to living, emphasized at each phase.

During the procession, the deceased towers above the rest of the funerary participants, with his or her ancestors dominating the next register in the visual hierarchy while simultaneously upsetting the symmetrical, horizontal balance of the cortege. The ancestors lead the way in a crescendo that culminates with the exclamatory full stop of the deceased, elevated on the funeral bier.

---

[14] See Steinby 1996, Clarke 1968: 147–148, and Nielsen et al. 1992 for the modifications that led to Temple IA, the version with columns removed and platform added.

[15] See Pina Polo 2009: 100, who asserts, "The funeral of an aristocrat in Rome was conceived as a theatrical representation, a genuine dramatization of memory where actors and real people, both dead and alive, intermingled to make up a collective drama which was both a farewell to the deceased and an overcoming of his absence."

At the Rostra, the deceased and the ancestors climb higher, to a level in direct semiotic rivalry with the surrounding competitive visual hierarchy. Whether the deceased or the ancestors are featured is partly a familial decision, but in either case, this is the moment where the past is emphasized. A window into the future is also opened: the *laudator*, if a member of the family, has now joined the illustrious group in this elevated register. The rest of the family remains below.

At the *ludi*, an additional elevation may have occurred. It can never be proven with certainty, but the preponderance of evidence suggests that the elevated platforms of the Forum offer one last opportunity for the family to shine. Tribunals, temple podia, *maeniana*, and even the Rostra itself might have accommodated the sponsoring family. The deceased was no longer a participant and neither were the ancestors. The living family replaced them instead. By climbing up to occupy the upper visual register, the family, for the first time during the funeral performance, joined the same vertical level of competitive imagery recently occupied by representational family members of the past. Thus it offered a visual confirmation that the family would carry on, cashing in on the symbolic capital of the family's heritage by physically occupying the same stage and the same elevated visual register as the ancestors who had come before. In addition, the family engaged directly in a visual competition with the rest of the competitive imagery of the Forum.

Considering the three events, *pompa*, *laudatio*, and *ludi*, as a cohesive whole reveals the Forum itself to be a critical player in each act. The symbolic capital deposited by the leading political players of the family is withdrawn at critical stages during each performance. In the procession, connections to monuments dedicated by family members or symbolic connections to religious or civic traditions are made explicit by the route of the procession, or by secondary or tertiary branches of the procession that deliver the *imagines* of the deceased. Similarly, during the *laudatio*, these visual connections are exploited. Perhaps, as might have been the case during the funeral of Paullus, these connections were exploited by interacting with monuments constructed during his own magistracy, or simply by capitalizing on the one opportunity to place the family's accumulated savings of symbolic capital on the most visible stage in the city, the Rostra. Thus, *imagines* and deceased, in full regalia, are visible and quantifiable withdrawals of this capital.

The same rules apply to the third act: at the games, the family took center stage. On elevated platforms, on *maeniana*, or even on the Rostra, the presence of the family was highlighted. Did the family watch from its own *maeniana*? Prior to the addition of a basilica to the city, did the family who owned a home surrounding the Forum, like that of Scipio Africanus, watch prior games from private balconies on their own *domus*?

The fundamental principle, however, is to ensure familial prominence within the potent semiotic landscape of the Forum. The gladiatorial games were a means to an end. It is curious that the limited textual evidence about the staging of gladiatorial games points to an extraordinarily consistent pattern of growth, when demonstrations of lavish expenditure are recorded. To put on a larger spectacle of gladiators involved, for the most part, hiring more gladiators. The spatial-temporal consequences of this conclusion have not been emphasized enough: more pairs yield *more* fights, which require *more* time. One last comparison to the triumph is useful. Triumphs were marked by the quantity of gold, booty, and prisoners on display, but they were also measured in the historic record by a simple metric: not length of procession in linear feet, but by number of days. The more days an event could occupy, the more impressive the historic report. At the *ludi funebres*, multiple pairs *could* have fought in the Forum simultaneously. Mock naval battles *could* have been staged, but they apparently were not.

There is also no record, before Plutarch's note on 123 BCE, of the construction of temporary stands for funeral games. In fact, the use of an enclosed, amphitheater-like structure is precisely the vehicle one might use to cut off the visual intrusions of the surrounding space. Such is the view often applied to the monumental Roman theater and its *scaenae frons*. These constructions exist to focus the gaze inward. For gladiatorial games held in the Forum in 160 BCE at the funeral of L. Aemilius Paullus, the goal, in part, was the opposite: to focus the gaze of the audience on the visible presence of the deceased's family at the games and on the symbols of familial accomplishment visible throughout the Forum. In the second century BCE, gladiators had not yet become celebrity superstars. They were merely combatants taking part in a larger semiotic argument. The family, not the fighters, were the stars. The gladiators were the entertainment, but the historical record preserves only their numbers and those who paid for them.

Though the development of the form of the amphitheater may ultimately derive from temporary seating constructed in the Forum on or after 123 BCE, there is an alternative narrative based instead on the model of the funeral proposed above. Gladiatorial activity outside Rome is an epiphenomenon derived from a similar but fundamentally different activity from that of funerary *munera gladiatoria* held within the eternal city. The chronological development of the monumental amphitheater outside Rome, and its association with Roman military colonies is complementary to funeral games at Rome. The monumental amphitheater represented the development of the games as independent spectacle. Amphitheaters were sponsored by those who saw no need to connect to the semiotic landscape of their local forum. Instead the monuments were potentially constructed as a means to avoid engaging with the symbolic capital on deposit in regional *fora*. These new monuments, like a monumental theater, offered those whose families did not have a wealth of symbolic capital a way to isolate the audience, and to focus their attention solely on the sponsored show.

Three Acts: State, Ancestors, Family

The complete funeral of Lucius Aemilius Paullus Macedonicus unfolded in three parts, each progressing from the last, and each guided by specific, but distinct cultural determinants. The first two acts followed a loosely defined script that was determined almost entirely by actions taken in the past. The first act, the procession, followed a route whose destination and whose composition was governed by tradition. It originated from the house, a location established by the deceased or by one of his ancestors when it was first purchased. Custom and accomplishment designated the Rostra as a destination. The presence of ancestors, the chariots, their garb as well as that of the deceased were all virtually prescribed by custom. The script for the second act was largely determined by those who had come before. What was said at the Rostra was the direct result of the actions (actual or legendary) of those who were claimed as ancestors. The surviving family could have omitted or added ancestors, embellished or omitted certain events, but the broad strokes of the funeral eulogy must have been virtually predetermined by the recorded accomplishments of the deceased and ancestors on the stage. The third act, however, could have deviated from a predetermined script. In fact, it was the one element where the survivors were in greater control. They decided whether there would be games and how much they wished to spend. They decided what those *ludi* would comprise. Accomplishments of the deceased and of the ancestors did not directly matter for this act. Instead, the present family was in charge and determined the length of the event and who might take the stage.

The funeral also served a necessary and pragmatic purpose, to bring the deceased to the various nodal points of the overall show. When it included ancestors and chariots, it also signified that this particular funeral was similar to all important *ludi* at Rome: it began with a procession. The procession transitioned from the domestic space to the more public sphere. It transformed the occasion from one held at the home, centered on the family, to one held in the shared public space of all Rome: the Roman Forum. Upon arrival in the Forum, at the Speaker's Platform, the Rostra, the second stage of the event began.

The funeral eulogy was an event driven by custom. It publicly integrated the deceased and (re)integrated his family into the temporally, politically, and historically charged space of the Roman Forum. It also situated the deceased within a larger historical context. The deceased, his accomplishments or lack thereof, were put in dialog with the rest of the space and with the history of Rome itself. The story of the family was retold, and the built environment aided that retelling. The *laudatio funebris*, for all its variability, followed a generic script of a kind: one's ancestors in effect determined the course of the event, how it looked and what was said. The *res gestae* of Rome itself briefly served as the puppeteer. The deceased was partly the star of this show, but so were the ancestors. The family and the orator played lesser roles. The living were there to praise the dead, integrate the deceased into the line-up of ancestors, and to celebrate the past. The orator—most often a younger son—was a visible part of the show, but he was not its focus.

For the living family, the funeral games were the critical third act, which signaled a substantial transformation in purpose and in roles played. It was an event scripted by the living to indicate a transition from the past to the present. The first two events centered on the deceased and those who had died before—that script was written by those players, derived directly from their (purported) accomplishments. While there was some choice available to the living with regard to what might be said and who might be praised, the presence of each waxen mask within a cabinet in the house ultimately determined the totality of the props employed. In contrast, the events at the *ludi funebres* were entirely determined by the living. Politicians of the first century had begun to exploit the full effect of this aspect of the *ludi*, whereas in 160 BCE, funeral tradition still held sway. For Paullus, the games were staged in honor of the deceased, directly after the funeral, but the decision to hold the games was distinctly one made by Paullus' children, who wished, despite their relatively lean inheritance, to hold gladiatorial matches at such a scale as to be recorded by Polybius. Moreover, they also decided to stage at least two plays. The funeral *ludi* were functionally a means to circumvent the usual ways one might sponsor public *ludi*, which were performed as part of the public and religious calendar of Rome and overseen by elected officials. Instead, one could offer entirely private *ludi*, ostensibly in celebration of one man, but overtly a celebration of one family. It was a demonstration that the surviving family, more specifically, Paullus' two surviving male children, were still political players in Rome, with means enough to put on a show and to give a "gift" to the people—the voting populace—of the city. Funerals allowed for a distinctive gift that superseded the regular *ludi*, however: not only were there plays, there were gladiators.

Three Acts, Not Two

The most curious feature of this investigation is that it derives almost all its key material from extant textual descriptions, yet it does not privilege the words delivered in the Roman Forum. The temptation for scholars, who all write and appreciate the written word, to privilege texts in source material, is well known, but it is also a feature of modern interpretation that the importance of words delivered and performed are unduly privileged. Why else would gladiatorial combat, a type of event that would one day produce the most iconic Roman architectural form, the amphitheater, be considered a relatively minor element in a Roman funeral in comparison to an event centered on the spoken word? The funeral's highlight was not merely the *laudatio funebris*, but it was the entire funerary event. In the case of Paullus, and perhaps for many of his contemporaries, his funeral comprised a procession, a speech, and multi-day games.

In sum, act one, the procession replete with chariots and the regalia of a triumph, put the funeral in dialog with major state-sponsored festivals. Act two, the funeral eulogy, focused on the deceased, the family, the patriline, and its role in shaping Rome. Act three was a celebration of the survivors, and it was overtly a gift from the surviving family to the people. The first two acts for this play highlighted the past, whereas the third act turned directly to the present: though a significant leader of the family had died, his children could demonstrate explicitly, through every pair of gladiators hired, through every day of extended celebration, through each play, through public dining and distribution of food, how wealthy, powerful and capable they were to carry on. And for the two surviving children of Paullus, they did so with his monumental achievements and those of his ancestors, clearly and visibly supporting them, represented throughout the entirety of the Roman Forum.

The funeral of Lucius Aemilius Paullus, a complete example of the funerary event, engaged fully with the Forum, was exemplary for its time, and clearly illustrates the cultural, political, and historical importance of a spectacular three-act Roman aristocratic funeral.

APPENDIX A

Applied Digital Humanities

COMPUTATIONAL METHODS AND PIPELINE

During the course of this project, I used many tools employed by practitioners of Digital Humanities to wrangle and represent the data available. The built environment was constructed using GIS, procedural modeling rules, 3D modeling tools and simple rendering packages.[1] Experiments were carried out using avatar-based, virtual world technology. Prosopographical material was harnessed by using graph-based queries on an open-rdf database to reconstruct family trees, patrilines, and assemblages of *imagines*. Each of these aspects of the project merits their own space and publication. I do not want details related to these various projects to distract from the argument of this book. I also wish to avoid discussing the potential of each of the tools employed, something I am happy to do in other contexts; instead I have focused entirely on results. This is not to say that each of the above methods and how I specifically employed them is above scrutiny. It is simply the case that I intend to engage those conversations elsewhere, in different publication modes and environments.

This study, the first to consider the totality of the aristocratic funeral of the second century BCE specifically within the context of the Forum, raises as many

[1] Basemap georeferenced in Erdas Imagine; archaeological and reconstruction plans georeferenced and stored in ESRI ArcMap; building footprints traced and stored in ESRI ArcMap; 3D forms, procedurally generated in ESRI City Engine, with rules developed with the Roman City Ruleset in collaboration with Marie Saldaña and outlined in Saldaña 2015; 2D forms created in Adobe Illustrator; all final image modification in Adobe Photoshop; custom software written in collaboration with Benjamin Niedzielski extracted data from the *DPRR* to reconstruct and visual hypothetical family trees and funeral assemblages of Paullus and coeval magistrates; the 3D models with results from the reconstructed family trees were imported into a custom Unity3D virtual world for experimentation; conclusions drawn from virtual world experiments were rendered in and exported from Trimble Sketchup; this workflow generated all 3D images in this book.

questions as it answers. In so doing, however, it also creates the opportunity for reexamination of scholarly consensus by forcing additional layers of context, precision and spatial accuracy into the argument. Using time and space to highlight the topographic surroundings creates new evidence.

First-person examinations, aided by virtual *in situ* argumentation offer effective means of interrogating evidence at a different scale and from a radically different perspective.[2] Bird's-eye views provide a general context, but the ability to inhabit a virtual laboratory of visualized ideas triggers a different cognitive approach to the investigation. One learns by traversing the virtual environment. Ideas are generated from the kinetic process connected to static views. Once represented in visual form, ideas can be tested and evaluated.

Many times it is the process of exploration that triggers narrative.[3] Just as the act of constructing a narrative set in historical times forces the scholar to address new issues within a different context, e.g., where will the protagonist go to the toilet? What exactly was fifth-floor apartment life like? How long would it have taken to walk from the Circus to the Forum?, the digital explorations and the process of modeling generate ideas.[4] The final, static visualization is often less important than the process employed.

When developing arguments on spectacle, words are not enough. A textual description of the funeral process, for example, might *seem* clear, *prima facie*. Nonetheless, each reader envisions an independent image. There is no control to ensure that a reader can engage fully with the argument set forth. One may have had preconceptions about the general staging possibilities for the *pompa*, but such ideas, until visualized, resemble the bare outline of a textual argument. They lack substance and refutability. The visualization supplies both.

The geo-temporal framework of a multi-dimensional, geographically-aware research environment enables rigorous inquiry.[5] In this study, the GIS provided a baseline set of coordinates to ground-truth these tinker toy models. Maps and plans were georeferenced, and all building footprints were drawn in accordance with boundaries set by geographic coordinates. The GIS provides a mechanism for accurately documenting real-world boundaries, such as the archaeological evidence and historical ground elevations. It also enables rapid overlay of disparate source material. One can create 3D representations from a non-georeferenced basemap, and those representations will be indistinguishable from those derived from a GIS.

[2] For an outline of the real-time laboratory within which some of this research developed, see Johanson 2015.

[3] For an example that follows two walks through the Roman funerary landscape at two distinct time periods, see Johanson 2011.

[4] K. Hopkins 2000: 1–45, esp. 44–45, reminds us that such investigations are always limited by an inability to grasp the "wide range of different experiences and understandings" that real Romans inevitably had.

[5] Johanson 2009 outlines the foundational elements for how this project models the funeral of Paullus.

Nonetheless, working within a georeferenced system allows one to include multiple archaeological plans within one mapping platform while still adhering to a shared global coordinate system. This visualized evidence based on an underlying empirical system constrains the hypothetical investigation. The method demands accuracy and provides a means for refutability. The shared coordinate system of the digital laboratory differentiates the images employed in the argument from exploratory, free-hand sketches: in short, the developer can always find ground truths by comparing to past and current satellite imagery and to other georeferenced data. In addition, for this project, the GIS was essential, since the models were procedurally generated based on rules applied to footprints traced within the GIS platform.[6]

The simple act of modeling an idea advances the argument. Each image, which is a distinct visual interrogation of evidence, ensures clarity: the idea envisioned by the author is the same as that which can be seen and understood by the reader. Both work from the same image. Images present cognitive challenges, however. It is possible that upon seeing a visualization of a historic event, the reader might think, "Yes, that is how *I* imagined the event. Nothing new here. It is *just* an image." Prior to the moment when the reader encountered the image, he or she may have developed a mental picture of the phenomenon, but the visual argument has not yet been made. The creation of a three-dimensional image transforms the thought experiment into a new form of evidence. A verbal description of an *ad hoc* arena defined by *cancelli* is merely a suggestion of a possibility. The visualization in geotemporal space is a more rigorous test of *probability* and a verifiable and citable argument in its own right.

In this project I explore the use of modeling to investigate socio-historical phenomena. A subset of the visualized data is "accurate," but all of it should be considered a "useful fiction."[7] These fictions are not intended to change how one perceives the topography of the Roman Forum—though cognitive science suggests that they may—rather they were created as a means of aggregating, representing, and exploring knowledge. I do not wish to make arguments about the topography of the Roman Forum; rather, for this study, I only aim to work within a topographic "text" established by others.[8]

Modeling generates more questions, and therein lies its chief strength. By visualizing evidence with a data-oriented, methodological approach, an argument can take on new levels of complexity. Event-based studies, such as of a funeral, a triumph, or an oratorical performance, can investigate thousands of hypothetical

---

[6] Saldaña and Johanson 2013 and Saldaña 2015 describe the methodology employed.

[7] For "useful fiction," see McCarty 2007. For additional reflection on process and modeling, see McCarty 2004, McCarty 2013, and Johanson 2009.

[8] I have used the maps and reconstructions generated by others as the basis for the Forum of 160BCE represented in this book; this new model functions like a critical edition, as discussed in Schreibman and Papadopoulos 2019. Nonetheless, it also differs in that it was used to generate images for a specific argument and does not yet stand on its own as a separate, published "text" of the city center.

scenarios. Unfortunately, the underlying textual and archaeological evidence ultimately precludes conclusive results. This is, of course, the same problem that all historical investigations must face. We will never know how exactly the funeral route was manipulated, and, in fact, have only explored a small subset of the possible routes. Nonetheless, the act of modeling has let us manipulate a multiplicity of possible variables in order to assess their likelihood and effect. By visualizing hypotheses, over time, some will be more easily cast aside. As others engage with these problems with similar methodologies, their investigations can literally—if the same data is used—build upon the digital foundations of previous studies.

APPENDIX B

Representing the Roman Forum of 160 BCE

This book is not intended to participate directly in conversations that reshape our understanding of Roman topography. Within my argument above concerning the Roman funeral, I acknowledge divergent views regarding the location of various buildings within the Forum, but I avoid arguing against any one interpretation. Nonetheless, to work within a 3D context, one must decide what to represent and what to omit. I have taken a relatively conservative approach, though doubtless there remain many valid objections to the abstract models I present. My aim is to engage with scholarly conversations focused on spectacle and funerary practice; if interpretation of these events within topographic context leads to modified reconstructions of specific buildings, then that will be a fortuitous residual effect.

In this short appendix, I will outline the specific process and data that created the 3D representations. Above all, these 3D representations should be viewed as abstract 3D versions of a simple 2D plan. They are not intended to be scientifically accurate, though, as you will see, the methodology employed forces the representations to adhere to specific boundaries. The process to develop the 3D model begins in a layered GIS, consisting of overlapping maps and plans. The basemaps for the area are the 1:500 cadastral surveys of the modern city of Rome created by S.A.R.A. Nistri. The four corners of each 1:500 plan have been assigned geographic coordinates by S.A.R.A. Nistri in the Universal Transverse Mercator (UTM) projected coordinate system. This geographic information was used to connect these 2D plans to the coordinate system of the GIS.[1] Plans from site-specific archaeological reports, topographical dictionaries, and reference maps generated by the

[1] Erdas Imagine was used to mosaic the individual 1:500 scale plans together into one, tileable, georeferenced image. ESRI ArcMap was used to manage the GIS and to georeference the basemaps.

scholarly community were then each georeferenced into the system by hand. This process entailed the digital equivalent of the analog process of rubber sheeting, in which one stretches a plan to fit to an existing basemap. Two simple methodologies were employed depending on the state of the source map: 1) if the source map was internally consistent, without distortion, then it was placed with a three-point fit, wherein three known locations were matched between basemap and secondary map, and then the secondary map was placed, rotated, and scaled so that the selected points matched up with a relative degree of precision. 2) if the source map appeared to be distorted, due to printing error, or due to spatial inconsistencies in the reference plan used in its reconstruction, then this secondary plan was georeferenced via a polynomial fit, wherein eight or nine known, shared points in both the basemap and the secondary map were matched, and the secondary map was stretched and distorted to force a fit.

These georeferenced maps function as a precise and deterministic control for the construction of the 3D model. For each monument visualized, a polygonal footprint was traced over the relevant georeferenced source plan. For each monument, the relevant figure below shows which plan was used and how that plan conforms to the underlying basemap, and how the outline for the footprint adheres to those plans. For example, to build the Temple of Castor and Pollux, the plan for Temple IA (Nielsen et al. 1992: 83 fig. 61) was georeferenced over the basemap from S.A.R.A. Nistri. A polygon was then traced over this figure to create a footprint for the 3D building. This footprint was then assigned a set of data attributes required by the Roman City Ruleset, such as name, building type, cella type, base elevation, number of steps, rise of steps, date of construction, style, columnar diameter, source bibliography. For the Temple of Castor and Pollux, the elevation of the podium was roughly 15.6m asl according to Nielsen 1990: 99. Using the Roman City Ruleset, a base elevation of 11.8m asl was given, to plant it in the Forum floor, 14 steps were assigned with a rise of .275m each, which results in a podium that is 15.65 meters high.[2] (See fig. B.2.) The process was repeated for each monument listed below. The majority of monuments in the 3D model traced footprints directly from Purcell 1995b fig. 153, which reprints the original work of Broise and David 1983: 183–185.[3] The base elevation changes depending on the topography of the physical landscape. The majority of the monuments surrounding the Forum plaza assume a base elevation of 11.8m asl; if no base elevation is listed, then the standard 11.8m asl was applied. Monuments placed on a slope are necessarily starting from higher ground, but that elevation is somewhat arbitrary.

The physical topography for the site is controlled in a similar manner. Using georeferenced maps, two types of topographic documentation are recorded: contour

[2] Frank and Stevens 1925: 82n3 cites the "average Oscan foot-rule" of .275m as opposed to the later Roman foot rule of .298m.

[3] There is no scholarly reason to use one source over the other; they are identical. The reprinted version in the *LTUR* was perhaps slightly easier to scan and was therefore selected.

lines and point elevations. The contour lines, themselves interpretations made by the author of the original, georeferenced map, are traced and a floating point number field containing the elevation is associated with the polyline data type. Point elevations, taken from core samples or from extant archaeological remains, likewise are marked as a vertex data type and associated with a float data field that contains the reported elevation for that point. This elevation information, in point and line format is combined and evaluated computationally to create an approximation of the terrain for the site. Imagine a standard interactive object in any museum of science, the classic pinscreen. When you push your hands into the object, a simulacrum of your hand, delineated by a thousand pin tips is formed on the opposite side. If you were to carefully place aluminum foil over these pins, you would have a seamless sloping and undulating surface. So the three-dimensional terrain is generated from a collection of points and contour lines. (See fig. B.1.)

For readers who wish to cite the figures in this book for specific topographical arguments, I suggest that this appendix is reviewed and the relevant figures below are cited as well, so that the data used to generate the 3D built environment is clearly understood.

For effective use of these images, see the online versions at escholarship.org.

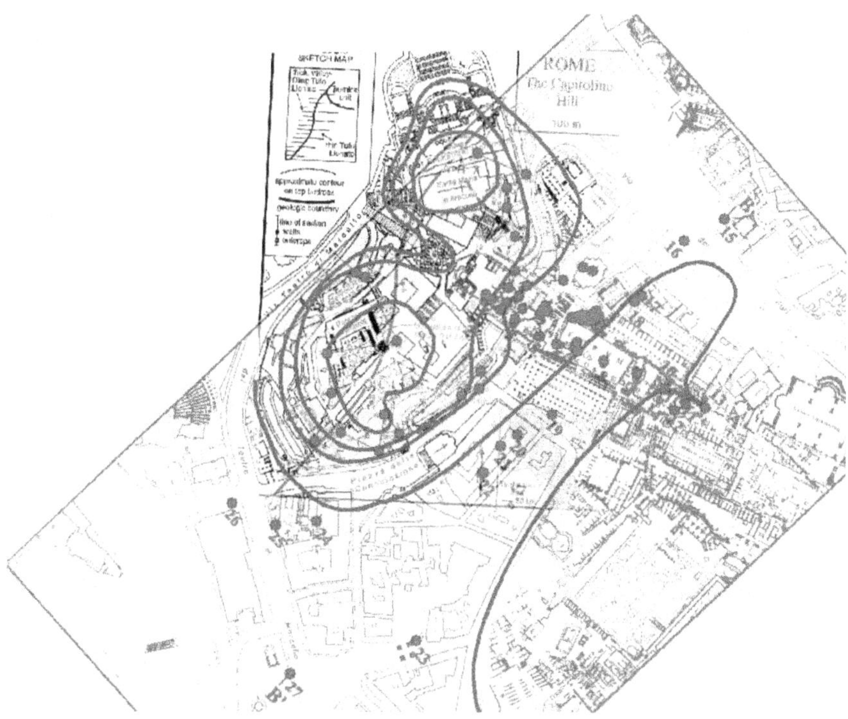

FIGURE B.1 Physical Topopgraphy: DEM. The Digital Elevation Model was created with core and contour data merged from the following sources: Ammerman 1990: 629 fig. 2, Alvarez et al. 1996: 752 fig. 1, Ammerman 1996: 126 fig. 1 and 131 fig. 3, Ammerman and Filippi 2004: 12 fig. 3.

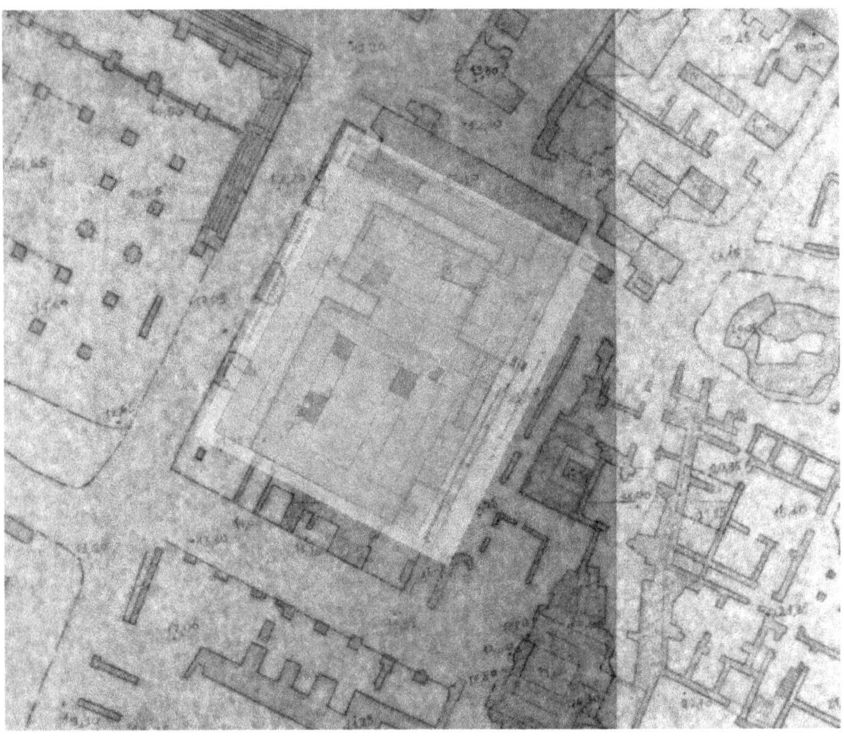

FIGURE B.2 Aedes Castrorum: footprint traced from Nielsen et al. 1992: 83 fig. 61. Podium was roughly 15.6m asl Nielsen 1990: 99. Roman City Ruleset base elevation: 11.8m asl. 14 steps, .275m rise.

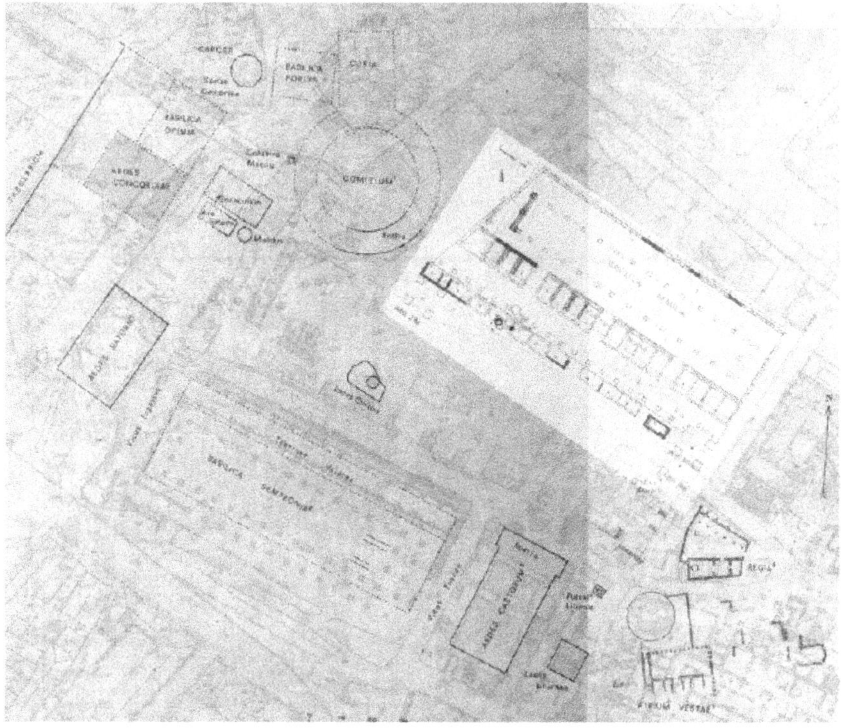

FIGURE B.3 Aedes Concordiae: footprint traced from Purcell 1995b fig. 153. Podium height arbitrarily assigned to rise above ground level. Roman City Ruleset base elevation: 16m asl. 20 steps, .275m rise.

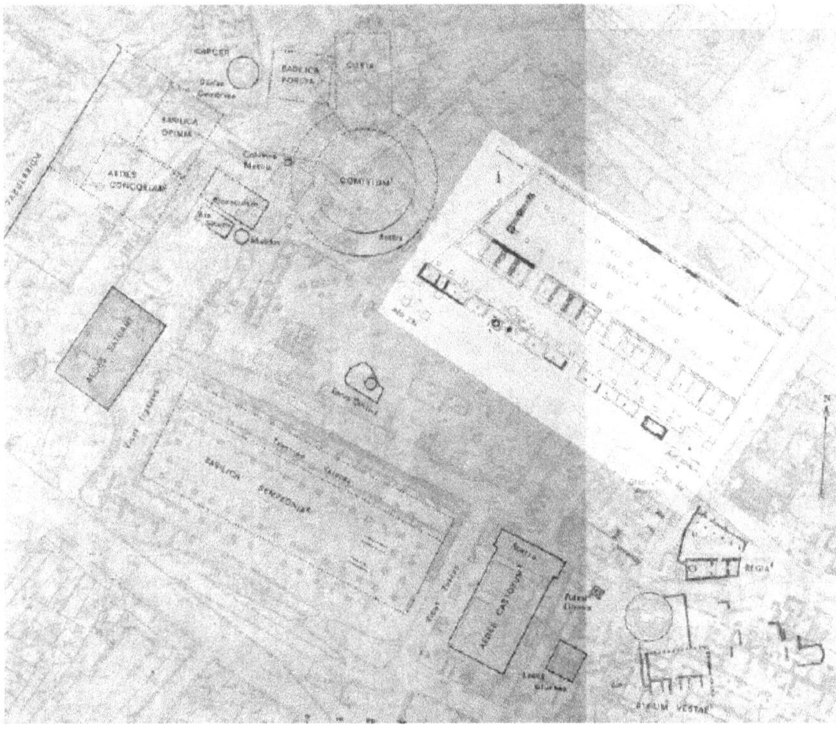

FIGURE B.4 Aedes Saturni: footprint traced from Purcell 1995b fig. 153. Extant podium height, not coeval to 160 BCE: 25m asl, Pensabene 1984 pl. 1. Roman City Ruleset base elevation: 16.2m asl. 20 steps, .275m rise.

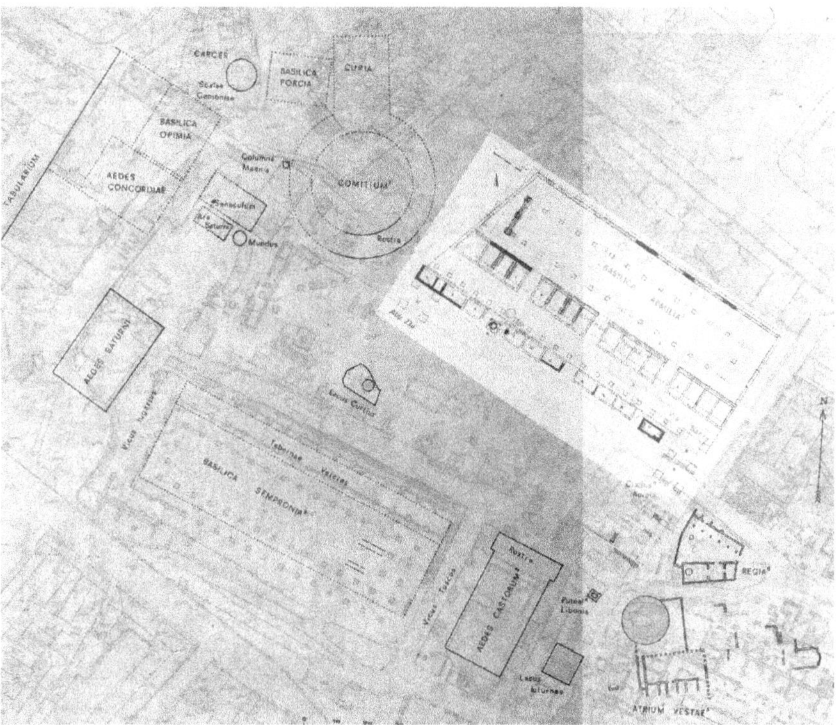

FIGURE B.5 Aedes Vestae: footprint traced from Purcell 1995b fig. 153.

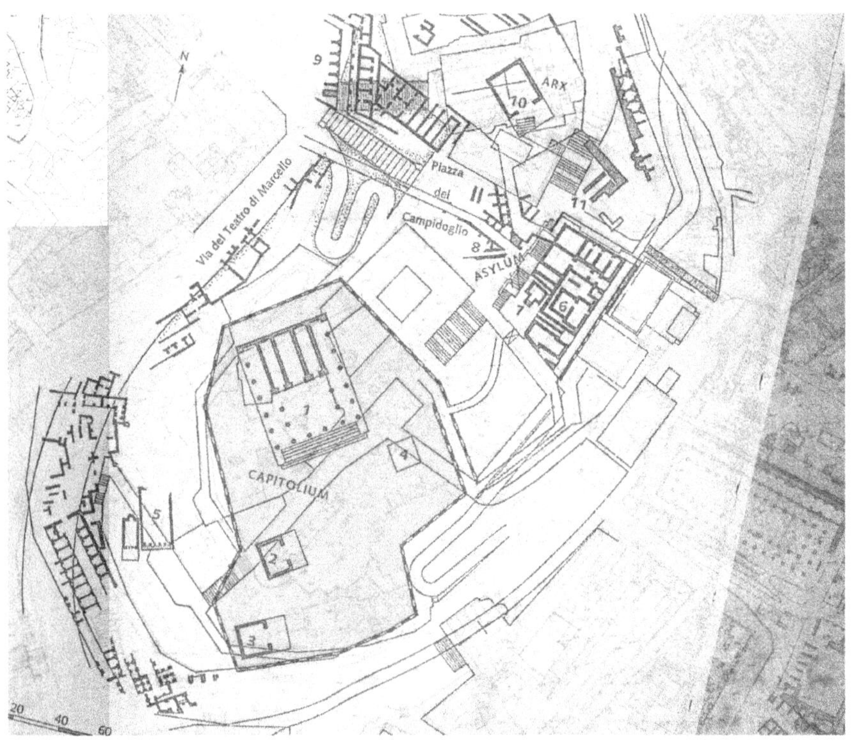

FIGURE B.6 Area Capitolina: footprint traced from Coarelli 2007: 28 fig. 10. Roman City Ruleset base elevation: 45m asl. 21 steps, .275m rise.

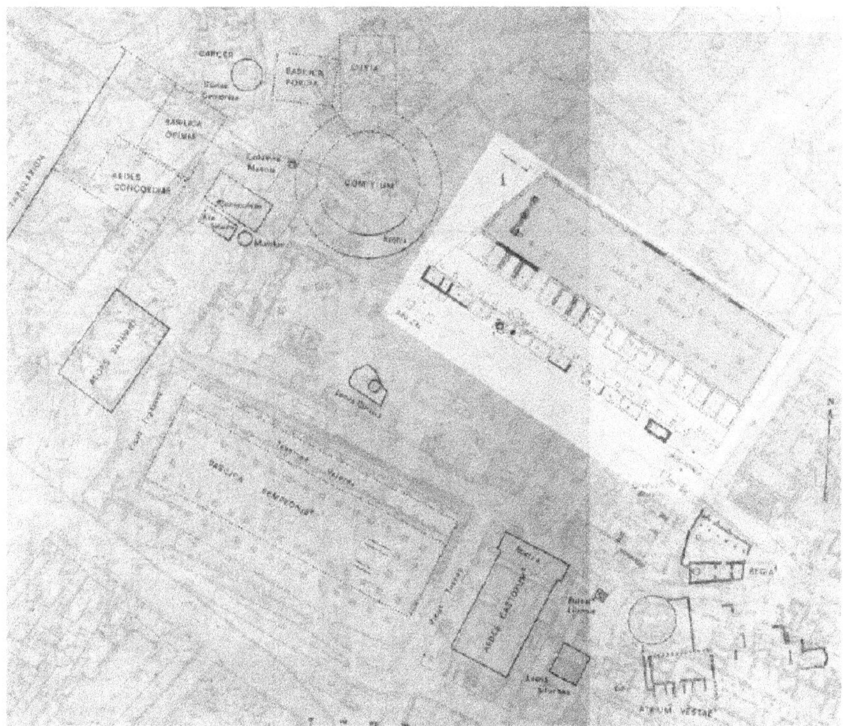

FIGURE B.7 Basilica Aemilia: footprint traced from Freyberger 2012 fig. 23a.

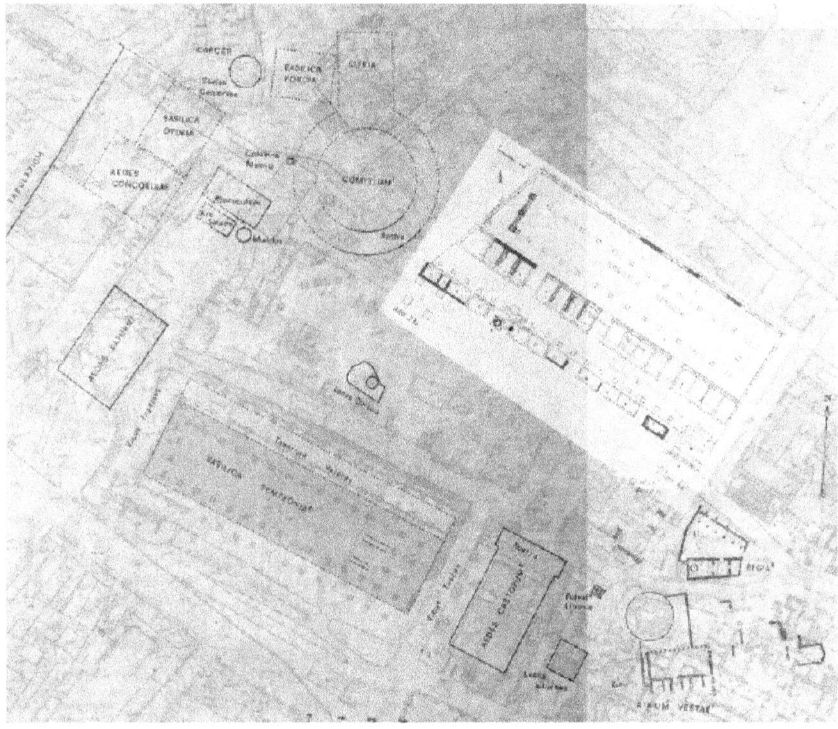

FIGURE B.8 Basilica Sempronia: footprint traced from Purcell 1995b fig. 153.

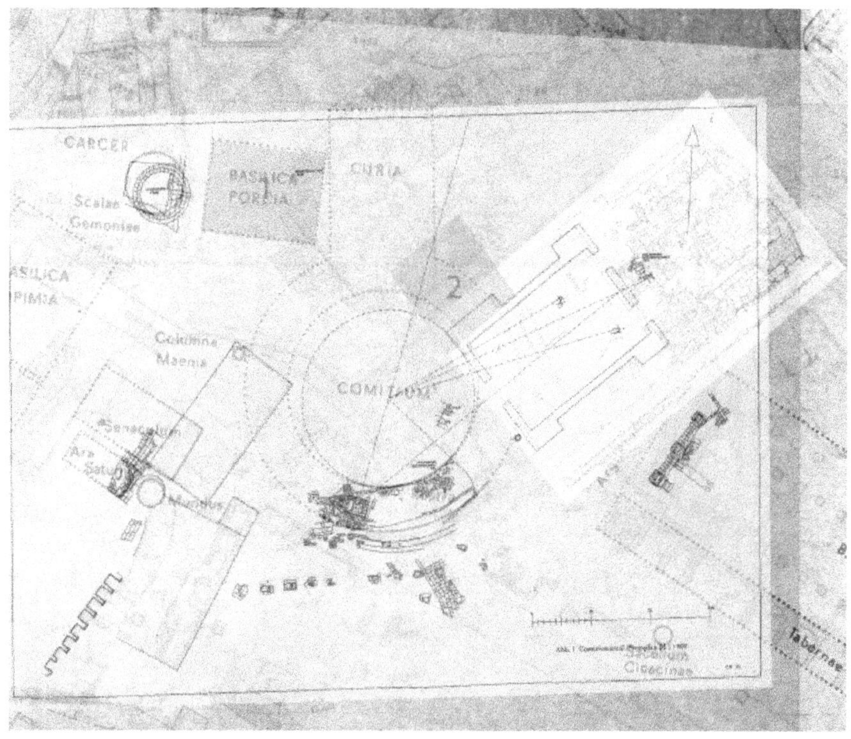

FIGURE B.9 Basilica Porcia: footprint traced from Purcell 1995b fig. 153. Roman City Ruleset base elevation 19m asl, from Amici 2004: 361 fig. 11, near remains "W."

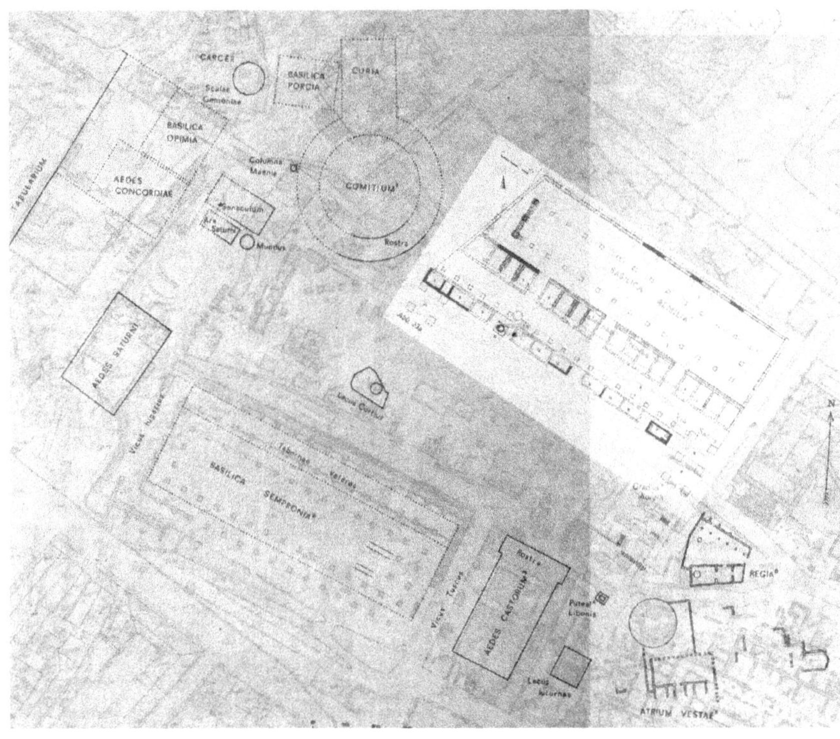

FIGURE B.10 Columna Maenia: footprint traced from Purcell 1995b fig. 153. Roman City Ruleset base elevation: 16m, following surrounding topography.

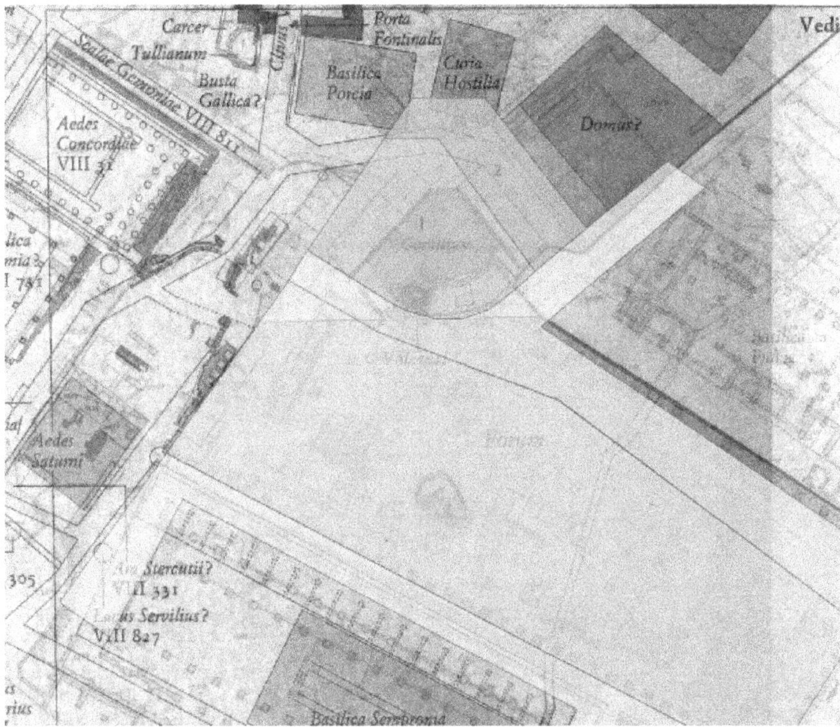

FIGURE B.11 Comitium: footprint traced to fit within bounds of surrounding Curia Hostilia and Basilica Porcia according to Carandini and Carafa 2012 fig. 15.

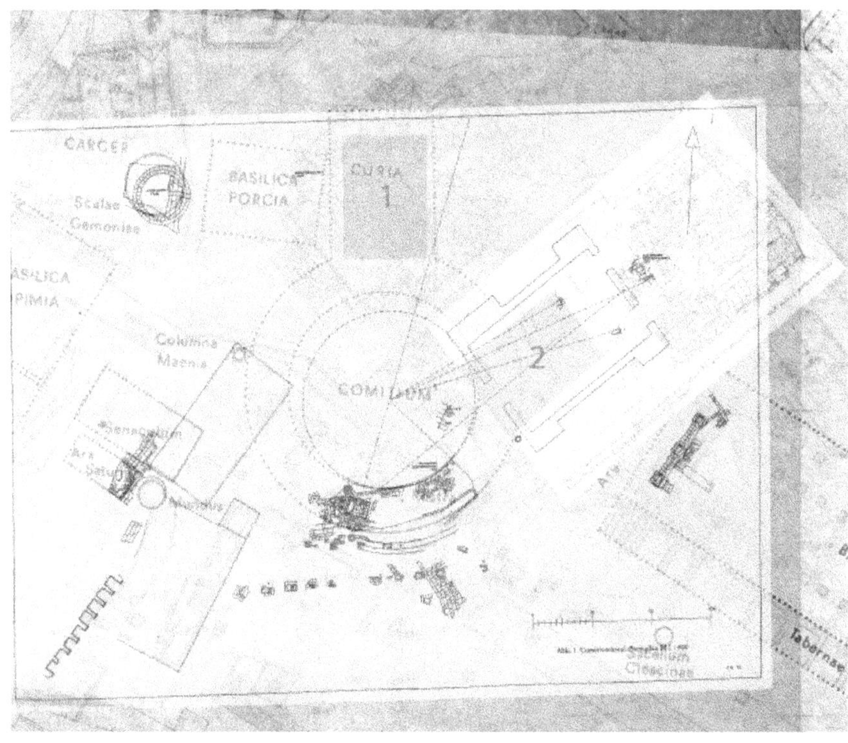

FIGURE B.12 Curia Hostilia: footprint (location 1) traced from Purcell 1995b fig. 153. Roman Ruleset base elevation: 14.5m roughly aligning with Amici 2004: 361 fig. 11, "X" at 14m but adapted to fit surrounding topography. *N.b.*, I used this elevation to fit the traditional reconstruction into the physical topography. Amici argues, with justification, for location 2 (above), not used in this reconstruction, but derived from Krause 1981 pl. 1 and Amici 2007: 161 fig. 1.

FIGURE B.13 *Domus*: footprints of houses were traced from Carandini 2003 pl. 32.

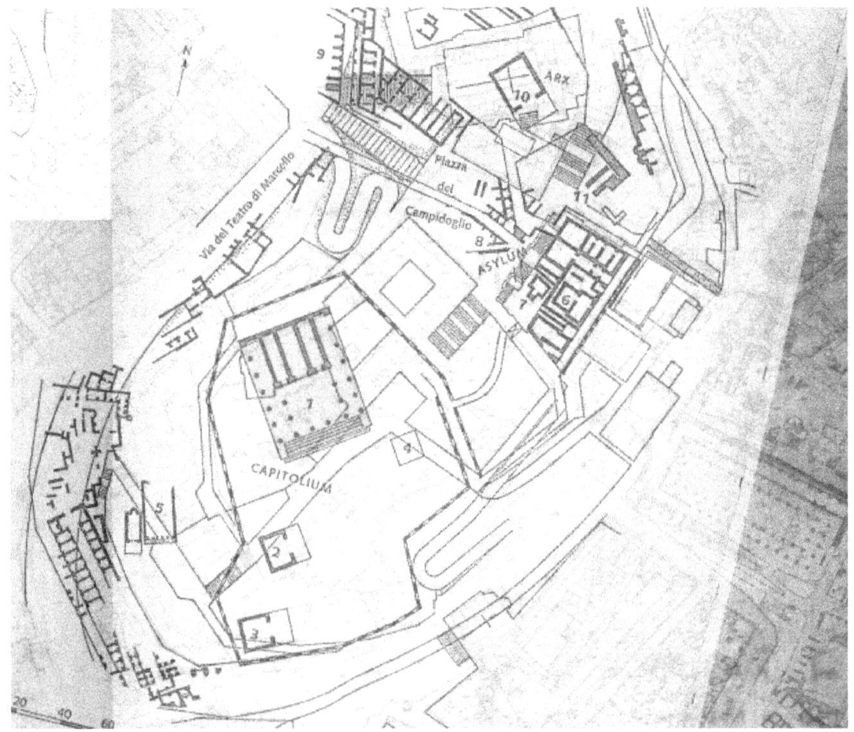

FIGURE B.14 Aedes Iovis Optimi Maximi: footprint was traced from Coarelli 2007: 28 fig. 10. Roman City Ruleset base elevation: 45m, derived from Haselberger, Romano, and Dumser 2002: 21 steps, .275m rise.

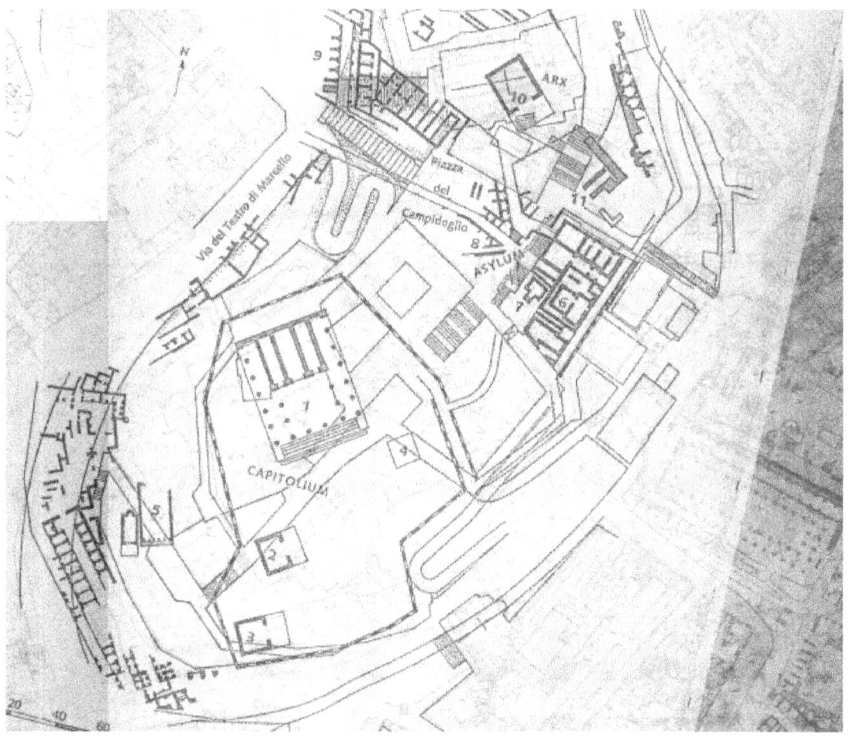

FIGURE B.15 Aedes Iunonis Monetae: footprint was traced from Coarelli 2007: 28 fig. 10. Roman Ruleset base elevation derived from Haselberger, Romano, and Dumser 2002: 40m. 7 steps, .275m rise.

FIGURE B.16 Lacus Iuturnae: footprint traced from Purcell 1995b fig. 153.

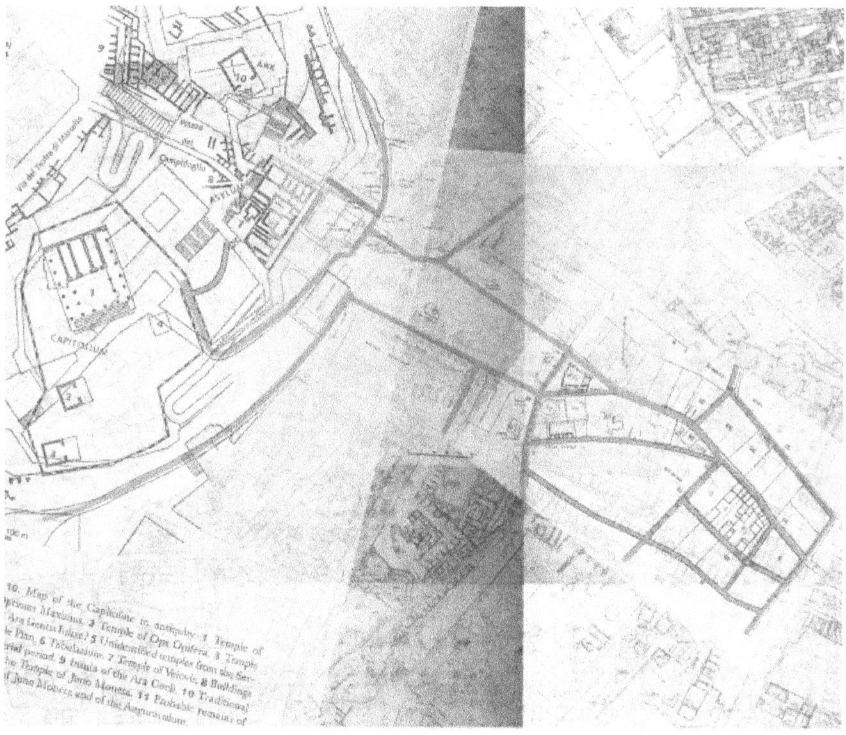

FIGURE B.17 Road Network: footprint traced (approximately) from Carandini 2003 pl. 32, Coarelli 2007: 28 fig. 10, Purcell 1995b fig. 153.

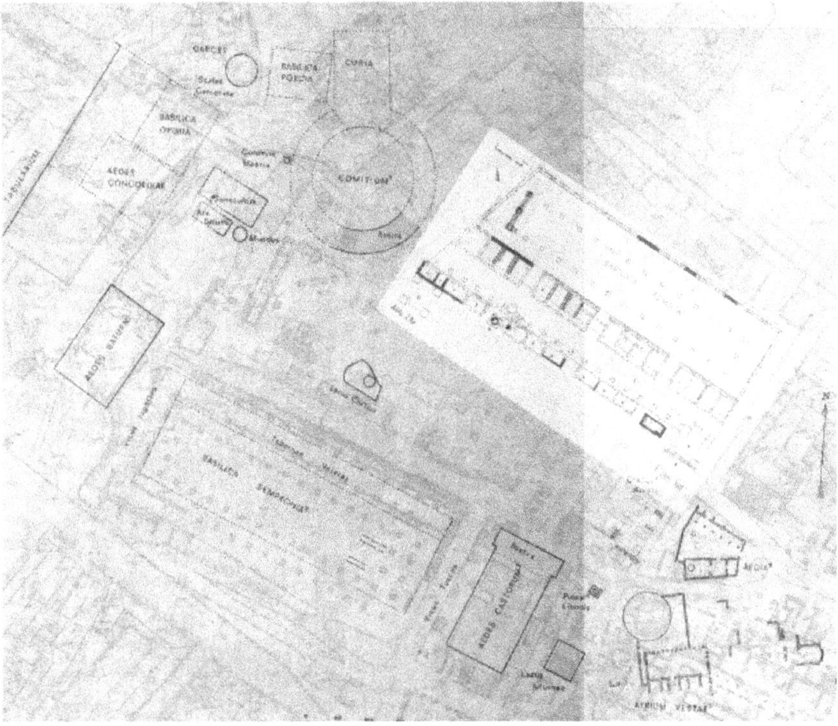

FIGURE B.18 Rostra: Non-procedural model follows outline in Krause 1981 pl. 1, georeferenced with Purcell 1995b fig. 153. Its platform is 2.5 meters above the Forum pavers, see above p. 47n93 and Morstein-Marx 2004: 51n55.

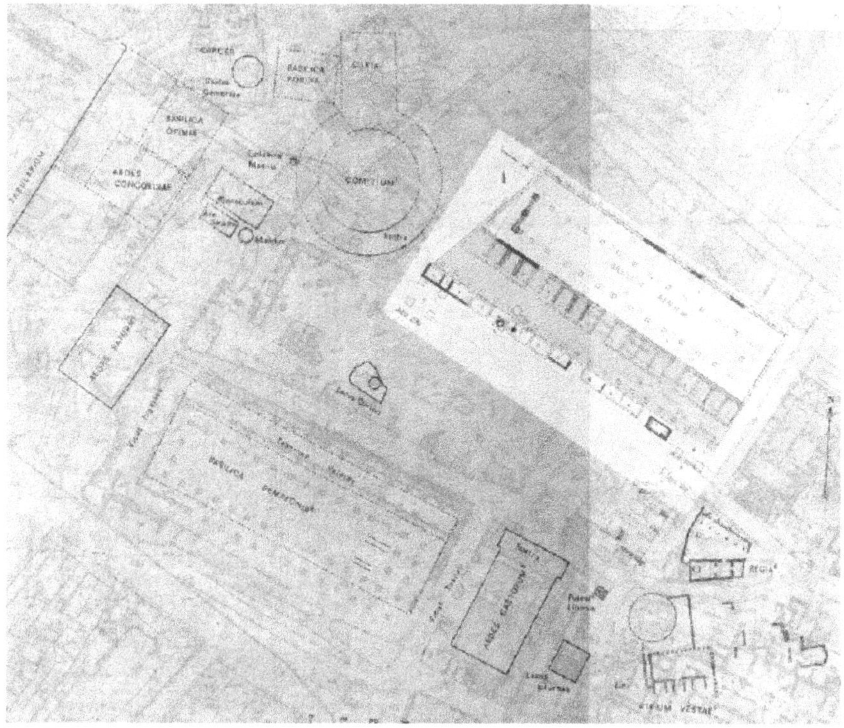

FIGURE B.19 Tabernae Novae: footprint traced from Freyberger 2012 fig. 23a.

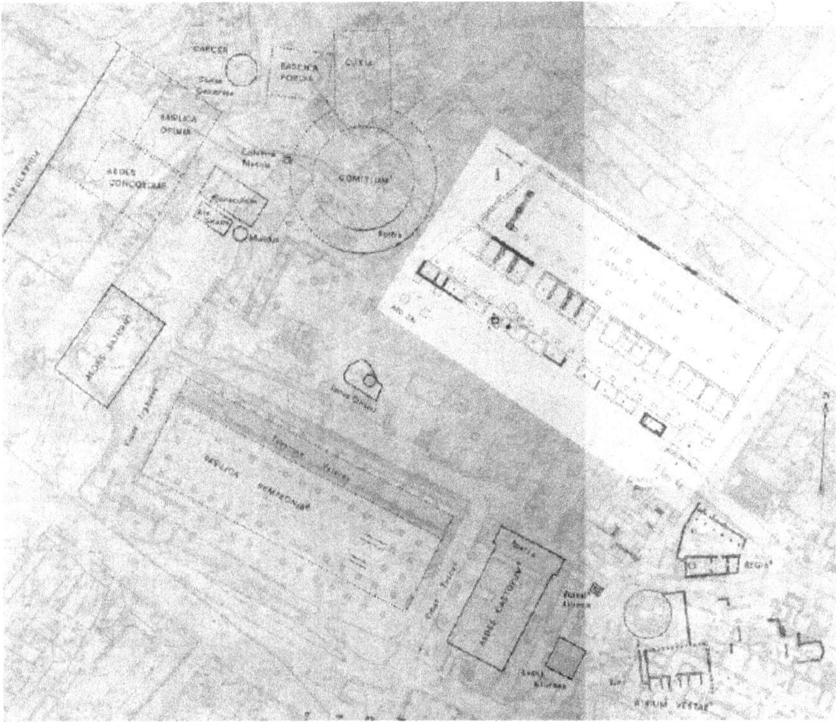

FIGURE B.20 Tabernae Veteres: footprint traced from Purcell 1995b fig. 153.

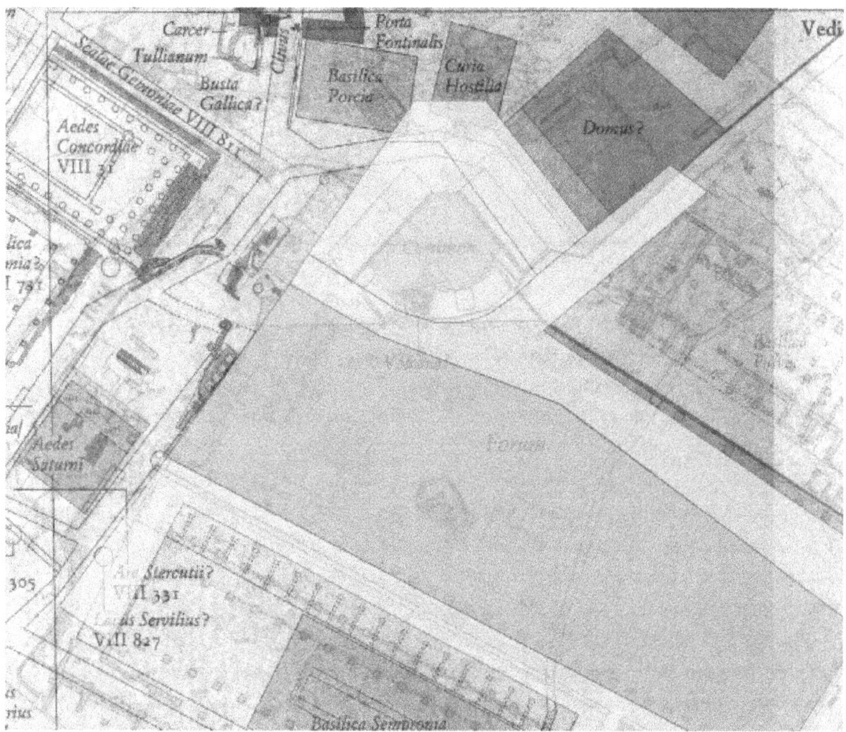

FIGURE B.21 Forum Romanum Central Plaza: 11.8m asl from Richardson 1992: 172; outline of plaza, Carandini and Carafa 2012 fig. 15.

BIBLIOGRAPHY

Aldrete, Gregory S. 1999. *Gestures and Acclamations in Ancient Rome.* Baltimore: The Johns Hopkins University Press.

Alvarez, Walter, Albert J. Ammerman, Paul R. Renne, Daniel B. Karner, Nicola Terrenato, and Alessandro Montanari. 1996. "Quaternary Fluvial-Volcanic Stratigraphy and Geochronology of the Capitoline Hill in Rome." *Geology* 24: 751–754.

Amici, Carla Maria. 1995. "Atrium libertatis." *Rendiconti della Pontificia Accademia di Archeologia* 68: 295–321.

Amici, Carla Maria. 2004. "Evoluzione architettonica del comizio a Roma." *Rendiconti della Pontificia Accademia di Archeologia* 77: 351–379.

Amici, Carla Maria. 2007. *Lo scavo didattico della zona retrostante la curia (foro di Cesare): campagne di scavo 1961-1970.* Roma: Bonsignori.

Ammerman, Albert J. 1990. "On the Origins of the Forum Romanum." *American Journal of Archaeology* 94: 627–645.

Ammerman, Albert J. 1996. "The Comitium in Rome From the Beginning." *American Journal of Archaeology* 100: 121–136.

Ammerman, Albert J., and Dunia Filippi. 2004. "Dal Tevere all'Argileto: nuove osservazioni." *Bullettino della Commissione Archeologica Comunale di Roma* 105: 7–28.

Anderson, James C. 1997. *Roman Architecture and Society.* Ancient Society and History. Baltimore: Johns Hopkins University Press.

Arce, Javier. 1990. Funus Imperatorum*: los funerales de los emperadores romanos.* Alianza forma. Madrid: Alianza.

Arce, Javier. 2000. *Memoria de los antepasados: puesta en escena y desarrollo del elogio fúnebre Romano.* Madrid: Electa.

Astin, A. E. 1957. "The Lex Annalis Before Sulla." *Latomus* 16: 588–613.

Astin, A. E. 1978. *Cato the Censor.* Oxford: Oxford University Press.

Badian, E. 1971. "The Family and Early Career of T. Quinctius Flamininus." *Journal of Roman Studies* 61: 102–111.

Badian, E. 1980. "Notes on the *Laudatio* of Agrippa." *Classical Journal* 76: 97–109.

Bakhtin, M. M. 1984. *Rabelais and His World.* Reprint of original 1968. Translated by Hélène Iswolsky. Indiana University Press.

Bauer, H. 1993. "Basilica Paul(l)i." In *LTUR,* 1: 183–187.

Beacham, Richard C. 1992. *The Roman Theatre and Its Audience.* Cambridge, Mass.: Harvard University Press.

Beacham, Richard C. 1999. *Spectacle Entertainments of Early Imperial Rome.* New Haven: Yale University Press.

Beagon, Mary. 2005. *The Elder Pliny on the Human Animal: Natural History, Book 7.* Oxford University Press.

Beard, Mary. 2003. "The Triumph of the Absurd: Roman Street Theatre." In *Rome the Cosmopolis,* edited by Catharine Edwards and Greg Woolf, 21–43. New York: Cambridge University Press.

Beard, Mary. 2007. *The Roman Triumph.* Cambridge, Mass.: Belknap Press of Harvard University Press.

Beck, Hans. 2018. "Of Fragments and Feelings: Roman Funeral Oratory Revisited." In Gray, Balbo, Marshall, and Steel 2018, 263–280.

Bergmann, Bettina Ann. 1999. "Introduction: The Art of Ancient Spectacle." In Bergmann and Kondoleon 1999, 9–36.

Bergmann, Bettina Ann, and Christine Kondoleon. 1999. *The Art of Ancient Spectacle.* New Haven: Yale University Press.

Bettini, Maurizio. 1991. *Anthropology and Roman Culture: Kinship, Time, Images of the Soul.* Ancient Society and History. Baltimore: The Johns Hopkins University Press.

Bettini, Maurizio. 2005. "Death and its Double. *Imagines, Ridiculum* and *Honos* in the Roman Aristocratic Funeral." In *Hoping for Continuity: Childhood, Education and Death in Antiquity and the Middle Ages,* edited by Katarina Mustakallio, 33: 191–202. Acta Instituti Romani Finlandiae. Rome: Institutum Romanum Finlandiae.

Birdsell, D., and L. Groarke. 1996. "Toward A Theory of Visual Argument." *Argumentation and Advocacy: The Journal of the American Forensic Association* 33.

Blasi, Massimo. 2010. "La 'memoria mascherata.' I MIMHTAÍ e la rappresentazione del defunto ai funerali gentilizi romani." *Scienze dell'Antichità* 16: 181–199.

Blasi, Massimo. 2012. *Strategie funerarie: onori funebri pubblici e lotta politica nella Roma medio e tardorepubblicana, 230-27 a.C.*

Bodel, John. 1986. "Graveyards and Groves: A Study of the Lex Lucerina." *American Journal of Ancient History* 11: 1–133.

Bodel, John. 1999. "Death on Display: Looking at Roman Funerals." In Bergmann and Kondoleon 1999, 259–282.

Bodel, John. 2000. "Dealing With the Dead: Undertakers, Executioners and Potter's Fields in Ancient Rome." In Hope and Marshall 2000, 128–151.

Bodel, John. 2004. "The Organization of the Funerary Trade at Puteoli and Cumae." In *Libitina e dintorni: Libitina e i luci sepolcrali, le leges libitinariae campane, iura sepulcrorum: vecchie e nuove iscrizioni: atti dell'XI Rencontre franco-italienne sur l'épigraphie,* edited by Silvio Panciera, 147–168. Roma: Quasar.

Bodel, John. 2024. "Libitina's Laborers: Praeficae and the Origins of the Roman Funerary Trade." In *Working Lives in Ancient Rome,* edited by Del A. Maticic and Jordan Rogers, 309–335. Cham: Springer Nature Switzerland.

Boethius, Axel. 1945. "*Maeniana*. A Study of the Forum Romanum of the Fourth Century B.C." *Eranos* 43: 89–110.

Bonnefond-Coudry, Marianne. 1989. *Le Sénat de la République romaine: de la guerre d'Hannibal à Auguste: pratiques délibératives et prise de décision.* Bibliothèque des Écoles françaises d'Athènes et de Rome 273. Rome: École française de Rome.

Bradley, John. 2017. "DPRR RDF: Documentation Website." Accessed August 13, 2025. http://www.romanrepublic.ac.uk/rdf/doc.

Bravo, José Román. 2006. "¿Terencio en el comicio? Reflexiones sobre la primera y segunda representación de la *Hecyra*." In *Estudios sobre Terencio,* edited by Andrés Pociña Pérez, Beatriz Rabaza, and María de Fátima Silva, 185–232. Granada: Universidad de Granada.

Brennan, T. Corey. 2000. *The Praetorship in the Roman Republic.* Oxford: Oxford University Press.

Brilliant, Richard. 1999. "'Let the Trumpets Roar!' the Roman Triumph." In Bergmann and Kondoleon 1999, 223–230.

Brink, C. O. 1981. *Horace on Poetry.* Vol. 2. Cambridge: University Press.

Broise, Henri, and Jean-Michel David. 1983. "Un plan du forum républicain." *Architecture et société. De l'archaïsme grec à la fin de la République. Actes du Colloque international organisé par le Centre national de la recherche scientifique et l'École française de Rome (Rome 2–4 décembre 1980),* Publications de l'École française de Rome, 66: 243–245.

Broughton, T. Robert S. 1968. *The Magistrates of the Roman Republic.* Vol. 1. New York: American Philological Association.

Brown, Frank Edward. 1980. *Cosa, the Making of a Roman Town.* Ann Arbor: University of Michigan Press.

Brown, Frank Edward. 1993. *Cosa III: The Buildings of the Forum: Colony, Municipium, and Village.* University Park, Pennsylvania: Published for the American Academy in Rome by Pennsylvania State University Press.

Bruni, Valerio. 2024. "La Basilica Aemilia e il lato settentrionale del Foro Romano dalla media repubblica al primo impero." *Mitteilungen des Deutschen Archäologischen Instituts. Römische Abteilung* 130.

Butler, Shane. 2009. "Cicero's Capita." *Litterae Caelestes* 3: 9–48.

Callebat, Louis, and Philippe Fleury, eds. 1995. *Dictionnaire des termes techniques du De Architectura de Vitruve.* Alpha-Omega. Hildesheim: Olms-Weidmann.

Campbell, Virginia L. 2021. "*Pompa* in Pompeii: Experiencing a Funeral Procession in the Ancient City." *Open Arts Journal,* no. 10, 145–159.

Carafa, Paolo. 1998. *Il comizio di Roma dalle origini all'etá di Augusto.* Roma: "L'Erma" di Bretschneider.

Carandini, Andrea. 2003. *La nascita di Roma: dèi, lari, eroi e uomini all'alba di una civiltà.* Biblioteca di cultura storica 219. Torino: Guilio Einaudi.

Carandini, Andrea. 2004. *Palatino, Velia e Sacra via: paesaggi urbani attraverso il tempo.* Workshop di archeologia classica. Quaderni 1. Roma: Edizioni dell'Ateneo.

Carandini, Andrea, and Paolo Carafa, eds. 1995. *Palatium e sacra via*. Roma: Istituto Poligrafico e Zecca dello Stato.

Carandini, Andrea, and Paolo Carafa, eds. 2012. *Atlante di Roma antica: biografia e ritratti della città*. Milano: Mondadori Electa.

Carawan, Edwin M. 1984. "The Tragic History of Marcellus and Livy's Characterization." *Classical Journal* 80: 131–141.

Carroll, Maureen. 2011. "The Mourning Was Very Good: Liberation and Liberality in Roman Funerary Commemoration." In Hope 2011, 126–148.

Carter, Michael J. 2003. "Gladiatorial Ranking and the '*SC de Pretiis Gladiatorum Minuendis*'(CIL II 6278 = ILS 5163)." *Phoenix* 57: 83–114.

Carter, Michael J. 2009. "Gladiators and Monomachoi: Greek Attitudes to a Roman 'Cultural Performance.'" *The International Journal of the History of Sport* 26: 298–322.

Cassanelli, Roberto, and David Massimiliano. 2002. *Ruins of Ancient Rome: The Drawings of French Architects Who Won the Prix De Rome, 1796–1924*. Los Angeles: J.P. Getty Museum.

Churchill, J. Bradford. 1999. "*Ex qua quod vellent facerent*: Roman magistrates' authority over *praeda* and *manubiae*." *Transactions of the American Philological Association* 129: 85–116.

Clarke, G. W. 1968. "The Dioscuri of the Lacus Iuturnae." *Latomus: revue d'études latines* 27: 147–148.

Coarelli, Filippo. 1972. "Il sepolcro degli Scipioni." *Dialoghi di Archeologia* (Roma), 36–106.

Coarelli, Filippo. 1977. "Il comizio dalle origine alla fine della repubblica." *La Parola del Passato: Rivista di Studi Antichi* 32: 166–238.

Coarelli, Filippo. 1983. *Il foro romano*. Vol. 1. Roma: Quasar.

Coarelli, Filippo. 1985. *Il foro romano*. Vol. 2. Roma: Quasar.

Coarelli, Filippo. 1993. "Carcer." In *LTUR*, 1: 236–237.

Coarelli, Filippo. 1998. "Comitium e comitia: l'assemblea e il voto a Roma in età repubblicana." In *Venticinque secoli dopo l'invenzione della democrazia*, edited by Luciano Canfora, 133–143. Pæstum: Fondazione Paestum.

Coarelli, Filippo. 1999. "Saturnus, Aedes." In *LTUR*, 4: 234–236.

Coarelli, Filippo. 2001. "Gli anfiteatri a Roma prima del Colosseo." In *Sangue e arena*, edited by A. La Regina, 43–47. Milano: Electa.

Coarelli, Filippo. 2007. *Rome and Environs: An Archaeological Guide*. Berkeley: University of California Press.

Coarelli, Filippo. 2014. "Il Foro Traiano e l'Atrium Libertatis." *Ephemeris Dacoromana* 16: 45–72.

Coleman, Kathleen M. 2003. "Euergetism in Its Place: Where Was the Amphitheatre in Augustan Rome?" In Lomas and Cornell 2003, 61–88.

Coleman, Kathleen M., ed. 2006. *Martial: Liber Spectaculorum*. New York: Oxford University Press.

Connolly, Joy. 2006. "Crowd Politics: The Myth of the 'Populus Romanus.'" In *Crowds*, edited by Jeffrey Thompson Schnapp and Matthew Tiews, 77–96. Stanford University Press.

Connolly, Joy. 2007. *The State of Speech: Rhetoric and Political Thought in Ancient Rome*. Princeton, N.J.: Princeton University Press.

Corbett, J. H. 1970. "L. Metellus (Cos. 251, 247), Agrarian Commissioner." *Classical Review* 20: 7–8.

Courtney, E. 1995. *Musa Lapidaria: A Selection of Latin Verse Inscriptions.* Atlanta, Ga.: Scholars Press.

Courtney, E. 1999. *Archaic Latin Prose.* American Classical Studies. Atlanta, Ga.: Scholars Press.

Craig, Christopher P. 2002. "A Survey of Selected Recent Work on Cicero's Rhetorica and Speeches." In *Brill's Companion to Cicero: Oratory and Rhetoric,* edited by James May, 503–31. Leiden: Brill.

Crawford, Michael H. 1974. *Roman Republican Coinage.* London: Cambridge University Press.

Crawford, O. C. 1941. "*Laudatio Funebris.*" *Classical Journal* 37: 17–27.

Čulík-Baird, Hannah. 2022. *Cicero and the Early Latin Poets.* Cambridge: Cambridge University Press.

Davies, Penelope J. E. 2000. *Death and the Emperor: Roman Imperial Funerary Monuments, From Augustus to Marcus Aurelius.* New York: Cambridge University Press.

Davies, Penelope J. E. 2017. *Architecture and Politics in Republican Rome.* Cambridge: Cambridge University Press.

Dodge, Hazel. 2011. *Spectacle in the Roman World.* Classical world series. London: Bristol Classical Press.

Döring, Moritz. 1843. *C. Plinii Caecilii Secundi epistolae, mit kritisch berichtigtem Text.* Freyberg: Engelhardt.

Duckworth, G. 1955. "Plautus and the Basilica Aemilia." In *Ut pictura poesis: studia latina Petro Iohanni Enk septuagenario oblata,* edited by P. de Jonge, 58–65. Leiden: Brill.

Dufallo, Basil. 2007. *The Ghosts of the Past: Latin Literature, the Dead, and Rome's Transition to a Principate.* Columbus: Ohio State University Press.

Dugan, John. 2001. "How to Make (And Break) a Cicero: Epideixis, Textuality, and Self-Fashioning in the *Pro Archia* and *In Pisonem.*" *Classical Antiquity* 20: 35–78.

Dumser, Elisha Ann. 2005. "Review: Palatino, Velia e Sacra Via. Paesaggi urbani attraverso il tempo. Workshop di archeologia classica." *Bryn Mawr Classical Review* 2005.08.18.

Dupont, Florence. 1987. "Les morts et la mémoire: le masque funèbre." In *La Mort, les morts et l'au-delà dans le monde romain: actes du colloque de Caen, 20–22 novembre 1985,* edited by François Hinard, 167–172. Caen: Centre de publications de l'Université de Caen.

Durry, Marcel. 1942. "'*Laudatio funebris*' et rhétorique." *Revue de Philologie* 16: 105–114.

Durry, Marcel. 1950. *Éloge funèbre d'une matrone Romaine (éloge dit de Turia).* Collection des universités de France. Paris: Belles Lettres.

Dutsch, Dorota. 2008. "Nenia: Gender, Genre, and Lament in Ancient Rome." In *Lament: Studies in the Ancient Mediterranean and Beyond,* edited by Ann Suter, 258–279. New York: Oxford University Press.

Dyck, Andrew R. 2003. *A Commentary on Cicero, De Legibus.* Ann Arbor: University of Michigan Press.

Eck, Werner. 1995. "Domus: L. Aemilius Paullus." In *LTUR,* 2: 26.

Eckstein, Arthur M. 1994. *Moral Vision in the Histories of Polybius.* Hellenistic Culture and Society 16. Berkeley: University of California Press.

Edmondson, Jonathan. 1996. "Dynamic Arenas: Gladitorial Presentations in the City of Rome and the Construction of Roman Society During the Early Empire." In *Roman Theater and Society: E. Togo Salmon Papers,* edited by William J. Slater, 1: 69–112. Ann Arbor: University of Michigan.

Edwards, Catharine. 1993. *The Politics of Immorality in Ancient Rome.* Cambridge: Cambridge University Press.

Edwards, Catharine. 2007. *Death in Ancient Rome.* New Haven: Yale University Press.

Fantham, Elaine. 2004. *The Roman World of Cicero's* De Oratore. Oxford: Oxford University Press.

Farney, Gary D. 2007. *Ethnic Identity and Aristocratic Competition in Republican Rome.* New York: Cambridge University Press.

Farney, Gary D. 2023. "The Cornelii and Jupiter: A Case Study in the Manipulation of Traditional Religion by an Aristocratic Roman Kinship Group." *Greece & Rome* 70: 50–70.

Favro, Diane. 1994. "The Street Triumphant: The Urban Impact of Roman Triumphal Parades." In *Streets: Critical Perspectives on Public Space,* edited by Zeynep Çelik, Diane Favro, and Richard Ingersoll, 151–164. Berkeley: University of California Press.

Favro, Diane, and Christopher Johanson. 2010. "Death in Motion: Funeral Processions in the Roman Forum." *Journal of the Society of Architectural Historians* 69: 12–37.

Fears, J. Rufus. 1981. "The Cult of Jupiter and Roman Imperial Ideology." In *Aufsteig und Niedergang der Römischen Welt,* 3–141. II.17.1. Berlin; New York: De Gruyter.

Feldherr, Andrew. 1998. *Spectacle and Society in Livy's History.* Berkeley: University of California Press.

Feldherr, Andrew. 2000. "*Non inter nota sepulcra*: Catullus 101 and Roman Funerary Ritual." *Classical Antiquity* 19: 209–231.

Fentress, Elizabeth. 2000. *Romanization and the City: Creation, Transformations, and Failures: Proceedings of a Conference Held at the American Academy in Rome to Celebrate the 50th Anniversary of the Excavations at Cosa.* Portsmouth, R.I.: Journal of Roman Archaeology.

Ferroni, Anna Maria. 1993. "Concordia, Aedes." In *LTUR,* 1: 316–320.

Filippi, Dunia. 2004. "Ricerche e scavi in corso sulle pendici settentrionali del Palatino." *Journal of the Fasti Online.*

Fiorelli, Giuseppe. 1879. "Maggio." *Notizie degli scavi di antichità* (Roma), 125–166.

Flaig, Egon. 1995. "Die *Pompa funebris.* Adlige Konkurrenz und annalistische Erinnerung in der römischen Republik." In *Memoria als Kultur,* edited by Otto Gerhard Oexle, 121: 115–148. Veröffentlichungen des Max-Planck-Instituts für Geschichte. Göttingen: Vandenhoeck & Ruprecht.

Flaig, Egon. 2003. *Ritualisierte Politik: Zeichen, Gesten und Herrschaft im alten Rom.* Historische Semantik. Göttingen: Vandenhoeck & Ruprecht.

Flower, Harriet I. 1996. *Ancestor Masks and Aristocratic Power in Roman Culture.* Oxford: Oxford University Press.

Flower, Harriet I. 2004. "Spectacle and Political Culture in the Roman Republic." In *The Cambridge Companion to the Roman Republic,* edited by Harriet I. Flower, 322–343. Cambridge: Cambridge University Press.

Flower, Harriet I. 2007. "Debating the Political Culture of the Roman Republic." *Journal of Roman Archaeology* 20: 409–412.

Franchi [Dell'Orto], Luisa. 1966. "Rilievo con pompa funebre e rilievo con gladiatori al museo dell'Aquila." In *Sculture municipali dell'area sabellica tra l'età di Cesare e quella di Nerone,* edited by R. Bianchi Bandinelli, 10: 23–32. Studi Miscellanei. Rome: Instituto Geografico Tiberino de Stefano.

Frank, Tenney. 1925. "*Pro rostris, pro aede, pro tribunali.*" *Rivista di Filologia e di Istruzione Classica* 53: 105–106.

Frank, Tenney, and Gorham Phillips Stevens. 1925. "The First and Second Temples of Castor at Rome." *Memoirs of the American Academy in Rome* 5: 79–102.

Freyberger, Klaus Stefan. 2012. *Das Forum Romanum: Spiegel der Stadtgeschichte des antiken Rom.* In collaboration with Christine Ertel. Darmstadt: Philipp Von Zabern.

Freyberger, Klaus Stefan. 2013. "Die Basilica Aemilia auf dem Forum Romanum." In *Dichter, Denker, Denkmäler: Beiträge zum altsprachlichen Unterricht,* 141–175. Speyer: Kartoffeldruck-Verlag.

Fries, Jutta. 1985. *Der Zweikampf: historische und literarische Aspekte seiner Darstellung bei T. Livius.* Beiträge zur klassischen Philologie 169. Meisenheim: A. Hain.

Futrell, Alison. 2000. *Blood in the Arena: The Spectacle of Roman Power.* Austin: University of Texas Press.

Gabucci, Ada, and Filippo Coarelli. 2001. *The Colosseum.* Translated by Mary Becker. Los Angeles: J. Paul Getty Museum.

Galinsky, G. Karl. 1966. "Scipionic Themes in Plautus' Amphitruo." *Transactions and Proceedings of the American Philological Association* 97: 203–235.

Gallagher, Winifred. 1993. *The Power of Place: How Our Surroundings Shape Our Thoughts, Emotions, and Actions.* New York: Poseidon Press.

Gargola, Daniel J. 1995. *Lands, Laws & Gods: Magistrates & Ceremony in the Regulation of Public Lands in Republican Rome.* Chapel Hill: University of North Carolina Press.

Geertz, Clifford. 1973. "Thick Description: Toward an Interpretive Theory of Culture." In *The Interpretation of Cultures: Selected Essays,* 3–30. New York: Basic Books.

Gerding, Henrik, and Nicolò Dell'Unto. 2022. "The Basilica Sempronia and the Forum Romanum." *Opuscula (Stockholm)* 15: 157–188.

Gilula, Dwora. 1981. "Who's Afraid of Rope-Walkers and Gladiators? (Ter. *Hec.* 1-57)." *Athenaeum* 49: 29–37.

Gilula, Dwora. 1989. "When did L. Aemilius Paullus actually die?" *Athenaeum* 67: 283–287.

Giuliani, Cairoli F. 1990. *L'edilizia nell'antichità.* Roma: La Nuova Italia Scientifica.

Gjerstad, Einar. 1941. "Il comizio romano nell'età repubblicana." *Opuscula Archaeologia* 2: 97–158.

Gjerstad, Einar. 1960. *Early Rome III: Fortifications, Domestic Architecture, Sanctuaries, Stratigraphic Excavations.* Vol. 3. Lund: C. W. K. Gleerup.

Goldberg, Sander M. 1998. "Plautus on the Palatine." *Journal of Roman Studies* 88: 1–20.

Goldberg, Sander M. 2005. *Constructing Literature in the Roman Republic: Poetry and Its Reception.* New York: Cambridge University Press.

Goldberg, Sander M. 2013. *Terence:* Hecyra. Cambridge Greek and Latin Classics. Cambridge; New York: Cambridge University Press.

Goldberg, Sander M. 2018. "Theater Without Theaters: Seeing Plays the Roman Way." *TAPA* 148: 139–172.

Golvin, Jean-Claude. 1988. *L'amphithéâtre romain: essai sur la théorisation de sa forme et de ses fonctions.* Paris: Boccard.

Gorski, Gilbert J., and James E. Packer. 2015. *The Roman Forum: A Reconstruction and Architectural Guide.* Cambridge: Cambridge University Press.

Gray, Christa, Andrea Balbo, Richard M. A. Marshall, and Catherine E. W. Steel, eds. 2018. *Reading Republican Oratory: Reconstructions, Contexts, Receptions.* Oxford: Oxford University Press.

Green, R. P. H. 1971. "Review: Death and Burial in the Roman World." *Journal of Roman Studies* 61: 283–284.

Gronewald, Michael. 1983. "Ein neues Fragment der *Laudatio Funebris* des Augustus auf Agrippa." *ZPE* 52: 61–62.

Gros, Pierre. 2001. *L'architecture romaine du début du IIIe siècle av. J.-C. à la fin du Haut-Empire. Maisons, palais, villas et tombeaux.* Vol. 2. Les manuels d'art et d'archéologie antiques. Paris: Picard.

Gruen, Erich S. 1990. *Studies in Greek Culture and Roman Policy.* Cincinnati Classical Studies. New York: E.J. Brill.

Gruen, Erich S. 1992. *Culture and National Identity in Republican Rome.* Ithaca, New York: Cornell University Press.

Guidi, Gabriele. 2015. "Relief with *Bustuarii* from Amiternum: 3D Model by Computer Vision and Reverse Engineering Lab." Sketchfab, October 13, 2015. Accessed March 4, 2026. https://skfb.ly/6YpVM.

Guilhembet, J.P. 1996. "Les résidences urbaines des sénateurs romains des Gracques à Auguste: la maison dans la Ville." *L'Information historique* 58: 185–197.

Hall, Jonathan. 2004. "Cicero and Quintilian on the Oratorical Use of Hand Gestures." *Classical Quarterly* 54: 143–160.

Hall, Jonathan. 2014. *Cicero's Use of Judicial Theater.* Ann Arbor: University of Michigan Press.

Hanses, Mathias. 2020. "Men Among Monuments: Roman Topography and Roman Memory in Plautus' *Curculio.*" *Classical Philology* 115: 630–658.

Hanson, John Arthur. 1959. *Roman Theater-Temples.* Princeton, N.J.: Princeton University Press.

Harrison, S. J. 1989. "Augustus, the Poets, and the *Spolia Opima.*" *Classical Quarterly,* New Series, 39: 408–414.

Haselberger, Lothar. 1997. "Architectural Likenesses: Models and Plans of Architecture in Classical Antiquity." *Journal of Roman Archaeology* 10: 77–94.

Haselberger, Lothar, David Gilman Romano, and Elisha Ann Dumser. 2002. *Mapping Augustan Rome.* Journal of Roman Archaeology. Supplementary Series, no. 50. Portsmouth, R.I: Journal of Roman Archaeology.

Haslam, Michael W. 1980. "Augustus' Funeral Oration for Agrippa." *Classical Journal* 75: 193–199.

Hayden, Dolores. 1997. *The Power of Place: Urban Landscapes as Public History.* Cambridge, Mass: MIT Press.

Hemelrijk, Emily A. 2004. "Masculinity and Femininity in the *Laudatio Turiae*." *Classical Quarterly* 54: 185–197.

Heyworth, S.J. 2011. "Roman Topography and Latin Diction." *Papers of the British School at Rome* 79: 43–69.

Hodgman, John. 2008. "Comics." *The New York Times* (June 1, 2008).

Hölkeskamp, Karl-Joachim. 2004. *Rekonstruktionen einer Republik: die politische Kultur des antiken Rom und die Forschung der letzten Jahrzehnte.* München: R. Oldenbourg.

Hölkeskamp, Karl-Joachim. 2010. *Reconstructing the Roman Republic: An Ancient Political Culture and Modern Research.* Translated by Henry Heitmann-Gordon. Princeton, N.J: Princeton University Press.

Hölkeskamp, Karl-Joachim. 2023. *Theater der Macht: Die Inszenierung der Politik in der römischen Republik.* München: C.H. Beck.

Holleran, Claire. 2003. "Public Entertainment Venues in Rome and Italy." In Lomas and Cornell 2003, 46–60.

Holliday, Peter James. 2002. *The Origins of Roman Historical Commemoration in the Visual Arts.* New York: Cambridge University Press.

Hope, Valerie M. 2007. *Death in Ancient Rome: A Source Book.* London: Routledge.

Hope, Valerie M. 2011. *Memory and Mourning: Studies on Roman Death.* Oxford; Oakville, Conn.: Oxbow Books.

Hope, Valerie M. 2018. "Funerary Practice in the City of Rome." In *A Companion to the City of Rome,* 383–401. Wiley-Blackwell.

Hope, Valerie M. 2025. *The Roman Mourner: Funeral Rites, Gender and the Body.* London: Bloomsbury Publishing.

Hope, Valerie M., and Eireann Marshall. 2000. *Death and Disease in the Ancient City.* Routledge Classical Monographs. London: Routledge.

Hopkins, John North. 2007. "The Cloaca Maxima and the Monumental Manipulation of Water in Archaic Rome." *Aquae urbis Romae: the waters of the city of Rome* 4: 1–15.

Hopkins, John North. 2016. *The Genesis of Roman Architecture.* New Haven; London: Yale University Press.

Hopkins, Keith. 1983. *Death and Renewal.* New York: Cambridge University Press.

Hopkins, Keith. 2000. *A World Full of Gods: The Strange Triumph of Christianity.* New York: Free Press.

Horsfall, Nicholas. 1982. "Review: *Laudatio funebris*: Interpretationen und Untersuchungen zur Entwicklung der Römischen Leichenrede." *Classical Review* 32: 36–38.

Horsfall, Nicholas. 1983. "Some Problems in The '*Laudatio Turiae*'." *Bulletin of the Institute of Classical Studies* 30: 85–98.

Horsfall, Nicholas. 2003. *The Culture of the Roman Plebs.* London: Duckworth.

Hughes, Alan. 1996. "Comic Stages in Magna Graecia: The Evidence of the Vases." *Theatre Research International* 21: 95–107.

Hurst, Henry, and Dora Cirone. 2003. "Excavations of the Pre-Neronian Nova Via, Rome." *Papers of the British School at Rome* 71: 17–84.

Iacopi, Irene. 1993. "Basilica Sempronia." In *LTUR,* 1: 187–188.

Johanson, Christopher. 2009. "Visualizing History: Modeling in the Eternal City." *Visual Resources: An International Journal of Documentation* 25: 403–418.

Johanson, Christopher. 2011. "A Walk With the Dead." In *A Companion to Families in the Greek and Roman Worlds,* edited by Beryl Rawson, 408–430. Oxford: Wiley-Blackwell.

Johanson, Christopher. 2015. "Making Virtual Worlds." In *A New Companion to Digital Humanities,* edited by Susan Schreibman, Ray Siemens, and John Unsworth, 110–126. John Wiley & Sons, Ltd.

Jory, E. J. 1986. "Gladiators in the Theatre." *Classical Quarterly* 36: 537–539.

Kaster, Robert A., ed. 2006. *Cicero: Speech on Behalf of Publius Sestius.* Oxford; New York: Oxford University Press.

Keating, Frank. 2010. "Heenan v Sayers: The Fight That Changed Boxing Forever." *The Guardian* (April 14, 2010).

Kehoe, Patrick E. 1989. "Was Book 5 Once in a Different Place in the Aeneid?" *American Journal of Philology* 110: 246–263.

Keillor, Garrison. 1999. *Prairie Home Commonplace Book: 25 Years on the Air with Garrison Keillor.* Highbridge.

Kennedy, George Alexander. 1994. *A New History of Classical Rhetoric.* Princeton, N.J.: Princeton University Press.

Kierdorf, Wilhelm. 1980. Laudatio funebris*: Interpretationen und Untersuchungen zur Entwicklung der Römischen Leichenrede.* Beiträge zur klassischen Philologie 106. Meisenheim am Glan: Hain.

King, Charles W. 2020. *The Ancient Roman Afterlife: Di Manes, Belief, and the Cult of the Dead.* University of Texas Press.

Köhne, Eckart. 2000a. *Gladiators and Caesars: The Power of Spectacle in Ancient Rome.* Berkeley: University of California Press.

Köhne, Eckart. 2000b. "The Politics of Entertainment." In Köhne 2000a, 8–30.

Koenen, L. 1970. "Die *Laudatio funebris* des Augustus für Agrippa auf einem neuen Papyrus (P. Colon. Inv. Nr., 4701)." *Zeitschrift für Papyrologie und Epigraphik* 5: 224–283.

Kondratieff, Eric J. 2009. "Reading Rome's Evolving Civic Landscape in Context: Tribunes of the Plebs and the Praetor's Tribunal." *Phoenix* 63: 322–360.

Kopij, Kamil, Kaja Głomb, and Szymon Popławski. 2023. "More Than Words: A Study on the Visibility of Hand Gestures in Public Spaces: Case Studies of Forum Romanum and Mayan Tikal." *Virtual Archaeology Review* 14: 1–13.

Kopij, Kamil, and Adam Pilch. 2019. "The Acoustics of Contiones, or How Many Romans Could Have Heard Speakers." *Open Archaeology* 5: 340–349.

Krause, Clemens. 1976. "Zur baulichen Gestalt des Republikanischen Comitiums." *Mitteilungen des Deutschen Archäologischen Instituts. Römische Abteilung* 83: 31–69.

Krause, Clemens. 1981. "Per una ricostruzione grafica del comizio." *La Parola del Passato: Rivista di Studi Antichi* 36: 71–72.

Kruschwitz, Peter. 2002. *Carmina Saturnia epigraphica: Einleitung, Text und Kommentar zu den Saturnischen Versinschriften.* Hermes Einzelschriften 84. Stuttgart: Steiner.

Künzl, Ernst. 1988. *Der römische Triumph: Siegesfeiern im antiken Rom.* Beck's archäologische Bibliothek. München: C.H. Beck.

Kyle, Donald. 2001. *Spectacles of Death in Ancient Rome.* New York: Routledge.

La Regina, A. 1968. "L'elogio di Scipione Barbato." *Dialoghi di Archeologia* 2: 173–190.

Lajolo, Giovanni. 2008. "Discorso al termine della processione in onore di Maria SS. Liberatrice." Stato della Città del Vaticano, May 25, 2008. https://web.archive.org/web/20120610073510/http://www.vaticanstate.va/IT/Stato_e_Governo/StrutturadelGovernatorato/Presidenza/Presidente/2008/25_maggio_2008.htm.

Lake, Randall A., and Barbara A. Pickering. 1998. "Argumentation, the Visual, and the Possibility of Refutation: An Exploration." *Argumentation* 12: 79–93.

Laurence, Ray. 1994. *Roman Pompeii: Space and Society.* New York: Routledge.

Leeman, A. D., and Harm. Pinkster. 1981. *De oratore libri III.* Wissenschaftliche Kommentare zu griechischen und lateinischen Schriftstellern. Heidelberg: Winter.

Lehmann-Hartleben, Karl. 1938. "*Maenianum* and *Basilica*." *American Journal of Philology* 59: 280–96.

Levison, John R. 2002. "The Roman Character of Funerals in the Writings of Josephus." *Journal for the Study of Judaism* 33: 245–277.

Lindsay, Hugh. 2000. "Death-Pollution and Funerals in the City of Rome." In Hope and Marshall 2000, 85–103.

Lippold, Adolf. 1963. *Consules: Untersuchungen zur Geschichte des römischen Konsulates von 264 bis 201 v. Chr.* Antiquitas 8. Bonn: R. Habelt.

Lomas, Kathryn, and Tim Cornell, eds. 2003. *Bread and Circuses: Euergetism and Municipal Patronage in Roman Italy.* New York: Routledge.

LTUR = Steinby, Eva Margareta. 1993–2000. *Lexicon Topographicum Urbis Romae.* 6 vols. Roma: Edizioni Quasar.

Lugli, Giuseppe. 1946. *Roma antica: il centro monumentale.* Roma: G. Bardi.

MacMullen, Ramsay. 1980. "Romans in Tears." *Classical Philology* 75: 254–255.

Makin, E. 1921. "The Triumphal Route, with Particular Reference to the Flavian Triumph." *Journal of Roman Studies* 11: 25–36.

Malakoff. 1860. "The Great Fight; Full Particulars. Thirty-Seven Rounds Fought." *New York Times* (New York) (April 30, 1860): 8.

Malcovati, Enrica. 1976. *Oratorum Romanorum fragmenta.* 4th ed. Corpus scriptorum Latinorum Paravianum. Torino: Paravia.

Mankin, David. 1995. *Horace: Epodes.* Cambridge Greek and Latin Classics. Cambridge: Cambridge University Press.

Manning, C. E. 1981. *On Seneca's "Ad Marciam."* Leiden: Brill.

Manuwald, Gesine. 2019. *Fragmentary Republican Latin. Volume III: Oratory, Part 1.* Loeb Classical Library 540. Cambridge, MA: Harvard University Press.

Marin, L. 1987. "Notes on a Semiotic Approach to Parade, Cortege and Procession." In *Time out of Time: Essays on the Festival,* edited by A. Falassi, 220–228. University of New Mexico Press.

Marks, Raymond. 2005. *From Republic to Empire: Scipio Africanus in the Punica of Silius Italicus.* Studien zur klassischen Philologie 152. Frankfurt am Main; New York: Peter Lang.

Marshall, C. W. 2006. *The Stagecraft and Performance of Roman Comedy.* Cambridge: Cambridge University Press.

McCarty, Willard. 2004. "Modeling: A Study in Words and Meanings." In *A Companion to Digital Humanities,* edited by Susan Schreibman, Raymond George Siemens, and

John Unsworth, 254–270. Blackwell companions to literature and culture. Malden, Mass: Blackwell Pub.

McCarty, Willard. 2007. "What's Going On?" In *Institute for Digital Research and Education, University of California at Los Angeles.*

McCarty, Willard. 2013. "Knowing …: Modeling in Literary Studies." In *A Companion to Digital Literary Studies,* edited by Ray Siemens and Susan Schreibman, 389–401. Malden, Mass.: Wiley-Blackwell.

Mee, Bob. 2001. *Bare Fists: The History of Bare-Knuckle Prize-Fighting.* Woodstock, N.Y: Overlook Press.

Mere, L. B. van der. 1982. "*Ludi scenici et gladiatorum munus*: A Terracotta Arula in Florence." *Bulletin Antieke Beschaving* 57: 87–99.

Millar, Fergus. 1998. *The Crowd in Rome in the Late Republic.* Ann Arbor: University of Michigan Press.

Moore, Daniel Walker. 2020. *Polybius: Experience and the Lessons of History.* Historiography of Rome and Its Empire 6. Leiden: Brill.

Moore, Timothy J. 1991. "*Palliata Togata*: Plautus, *Curculio* 462–86." *American Journal of Philology* 112: 343–362.

Morris, Ian. 1992. *Death-Ritual and Social Structure in Classical Antiquity.* New York: Cambridge University Press.

Morstein-Marx, Robert. 2004. *Mass Oratory and Political Power in the Late Roman Republic.* Cambridge: Cambridge University Press.

Morstein-Marx, Robert, and Kaine Byrne. 2025. "The End of the Wax *Imagines*." *Historia: Zeitschrift für alte Geschichte* 74: 329–348.

Mouritsen, Henrik. 2001. *Plebs and Politics in the Late Roman Republic.* Cambridge: Cambridge University Press.

Muth, Susanne. n.d. "Digitales Forum Romanum." Accessed June 18, 2025. https://www.projekte.hu-berlin.de/de/digitales-forum-romanum.

Mynors, Roger. 1963. *C. Plini Caecili Secundi. Epistularum libri decem.* Scriptorum classicorum bibliotheca Oxoniensis. Oxford: Oxford University Press.

Narducci, Emanuele. 1997. *Cicerone e l'eloquenza romana: retorica e progetto culturale.* Roma: Laterza.

Nash, Ernest. 1961. *Pictorial Dictionary of Ancient Rome.* New York: Praeger.

Nielsen, Inge. 1990. "The Forum Paving and the Temple of Castor and Pollux." *Analecta Romana Instituti Danici* 19: 89–104.

Nielsen, Inge. 1993. "Castor, Aedes, Templum." In *LTUR,* 1: 332–334.

Nielsen, Inge, Birte Poulsen, Pia Guldager Bilde, and Carl Nylander. 1992. *The Temple of Castor and Pollux.* Lavori e studi di archeologia 17. Roma: Edizioni De Luca.

Oakley, S. P. 1985. "Single Combat in the Roman Republic." *Classical Quarterly,* New Series, 35: 392–410.

Oakley, S. P. 1987. "Review: Livy's Duels." *Classical Review,* New Series, 37: 34–36.

Oakley, S. P. 1998. *A Commentary on Livy, Books VI-X.* Vol. 2. Oxford: Clarendon Press.

Ochs, Donovan J. 1993. *Consolatory Rhetoric: Grief, Symbol, and Ritual in the Greco-Roman Era.* Columbia: University of South Carolina Press.

Ogilvie, R. M. 1965. *A Commentary on Livy, Books 1-5.* Oxford: Clarendon Press.

Olsen, Dale A. 1979. "Public Concerts in Early America." *Music Educators Journal* 65: 48–59.

Osgood, Josiah. 2014. *Turia: A Roman Woman's Civil War.* Women in Antiquity. Oxford: Oxford University Press.

Östenberg, Ida. 2021. "The Arch of Titus: Triumph, Funeral, and Apotheosis in Ancient Rome." In *The Arch of Titus: from Jerusalem to Rome—and Back,* edited by Steven Fine, 33–41. Leiden: Brill.

Östenberg, Ida. 2023. "Gendering the Funeral: Public Obsequies Held for Elite Women in Rome." In *Gendering Roman Imperialism,* by Hannah Cornwell and Greg Woolf, 39–57. Impact of Empire 43. Leiden: Brill.

Papi, E. 1995a. "Domus est quae nulli villarum mearum cedat (Cic. Epist. 5.6.18). Osservazioni sulle residenze del Palatino alla metà del I secolo a.C." In *Horti romani: atti del convegno internazionale: Roma, 4–6 maggio 1995,* edited by M. Cima and E. La Rocca, 45–67. Roma: "L'Erma" di Bretschneider.

Papi, E. 1995b. "Domus: P. Cornelius Scipio Africanus." In *LTUR,* 2: 88.

Papini, Massimiliano. 2004. *Munera gladiatoria e venationes nel mondo delle immagini.* Roma: Accademia nazionale dei Lincei.

Parker, Holt N. 1996. "Plautus vs. Terence: Audience and Popularity Re-Examined." *American Journal of Philology* 117: 585–617.

Pascal, Carlo. 1894. "I ludi funebri romani." *Rendiconti della Reale Accademia dei Lincei: Classe di Scienze Morali, Storiche* 3: 290–302.

Paton, W. R. 1975. *Polybius: The Histories.* Cambridge, Mass: Harvard University Press.

Pensabene, Patrizio. 1984. *Tempio di Saturno: architettura e decorazione.* Roma: De Luca.

Pepe, Cristina. 2018. "Fragments of Epideictic Oratory: The Exemplary Case of the *Laudatio Funebris* for Women." In Gray, Balbo, Marshall, and Steel 2018, 281–296.

Pina Polo, Francisco. 2009. "Eminent Corpses: Roman Aristocracy's Passing From Life to History." In *Formae mortis: el tránsito de la vida a la muerte en las sociedades antiguas,* edited by Francisco Marco Simón, Francisco Pina Polo, and José Remesal Rodríguez, 89–100. Zaragoza: Institución Fernando el Católico, Fundación de la Diputación de Zaragoza.

Plass, Paul. 1995. *The Game of Death in Ancient Rome: Arena Sport and Political Suicide.* Madison, Wisconsin: University of Wisconsin Press.

Popkin, Maggie L. 2016. *The Architecture of the Roman Triumph: Monuments, Memory, and Identity.* New York: Cambridge University Press.

Potter, D. S. 1999. "Entertainers in the Roman Empire." In *Life, Death, and Entertainment in the Roman Empire,* edited by D. S. Potter and D. J. Mattingly, 256–325. Ann Arbor: University of Michigan Press.

Powell, J. G. F. 1988. *Cato Maior de senectute.* Cambridge Classical Texts and Commentaries 28. Cambridge: Cambridge University Press.

Purcell, Nicholas. 1983. "The Apparitores: A Study in Social Mobility." *Papers of the British School at Rome* 51: 125–73.

Purcell, Nicholas. 1989. "Rediscovering the Roman Forum." *Journal of Roman Archaeology* 2: 156–166.

Purcell, Nicholas. 1995a. "Forum Romanum (the Imperial period)." In *LTUR,* 2: 336–342.

Purcell, Nicholas. 1995b. "Forum Romanum (the Republican period)." In *LTUR*, 2: 325–336.

Purcell, Nicholas. 1999. "Does Caesar Mime?" In Bergmann and Kondoleon 1999, 181–193.

Purcell, Nicholas. 2022. "Historians in the Forum." In *Rethinking the Roman City: The Spatial Turn and the Archaeology of Roman Italy*, by Dunia Filippi, 177–212. Studies in Roman Space and Urbanism. Abingdon: Routledge.

Ramage, E. S. 2006. "Funeral Eulogy and Propaganda in the Roman Republic." *Athenaeum* 94: 39–64.

Ramsey, J. T. 2003. *Cicero: Philippics I-II*. Cambridge Greek and Latin Classics. Cambridge: Cambridge University Press.

Rawson, Beryl. 2002. "The Express Route to Hades." In *Thinking Like a Lawyer: Essays on Legal History and General History for John Crook on His Eightieth Birthday*, edited by Paul McKechnie, 81–112. Leiden: Brill.

Rich, J. W. 1999. "Drusus and the *Spolia Opima*." *Classical Quarterly* 49: 544–555.

Richardson, Lawrence. 1980. "The Approach to the Temple of Saturn in Rome." *American Journal of Archaeology* 84: 51–62.

Richardson, Lawrence. 1988. *Pompeii: An Architectural History*. Baltimore: Johns Hopkins University Press.

Richardson, Lawrence. 1992. *A New Topographical Dictionary of Ancient Rome*. Baltimore: The Johns Hopkins University Press.

Richlin, Amy. 2014. "Emotional Work: Lamenting the Roman Dead." In *Arguments with Silence: Writing the History of Roman Women*, 267–288. Ann Arbor: University of Michigan Press.

Robertson, Campbell, and Frances Robles. 2014. "Rite of the Sitting Dead: Funeral Poses Mimic Life." *The New York Times* (June 21, 2014).

Roche, R. A. P., M. A. Mangaoang, S. Commins, and S. M. O'Mara. 2005. "Hippocampal Contributions to Neurocognitive Mapping in Humans: A New Model." *Hippocampus* 15: 622–641.

Roller, Matthew B. 2010. "Demolished Houses, Monumentality, and Memory in Roman Culture." *Classical Antiquity* 29: 117–180.

Roller, Matthew B. 2013. "On the Intersignification of Monuments in Augustan Rome." *American Journal of Philology* 134: 119–131.

Roque, Georges. 2012. "Visual Argumentation: A Further Reappraisal." In *Topical Themes in Argumentation Theory*, edited by Frans H. van Eemeren and Bart Garssen, 273–288. Argumentation Library. Springer Netherlands.

Rose, Peter. 2005. "Spectator and Spectator Comfort." *Papers of the British School at Rome* 73: 99–130.

Rosenstein, Nathan Stewart. 1990. *Imperatores victi: military defeat and aristocratic competition in the middle and late Republic*. Berkeley: University of California Press.

Ruebel, James S. 1991. "Politics and Folktale in the Classical World." *Asian Folklore Studies* 50: 5–33.

Rüpke, Jorg. 2006. "Triumphator and Ancestor Rituals Between Symbolic Anthropology and Magic." *Numen* 53: 251–289.

Ruscha, Edward. 1966. *Every Building on the Sunset Strip*. Los Angeles, California: Edward Ruscha.

Russell, Amy. 2016. *The Politics of Public Space in Republican Rome.* Cambridge: Cambridge University Press.

Saldaña, Marie. 2015. "An Integrated Approach to the Procedural Modeling of Ancient Cities and Buildings." *Digital Scholarship in the Humanities* 30 (suppl. 1): 148–163.

Saldaña, Marie, and Christopher Johanson. 2013. "Procedural Modeling for Rapid-Prototyping of Multiple Building Phases." *ISPRS - International Archives of the Photogrammetry, Remote Sensing and Spatial Information Sciences* XL-5/W1: 205–210.

Salvador-Amores, Analyn. 2018. "Understanding the Materiality of Death Rituals in Bontoc Society, Northern Philippines." *The Cordillera Review* 8 (2): 1–20.

Sandbach, F. H. 1982. "How Terence's *Hecyra* Failed." *Classical Quarterly* 32: 134–135.

Saunders, Catharine. 1913. "The Site of Dramatic Performances at Rome in the Times of Plautus and Terence." *Transactions and Proceedings of the American Philological Association* 44: 87–97.

Scheid, J. 1984. "Contraria facere: renversements et déplacements dans les rites." *AION, Sezione di Archeologia e Storia Antica* 6: 117–39.

Schilling, Robert. 1977. *Pliny: histoire naturelle: livre VII.* Collection des universités de France. Paris: Belles Lettres.

Schreibman, Susan, and Costas Papadopoulos. 2019. "Textuality in 3D: Three-Dimensional (Re)constructions as Digital Scholarly Editions." *International Journal of Digital Humanities* 1: 221–233.

Scott, Russel T. 1995. "Domus Publica." In *LTUR*, 2: 165–166.

Scott-Kilvert, Ian. 1979. *The Rise of the Roman Empire.* Penguin Classics. Harmondsworth: Penguin.

Sehlmeyer, Markus. 1999. *Stadtrömische Ehrenstatuen der Republikanischen Zeit: Historizität und Kontext von symbolen nobilitären Standesbewusstseins.* Historia Einzelschriften 130. Stuttgart: Franz Steiner.

Senseney, J. R. 2007. "Review: The Architecture of Roman Temples: The Republic to the Middle Empire." *American Journal of Archaeology* 111: 384.

Sharrock, Alison. 2009. *Reading Roman Comedy: Poetics and Playfulness in Plautus and Terence.* The W. B. Stanford Memorial Lectures. Cambridge: Cambridge University Press.

Shatzman, I. 1972. "The Roman General's Authority Over Booty." *Historia* 21: 177–205.

Shuckburgh, Evelyn S. 1962. *The Histories of Polybius.* Reprint of original 1889. Indiana University Greek and Latin Classics. Bloomington: Indiana University Press.

Smith, Christopher. 2006. *The Roman Clan: The Gens From Ancient Ideology to Modern Anthropology.* New York: Cambridge University Press.

Sommer, Michael. 2013. "Scipio Aemilianus, Polybius, and the Quest for Friendship in Second-Century Rome." In *Polybius and His World: Essays in Memory of F. W. Walbank*, edited by Bruce Gibson and Thomas Harrison, 307–318. Oxford: Oxford University Press.

Stambaugh, John E. 1988. *The Ancient Roman City.* Baltimore: The Johns Hopkins University Press.

Stamper, John W. 2005. *The Architecture of Roman Temples: The Republic to the Middle Empire.* Cambridge: Cambridge University Press.

Steele, R. B. 1904. "The Historical Attitude of Livy." *American Journal of Philology* 25: 15–44.

Steinby, Eva Margareta. 1993a. "Basilica Aemilia." In *LTUR*, 1: 167–168.

Steinby, Eva Margareta. 1993b. "Basilica Porcia." In *LTUR*, 1: 187.

Steinby, Eva Margareta. 1996. "Lacus Iuturnae." In *LTUR*, 3: 168–170.

Steinby, Eva Margareta. 2012. *Edilizia pubblica e potere politico nella Roma repubblicana*. Roma; Milano: Jaca Book.

Sumi, Geoffrey S. 2002. "Impersonating the Dead: Mimes at Roman Funerals." *American Journal of Philology* 123: 559–585.

Sumi, Geoffrey S. 2005. *Ceremony and Power: Performing Politics in Rome Between Republic and Empire*. Ann Arbor: University of Michigan Press.

Sumi, Geoffrey S. 2009. "Monuments and Memory: The Aedes Castoris in the Formation of Augustan Ideology." *Classical Quarterly* 59: 167–186.

Swan, Peter Michael. 2004. *The Augustan Succession: An Historical Commentary on Cassius Dio's Roman History Books 55–56 (9 B.C.–A.D. 14)*. Oxford: Oxford University Press.

Taylor, Lily Ross. 1966. *Roman Voting Assemblies from the Hannibalic War to the Dictatorship of Caesar*. Jerome Lectures 8. Ann Arbor: University of Michigan Press.

The Annual Register. 1861. London: Rivingtons.

Torelli, Mario. 1999. "*Funera Tusca*: Reality and Representation in Archaic Tarquinian Painting." In Bergmann and Kondoleon 1999, 147–161.

Toynbee, J. M. C. 1996. *Death and Burial in the Roman World*. Reprint of original 1971. Baltimore: The Johns Hopkins University Press.

Tumolesi, Patrizia Sabbatini. 1980. *Gladiatorum paria: annunci di spettacoli gladiatorii a Pompeii*. Roma: Edizioni di storia e letteratura.

Van Sickle, John. 1987. "The Elogia of the Cornelii Scipiones and the Origin of Epigram at Rome." *American Journal of Philology* 108: 41–55.

Van Sickle, John. 1988. "The First Hellenistic Epigrams at Rome." In *Vir Bonus Discendi Peritus: Studies in Celebration of Otto Skutsch's Eightieth Birthday*, edited by Nicholas Horsfall, 132–156. London: University of London, Institute of Classical Studies.

Vasaly, Ann. 1993. *Representations: Images of the World in Ciceronian Oratory*. Berkeley: University of California Press.

Versnel, Hendrik Simon. 1970. *Triumphus: An Inquiry Into the Origin, Development and Meaning of the Roman Triumph*. Leiden: Brill.

Ville, Georges. 1981. *La gladiature en Occident des origines à la mort de Domitien*. Bibliothèque des Écoles françaises d'Athènes et de Rome 245. Roma: École française de Rome.

Vismara, Cinzia. 2001. "The World of the Gladiators." In Gabucci and Coarelli 2001, 21–55.

Vollmer, Friedrich. 1891. "*Laudationum funebrium Romanorum historia et reliquiarum editio*." *Jahrbücher für classische Philologie. Suppl.* 18: 445–528.

Walbank, F. W. 1970. *A Historical Commentary on Polybius*. Vol. 1. Oxford: Clarendon Press.

Wallace-Hadrill, Andrew. 1990. "Roman Arches and Greek Honours: The Language of Power at Rome." *Proceedings of the Cambridge Philological Society* 36: 143–181.

Wallace-Hadrill, Andrew. 1994. *Houses and Society in Pompeii and Herculaneum*. Princeton, N.J.: Princeton University Press.

Wallace-Hadrill, Andrew. 2001. "Emperors and Houses in Rome." In *Childhood, Class and Kin in the Roman World*, edited by Suzanne Dixon, 128–144. London: Routledge.

Wallace-Hadrill, Andrew. 2003. "Domus and Insulae in Rome: Families and Housefuls." In *Early Christian Families in Context: An Interdisciplinary Dialogue,* edited by David L. Balch and Carolyn Osiek, 3–18. Grand Rapids, Mich.: W.B. Eerdmans Pub. Co.

Weinstock, Stefan. 1971. *Divus Julius.* Oxford: Clarendon Press.

Welch, Katherine E. 1994. "The Roman Arena in Late-Republican Italy: A New Interpretation." *Journal of Roman Archaeology* 7: 59–79.

Welch, Katherine E. 2003. "A New View of the Origins of the Basilica: The Atrium Regium, Graecostasis, and Roman Diplomacy." *Journal of Roman Archaeology* 16: 5–34.

Welch, Katherine E. 2007. *The Roman Amphitheatre: From Its Origins to the Colosseum.* Cambridge: Cambridge University Press.

Wesch-Klein, Gabriele. 1993. Funus Publicum*: eine Studie zur öffentlichen Beisetzung und Gewährung von Ehrengräbern in Rom und den Westprovinzen.* Heidelberger althistorische Beiträge und epigraphische Studien 14. Stuttgart: Franz Steiner.

Wiedemann, Thomas. 1992. *Emperors and Gladiators.* London: Routledge.

Wiles, David. 2003. *A Short History of Western Performance Space.* New York: Cambridge University Press.

Wilskman, Anna-Maria. 2024. "From Honour to Dishonour: The Different Readings of Columna Maenia." In *Running Rome and Its Empire,* in collaboration with Antonio Lopez Garcia, 235–250. Routledge.

Winkes, Rolf. 1979. "Pliny's Chapter on Roman Funeral Customs in the Light of Clipeatae Imagines." *American Journal of Archaeology* 83: 481–484.

Wiseman, T. P. 1964. "Some Republican Senators and Their Tribes." *Classical Quarterly,* New Series, 14: 122–133.

Wiseman, T. P. 1994. "*Conspicui Postes Tectaque Digna Deo*: the Public Image of Aristocratic and Imperial Houses in the Late Republic and Early Empire." In *Historiography and Imagination: Eight Essays on Roman Culture.* 98–115. Exeter: University of Exeter Press.

Wiseman, T. P. 1995. *Remus: A Roman Myth.* Cambridge: Cambridge University Press.

Wiseman, T. P. 1996. "The Minucii and Their Monument." In Imperium sine fine*: T. Robert S. Broughton and the Roman Republic,* edited by T. Robert S. Broughton and Jerzy Linderski, 57–74. Stuttgart: F. Steiner Verlag.

Wiseman, T. P. 2004. "Where Was the Nova Via?" *Papers of the British School at Rome* 72: 164–184.

Wistrand, Erik Karl Hilding. 1976. *The So-Called* Laudatio Turiae*: Introduction, Text, Translation, Commentary.* Göteborg: Acta Universitatis Gothoburgensis.

Zanker, Paul. 2004. *Die Apotheose der römischen Kaiser: Ritual und städtische Bühne.* München: Carl Friedrich von Siemens Stiftung.

Zarmakoupi, Mantha. 2006. "Review: The Architecture of Roman Temples: The Republic to the Middle Empire." *Bryn Mawr Classical Review* 2006.04.22.

Zevi, F. 1970. "Considerazioni sull'elogio di Scipione Barbato." *Studi Miscellanei* 15: 63–74.

Ziółkowski, Adam. 2004. *Sacra Via: Twenty Years After.* Warsaw: Fundacja im. Rafala Taubenschlaga.

INDEX LOCORUM

GENERAL INDEX

TEXT
10/12.5 Minion Pro, with New Athena Unicode

DISPLAY
Minion Pro

COMPOSITOR
Christopher John Johanson, using XeLaTeX and the memoir class
via the custom ccsdesign package

PRINTING AND BINDING
Printed on demand

www.ingramcontent.com/pod-product-compliance
Lightning Source LLC
LaVergne TN
LVHW010053110826
845155LV00028B/324

* 9 7 8 1 9 3 9 9 2 6 2 0 3 *